Vienna

D0104327

"All you've got to do is decide to go
and the hardest part is over.

So go!"

TONY WHEELER, COFOUNDER – LONELY PLANET

THIS EDITION WRITTEN AND RESEARCHED BY
Anthony Haywood,
Kerry Christiani, Marc Di Duca

Contents

(left) **Burggarten p68**
Visit the Mozart statue.

(above) **Kunsthistorisches Museum p113**
Admire famed artworks in a sumptuous palace.

(right) **Sacher Torte**
Sample a piece at Hotel Sacher (p201).

Prater &
East of the Danube
p162

Alsergrund &
the University District
p132

Stephansdom &
the Historic
Centre
p73

The Hofburg
& Around
p58

The Museum District
& Neubau
p111

Schloss Belvedere
to the Canal
p145

Karlsplatz &
Around Naschmarkt
p93

Schloss
Schönbrunn &
Around
p173

Welcome to Vienna

Vienna is packed with imperial history; at the same time it has exciting contemporary museums and lively eating and nightlife scenes.

Imperial Grandeur

Few cities can boast the imperial grandeur of Vienna, once the centre of the powerful Habsburg monarchy. Lipizzaner stallions performing elegant equine ballet, the angelic tones of the Vienna Boys' Choir drifting across a courtyard, outrageously opulent palaces such as Schloss Belvedere and Schloss Schönbrunn, and the monumental Hofburg complex – as a visitor today, you feel grandeur everywhere in Vienna.

City of Music

Vienna is one the most musical cities in the world. This is partly due to the vast number of great composers and musicians who were born here or lived and worked here. Visiting Austria's capital therefore means experiencing the works of Mozart, Haydn, Schubert, Beethoven, Johann Strauss (both father and son), Liszt, Brahms, Bruckner and many others in venues such as the Staatsoper and Musikverein. The music of Bach and Händel continues to be performed in Vienna's historic churches today, and Vienna's Collection of Ancient Musical Instruments, paired with a visit to the Haus der Musik, takes you deeper into the texture of music and how it is created. Venues for classical music are augmented by some great clubs and live rock and jazz places.

Living Well

It's hard to imagine a more livable city than Vienna. This is a metropolis where regulars sit in cosy coffee houses and offer credible solutions to world chaos over the noble bean; where *Beisln* (bistro pubs) serve delicious brews, wines and traditional food; where talented chefs are taking the capital in new culinary directions; and where an efficient transport system will ferry you across town from a restaurant to a post-dinner drink in no time at all. It's safe, it has lots of bicycle tracks and it even has its own droll sense of humour.

New Old City

Vienna is a city where postmodernist and contemporary architectural designs contrast and fuse with the monumental and historic. The MuseumsQuartier is a perfect example, with modern museum architecture integrated into a public space created around former stables for the Habsburgs' horses. Twentieth-century designs such as Loos American Bar are little short of inspiring, while contemporary Vienna is constantly being given new and exciting infrastructural designs such as the new Twin City Liners boat landing (with the restaurant, bar and cafe Motto am Fluss) and the enormous *Hauptbahnhof* (main train station).

Why I Love Vienna

By Anthony Haywood, Author

Buzzing restaurants, coffee houses like living rooms, *Beisln,* innovative museums, absurdly pompous architecture and the sheer quality of life. These are just some of the reasons why I love Vienna. But what I especially love is exploring the capital by foot. Some evenings I like to walk through the courtyards of the historic centre, other nights I'll explore the idiosyncratic *Vorstadt* districts – places like Margareten, Neubau, Josefstadt and Leopoldstadt where the rawness of ordinary life washes to the surface. Vienna is a large, variegated city, but it's still one you can easily walk through to discover new sides.

For more about our authors, see p272.

Above: Kunsthistorisches Museum (p113)

Vienna's
Top 10

Schloss Schönbrunn *(p175)*

1 The magnificent rococo former summer palace and gardens of the Habsburgs are a perfect place to experience the pomp, circumstance and gracious legacy of Austria's former monarchs. A visit to 40 of the palace's lavishly appointed rooms reveals the lifestyle and the eccentricities of Europe's most powerful family, right down to Empress Elisabeth's obsession with her figure. Beyond the palace, Schloss Schönbrunn Gardens invite a stroll past pseudo-Roman ruins, along bucolic paths winding through leafy woods and a stopover in Gloriette.

◉ *Schloss Schönbrunn & Around*

Kunsthistorisches Museum *(p113)*

2 As well as accumulating vassal lands, the Habsburgs assembled one of Europe's finest collections of art and artefacts. The majestic highlight of this museum is the Picture Gallery, an encounter with a vast and emotionally powerful collection of works by grand masters, such as Pieter Bruegel the Elder's evocative and 'industrial' *Tower of Babel* from the 16th century, or the bright plenitude of Giuseppe Arcimboldo's *Summer.*

◉ *The Museum District & Neubau*

SYLVAIN SONNET / GETTY IMAGES ©

3

5

Schloss Belvedere
(p147)

3 Living up to its Italian-esque name 'beautiful view', this palace and garden ensemble is deceptively close to Vienna's centre while still creating a feeling of being worlds apart. Symmetrical, finely sculpted and manicured gardens inspired by France's Versailles connect two exquisite palaces dedicated to Austrian art, complemented by design interiors so stately that these are worthy of a visit in their own right. Altogether, Schloss Belvedere and gardens bring together an astonishing who's who of Austrian art with the finest of 18th-century palace architecture and landscaping. Not to be missed here is Gustav Klimt's painting *The Kiss.*

⊙ *Schloss Belvedere to the Canal*

Ringstrasse Tram Tour *(p29)*

4 Jump on a tram and explore the Ringstrasse, one of Europe's most unusual streets. This circular boulevard of magnificent state buildings, palaces and majestic hotels was carved out of the space once occupied by fortifications protecting Vienna from Ottoman Turk attack in the 16th century. Today, monumental 19th-century architectural masterpieces boldly rise up along the flanks, encircling most of the central Innere Stadt and separating the centre from the gritty, character-laden *Vorstädte* (inner suburbs).

⊙ *Guided Tours & Walks*

Prater & the Ferris Wheel *(p164)*

5 There are larger and more hair-raising Ferris wheels, but this icon in Vienna's Prater has the most character. Graham Greene sent his fictional character Harry Lime up here for a slow rotation in *The Third Man,* the film from 1949, and little about it has changed since then. A ride takes you high above the beautiful green open spaces of the Prater, giving you a bird's-eye view of the city and the expanse of wooded parkland and meadows that you can explore on in-line skates, by bicycle or on a walk after hitting ground level.

⊙ *Prater & East of the Danube*

Stephansdom (p75)

6 Rising out of the centre as a Gothic reminder of another age, St Stephan's Cathedral is the heart and soul of Vienna. The cathedral boasts a magnificent main nave and a fascinating cluster of other religious attractions below, inside and on top of it. Below are the catacombs, with their eerie collection of the deceased; inside are the cathedral treasures of reliquaries and religious art, which are part of a special exhibition; and rising above it to dizzying heights is the South Tower with its viewing stage offering the most spectacular views over town.

◉ *Stephansdom & the Historic Centre*

The Hofburg (p60)

7 The impressive former wintering ground of the Habsburg monarchs for over 700 years not only boasts a fine collection of museums, it's also a living palace that today is home to the Austrian president, Austria's National Library and public offices. A leisurely stroll through the palace complex is an encounter with one gracious or monumental building, statue and square after another, taking in highlights such as the Swiss Courtyard, the grotesquely proportioned Heldenplatz and the diminutive arches of the Outer Palace Gate.

◉ *The Hofburg & Around*

6

Coffee Houses *(p37)*

8 Great works of art or arts of living have been created in these 'living rooms' of the Viennese, run by laconic and insouciant waiters who rule the tables the way the Habsburgs once ruled the world. Drop by, wade through the endless coffee menu, read the world press and trade the latest gossip in Vienna's cosy answer to a home away from home. CAFÉ CENTRAL (P141)

🍷 *Coffee Houses & Cake Shops*

Vienna Boys' Choir *(p47)*

9 When Maximilian I founded the Vienna Boys' Choir in 1498 he replaced castrati with young boys whose voices had not broken, creating the world's most celebrated choir. Today the celestial tones of this choir echo through the Imperial Chapel of the Hofburg, where the choir performs classical music by Schubert, Mozart and other musical greats during holy Mass; it also stages an eclectic program of classical and contemporary music across town in MuTh, its own dedicated performing space.

⭐ *Entertainment*

Beisln *(p32)*

10 Imagine wood-panelled dens where godfather-like shakers and movers from the *Vorstädte* plot their next town-hall coup; imagine wallpaper in original 1970s shades clinging to walls, and hearty food such as sweetmeats, offal, goulash, Wiener Schnitzel and other favourites. This Viennese tradition is something like a bistro pub but much more, with a feel and mood you can almost scratch off the wooden tables. Linger over a beer or glass of wine, enjoy the filling food and soak up the unique atmosphere. A new breed of neo-*Beisln,* with a slightly upmarket edge, has even emerged from this worthy tradition. GLACIS BEISL (P127)

🍴 *Eating*

What's New

Motto am Fluss

Motto, in the Margareten Vorstadt (inner suburb), has for many years been a household name among food aficionados in Vienna. Now another fascinating Motto augments this on the Danube Canal, inside the Wien-City ferry terminal. The tastefully designed Motto am Fluss is a restaurant, bar and cafe, which resembles a luxury cruiser, with exposed iron struts and waterside windows offering wonderful views over the Danube Canal. (p85)

Klimt Villa

Dip into the sensual world of Vienna's most famous Secessionist at the neo-baroque Klimt Villa in Hietzing. (p179)

25hours Hotel

Roll up for a circus-themed extravaganza of a sleep at the 25hours Hotel, with bigtop views of Vienna. (p204)

Kunstkammer

Marvel at Renaissance and baroque wonders in the Kunsthistorisches Museum's new Kunstkammer, a cabinet of art and curiosities. (p115)

Phantastenmuseum Wien

Hidden away inside Palais Palffy in the shadows of the Hofburg, the new Phantastenmuseum Wien fills a gap for fantastic realism in Vienna's museum landscape. (p68)

Cafe Neko

Cat cafes are common in Japan, but Cafe Neko is the only one in Vienna. Feline friends roam around and gaze down from the elevated walkway upon the disgracefully fallible but admiring human species. (p90)

Tian

Sleek, modern and with a bar area, Tian serves some of Vienna's best vegetarian food. Ingredients are organic and it's all aimed at sustainability. (p86)

Therme Wien

Factor in a rest day of thermal bubbles at the new Therme Wien day spa south of the centre. (p158)

MuTh

Hear the Vienna Boys' Choir hit angelic high notes at MuTh, their new home in the Augarten. (p170)

Madame Tussauds Vienna

Mozart, Emperor Franz Joseph, Freud and Falco hang out under one roof at Madame Tussauds Vienna, the waxwork wonderland in the Prater. (p166)

For more recommendations and reviews, see **lonelyplanet .com/vienna**

Need to Know

For more information, see Survival Guide (p227)

Currency
Euro (€)

Language
German

Visas
Generally not required for stays of up to 90 days (or not at all for EU nationals); some nationalities need a Schengen Visa.

Money
ATMs widespread, not all 24 hour. Payment in cash usual, credit cards often not accepted.

Mobile Phones
Mobile phones use GSM900/800 and 3G2100. Australian, Chinese, European (and Russian) just need a local SIM card. US phones must be tri-band, Japanese quad-band.

Time
Central European Time (GMT/UTC plus one hour)

Tourist Information
Tourist Info Wien (Map p254; ☑245 55; www.wien.info; 01, Albertinaplatz; ☉9am-7pm; ☎; ⓜStephansplatz, ⬛D, 1, 2, 71 Kärntner Ring/Oper) office in arrival hall at the airport and the city office, with hotel booking, info and free maps.

Daily Costs

Budget:
Less than €80

➡ Dorm bed, shared apartment or cheap double per person: €25

➡ Self-catering or lunchtime specials: €6–12

➡ Visit cheap museums (€4) and free sights; drink at happy hours

Midrange:
€80–160

➡ Hotel single: €60–90; per person double: €40–100

➡ Two-course midrange meal with glass of wine: €30

➡ High profile museums (€12) and day trips

Top end:
Over €160

➡ Upmarket hotel double: from €200

➡ Eat superbly, enjoying several courses with wine for €70

➡ High-profile museums, opera, clubs and wine bars

Advance Planning

Three months before Reserve tickets for Staatsoper seating, Vienna Boys' Choir, the Spanish Riding School and top-flight events.

One month before Make reservations for top-shelf restaurants; use www.wien.info and venue websites for event planning. Book hotel in summer.

One week before Check out Falter (www.falter.at) for tips, reserve table in favourite classy restaurant for Friday or Saturday night.

Useful Websites

➡ **Tourist Info Wien** (www.wien.info) Information, hotel booking, events, special interest.

➡ **Falter** (www.falter.at) Eating and entertainment listings, special interest.

➡ **Lonely Planet** (lonelyplanet.com/vienna) Destination information, hotel bookings, traveller forum and more.

➡ **Vienna Webservice** (www.wien.gv.at) Official Vienna city council website.

WHE N TO GO
• •

July and August are busy. April–May and September–October are attractive shoulder seasons. November can be drizzly; December–March often brings snow.

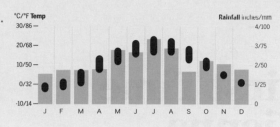

°C/°F Temp
30/86 —
20/68 —
10/50 —
0/32 —
-10/14 —

J F M A M J J A S O N D

Rainfall inches/mm
4/100
3/75
2/50
1/25
0

Arriving in Vienna

Vienna International Airport
City Airport Train (CAT) leaves the airport half-hourly from 6.06am till 11.36pm 365 days. The S7 suburban train is cheaper and takes 30 minutes. Expect to pay €36 to €50 for a taxi.

Vienna Hauptbahnhof Due to be fully completed in January 2015. Until then, many services arrive in Wien-Meidling and Westbahnhof. Trains from Bratislava and some other parts of Austria already arrive at Hauptbahnhof. Trains from Germany and western Austria arrive at Westbahnhof until Hauptbahnhof station is fully operational. A taxi to the centre costs about €10. All stations are quite safe late at night and have good connections with the centre and suburbs.

For much more on **arrival** see p228

Getting Around

➡ **U-Bahn** Fast, comfortable and safe. U-Bahn runs all night on weekends (Friday through to Sunday night or early Monday morning). Tickets are bought at machines or windows at stations.

➡ **Tram** Slower but more enjoyable. Depending on route, runs from around 5.15am to about 12.30am. Tickets are bought from kiosks or from the driver (more expensive). Validate ticket when boarding.

➡ **Bus** Reliable, punctual, several very useful routes for visitors, sometimes sporadic or nonexistent on weekends. Tickets can bought from the driver or from tobacconists. Validate on boarding.

➡ **Night Bus** Useful for outer areas especially. Main hubs for night buses are located at Schwedenplatz, Schottentor and Kärntner Ring/Oper.

For much more on **getting around** see p229

Sleeping

During the summer months, book at least a few days ahead for any accommodation, and at least a few weeks ahead for popular hotels (especially those close to the centre). Except over Christmas, New Year, Easter and during large trade fairs, a day or two ahead or no booking is required from late October to March. The most convenient places are in the centre, inside the Gürtel or near U-Bahn stations just outside it. Short notice booking on hotel booking portals are possible but many offerings are far from the centre.

Useful Websites

➡ **Tourist Info Wien** (www. wien.info) Hotel booking service, small extra charge.

➡ **Hostelworld.com** (www. hostelworld.com) Only hostels.

➡ **Booking.com** (www. booking.com) One of many good portals.

For much more on **sleeping** see p198

First Time Vienna

For more information, see Survival Guide (p227)

Checklist

➡ Make sure your passport is valid for at least six months past your arrival date

➡ Make sure you have a visa if you need one (see p235)

➡ Arrange travel insurance, and medical insurance if needed

➡ Check airline baggage restrictions

➡ Check your credit/debit card can be used with ATMs internationally

➡ Make copies of all important documents and cards (store online or in hard copy)

➡ Set mobile phone and apps so phone doesn't data roam (see p234)

What to Pack

➡ Comfortable walking shoes for exploration (with profile for ice in winter)

➡ Umbrella or rain jacket

➡ Decent shoes and jacket for going out – the Viennese dress up

➡ Day pack

➡ Electrical adaptor if needed (see p232)

Top Tips for Your Trip

➡ Walk in the central neighbourhoods. The Innere Stadt is deceptively small and most places are a short walk from Stephansplatz. Save time outside the centre by taking public transport, using a public transport pass. It's easy to cross town on a tram or metro and then explore a neighbourhood hub.

➡ Spend time in the coffee houses and *Beisln* (bistro pubs), which are unique to Vienna. Build them into your daily routine; seek respite from bad weather in a coffee house, read the paper and get a feel for the city.

➡ Explore areas in the evening or at night – it gives you a different feel for Vienna.

What to Wear

Winter can be cold and the ground icy, so several layers of warm clothing and good shoes are essential, along with gloves, scarf and a woollen cap or a hat. In summer, wear layers you can peel off and make sure you have something for occasional rain showers. The Viennese tend to dress up well in the evening or at good restaurants, but smart jeans are fine even for upmarket clubs and restaurants if combined with a good shirt or blouse.

Be Forewarned

Vienna is a very safe city and generally women and men will have no trouble walking around at night.

➡ Karlsplatz station and Gumpendorfer Strasse can be populated with off-their-head lingerers late at night.

➡ The Prater and Praterstern can get dodgy at night. Ausstellungsstrasse is best avoided due to street walkers and kerb-crawlers.

➡ The Gürtel has a heavy sprinkling of red-light clubs. North of Westbahnhof along the Neubaugürtel has a very high density (but gets better around Thaliastrasse), and directly south to Gumpendorfer Strasse is plain seedy.

➡ S-Bahn and tram stops along Margareten and Wiedner Gürtel can be seedy.

Money

ATMs are located all over the city, though not all are open 24 hours. Travellers cheques are generally no longer accepted and credit cards are not as widely accepted as in many other European countries – not even in some midrange restaurants (and sometimes not in budget hotels). You can change money in banks or post offices, but the cheapest method is using credit cards in ATMs.

For more information, see p233.

Taxes & Refunds

Austria has a consumer tax of 20% on most items, 10% for goods such as foodstuffs. This is always included in the price but almost always listed separately on a formal receipt. Visitors from outside the EU can claim back the tax for individual purchases over €75.01. After processing fees, the deduction is usually around 13% of the consumer tax.

Tipping

Tipping is usual in Vienna but not an essential part of a person's income as it is in countries such as the USA. About 5% to 10% for service is usual if you are satisfied, done by rounding up a bill, or €1 or €2 in good hotels for porters.

Wiener Neustadt altarpiece, Stephansdom (p75)

Etiquette

The Viennese may be laconic and ironic wits with a morbid bent, but they're polite about it unless you catch one on a big grump.

➡ Stick to the polite *Sie* (you) form unless you know someone well or are of a similar age in a young-ish scene. Never use *du* with shop assistants or waiters.

➡ Give your surname at the start of any telephone call (it's rude or brusque not to), especially when calling to reserve a room or table.

➡ *Grüss Gott* or the less formal *Servus!* are the usual forms of greeting; *Guten Tag* is also common.

➡ When entering a breakfast room, it's usual to acknowledge others by saying *'Guten Morgen'* when you walk in and *'Auf Wiedersehen'* on leaving.

Top Itineraries

Day One

Stephansdom & the Historic Centre (p73)

 Start your day with a visit to Stephansdom, taking a stroll through the interior of the church and admiring the **Domschatz** cathedral treasures. For a bird's-eye view of Vienna, climb the **cathedral south tower** to the platform. Alternatively, take in one of the other cathedral sights, such as the **Katakomben** (catacombs). Use the rest of the morning to stroll the narrow streets around the cathedral.

 Lunch Deli food and a glass of wine at Zum Schwarzen Kameel (p87).

The Hofburg & Around (p58)

Make your way along **Graben** and Kohlmarkt to the **Hofburg**, where one of the nicest things to do is simply to wander through and soak up the grandeur of this Habsburg architectural masterpiece. Choose one or two of the museums here, such as the **Kaiserappartements**.

Dinner Restaurant Herrlich (p69): traditional but classy Viennese cuisine.

The Museum District & Neubau (p111)

Especially on a warm summer evening, this public space framed by historic and contemporary architecture is great for people-watching and enjoying an outdoor drink. Stroll off the drink on floodlit **Maria-Theresian-Platz** or behind the **MuseumsQuartier** in cobblestone **Spittelberg**.

Day Two

The Museum District & Neubau (p111)

 After sniffing morning air and perhaps a coffee kick-start in the MuseumsQuartier, cross the road to the **Kunsthistorisches Museum**, where you can plan on spending a whole morning.

Lunch Head back into the MuseumsQuartier or deeper into Neubau.

The Museum District & Neubau (p111)

After several hours of grand masters, the afternoon is a good time to change artistic direction and explore at least one of the museums in the MuseumsQuartier. The light, bright **Leopold Museum** is a good choice. **MUMOK** will be a complete contrast, with works that shock (and some consider shocking). Take time again to relax, either by strolling to **Café Sperl** between museums or resting up in the MuseumsQuartier itself.

 Dinner Motto am Fluss (p85): hip lounge ambience on the Danube Canal.

Stephansdom & the Historic Centre (p73)

It's hard to pull yourself away from the post-dinner cocktail lounge at Motto am Fluss but explore the streets and bar scene in the evening in the centre, also hitting architectural delights such as **Loos American Bar** or **Kruger's American Bar**.

Café Sperl (p104)

Day Three

Schloss Belvedere to the Canal (p145)

 Plan on spending the whole morning here, dividing your time between the galleries and strolling along the clean lines of Schloss Belvedere's French-style **gardens**. **Lower Belvedere** is a palatial temple to the gentry augmented by galleries for temporary exhibitions, while a walk through **Upper Belvedere** takes you through a who's who of Austrian art.

> **Lunch** Meierei im Stadtpark (p158) for possibly Austria's best goulash.

Prater & East of the Danube (p162)

 After the opulence and art of Schloss Belvedere, the tone is somewhat lower in the Prater, Vienna's playground of woods, meadows and – with the **Würstelprater** – sideshow attractions. The crowd screamer here, however, is the Ferris wheel, which takes you up into the lofty heights of Leopoldstadt.

> **Dinner** An eatery around Karmelitermarkt or nearby in Leopoldstadt.

Prater & East of the Danube (p162)

 Leopoldstadt is not overflowing with drinking and nightlife options, but it has a fair sprinkling you can relax in. It's also home to the Pratersauna, one of the city's better clubs.

Day Four

Schloss Schönbrunn & Around (p173)

 Take a tour and walk in the grounds of **Schloss Schönbrunn**, not forgetting to detour to **Gloriette**, with magnificent views over the palace grounds toward the city. In warm weather, loiter and stroll at leisure through the grounds and take side trails; otherwise, limit outdoor meanderings to highlights.

> **Lunch** This is a good chance to head to the Naschmarkt (p110).

Karlsplatz & Around Naschmarkt (p93)

 From Naschmarkt stroll to the **Karlskirche** and take the lift into the dome where there's a stunning fresco by Johann Michael Rottmayr. On reaching the upper landing stage, take the steps up the scaffolding to the top viewing platform. After the Karlskirche, you might feel like a coffee in the **Cafe Drechsler**, with its off-beat buzz and design interior.

> **Dinner** An eatery in Margareten's Schlossquadrat, like Silberwirt (p104).

Karlsplatz & Around Naschmarkt (p93)

 Each of Vienna's *Vorstädte* (inner suburbs between the Ringstrasse and the Gürtel) has a character of its own, and the two districts Margareten (the 5th district) and Mariahilf (the 6th), both flanking the trickling Wien river, offer plenty of nightlife and drinking opportunities. Stroll, explore, sip and enjoy.

If You Like...

Great Works of Art

Kunsthistorisches Museum There are masterpieces in every room at Vienna's best museum for works by grand masters. (p113)

Leopold Museum A stunning collection of works with a strong focus on Schiele, Kokoschka, Gerstl and other expressionists. (p119)

MUMOK The Museum of Modern Art shocks, seduces and repels with a collection covering virtually all 20th- and 21st-century movements. (p120)

Schloss Belvedere The ensemble of galleries here focuses on the pantheon of Austrian artists from the Middle Ages to the present, complemented by world-class special exhibitions. (p147)

Kunsthalle Showcases local and international artists in changing exhibitions. (p120)

Albertina The attractive state apartments are augmented by copies from the graphics collection and the outstanding Batliner Collection. (p66)

Reliquiaries & Religious Art Highlights are housed in Stephansdom (St Stephan's Cathedral) until the Dom- & Diözesanmuseum reopens around 2015. (p76)

Classical Music

Musikverein Oft-used by the Vienna Philharmonic Orchestra, this concert hall is among the world's very best for acoustics. (p108)

Staatsoper Vienna's famous opera venue doesn't necessarily tear holes in your pocket. (p108)

GÜNTER LENZ / IMAGEBROKER ©

Albertina (p66)

Konzerthaus Top-flight classical concerts are staged here. (p161)

Live Music & Clubs

Porgy & Bess Vienna's most popular jazz club has a velvety vibe. (p90)

Arena A former slaughterhouse with outdoor and indoor spaces. (p47)

Flex Great local and international DJs on the Danube Canal. (p141)

Pratersauna This former sauna has been resurrected as a pool, bistro and club in one. (p170)

Getting Active

Donauinsel & Alte Donau Prime recreation areas for activities. (p170)

Wienerwald A paradise for walkers and cyclists, with the added attraction of being able to visit *Heurigen* (wine taverns). (p171)

Prater Small but central expanse of forest trails. (p164)

Flakturm In summer the *Flakturm* (flak tower) housing the Haus des Meeres has a climbing wall on one side. (p168)

Grand Architecture

Hofburg One monument after another is revealed in the Habsburg's home from 1279 to 1918. (p60)

Schloss Belvedere Built for military strategist Prince Eugene of Savoy, the Belvedere today doubles as an art gallery. (p147)

Ringstrasse An impressive array of 19th-century masterpieces

that can be enjoyed from the comfort of a tram. (p29)

Schloss Schönbrunn Around 40 of the palace's 1441 rooms are open to the public, and the Gloriette offers wonderful views. (p175)

Churches

Stephansdom Vienna's landmark Gothic cathedral is one of Europe's finest. (p75)

Karlskirche Brings together baroque magnificence and an ascension 70m into the cupola. (p95)

Peterskirche This sublime church invites contemplation beneath a dome fresco by Rottmayr. (p77)

Franziskanerkirche The beauty of this church is its deceptive *trompe-l'œil* dome. (p83)

Kapuzinerkirche (Kaisergruft) Contains the bodies – minus their hearts and organs – of the Habsburg family. (p66)

The Habsburg Heritage

Kaiserappartements Located in the Hofburg, the former imperial apartments house the Sisi Museum, which tells the story of Empress Elisabeth. (p60)

Schloss Schönbrunn Tours take you through this opulent palace and tell you all about the palace rooms and former imperial residents. (p175)

Kapuzinerkirche The crypt contains the bodies of almost every royal Habsburg. (p66)

Augustinerkirche Before being sealed in a tomb, the Habsburgs were relieved of

For more top Vienna spots, see the following:
➡ Guided Tours & Walks (p28)
➡ Eating (p31)
➡ Coffee Houses & Cake Shops (p37)
➡ Drinking & Nightlife (p42)
➡ Entertainment (p45)
➡ Shopping (p48)
➡ Sports & Activities (p51)

PLAN YOUR TRIP IF YOU LIKE...

their hearts, which are stored in urns here. (p67)

Markets

Naschmarkt Vienna's largest and most famous market is a medley of local and exotic fruits and vegetables, gourmet and ethnic foods, and food stands that have grown into fully fledged restaurants. (p110)

Brunnenmarkt This fruit, vegetable and foodstuff market reflects its location right in the middle of the Turkish district. Expect strong character and working-class charm. (p138)

Karmelitermarkt This food market with a cluster of small restaurants is so genuine that you can still buy delicious spicy horse-meat sausages here. Weeping with local flavour in Leopoldstadt. (p169)

Freyung Market A small, fine market with organic produce in the Innere Stadt. (p144)

Rochusmarkt A hub of activity in the Landstrasse district. (p159)

Month by Month

TOP EVENTS

Wiener Festwochen, May to mid-June

OsterKlang Festival, around Easter

Donauinselfest, June

Jazz Fest Wien, July

Christkindlmärkte, mid-November

January

One of the coldest but least expensive months; rooms are available at short notice and the winter cultural scene is lively.

 **Wiener Eistraum**

From January to about mid-March the square in front of Vienna's Rathaus turns into a massive ice rink (www.wienereistraum.com).

February

Days are still short, dark and often snowy. Crowds are still down but the cultural scene is going strong.

⭐ Fasching

The Fasching season, a carnival time of costumes and parties, runs from November to Ash Wednesday but things climax in February.

☆ Opernball

Of the 300 or so balls held in January and February, the Opernball (Opera Ball) in February is Vienna's most lavish and renowned.

March

Days are getting longer and, especially by late March, often it's even warm enough to sit outdoors in the sun.

⭐ Frühlingsfestival

Alternating each year between the Musikverein and the Konzerthaus concert halls, this spring festival of classical concerts can begin in late March or early April and run into May.

April

Vienna's tourist season starts at Easter. Weather is changeable. Book very early for Easter and in advance from now on for most accommodation.

⭐ OsterKlang Festival

Orchestral and chamber music recitals fill some of Vienna's best music halls during the OsterKlang Festival (www.osterklang.at) held around Easter each year.

May

May can be a lovely time to travel. Cycling is possible, the Danube cruises are frequent and it's warm enough to ponder an excursion to the Wachau.

☆ Life Ball

This AIDS charity event (www.lifeball.org) is a highlight of the ball season and is often graced by international celebrities. It's held in the Rathaus around the middle of May or as late as July.

June

Good weather but the big-hitting sights in central Vienna start to get crowded. A great time for activities or excursions to the Wachau.

⭐ Wiener Festwochen

Wiener Festwochen (Vienna Festival; www.festwochen.or.at) hosts a program of arts, based in various venues around town, from May to mid-June.

☆ Identities: Queer Film Festival

Identities (www.identities. at) showcases queer movies from around the world. It normally takes place at the beginning of June every second year (2015 is an on-year).

✯ Donauinselfest

Held over three days on a weekend in late June, the Donauinselfest (www.donauinselfest.at) on the Danube Island features a feast of rock, pop, folk and country performers, attracting three million onlookers. Best of all, it's free!

✯ Regenbogen Parade

In late June Vienna is taken over by the Regenbogen Parade (Rainbow Parade; www.hosiwien.at), a predominantly gay and lesbian festival attracting some 150,000 people.

July

School holidays begin and Vienna can be hot and crowded. Enjoy the outdoors, take an excursion into the country, relax in a *Heuriger* (wine tavern) and dine outdoors.

☆ Jazz Fest Wien

From the end of June to mid-July, Vienna relaxes to the smooth sound of jazz, blues and soul during the Jazz Fest Wien (www.vien najazz.org) at venues across town.

☆ ImPulsTanz

Vienna's premier avantgarde dance festival, ImPulsTanz (www.impulstanz. com) attracts troupes between mid-July and mid-August at theatres across Vienna.

☆ Musikfilm Festival

Screenings of operettas, operas and concerts outside the Rathaus in July and August.

September

Temperatures are falling and the crowds are tailing off at museums. School holidays have finished.

☆ Vienna Fair

Held in September or October, this is Austria's prime contemporary art fair (www.viennafair.at), with Eastern European artists in particular well represented. It's held at the trade fair grounds.

October

***Goldener Oktober* – the sun reflects the golden browns of autumn and in a good year you can sit outside, but it can get cold at night. The cultural scene is moving onto winter programs.**

☆ Viennale Film Festival

This is the country's best film festival. The Viennale Film Festival (www.viennale.at) features fringe and independent films from around the world, with screenings around the city.

November

Vienna can be grey and wet in November. Get into the restaurant, coffeehouse and cultural scenes; don't expect to spend much time outdoors, and only do city excursions (eg Bratislava).

☆ Wien Modern Festival

Wien Modern (www.wienmodern.at) festival features modern classical and avantgarde music from mid-October to mid-November.

December

Another good month for culture and the good life indoors, with one exception: the Christmas markets. A quintessential experience is to wrap up against the cold and sip mulled wine.

🎁 Christkindlmärkte

Vienna's much-loved Christmas market season runs from mid-November to Christmas Day.

✯ Silvester

The city council transforms the Innere Stadt into one huge party venue for Silvester (New Year's Eve).

☆ Le Grand Bal

Le Grand Bal (www. legrandbal.at), held on New Year's Eve at the Hofburg, offers more opportunities for haute-couture hobnobbing than you ever thought possible (or bearable).

With Kids

Vienna has lots of attractions for kids, and many of the museums in the city go out of their way to gear their exhibitions towards children. Language can be a hitch, though; in that case museums with hands-on and high visual appeal are best.

Museums

In addition to the spaces created for kids in the MuseumsQuartier (see following), four museums have exhibitions that are well suited to children. The Haus der Musik (p82) has lots of practical exhibits for almost all ages to promote an understanding of music. The Naturhistorisches Museum (p122) has a new anthropology section where you can have a photo of yourself taken as a prehistoric human and delve into forensics. The Museum für Völkerkunde (p65) has fascinating exhibits on indigenous cultures of the world, put together with kids in mind, while the Technisches Museum (p179) has lots of hands-on exhibits to promote the understanding of science and technology.

MuseumsQuartier for Kids

WienXtra-Kinderinfo (p235) Information centre.

Zoom (p121) Exhibition sections and programs of hands-on arts and crafts (from eight months to 14 years old).

Dschungel Wien (p120) Children's theatre with dance and occasional English performances.

Playgrounds & Open Space

Playgrounds are everywhere, but the Jesuitenwiese (p165) in the Prater – along Hauptallee, about 1.5km east of Praterstern – has a good one with a Wild West theme, while on the Donauinsel (p170) there's the Wasserspielplatz Donauinsel where toddlers can paddle and kids can dart across water on flying foxes and cross suspension bridges (U-Bahn station Donauinsel, then walk seven minutes downriver). Inside the MuseumsQuartier (p119) there's a sand pit from about May to September, as well as various events. Wiener Eistraum (p131) has fantastic winter ice skating.

Schloss Schönbrunn

Your six- to 12-year-old will need to speak German to understand the 1.5-hour tour about the Habsburg children. A visit to the Children's Museum (p178) is more accessible. The Marionetten Theater (p182) combines marionettes with Mozart and the music of other legendary composers.

The maze at Schloss Schönbrunn is good fun for everyone, and the so-called Labyrinthikon playground is designed for kids, but adults have just as much fun at the 14 playing stops for climbing, crawling and educational exploration.

Like a Local

Vienna is a very liveable city and the best ways to enjoy it are as the Viennese do – picnicking in parks and woods in summer, soaking up the cultural vibe in winter, and making the most of the city's Beisln, coffee houses, and great dining and drinking scenes.

MuseumsQuartier (p119)

Drinking Like a Local

The magic words for wine drinkers are *ein Achterl* (an eighth of a litre), which is the most common serving in Vienna. The wine is always delivered with a glass of tap water (*Leitungswasser*), but on finer occasions mineral water is usually the thing to order. Beer drinkers can choose *ein kleines* (0.2L to 0.3L), *ein grosses* (0.5L), *ein helles* (clear, light flavoured), *ein dunkeles* (dark) and much more. Coffee is rocket science in Vienna, with a profusion of varieties. Just because a place serves food doesn't mean you cannot drop in just for a drink there. After 10pm many morph into bars or even small 'clubs' with a resident DJ.

Vienna in Winter

Despite cold weather and often grey skies, Vienna is a remarkably active city in winter. Obviously, local pursuits are of the indoor variety, but this is also the main arts and performance season. The Viennese settle into the enjoyable warmth of classical venues such as the Staatsoper, or make the most of the bars, clubs and live music venues. The idea is not to seek the outdoors or expect much outdoor activity but to adapt to this winter lifestyle. One of the few exceptions when the Viennese linger outdoors in winter is the lead-up to Christmas, when *Christkindlmärkte* (Christmas markets) spring up all over Vienna. A large one is held on Maria-Theresien-Platz; quaint but lively ones are in Spittelberg and in the courtyard of Heiligenkreuzerhof.

The Summer Scene

The summer months, especially July and August, are when the Viennese emerge from the indoor venues and flock onto the streets. Restaurant tables sprout up and spread across the squares and footpaths, filled with voluble Viennese soaking up warmth and sunshine. The main courtyard of the MuseumsQuartier is often packed with warm-weather worshippers lounging about on brightly painted concrete forms that double as seating (they are repainted every year in a different colour). The Altes AKH university campus is another popular outdoor area in summer, and Yppenplatz has a good constellation of bars and cafes with outdoor seating. Each summer the large Summer Stage emerges alongside the Danube Canal. Nearby Flex (p141), Motto am Fluss (p85) and the world-class beach bar Strandbar Herrmann (p160) bring the canal to life. Across the canal, the Prater and the Danube Island (on the Danube River) are green havens popular for picnics and activities such as inline skating.

Eating Like a Local

The most local of local experiences is to eat in a *Beisl* (something like a bistro pub serving wine, beer and hearty food) or in one of the coffee houses that serve traditional food, such as Café Sperl (p104). Don't miss out on either of these experiences, but also make sure you plunge into the more formal Viennese restaurant scene too. A pre-dinner drink, a good meal, followed by a bar and club can make a great night out in Vienna. Visit the markets, try a horsemeat sausage at Karmelitermarkt (p169) or some of the delicacies of Naschmarkt (p110) or Brunnenmarkt (p138). The restaurants around these markets also have a nice local feel. Don't forget to pre-book for the evening in the more formal or popular places, especially on Friday and Saturday nights. For more, see p33.

Getting Around Town

In summer, cycling is a great way to move through the city. Bikes can be hired from stands around the city, or by the day or longer from various operators. The network of marked bike paths is excellent, with over 1200km threading through the 21 districts. Make the most of the U-Bahn, which runs all night on Friday and Saturday, complemented by night buses. Trams don't run as late as the U-Bahn but they are a great way to move around and see the city.

Dress up or Dress Down?

The Viennese like to dress up and dress down. Regardless of the direction, however, they think about how they dress and most make a fashionable or styled impression. Clean or well-polished shoes are important in this part of Europe. All-purpose wear, like joggers and street-wear trousers, are worn by young Viennese but are less common as you move up the age scale. You can get by with this – less so in shorts – in a *Beisl* at lunchtime, but you'll want to wear a nice pair of pants to avoid feeling out of place in the evening.

Staying in Touch

Coffee houses usually have a good selection of press. Among the local Austrian papers, sensationalist *Kronen Zeitung* and free *Heute* have the largest circulation. Serious papers include the leftish *Der Standard* and right-wing *Die Presse*. *Augustin* is a street newspaper partially produced and sold by the homeless. The weekly *Falter* is the indispensable German-language entertainment magazine, with listings from Friday to the following Thursday, articles and reviews.

For Free

Although most sights such as museums are pay-for-entry, it's still possible to carve out an enjoyable and interesting trip based around sights and activities that are free or very inexpensive, or simply by soaking up the mood and vibe of street life.

Free Museums & Exhibitions

Some museums are free for those under 19 years and, if you're interested in modern or contemporary art, drop into any of the free private art galleries scattered throughout the Innere Stadt. The following are free:

Dorotheum (p71) Sensational auction house packed with everything from paintings to furnishings and household objects.

Archiv des Österreichischen Widerstands (p79) Exhibition documenting the antifascist resistance movement under Nazi rule.

Bawag Contemporary/Bawag Foundation (p85) A private space with a contemporary focus.

Neidhart-Fresken (p79) Frescoes surviving from the 14th century.

Schloss Belvedere Gardens (p149) Exquisitely laid out gardens between Upper and Lower Belvedere palaces.

Schloss Schönbrunn Gardens (p177) Expansive gardens, manicured and adorned in some parts, but also with pleasant wooded parkland.

Museum für Angewandte Kunst (p153) Tuesday from 6pm to 10pm. Vienna's best collection of applied arts.

Free Public Buildings, Parks & Churches

Simply walk or catch a tram around the Ringstrasse (p29), or stroll through the Innere Stadt. The best of the Ringstrasse is around the Parlament (p125) and University Main Building (p134); beyond these also check out the Altes AKH and Bethaus, especially the Christmas market, and the charming Servitenviertel (p137). The northern side-aisle of Stephansdom (p75) is free, and the Justizpalast (p125) is great for a visit if you're not on trial (views are good from the canteen). The Hofburg (p60) is the most magnificent of the free highlights. Most churches are free and the Rathaus (p123) has free guided tours.

Servitenkirche & Servitenviertel (p137) Wonderfully quiet church grounds and quarter around it.

Prater (p164) Vienna's park and woodland across the Danube Canal.

Donauinsel (p170) An island and recreation area in the middle of the Danube River.

Augarten (p166) Eighteenth-century parkland with paths and meadows.

Hietzinger Friedhof (p180) Burial place of Gustav Klimt, Otto Wagner and other notable Viennese.

Free Entertainment

Rathausplatz has the biggest bashes, including the Musikfilm Festival, but also lots of free concerts and activities in summer. Good places for people-watching and soaking up the vibe in summer are the MuseumsQuartier, Donauinsel (p170), Prater (p164) and Naschmarkt (p97). Discos in the week are often dirt cheap or free, especially before midnight. Vienna also has a lot of drinking venues that are bars most of the time but morph late at night on the weekend into small discos, with a DJ spinning CDs in a corner. Mostly there's no space to dance, but you can wag your tail on the seat. Blue Box (p129) is one place.

Guided Tours & Walks

Vienna offers some great opportunities for guided exploration. Join a tour by bus, boat or on foot (perhaps even on a specific theme). Jump on a tram tour, tour a wine region outside town, or simply use our neighbourhood walks as a guide to explore interesting corners of the city.

Guided Walks

Vienna Tour Guides (www.wienguide.at; adult/child €14/7) A collection of highly knowledgeable guides who conduct over 60 different guided walking tours, some of which are in English. The monthly *Wiener Spaziergänge* (Vienna's Walking Tours) leaflet from tourist offices details all tours, departure points and tour languages.

Vienna Walks & Talks (⌕774 89 01; www.viennawalks.com) Offers the excellent Third Man Tour (€17) based on the film, and many more.

Bus Tours

Vienna Sightseeing Tours (Map p268; ⌕712 46 830; www.viennasightseeingtours.com; tours adult €39-109, child €15-45; ☺6.30am-7.30pm; ⓂSüdtiroler Platz/Wien Hauptbahnhof, ⓇD) Runs the Hop On Hop Off city tours and tours by the affiliated Cityrama. These take in Schloss Schönbrunn, plus some thematic (mostly music) tours in Vienna. Buses depart from Südtiroler Platz – Wiedner Gürtel/Laxenburger Strasse, but a shuttle leaves from outside the Staatsoper 30 minutes before each departure.

Hop On Hop Off (Vienna Sightseeing Tours; Map p256; ⌕712 46 830; www.viennasightseeing tours.com; 01, Opernring; 1hr/2hr/all-day ticket €13/16/20; ☺10am-5pm; ⓂKarlsplatz, ⓇD, 1, 2, 71 Kärntner Ring/Oper) Buses stop at 14 sights around Vienna. Tickets range from one hour to all day, and you can hop on and off as often as you wish. Buses circle the Innere Stadt, with detours to Stephans-platz. Others take you east of the Danube Canal, and to Schönbrunn and Schloss Belvedere. See the website for details.

Oldtimer Bus Tours (Map p254; ⌕503 74 43 12; www.oldtimertours.at; 01, Departure from Helden-platz; tours adult/child €19/12; ☺May–early Oct; ⓂMuseumsquartier, ⓇD, 1, 2, 71 Burgring) Vintage open-top (closed if rainy) oldtimer coaches trundle around the city centre and occasionally up to the Wienerwald (p171). Tours last an hour and leave from in front of the Hofburg at Heldenplatz daily at 11am, 12.30pm, 2pm and 4pm.

Redbus City Tours (Map p254; ⌕512 48 63; www.redbuscitytours.at; 01, Führichgasse 12; tours adult €14-24, child €7-12; ☺10am-7pm; ⓂKarls-platz, ⓇD, 1, 2 Kärntner Ring/Oper) One and a half hour tours of the main sights in around the Innere Stadt and 2½-hour tours of the city's big sights. Buses leave from outside the Albertina.

Boat Tours

DDSG Blue Danube (Map p252; ⌕588 80; www. ddsg-blue-danube.at; 01, Schwedenbrücke; adult/child from €19/9.50, under 10yr free; ☺tours 11am & 3pm Apr-Oct) Offers some of the most popular tours include circumnavigating Leopoldstadt and Brigittenau districts along the Danube Canal and the Danube or through the historic Nussdorf locks. Tour length starts from 1½ hours.

Wine Tours

Vienna Explorer (Map p252; ⌕890 9682; www. viennaexplorer.com; Franz-Josefs-Kai 45; Wachau bike tours €59-115, Vienna Segway/walking/bike tours €70/15/26; ⊙8.30am-7pm, tours Apr–Oct; MSchwedenplatz, ☐1 Salztorbrücke) Does bike tours through the Wachau vineyards, and walking and Segway tours in Vienna itself. It also rents out bikes for short-term (€12 per day) and long-term. The website gives tour dates and office opening times (it is open much of the year, and has a telephone service year-round).

Other Tours

Fiaker (20min/40min tour €55/80) A Fiaker is a traditional-style Viennese open carriage drawn by a pair of horses. Drivers generally speak English and point out places of interest en route. Lines of horses, carriages and bowler-hatted drivers can be found at Stephansplatz, Albertinaplatz and Heldenplatz at the Hofburg.

Ring Tram (Map p252; ☑790 91 00; www.wienerlinien.at; adult/child €7/4; ⊙10am-6pm) Continuous hop-on, hop-off guided tour of the Ringstrasse with video screens and commentary on a clockwise route stopping at 13 stations. You can get on and off at any stop on a tour that lasts 25 minutes without stops. The first tour leaves Kärntner Ring-Oper at 10am, the last from Schwarzenbergplatz at 5.28pm. See the Do-It-Yourself Ringstrasse Tram Tour in this chapter for a self-guided alternative.

City Segway Tours (Map p256; ☑729 72 34; www.citysegwaytours.com/vienna; tour adult €70; ⊙Apr–Oct; ☐59A, 62, MKarlsplatz, ☐D, 1, 2 Kärntner Ring/Oper) Run by Pedal Power (which conducts bicycle tours in and around Vienna), these Segway tours meet in front of the Staatsoper and cover the main city highlights including the Ringstrasse and the *Rathaus*, Hofburg and more.

Ringstrasse Tram Tour: Do-It-Yourself

Public trams are a cheap way to see the sights and enjoy a slice of everyday life in Vienna at the same time. This quintessential Vienna tram experience takes you past the city's palatial monuments.

Board tram 1 at Schwedenplatz (platform B) heading towards Stefan-Fadinger-Platz and immediately look out on the left for the **Monument to the Victims of Fascism** at the former Gestapo headquarters site.

On your left on the Ringstrasse will emerge Vienna's **Börse Palais (Stock Exchange)**, a handsome structure bedecked in dusty brick with white trimmings, designed by renowned Ringstrasse architect Theophil von Hansen.

NEIGHBOURHOOD WALKS

Use our guided walks and Local Life features in this book:
➡ Stephansdom & the Historic Centre (p84)
➡ Local Life: Karlsplatz & Around Naschmarkt (p98)
➡ Local Life: The Museum District & Neubau (p124)
➡ Local Life: Alsergrund & the University District (p138)
➡ Schloss Belvedere to the Canal (p155)

Pulling into Schottentor station you'll be accosted on your right by two stone-carved steeples reaching for the sky – the marvellous neo-Gothic Votivkirche (p136) is quite reminiscent of France's Chartres Cathedral.

When the spires of an arresting Flemish-Gothic edifice beck on your gaze on the right, you will have reached the *Rathaus* (p123) and Rathausplatz.

The neoclassical facade of Parlament (p125), Austria's parliament, with its majestic Greek pillars, will spill into view on the right, flanked by the **Athena Fountain** – the four figures lying at her feet represent the Danube, Inn, Elbe and Vltava, the four key rivers of the Austro-Hungarian Empire.

A majestic testament to Austria's 1813 triumph over Napoleon in Leipzig, the **Äusseres Burgtor (Outer Palace Gate)** will loom into view on the left – the Roman gate leads the way to the Hofburg (Imperial Palace).

Directly opposite the Burgtor is **Maria-Theresien-Platz**, anchored by a statue of Empress Maria Theresia, the only female to ascend to the Austrian throne. Note the bundle of papers clasped in her left hand – these are the Pragmatic Sanctions of 1713, which made it possible for women to rule the empire.

The marvellous neo-Renaissance Staatsoper (p108) (State Opera House) impresses the masses today, but when it was originally built the Viennese dubbed it 'the *Königgrätz* of architecture,' likening it to the 1866 military disaster of the same name.

The final stretch of the tram route (tram 2) continues past Stadtpark (p159) back to the Danube Canal and Schwedenplatz.

Ringstrasse Tram Tour

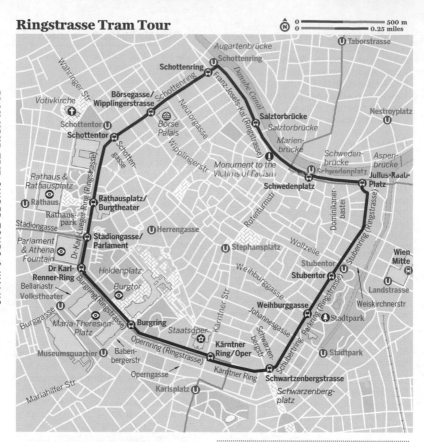

RINGSTRASSE TRAM PRACTICALITIES

You can tour the Ringstrasse on the tourist Ring Tram, but it's much cheaper to catch regular city trams below (without commentaries) if you already have a transport ticket.

Trams to catch Tram 1 heading northwest from Schwedenplatz, changing to tram 2 at Stadiongasse/Parlament, Dr-Karl-Renner-Ring, Burgring or Kärntner Ring-Oper to finish at Schwedenplatz.

Cost Use your normal transport ticket; 24-hour tickets are best (€6.70).

MORE INFORMATION

www.wien.info/en/sightseeing/tours-guides
Official portal with a comprehensive overview of tour options.

Tourist Info Wien (p235) Main tourist office, with walk-in service.

der Kunsthalle Wien und

HALLE | CAFE

Halle (p127)

Eating

One of the exciting ways to experience Vienna is through its lively eating scene. Many of Vienna's kitchens are run by a new generation of creative chefs who are steering traditional cuisine in new directions. At the same time, the eating experience in Vienna is also about ever-popular street sausage stands, Wiener Schnitzel in lively Beisln and favourites like goulash.

The Dining Scene

Vienna has a lively and changing culinary scene. The trend these days is to give traditional Austrian cuisine a lighter note. At the same time, new generations of chefs have turned to high-quality seasonal and local ingredients, coupled with the quick acceptance of new food ideas from local producers or from abroad.

The Viennese have also reaffirmed their love for traditional-style eateries, in particular *Beisln* (bistro pubs); these are augmented by a wide range of stylish restaurant-bars with design tones and well-prepared international cuisine to complement Austrian favourites like Wiener Schnitzel or goulash. Today, eating out in Vienna therefore often means being able to enjoy the best of both worlds – traditional as well as contemporary dining, with many places crossing effortlessly between the two.

Many Viennese restaurants serve the goat's cheeses and buffalo mozzarella of Robert Paget, who produces his cheeses in the Kamptal (Kamp Valley; a side valley of the

NEED TO KNOW

Price Ranges

The price guide we use is for a two-course meal, excluding drinks.

€	less than €15
€€	€15–30
€€€	more than €30

Opening Hours

➡ **Restaurants** 11am to 2.30pm or 3pm and 6pm to 11pm or midnight. Many close on Sunday or Monday.

➡ **Cafes** From 8am to midnight.

➡ **Beisln** From 11am or noon to 11pm or midnight.

Lunch Menu

Most restaurants have an inexpensive lunch menu (*Mittagsmenü*).

Dress Code

The Viennese take food and dress sense seriously. Dress reasonably well for dinner at top-shelf restaurants.

Mobile Phones

Switch off your phone, or at least the sound, in restaurants. Take calls away from your table.

Booking Tables

When this is highly advisable, we've noted it in reviews or included a telephone number. Also consider eating at fringe times.

Gedeck

Often restaurants charge €2 to €3 extra for the *Gedeck* (table setting), which includes bread and various sundries.

Smoking

Some places have separate areas for smokers, others are completely non-smoking or nonsmoking while food is served.

Online Resources

Visit www.falter.at (under 'Wien, wie es isst'), Vienna's quintessential foodie guide.

Danube) for the Viennese table. Snails also crop up regularly: Vienna once had a thriving snail industry, which today has been revived on the edge of town by Andreas Gugumuck at **Wiener Schnecke** (www.wienerschnecke.at; tour €10). Gugumuck integrates locally produced *Suppengrün* (soup vegetables such as turnips, carrots, leek and herbs) into his own snail production. Local soup vegetables as well as Gugumuck's snails (and even the caviar produced by snails) are often served in top-flight restaurants. Mangalitza ham available at Urbanek (p101), hams by **Thum Schinkenmanufaktur** (Map p256; http://thum-schinken.at) and beef from the Waldviertel region north of the Danube River are other local specialities featuring in a trend towards using fresh, high-quality ingredients produced locally. Much of this can be found at Vienna's Naschmarkt market. *Beisln* such as Silberwirt (p104) or Hollmann Salon (p88) are indicative of how *Beisln* are helping to lead this trend.

Street Food & Markets

The humble *Wurst* (sausage) is sold in up to a dozen varieties at stands throughout the city. It comes with a bread roll or chunk of bread, weighed down with *Senf* (sweet or hot mustard). As well as *Bratwurst* (fried sausage), consider *Burenwurst* (the boiled equivalent), *Debreziner* (spicy), or *Käsekrainer* (infused with cheese) – for some a culinary obscenity, for others a religion.

The largest and best-known of all markets is Naschmarkt (p110), which as well as having produce of all kinds is overflowing with food stalls; many of these are fully fledged restaurants. Other very good markets are Brunnenmarkt (p138), leading to Yppenplatz in Ottakring, and Karmelitermarkt (p169), east of the Danube Canal.

Beisln

Eat in a *Beisl* at least a couple of times during a visit. This unique eatery is usually a simple bistro pub featuring wood-panelling, plain tables, perhaps a ceramic oven, and hearty Viennese cuisine. Fairly recently, marginally more expensive neo-*Beisln* have emerged – eateries that have added a few new touches to old recipes. Revolutions have been hatched and thwarted over sweet meats in these atmospheric places.

Vegetarians & Vegans

Vegans are not well catered for in Vienna's restaurants, and the few places that serve vegan food are low-budget alternative-style eateries. Vegetarians, however, will have no problem finding dishes based on beans and other pulses, fruit and dairy products. Some of them, such as the burger eat-in and takeaway Die Burgermacher's (p126) meat and meatless burgers, and dishes at the midrange Hollmann Salon (p88), use organic ingredients. Naschmarkt and other farmers markets offer lots of choices for vegetarian picnics, takeaway or sit-down meals, and Biomarkt Maran stores have good vegetarian and organic selections of produce and packaged foodstuffs.

How to Eat & Drink Like a Local

Meals A typical breakfast for the Viennese consists of a *Semmel* (bread roll) with jam, ham or cheese (or all three). All but the cheapest hotels have buffets, though, with these as well as cereal, juice, eggs, right up the scale to a full English breakfast. Lunch is often the largest meal – often a lunch special (*Mittagsmenü* or *Tagesteller*) for around €7 to €11. In the evening, bread with cheese or ham and a beer or wine is usually eaten at home. Following the Viennese example is the least expensive way to eat.

Where to Eat The main choices are in a restaurant, *Beisl* (bistro pub), cafe or coffee house or *Heuriger* (wine tavern). Sausage stands abound, and Vienna also has employee canteens, such as on the top floor of the **Justizpalast** (p125).

Arriving In better establishments, a waiter will greet you and take your coat before showing you to a table. Once you're seated you'll have the chance to order a drink right away. The waiter is unlikely to return to take your order until you've closed your menu. In midrange and less formal places, it's usually fine to place your jacket over the back of your chair if you don't want to use the cloakroom.

Eating & Toasting Before starting to eat say *'Guten appetit!'* Before starting to drink, toast by clinking glasses while looking the person in the eye. Not to have eye contact is said to bring seven years of bad sex (you've been warned!). *'Zum Wohl'* (to well-being) is the generic toast.

Paying the Bill Many places don't accept credit cards. Tip 5% to 10% (or don't bother coming back) by rounding up the bill. If several of you are eating together, you will be asked *'Geht das zusammen oder getrennt?'* (Together or separately?). If paying separately, there's no need to pool the money: each diner pays the waiter and tips individually.

Tipping If the bill has been presented in a folder, you can leave the tip in the folder when you depart. It's also common to round up verbally by simply stating the amount and adding *'danke!'* or by saying *'das stimmt so'* (keep the change).

Visiting Heurigen

Heurigen are rustic wine taverns mostly on the outskirts of the city serving traditional food and young wine, usually in a courtyard setting. *Buschenschenken* are a variation on *Heurigen* and only exist in the countryside bordering the city. These are more like the original *Heurigen*, which bloomed after

---

VIENNESE SPECIALITIES

Vienna offers a strong range of traditional dishes. One or two are variations on dishes from other regions. Here's a shortlist of classics.

Schnitzel Wiener Schnitzel should always be crumbed veal, but pork is gaining ground in some places.

Goulash *Rindsgulasch* (beef goulash) is everywhere in Vienna but attains exquisite heights at Meierei im Stadtpark (p158).

Tafelspitz Traditionally this boiled prime beef swims in the juices of locally produced *Suppengrün* (fresh soup vegetables), before being served with *Kren* (horseradish) sauce.

Beuschel Offal, usually sliced lung and heart with a slightly creamy sauce; it's a *Beisl*-type dish.

Backhendl Fried, breaded chicken, often called *steirischer Backhendl* (Styrian fried chicken).

Zwiebelrostbraten Slices of roast beef smothered in gravy and fried onions.

Schinkenfleckerln Oven-baked ham and noodle casserole.

Bauernschmaus Platter of cold meats.

The undeniable monarchs of all desserts are *Kaiserschmarrn* (sweet pancake with raisins) and *Apfelstrudel* (apple strudel), but also look out for *Marillenknödel* (apricot dumplings) in summer.

Joseph II decreed in 1784 that producers could sell their own wine from the vineyard without obtaining a license – open less often (usually in September).

Heuriger Food & Ordering Choose from the buffet and staff will place it on your plate. Most food is sold by the decagram (dag) in portions of 10 dag (100 grams). Typically, you find a selection of warm and cold foods, such as roast pork in one or the other variety, blood sausage, meat loaf and a range of cured meats, lard and breads, pickled vegetables and salads such as *Schwarzwurzel-salat* (black salsify salad) and potato salad, as well as strudel for dessert.

Heuriger Wine The most important feature of any *Heuriger* is the wine, traditionally made by the owner and usually only a year old. *Sturm* (literally 'storm' for its cloudy appearance, perhaps even for its chaotic effects on drinkers) is yeasty because it is still fermenting. It's sold from around early September to the middle of October. A new vintage of bottled *Heuriger* wine is released each year on 11 November.

Where & When Apart from a handful of *Stadt-heurigen* in the city, *Heurigen* are concentrated in and around winegrowing regions on Vienna's fringes. Many are only open part of the year or every other month. Double check opening times online or by calling before heading out to avoid disappointment.

Transport & Map Some *Heurigen* are up to 20 minutes' walk from the public transport stop. Pick up the *Verkehrslinienplan für Wien* transport map (also showing streets in outer suburbs; €2.50) from any Wiener Linien service desk or use www.wienerlinien.at.

KAHLENBERG, GRINZING & DÖBLING

These three villages have a large concentration of *Heurigen* (especially Grinzing, where most cater to tour groups with kitsch live music and pseudo folk art beyond the pale). Those in Kahlenberg can easily be combined with a visit to the historical site on Kahlenberg proper.

For Grinzing take the U4 (or tram D) to Heiligenstadt and change to bus 38A; this continues on to Kahlenberg. You can also take tram D to the Grinzinger Strasse stop and change to the 38A there. For Döbling, take tram 38 from Schottentor.

Hirt (☑318 96 41; www.heuriger-hirt.at; 19, Eisernenhandgasse 165, Kahlenberg; ☺3-11pm Wed-Fri, noon-11pm Sat & Sun, closed Wed-Fri Nov-Mar; ☐38A Kahlenberg) Hidden among the vineyards on the eastern slopes of Kahlenberg, this is a simple *Heuriger* with few frills and pleasant views.

Sirbu (☑320 59 28; www.sirbu.at; Kahlenberger Strasse 210; ☺3-11pm Mon-Sat, mid-Apr–mid-Oct; ☐38A Kahlenberg) Far-reaching views across Vienna's urban expanse from its quiet spot, and a garden that's the perfect place on a sunny afternoon.

Reinprecht (☑320 14 71; www.heuriger-rein precht.at; 19, Cobenzlgasse 22; ☺3.30pm-midnight Mar-Oct, closed Mon-Fri Nov-Feb; ☐38A Grinzing) Like others in Grinzing, Reinprecht caters to the masses with its huge garden, enormous buffet and live music, but award-winning wines.

Weingut am Reisenberg (☑320 93 93; www. weingutamreisenberg.at; Oberer Reisenbergweg 15; ☺5pm-midnight Fri, 1pm-midnight Sat & Sun May-Sep, 6pm-midnight Wed-Sat Oct-Dec; ☐38A Oberer Reisenbergweg) Modern premises with huge windows and a styled, brick interior. Part of the new generation of *Heurigen*, with Italian cuisine and vegetarian dishes.

Zawodsky (☑320 79 78; www.zawodsky.at; 19, Reinischgasse 3, Döbling; ☺5pm-midnight Mon-Fri, from 2pm Sat & Sun, closed Mon-Wed Apr & Oct-Nov; ☐38 An den langen Lüssen) Stripped-back set up featuring picnic tables surrounded by apple trees and vineyards, and a small selection of hot and cold meats complemented by various salads.

STREBERSDORF & STAMMERSDORF

To the north across the Danube, the neighbourhoods of Strebersdorf and Stammersdorf produce around 30% of the city's wine, making it Vienna's largest winegrowing district. The *Heurigen* here are very traditional and authentic. For Strebersdorf, take the U6 to Floridsdorf U-Bahn station and tram 26 from there. For Stammersdorf take tram 31 from Schottenring U-Bahn station, or tram 30 from Floridsdorf U-Bahn station. Regional bus 228 also runs to Stammersdorf from Floridsdorf.

Göbel (www.weinbaugoebel.at; 21, Stammersdorfer Kellergasse 131, Stammersdorf; ☐228 Senderstrasse, ☐30, 31 Stammersdorfer Strasse) Combines quality wines (about 80% are reds) with a sleek architectural setting. Bus 228 drops you very close; the tram runs until late. See the website for opening times.

Eckert (☑292 25 96; www.eckert.co.at; Strebersdorfer Strasse 158; ☺from 4pm Mon-Fri, from 3pm Sat, 10am-5pm Sun, see website for dates;

🚇32A Mühlweg, 🚊26 Edmund-Hawranek-Platz)
An eclectic cross between a traditional *Heuriger*
and an art centre. Paintings by local artists adorn
the walls.

Weingut Schilling (📞292 41 89; www.
weingut-schilling.at; 21, Langenzersdorferstrasse
54, Strebersdorf; ⊘from 2pm Mon-Fri, from 3pm
Sat, from noon Sun, see website for dates; 🚊26
Edmund-Hawranek-Platz) With the spread of
vineyards rising over Bisamberg hill in full view
from its large garden, Schilling attracts many on
warm evenings.

Schmidt (📞292 66 88; www.heuriger-schmidt.
at; 21, Stammersdorfer Strasse 105, Stammersdorf; ⊘3pm-midnight Thu-Sat, from 2pm Sun,
see website for dates; 🚊31 Stammersdorf)
Stocks wonderful *Muskateller* and *Grüner
Veltliner* wines.

Wieninger (📞292 41 06; www.heuriger-
wieninger.at; 21, Stammersdorfer Strasse 78,
Stammersdorf; ⊘3pm-midnight Fri, from noon
Sat & Sun mid-Jan–late Dec, also 3pm-midnight
Thu early Apr-late Dec; 🚊30A, 🚊30, 31 Stammersdorf) Extensive buffet, fruity and light wines
in a local atmosphere.

NUSSDORF

Nussdorf has a string of inviting *Heurigen*.
Take tram D to the terminus.

Mayer am Pfarrplatz (📞370 12 87; www.
pfarrplatz.at; 19, Pfarrplatz 2, Nussdorf; ⊘4pm-
midnight Mon-Sat, from noon Sun; 🚊D Nussdorf)
Caters to tour groups but retains an authentic air.
Beethoven lived here in 1817. There's a children's
play area and live music from 7pm.

MAURER

A cluster of *Heurigen* is located southwest
of the centre and easily reached by tram 60
from Hietzing U-Bahn station.

Zahel (📞889 13 18; www.zahel.at; Maurer Hauptplatz 9; ⊘11.30am-midnight, see website for
dates; 🚊60 Maurer Hauptplatz) One of the oldest
Heurigen in Vienna, Zahel occupies a 250-year-
old farmhouse on Maurer Hauptplatz. The buffet
is laden with Viennese and seasonal cuisine and
wine is for sale to take home.

Edlmoser (📞889 86 80; www.edlmoser.at; 23,
Maurer Lange Gasse, Maurer; ⊘2.30pm-midnight,
see website for dates; 🚊60 Maurer-Lange-Gasse)
Run by dynamic young winemaker Michael
Edlmoser in a four-centuries-old house.

OTTAKRING

Most *Heurigen* to the west in Ottakring are
within the city's built-up area, but they offer
excellent views and peaceful gardens.

10er Marie (16, Ottakringerstrasse 222-224;
⊘3pm-midnight Mon-Sat; 🚇Ottakring, 🚊2, 10,
46 Ottakring) Vienna's oldest *Heuriger*, it's family-
run, rustic and attracts locals and visitors alike.

Buschenschank Huber (📞485 81 80; http://
sissi-huber.at; Roterdstrasse 5; ⊘3pm-midnight
Tue-Sat; 🚊10, 44 Dornbach/Güpferlingstrasse)
Slightly upmarket edge with a gargantuan buffet,
filling a mainly older crowd with a sensational
selection of salads, meats and sweets.

Buschenschank Stippert (📞486 89 17;
16, Ottakringerstrasse 225; ⊘3pm-midnight
Wed-Sat, 10am-1pm Sun; 🚇Ottakring, 🚊2, 10,
46 Ottakring) Blink and you'll think you've time-
travelled at this simple *Heuriger* with sassy staff
and a ceramic oven in the centre of the room.

Eating by Neighbourhood

➡ **Stephansdom & the Historic Centre** Packed
with options, especially around Stephansplatz
and streets leading down towards the Danube
Canal. (p85)

➡ **Karlsplatz & Around Naschmarkt** Myriad
food stalls and restaurants on Naschmarkt,
and lots of options in Margareten and Mariahilf
districts. (p101)

➡ **The Museum District & Neubau** Some of
the best eating in Vienna's *Vorstadt* districts,
especially in and behind MuseumsQuartier.
(p126)

➡ **Alsergrund & the University District**
Yppenplatz has a market and a good cluster of
eateries. There are many student places close to
the university campuses. (p137)

➡ **Schloss Belvedere to the Canal** One or two
gems, otherwise limited options; Hauptstrasse
Landstrasse has a good cluster. (p158)

➡ **Prater & East of the Danube** Most located
west of Karmeliterplatz and Taborstrasse
(around Karmelitermarkt), extending north
towards Augarten. (p167)

Lonely Planet's Top Choices

Silberwirt (p104) Stylish *Beisl* with tradition.

ON (p104) Relaxed Austro-Asian fusion.

Österreicher im MAK (p159) Back-to-the-roots Austrian cuisine.

Neni (p104) Middle Eastern in Naschmarkt.

Steirereck im Stadtpark (p159) Vienna's class act by the Wien River.

Die Burgermacher (p126) Delicious organic burgers.

Best by Budget

€

Bitzinger Würstelstand am Albertinaplatz (p69) Sausage stand opposite the opera.

Tongues (p101) Hole-in-the-wall vinyl shop meets organic nosh spot.

Pure Living Bakery (p180) NYC-style deli with a laid-back garden near Schönbrunn.

€€

Motto am Fluss (p85) Ultimate restaurant, bar and cafe on the canal.

Brezl Gwölb (p138) *Beisl* big on Gothic charm and Austrian home cooking.

€€€

Steirereck im Stadtpark (p159) Seasonal taste sensations at a two-Michelin-starred restaurant in Stadtpark.

Schnattl (p140) Elegant wood-panelled interior, seasonally changing menus and courtyard dining.

Meinl's Restaurant (p87) Exceptional quality through the seasons.

Best Seafood

Kornat (p87) Dalmatian with formal style and all-day kitchen.

Umar (p102) The best catch around Naschmarkt, with brilliantly fresh seafood and Wachau wines.

An-Do (p140) Relaxed Yppen-platz choice, with an aquarium of a menu.

Best Vegetarian

Tian (p86) Formal vegie with a cool cocktail bar.

Wiener Deewan (p137) 'Eat what you like, pay as you wish' Pakistani cuisine.

Hollerei (p180) Convivial vegie bistro near Schloss Schönbrunn.

Best Goulash

Meierei im Stadtpark (p158) Some speak of the world's best.

Café Drechsler (p105) DJs, Terence Conran cool with accomplished goulash.

Café Alt Wien (p88) Coffee house to sit in while writing home about goulash.

Best Asian

Yohm (p85) Creative pan-Asian and sushi.

Ra'mien (p103) Fresh spices and herbs give oomph to these noodle soups.

Kojiro (p103) Vienna's best sushi.

Chang Asian Noodles (p101) Slurp first-class noodle soup in an upbeat setting.

Best Schnitzels

Figlmüller (p86) Bills itself as the home of the schnitzel.

Gasthaus Wickerl (p140) Warm wooden *Beisl* decor and sizzling schnitzels.

Zum Alten Fassl (p102) Residential setting with private garden.

Ubl (p102) *Beisl* dishing up four types of schnitzel, all cooked to thin, golden perfection.

Best Beisln

Rustic

Beim Czaak (p85) Traditional to the back teeth.

Steman (p102) Friendly, high-ceilinged *Beisl*.

Zum Alten Fassl (p102) Falco once lived above this woody *Beisl*, which has a regionally focused menu.

Haas Beisl (p103) Meaty menu and a genuinely local vibe.

Figlmüller (p86) Large, bustling, touristy but ever popular.

Contemporary Atmosphere

Silberwirt (p104) Atmospheric with an accent on organic and local grub.

Tancredi (p103) Pared-down interior, seasonal menu and garden for summer dining.

Amerlingbeisl (p126) Courtyard dining in the Biedermeier heart of Spittelberg.

Hollmann Salon (p88) Partly organic meats, shared tables and young staff.

Patrons relax in a Viennese cafe

🍷 Coffee Houses & Cake Shops

Vienna's long-standing tradition of coffee houses and cake shops captures the spirit of Gemütlichkeit – that quintessential Austrian quality of cosiness and languid indulgence. Grand or humble, poster-plastered or chandelier-lit, this is where you can join the locals for whipped cream, gossip and a slice of living history.

NEED TO KNOW

Opening Hours

Coffee houses and cake shops tend to open for breakfast and close anywhere between 7pm and midnight; many close earlier on Sunday.

Coffee House Etiquette

➡ In more formal coffee houses wait to be seated, otherwise take your pick of the tables.

➡ There's no dress code per se, but smart-casual wear will help you blend in with the crowd at posh coffee houses.

➡ You're generally welcome to linger for as long as you please – waiters present the *Rechnung* (bill) when you ask for it.

➡ Some coffee houses have English menus, but failing that, you can sometimes choose from the counter.

➡ Viennese waiters are notoriously brusque, but a polite *Grüss Gott* (good day) and a smattering of German will stand you in good stead.

➡ Newspapers are freely available, often also in English.

How Much?

Prices vary but on average expect to pay between €2 and €5 for a coffee, between €3 and €4 for a slice of cake, and around €8 for a day special.

What to Order

Coffee and cake are obvious choices, but many *Kaffeehäuser* also serve *Frühstuck* (breakfast) and moderately priced *Tagesteller* (day specials) at lunch. Dishes tend to be hearty, along the lines of schnitzel, *Fiakergulasch* (beef goulash with egg, pickles and sausage) and *Tafelspitz* (boiled beef with horseradish). Snacks are available nearly all day.

Coffee Houses

Poet and playwright Bertolt Brecht once described Vienna as 'a small city built around a few coffee houses' where the locals 'sit together and read papers.' It's a simple observation but a perceptive one, for despite the overwhelming variety of coffee on offer, caffeine is secondary to the *Kaffeehaus* experience. In many ways coffee

Apfelstrudel (apple strudel)

is but an entrance ticket to a world where you can meet friends, browse newspapers, play games, put the world to rights, reflect and linger undisturbed for hours. Affectionately dubbed Vienna's 'living rooms,' many Wiener go misty eyed when you ask them about their favourite *Kaffeehaus*.

COFFEE HOUSE HISTORY

It all started with some mystery beans. Back at the Battle of Vienna in 1683, when Polish-Habsburg allies sent the Ottoman invaders packing, the Turks, so the story goes, left sacks of precious coffee beans at the city gates as they beat a hasty retreat. There was much speculation as to what these beans were, with most surmising camel feed or dung. King Jan III Sobieski handed over the beans to his military officer, Jerzy Franciszek Kulczycki, who recognised their value, having encountered coffee during time spent in captivity in Turkey. Adding a dash of milk and sweetening the aromatic blend to Viennese tastes, he soon opened Vienna's first coffee house: the Hof zur Blauen Flasche. In coffee house circles to this day, Kulczycki is considered something of a patron saint.

The Viennese were hooked and soon coffee houses began to pop up all over the city. By the late 18th century, *Kaffeehäuser* were in vogue in high society, with composers like Mozart and Beethoven giving public performances. They became places to meet, socialise and, on a practical level, warm up.

This boom continued in the 19th century thanks to the Habsburg's insatiable appetite for coffee, cake and palatial surrounds. *Sacher Torte* was created for Prince Klemens

Above: Cakes at Demel (p70)
Right: Café Drechsler (p105)

LONELY PLANET / GETTY IMAGES ©

Wenzel von Metternich in 1832 and swiftly became an imperial favourite. In the latter half of the century, grand coffee houses such as Landtmann, Central and Sperl opened their doors, setting a precedent with grand interiors adorned with chandeliers, Thonet chairs and marble-topped tables.

At the turn of the century, coffee houses attracted the greatest artists, musicians, writers and radical thinkers of the age – Mahler, Klimt, Freud, Trotsky and Otto Wagner. The 1950s signalled the end of an era for many *Kaffeehäuser* – a period the Viennese call the *Kaffeehaussterben* (coffee house death). Postwar, a new generation of Viennese had grown tired of the coffee house, which they saw as being antiquated and/or elitist. TVs and espresso bars also played a part in their closure, as did the scattering of Jews, many of whom were pivotal to making the coffee house a cultural institution. Luckily many of the best survived and the tradition later revived.

COFFEE HOUSE CULTURE

In 2011 Vienna's coffee houses were added to the Unesco list of Intangible Cultural Heritage, which defines them as 'places where time and space are consumed, but only the coffee is found on the bill'. Indeed, life may rush ahead outside, but the clocks are stuck in 1910 in the *Kaffeehaus*, where the spirit of unhurried gentility remains sacrosanct. Neither time nor trend obsessed, coffee houses are like a nostalgic balm for the stresses of modern life; they are places where life dissolves into the warm simplicity of a good cup of coffee, impromptu conversation and nostalgic daydreaming.

While the echoes of the past can still be felt keenly in the marble splendour of stalwarts like Central and Sperl, a growing number of coffee houses are ushering in a new age of creativity, from pretty cupcake shops to feline-focused cat cafes imported from Japan.

Another nod to the social importance of *Kaffeehäuser* is the Kaffeesiederball, staged by the coffee houses owners at the Hofburg in February, one of the most glittering events on the ball calendar.

For more on coffee house culture, see the boxed text on p160.

COFFEE DECODER

Ask for 'a coffee, please' and you may get a puzzled look. The following are fixtures on most menus:

Brauner Black but served with a tiny splash of cream; comes in *gross* (large) or *klein* (small).

Einspänner Strong coffee with whipped cream, served in a glass.

Verlängerter *Brauner* lengthened with hot water.

Mocca Sometimes spelled *Mokka* or *Schwarzer* – black coffee.

Melange The Viennese classic, served with milk and topped with milk froth or whipped cream, similar to a cappuccino.

Kapuziner With a little milk and perhaps a sprinkling of grated chocolate.

Eiskaffee Cold coffee with vanilla ice cream and whipped cream.

Maria Theresia With orange liqueur and whipped cream.

Türkische Comes in a copper pot with coffee grounds and sugar.

Cake Shops

Forget the schnitzel clichés, if the sweet-toothed Viennese could choose one last meal on earth, most would go straight for dessert. The city brims with *Konditoreien* (cake shops), where buttery aromas lure passers-by to counters brimming with fresh batches of cream-filled, chocolate-glazed, fruit-topped treats. In these mini temples of three o'clock indulgence, pastries, cakes and tortes are elevated to an art form.

Many cake shops also do a fine line in *Confiserie* (confectionery), producing their own sweets and chocolate. Sumptuous examples include Demel, one-time purveyor to the imperial and royal court, famous for its chocolate-nougat *Annatorte* and fragrant candied violets. The Viennese swear by the feather-light macaroons, chocolates and tortes at Oberlaa, while retro Aida time warps you back to the 1950s with its delectable cakes and pink-kissed interior.

Top of the charts in Viennese cakes is *Sacher Torte*. Emperor Franz Josef was partial to this rich iced chocolate cake – its sweetness offset by a tangy layer of apricot jam – and it's still a favourite at **Café Sacher** (Map p254; 01, Philharmonikerstrasse 4; ⊙8am-midnight) today. *Esterházytorte,* a marbled butter-cream and meringue torte, and flaky, quark-filled *Topfenstrudel* would also make the top 10. *Gugelhupf,* a ring-shaped marble cake, *Linzertorte,* a spiced tart filled with redcurrant jam, and good old apple strudel are as popular as ever, too.

Lonely Planet's Top Choices

Café Sperl (p104) The real deal coffee house: history, good food, games and faded grandeur.

Café Central (p141) A drop of opulence in vaulted, marble surrounds.

Café Leopold Hawelka (p69) Viennese character exudes from the walls of this convivial coffee house.

Demel (p70) Decadent cakes that once pleased the emperor's palate.

Sperlhof (p169) Offbeat and arty 1920s haunt.

Cafe Neko (p90) This Innere Stadt newcomer is the cat's whiskers.

Best Historic Coffee Houses

Café Sperl (p104) A blast of nostalgia and a game of billiards in this *Jugendstil* beauty.

Café Central (p141) Trotsky and Lenin once played chess under the soaring vaults here.

Café Landtmann (p142) Mahler and Marlene Dietrich loved this old-world classic near the Burgtheater.

Café Griensteidl (p70) Going strong since 1847, this *Jugendstil* gem was a literary magnet.

Café Leopold Hawelka (p69) Hundertwasser and Warhol once hung out at this warm, wood-panelled cafe.

Café Korb (p86) Freud's old haunt is now part gallery, part cafe.

Best Cakes & Sweets

Demel (p70) Cakes and tortes fit for royalty.

Café Sacher (p40) King of the *Sacher Torte*.

Oberlaa (p72) Beautifully wrapped chocolates and macaroons.

Aida (p89) 1950s decor and delectable cakes.

Diglas (p89) Legendary *Apfelstrudel* that flakes just so.

Best Local Coffee Houses

Café Alt Wien (p88) A dimly lit, arty haunt popular with students; located in the centre and has long hours.

Café am Heumarkt (p160) Old-school charmer near the Stadtpark.

Sperlhof (p169) Race back to the 1920s in this cafe with books, billiards and ping pong.

Café Jelinek (p106) Warm, down to earth and full of regulars.

Kleines Café (p88) Boho flair in this dinky cafe on Franziskanerplatz.

Best New-Wave Cafes

Cafe Neko (p90) A Japanese 'cat cafe' with a high purr factor.

Cupcakes Wien (p137) Pink is the colour at this fabulously girly cupcake parlour.

Phil (p105) Retro-cool cafe-bookshop on Gumpendorfer Strasse.

Café Drechsler (p105) DJ beats at Terence Conran–designed cafe open 23 hours a day.

Pure Living Bakery (p180) Boho-flavoured garden cafe near Schönbrunn.

Best Free Live Music

Café Bräunerhof (p71) Classical music from 3pm to 6pm on weekends.

Café Central (p141) A pianist plays from 5pm to 10pm daily.

Café Landtmann (p142) Live piano music tinkles from 8pm to 11pm Sunday to Tuesday.

Café Prückel (p88) Piano music from 7pm to 10pm on Monday, Wednesday and Friday in 1950s surrounds.

Diglas (p89) Bag a cosy booth to hear piano music from 7pm to 10pm Thursday to Saturday.

PLAN YOUR TRIP COFFEE HOUSES & CAKE SHOPS

Drinking & Nightlife

Vaulted wine cellars in situ since Mozart's day and boisterous beer gardens, boho student dives and dressy cocktail bars, retro and rooftop bars – there's nightlife to suit every mood and moment in Vienna. And in this city where history often waltzes with the cutting edge, you'll find many centuries-old bars have been given an avant-garde makeover without losing an ounce of character.

Vienna's Nightlife Hotspots

Reincarnated venues are very now, with their own distinctive flair and story to tell, such as former pet-grooming parlours, electrical shops and ruby-gold brothels that have been born again as bars. Also on the up are rooftop bars where you can swoon over skyline views while sipping a mojito. Retro bars with junk-shop charm are returning to vogue, too, in a city that loves to time travel to a different era over a drink or two.

Your options are limitless, but particularly lively stretches if you're devising a bar crawl include Gumpendorferstrasse in Mariahilf, between Naschmarkt and Mariahilferstrasse, Schleifmühlgasse in the Freihausviertel south of Naschmarkt (Wieden district) and the more touristy *Bermudadreieck* (Bermuda Triangle) in the Innere Stadt's old Jewish quarter. The Gürtel ring road is great for DJs and live music in bar-club hybrids under the railway arches.

Summer in the City

With the advent of summer, many revellers descend on outdoor venues. The bars and shady courtyards at Altes AKH university attract plenty, as does the market square Yppenplatz in Ottakring and the Freihausviertel in Wieden. The reinvention of the Danube Canal as a bar strip has been a huge success; Flex (p141) is a long-established location, but the likes of Strandbar Herrmann (p160) and Badeschiff (p92), pool by day, bar by night, have added an entirely new dimension to the waterway.

As spring ushers in summer, *Schanigärten* (courtyard gardens and pavement terraces) begin to pop up like wildflowers, luring the Viennese outdoors. There were 1800 at the last count.

Intimate Clubbing

While Vienna won't be stealing Berlin's clubbing crown anytime soon, the capital's relatively small scene still traverses the entire stylistic and musical spectrum, from chandelier-lit glamour to industrial-style grunge, with playlists skipping from indie through to house, electro, techno, R&B, reggae, metal and '80s pop. Clubs invariably feature excellent DJs, with both home-grown and international talent working the decks.

Bombastic venues are rare creatures here and the vibe is kept intimate and friendly in small clubs, where dress codes and bouncers are often refreshingly relaxed. The borders between bars and clubs are often blurred, with DJs amping up the atmosphere as the night wears on. Indeed, what the clubs here often lack in size, they make up for with alternative flair or unique locations, whether you're partying poolside in a former sauna-turned-club in the Prater, under the arches on the Gürtel or in a 1950s-style pavilion in the Volksgarten.

Microbreweries

Venues where the beer is always fresh, the atmosphere jovial and families are welcome, Vienna's microbreweries make for a great night out. Most offer a healthy selection of beers brewed on the premises (and proudly display the shining, brass brewing equipment), complemented by filling Austrian staples. Punters spill out into their courtyard gardens in summer.

Grape & Grain

While wine is the chosen drink of the Viennese, beer features heavily in the city's cultural make-up. Here's what you might order:

Blauburgunder Complex, fruity Pinot noir red.

Grüner Veltliner Strong, fresh white with hints of citrus and pear.

Riesling Fruity white with strong acidity.

Zweigelt Full-bodied red with intense cherry fruit aromas.

Dunkel Thick dark beer with a very rich flavour.

Helles Lager with a bite – clear and lightly hoppy.

Pils Crisp, strong and often bitter Pilsner beer.

Märzen Red-coloured beer with a strong malt taste.

Zwickel Unfiltered beer with a cloudy complexion.

Drinking & Nightlife by Neighbourhood

➜ **The Hofburg & Around** Old-world wine taverns, intimate cocktail bars and drinks with Hofburg views in the Burggarten and Volksgarten. (p69)

➜ **Stephansdom & the Historic Centre** Narrow lanes hide a mix of cellar bars, wine bars, pubs and serious cocktail bars. (p88)

➜ **Karlsplatz & Around Naschmarkt** Boho hood crammed with clubs, retro and alternative bars, especially along Gumpendorferstrasse. (p104)

➜ **The Museum District & Neubau** Arty bars with a spritz of culture and alfresco seating – hit Spittelberg for *Schanigärten*. (p128)

➜ **Alsergrund & the University District** Student pubs and all-night parties under the Gürtel viaduct. (p141)

➜ **Schloss Belvedere to the Canal** Bars by the Danube Canal and the odd microbrewery. (p160)

NEED TO KNOW

Opening Hours

Opening hours vary greatly and depend on season, with places often staying open later in summer. See individual listings for specific times.

➜ **Bars & Pubs** Generally open around 4pm or 5pm and close anywhere between midnight and 4am.

➜ **Clubs** Generally open between 6pm and 10pm and close roughly around 4am; many are only open Wednesday or Thursday through to Saturday.

Online Resources

➜ **Falter** (www.falter.at) Event and party listings.

➜ **Vienna Online** (http://party.vienna.at) Keep track of club nights with this event calendar.

➜ **Tourist Info Wien** (www.wien.info) Nightlife listings arranged by theme.

Drink Prices

Standard beer prices range from €2 to €5, depending on the location and venue (central Vienna tends to be more expensive). Local wine is quite reasonable – you can easily get a decent glass of Austrian wine for around €3, though prices rise at fancier wine bars. Expect to pay at least €7 for a simple mixed drink and around €9 and up for a cocktail.

Club Entry

Entry prices can and do vary wildly – from nothing to €15 – and depend on who's on the decks. Many small, intimate clubs offer free entry at least once a week.

Tipping

Tipping is standard: for smaller bills (under €10) it is customary to round up and add another euro if need be; for larger tabs, 5% to 10% is customary.

➜ **Prater & East of the Danube** Clubbing live-wire around Praterstern, rooftop haunts and relaxed cafe-bars around Karmelitermarkt. (p169)

➜ **Schloss Schönbrunn & Around** A smattering of cafe-bars and clubs. (p181)

Lonely Planet's Top Choices

Le Loft (p169) Map out Vienna from above at this super-sleek lounge bar.

Loos American Bar (p69) Find a cosy alcove for a cocktail at Loos' 1908 classic.

Volksgarten ClubDiskothek (p70) Party in the park at this glam club near the Hofburg.

Palmenhaus (p70) Cocktail sip in this palm house with great outdoor seating overlooking Burggarten.

Strandbar Herrmann (p160) Beach-side beers, DJs and films by the canal.

Tanzcafé Jenseits (p105) Brothel turned glamorously boho bar.

Best Riverside Bars

Strandbar Herrmann (p160) Lively 'beach' bar beside the Costa del Danube.

Urania (p161) Slick glass-walled bar overlooking the Danube Canal.

Best Wine Bars

Vis-à-vis (p88) Postage stamp of a wine bar tucked down a narrow passage.

Weinstube Josefstadt (p141) Atmospheric *Stadtheurigen* hiding in an oasis of a garden.

Villon (p69) The central district's deepest wine cellar has a light, modern ambience.

Sekt Comptoir (p105) Effervescent bar with Burgenland *Sekt* (sparkling wine) near the Naschmarkt.

Best Microbreweries

Siebensternbräu (p129) Cheery brewpub with hoppy beers and a warm-weather courtyard.

Wieden Bräu (p107) Helles, Märzen and hemp beers, plus summertime garden.

Salm Bräu (p161) Relaxed pick for home brews right by Schloss Belvedere.

Best Cocktail Bars

Loos American Bar (p69) Mixology magic in this minimalist, Adolf Loos–designed bar.

Kruger's American Bar (p88) Sip a classic margarita in this 1920s, wood-panelled den.

Barfly's Club (p106) Terrific cocktails in an intimate setting.

Lutz (p106) Modern contender with club chairs for conversing over a frozen mojito.

Best Retro Bars

Tanzcafé Jenseits (p105) Bordello-chic bar with a tiny dance floor.

Phil (p105) Retro-cool cafe-bar with a chilled vibe and books for browsing.

Wirr (p129) Vintage furnishings, local art and a downstairs club.

Mon Ami (p107) Former pet-grooming salon turned '60s-style bar.

Best Clubs

Volksgarten ClubDiskothek (p70) A popular house-spinning club.

Pratersauna (p170) Dance to electro by the poolside at this former sauna.

Fluc (p170) Turbo-charged Praterstern club with an alternative edge.

Donau (p129) Tucked-away techno club with a friendly crowd.

Best Rooftop Bars

Le Loft (p169) Knockout skyline views from this glass-clad bar on the 18th floor of the Sofitel.

Dachboden (p128) Big-top views of Vienna from the 25hours Hotel's rooftop bar.

Café Oben (p129) Landmark spot from this cafe atop Hauptbücherei Wien.

Sky Bar (p88) Vienna's most spectacular rooftop bar in the Innere Stadt.

Best Gay & Lesbian Hangouts

Café Berg (p142) Friendly, open and stocks gay books.

Café Savoy (p106) The atmosphere of a traditional Viennese cafe plus a little pizzazz.

Mango Bar (p107) Ever-popular bar open every night of the week.

Frauencafé (p129) A women-only favourite of Vienna's lesbian scene.

Best Schanigärten

Palmenhaus (p70) Slide into summer with DJ beats, barbecues and beers.

Volksgarten Pavillon (p70) Drink in Hofberg views and summer vibes from this pavilion's tree-shaded garden.

Café Leopold (p128) A terrace perfect for lapping up MuseumsQuartier's cultural buzz.

Kunsthallencafé (p106) Join an arty laid-back crowd on the decking.

★ Entertainment

Whether you're into opera, classical music and theatre or listening to live rock or jazz in one of the capital's music venues, Vienna offers lots of entertainment opportunities. It is home to the German-speaking world's oldest theatre, the Burgtheater, as well as the famous Vienna Boys' Choir and the Vienna Philharmonic Orchestra, which performs in the acoustically superb Musikverein.

Opera

Vienna is a world capital for opera, and a quick walk down Karntner Strasse from Stephansplatz to the Staatsoper will turn up more Mozart lookalikes than you can poke a baton at. The two main performance spaces are the Staatsoper, which closes in July and August, and Theater an der Wien (p108), which remains open during these months.

STAATSOPER TICKETS

The availability of tickets and how far in advance you need to book depends entirely on the popularity of a performance. To be sure of getting a seating ticket, book up to eight weeks in advance. For some performances, one month or a few weeks in advance is sufficient – book by phone, online or in person at the Bundestheaterkassen. The Bundestheaterkassen is an exclusive outlet for Staatsoper tickets, although you will see scalpers outside illegally offering tickets. Tickets for the Volksoper, Akademietheater and Burgtheater can also be bought here. For many performances, however, booking in person even a couple of days in advance is sufficient, if not for the best seats. The chances of getting seats on the day at the Abendkasse or in the foyer of the opera are quite low for most performances. The best alternative in that case is a standing room ticket.

If you need to pick up a purchased ticket at the *Abendkasse*, expect to queue for about 10 minutes. Depending on the popularity of a performance, the standing room queue will begin forming five hours or more before the performance begins, or you can get in almost immediately.

If you are in Vienna and don't have a ticket, it's best simply to drop by the Bundestheaterkassen. You can buy a ticket on the spot or staff can explain the best way to get one for the day you want.

The **Bundestheaterkassen** (Map p256; ☑514 44 7880; www.bundestheater.at; 01, Operngasse 2; ⊗8am-6pm Mon-Fri, 9am-noon Sat & Sun; Ⓜ Stephansplatz) office is located on Operngasse, on the west side of the Staatsoper. Tickets are available here for the Staatsoper two months prior to performance dates. Credit-card purchases can be made online or by telephone. For online bookings go to the Bundestheaterkassen website and click on the desired venue. The **Info unter den Arkaden** (Map p256; Herbert von Karajan-Platz 1; ⊗9am-1hr before performance begins Mon-Fri, 9am-5pm Sat) branch is located on the Kärntner Strasse side of the Staatsoper.

Staatsoper Telephone Bookings Call ☑+43 (1) 513 1 513 to reach the Bundestheaterkassen from outside Austria. From inside Austria, leave out the prefixes. Open 10am to 9pm daily.

Collecting Tickets Pick up tickets from the Bundestheaterkassen office using your ticket code. If you don't do this, the tickets must be collected at the *Abendkasse* (evening sales desk), which opens one hour before the performance. If you use the 'print at home' option on the internet, you'll be a given a certain time period during which you must print your ticket.

Abendkasse Located inside the Staatsoper, it opens one hour prior to performance and sells the leftover

NEED TO KNOW

→ **Opera** Staatsoper has no perform-ances in July and August. Theater an der Wien is open during these months.

→ **Cinema** Some cinemas have dis-counted admission on Monday.

Opening Hours

→ **Live Rock & Jazz** Usually starts at 8pm or 9pm.

Advance Booking

Highly advisable for classical cultural of-ferings, but there are also plenty of oppor-tunities to catch performances at short notice. Bookings for live rock and jazz are rarely required.

Ticket Organisations & Reservations

→ **Bundestheaterkassen** (p45) The official ticket office and exclusive out-let for the Staatsoper, Volksoper and Burgtheater.

→ **Wien-Ticket Pavillon** (p66) Charges anything from no commission up to a 6% levy. Tickets for all venues (but not for the Staatsoper, Burgtheater and Volksoper) are sold here.

→ **Jirsa Theater Karten Büro** (Map p260) Large ticketing office. Commis-sion of 25% on most opera, classical music and theatre tickets.

→ **Tourist Info Wien** (p235) Website with events calendar and all booking information.

→ **oeticket.com** Online sales for events as well as ticket sales and pick up in **oeticket Center MuseumsQuartier**.

Online Resources

→ **Falter** (www.falter.at) Weekly listings of all events.

→ **Tourist Info Wien** (http://events. wien.info/en) Produces a monthly listing of events and an annual events publica-tion, *Vienna Now or Never*.

contingent. Expect to queue for about 10 minutes here.

Staatsoper Foyer Sells tickets from 9am to two hours before performance Monday to Friday and 9am to noon Saturday.

Email Send email to kartenvertrieb@wiener-staatsoper.at.

Standing Room *Stehplätze* (room for 567 people) tickets are sold from an entrance on Operngasse, beginning 80 minutes before the performance. Downstairs/upstairs tickets cost €3/4.

Cost Seating costs from €10 to €197. About €45 is usual for an unimpeded view.

Classical Music

Opportunities to listen to classical music in Vienna abound. Churches are a hub for recitals of Bach and Händel especially, but also great venues for all sorts of classical music recitals. Vienna's Philharmonic Or-chestra is based in the Musikverein (p108).

Standing Room Costs €5.

Seating Cheapest is directly above the stage, with good views of the hall but not the orchestra. Everything up to €49 has partially obscured views, above €49 is with unimpeded views (ask when booking).

Return Tickets Although tickets are sold out years ahead, tickets of those who are unable to attend a particular performance are returned and sold for between €15 and €101. Depending on whether the Musikverein or the Wiener Phil-harmoniker has organised the concert, returned tickets can be bought from the Musikverein itself (seven weeks or less before the concert) or from the **Wiener Philharmoniker Karten- und Ballbüro** (Map p256) on the Monday before the performance or, for standing room tickets, go to the ticket booking office one hour before the performance.

Rock & Jazz

Vienna's rock and jazz scene is lively, with a strong local scene as well as international acts playing from the smallest bars to the largest arenas. See **Falter** (www.falter.at) for bands, venues and dates. The biggest bashes are the **Donauinselfest** (https://don-auinselfest.at) and **Jazz Fest Wien** (☑408 60 30; www.viennajazz.org).

Theatre

The Burgtheater (p130), Volkstheater (p130), Theater in der Josefstadt (p142) and **Akademietheater** (Map p268; 03, Lisztstrasse 1; ☑4A, ⓂStadtpark) are Vienna's prime theatre addresses in an innovative and lively scene. Sadly, options for non-German speakers are generally limited to Vienna's English Theatre (p130).

VIENNA BOYS' CHOIR

Founded by Maximilian I in 1498 as the imperial choir, the **Vienna Boys' Choir** (Wiener Sängerknaben; www.wienersaengerknaben.at) is the most famous of its type in the world. The experience will be very different depending on where you see the performance. The most formal occasions are held in the Burgkapelle, where the focus is obviously on sacred music. Performances at other venues might range from pop through to world music. Regardless of the setting and style of the performance, the thing that makes this choir so special remains the same: the beauty and choral harmony of the voices.

Performances

The choir sings during Sunday mass in the Burgkapelle (p61) in the Hofburg, but occasional concerts are also given during the week at other venues in Vienna and elsewhere. Sunday performances in the Burgkapelle are held from mid-September to June at 9.15am. Other performances are held in the Volksoper (p142) and in MuTH (p170), the choir's dedicated hall in Augarten. Regular two-hour Friday performances are usually held at 5.30pm in MuTH and last two hours.

The Vienna Boys' Choir website has links to the various venues alongside each performance date.

Tickets

Book tickets through the individual venue. Tickets for the Sunday performances at Burgkapelle cost €5 to €29 and can be booked through the **booking office** (Map p254; ☑533 99 27; www.hofburgkapelle.at; 01, Schweizerhof) by sending an email or fax. It's best to book about six weeks in advance.

For orders under €60, you pay cash when you pick up your tickets, which can be done from 11am to 1pm and 3pm to 5pm at the booking office of the chapel in the Schweizerhof of the Hofburg on the Friday before the performance. You can also pick them up between 8.15am and 8.45am on the Sunday, but this is less advisable as queues are long. If your order is €60 or more, you'll be sent the bank details for transferring the money. Credit cards and cheques aren't accepted. Seats costing €5 do not afford a view of the choir itself.

For a free *Stehplatz* (standing room space), simply show up by 8.30am. Uncollected tickets are also resold on the day. The queues for these and for standing-room tickets are long, so arrive very early – around 7am – and be prepared to wait.

Cinema

Both independent art-house films and Hollywood blockbusters are popular in Vienna. The website www.film.at, **Falter** (www.falter.at) and daily **Der Standard** (http://derstandard.at) newspapers are the best sources for listings. *OF* or *OV* following a film title means it will screen in the original language; *OmU* indicates the film is in the original language with German subtitles; and *OmenglU* and *OmeU* signify that it's in the original language with English subtitles.

THE VIENNALE

Vienna's annual international film festival, the 'fringe-like' **Viennale** (☑526 59 47; www.viennale.at), is the highlight of the city's celluloid calendar. For two weeks from mid-October cinemas screen works ranging from documentaries to short and feature films.

Ticket sales commence on the Saturday before the festival begins. You can book by credit card, online or via a special hotline number that is published on the website once sales begin. Tickets can be picked up at any of the booths set up around town, such as the **Viennale main booth** (Map p256; MuseumsQuartier, cnr Mariahilfer Strasse; ⊙10am-8pm; MMuseumsquartier).

OPEN-AIR CINEMA

Open-air cinema is popular in Vienna. The city hosts numerous such cinemas across town, the biggest of which is the **Musikfilm Festival** (01, Rathausplatz). **Kino Unter Sternen** (Cinema Under Stars; Map p; ☑0800-664 040; www.kinountersternen.at; ⬜5A, MKarlsplatz, ⬜2 Schwartzenbergstrasse) ꜰʀᴇᴇ, a highly popular outdoor cinema on Karlsplatz, hosts films from late June to mid-July. **Arena** (www.arena.co.at; 03, Baumgasse 80; MErdberg, Gasometer) has open-air screenings over three weeks in August, and **Kino wie noch nie** (Map p266; www.kinowienochnie.at; 02, Augarten; MTaborstrasse) has open-air screenings in July and August.

Shopping

Eclipsed by the trendsetting likes of Paris and London for many years, Vienna has spread its creative wings in the fashion and design world over the past decade. Whether you're browsing for hand-painted porcelain in the Innere Stadt, new-wave street-wear in Neubau or home-spun clothing in the Freihausviertel, you'll find inspiration, a passion for quality and an attentive eye for detail around almost every corner.

Vienna's Fashion & Design Scene

As one clued-up local pointed out, the Viennese have a love of life's fine details that extends to the way they shop, prizing quality of craftsmanship, eye-catching details and an individual sense of style over identikit high streets and throw-away products. The city is full of ateliers and independent boutiques where regulars are greeted by name and designers can often be seen at work, whether adding the finishing touches to a shift dress, knitting chunky beanies from silky merino wool or custom-making jewellery.

One of Europe's most dynamic, Vienna's contemporary fashion and design scene is fed by an influx of young up-and-coming creatives. This scene took root in the 7th district a few years back, and has spread fresh new shoots everywhere from Praterstrasse in the 2nd to Yppenplatz in the 16th today. Social consciousness is key, with many shops placing the accent on fair-trade materials and locally recycled or upcycled products – one man's junk becoming another man's treasure is big.

Also bang on trend are crossover enterprises. So you might, for instance, shop for vinyl before grabbing a wholesome lunch at Tongues (p101), flick through Babettes' (p98) globetrotting cookbooks before sampling a curry made with own-brand spices, or have your hair trimmed before spicing up your wardrobe with urban styles at Be a good girl (p131).

Market Mornings

One of the true joys of shopping in Vienna is milling around its markets first thing in the morning and having the chance to chat to the producers. With globalisation storming the world, it's refreshing to know that in Vienna the traditional market is still alive and kicking.

Almost every district has at least one market selling fresh produce from Monday to Saturday, many reflecting the ethnic diversity of their neighbourhood. Some host *Bauernmärkte* (farmers markets) on Saturday mornings, where growers from the surrounding countryside travel to the big city to sell their wares: fresh vegetables, tree-ripened fruit, cured hams, free-range eggs, homemade schnapps and cut flowers. Do as the laid-back Viennese do and linger for banter and brunch at a market-side cafe or deli.

Christmas Markets

From around mid-November to Christmas Eve, *Christkindlmärkte* (advent markets) breathe festive cheer into the city's squares, courtyards and cobbled lanes. Each has its own flair but all have *Glühwein* (mulled wine), *Maroni* (chestnuts) and twinkling trees. Below are some of our Christmas market favourites; www.wien.info lists exact dates and times.

Rathausplatz A whopper of a tree, 150 stalls and kid-pleasing activities from cookie-baking workshops to pony rides, all set against the atmospheric backdrop of the neo-Gothic Rathaus.

Schönbrunn Shop for nutcrackers, crib figurines and puppets at this handicraft market in the palace courtyard, with loads of events for the kids, and daily classical concerts at 6pm weekdays and 2pm weekends.

Spittelberg The cobbled lanes of this Biedermeier quarter set the scene for this market, beloved of the Viennese, where stalls sell quality arts and crafts.

Altes AKH Christmas Market (Map p262) A favourite of students, this small market occupies a corner of the Altes AKH university's largest courtyard. There are farm animals and a horse-drawn sleigh for the kids.

Altwiener Markt (Map p262; www.altwiener -markt.at) Choirs, puppet shows and storytelling for the little ones, and high-quality Austrian arts and crafts evoke an old-world feel at this market on Freyung.

Where to Shop

Kärntner Strasse The Innere Stadt's main shopping street and a real crowd puller.

Kohlmarkt A river of high-end glitz, flowing into a magnificent Hofburg view.

Neubau Track down the city's hottest designers along boutique-clogged streets like Kirchengasse, Lindengasse and Neubaugasse.

Mariahilfer Strasse Vienna's mile of high-street style, with big names and crowds.

Freihausviertel Lanes packed with home-grown fashion, design and speciality food stores, south of Naschmarkt.

Theobaldgasse Hole-in-the-wall shops purvey everything from fair-trade fashion to organic food.

Shopping by Neighbourhood

➡ **The Hofburg & Around** A nostalgic backstreet romp reveals fine porcelain, hat shops and one of Europe's best auction houses. (p71)

➡ **Stephansdom & the Historic Centre** Upper-crust Graben and Kohlmarkt fan into side-streets hiding Austrian design stores, jewellers and confectioners. (p90)

➡ **Karlsplatz & Around Naschmarkt** A picnic-basket banquet at the Naschmarkt and the Freihausviertel's idiosyncratic galleries, boutiques and speciality stores. (p109)

➡ **The Museum District & Neubau** Vienna's creative trailblazer – streets ahead of other

NEED TO KNOW

Opening Hours

Most shops open between 9am and 6.30pm Monday to Friday and until 5pm on Saturday. Some have extended hours on Thursday or Friday until around 8pm or 9pm.

Window Shopping Online

➡ **7tm** (www.7tm.at) For the lowdown on fashion and design in Neubau.

➡ **Guided Vienna** (www.guided-vienna. com) Pin down the city's hottest fashion and design by district.

➡ **Tourist Info Wien** (www.wien.info) Takes a comprehensive look at shopping in Vienna by theme and neighbourhood.

➡ **Spotted by Locals** (www.spotted bylocals.com/vienna) Up-to-the-minute recommendations written by locals.

➡ **Unlike Vienna** (http://unlike.net/ vienna) Has its ears to the ground for the latest shopping trends.

Tax-Free Shopping

➡ *Mehrwertsteuer* (MWST; value-added tax) is set at 20% for most goods.

➡ All non-EU visitors are entitled to a refund of the MWST on purchases over €75.01. To claim the tax, a tax-refund cheque must be filled out by the shop at the time of purchase, which must then be stamped by border officials when you leave the EU.

➡ Check www.globalblue.com for more details about how to obtain a refund.

Bargaining

Bargaining is a no-no in shops, although you can certainly haggle when buying secondhand. It's a must at the *Flohmarkt* (flea markets).

neighbourhoods when it comes to fashion and design. (p130)

➡ **Alsergrund & the University District** Farm-fresh goods at Freyung Market, delis and chocolatiers in the ever-so-grand Palais Ferstel. (p143)

➡ **Prater & East of the Danube** Karmelitermarkt and Praterstrasse for its growing crop of future-focused galleries, boutiques and design stores. (p170)

Lonely Planet's Top Choices

Naschmarkt (p110) Hands-down Vienna's best food market and street nosh.

Art Up (p91) Where the rising stars of Austria's fashion and design scene shine.

Freaks & Icons (p124) Exquisitely tailored fashion with a razor-sharp edge.

Henzls Ernte (p98) Garden veg and foraged herbs go into delectable spreads, sugars and salts.

Dorotheum (p71) Hammer time at this giant treasure chest of an auction house.

Gabarage Upcycling Design (p110) Reborn cast-offs become cutting-edge design.

Best Fashion & Accessories

Mein Design (p109) Fresh-faced fashion and accessories with a sustainable focus.

Be a good girl (p131) Urban street-wear meets hair salon.

Atelier Naske (p91) Elke creates jewellery as delicately beautiful as the materials she uses.

Ina Kent (p125) Silky soft leather bags made from vegetable-tanned leather.

Best Design

Das Möbel (p130) Furniture on the cusp of cool at a try-before-you-buy cafe.

Österreichische Werkstätten (p71) A showcase for top-quality Austrian design.

Best Edible Gifts

Austrian Delights (p91) What it says on the tin: organic, home-made Austrian treats.

Staud's (p139) Hans Staud's wine jellies, apricot jams and chutneys are the bee's knees.

Manner (p92) Vienna's favourite hazelnut wafers – enough said.

Blühendes Konfekt (p109) Say it with a bouquet of chocolate-dipped herbs or candied flowers.

Unger und Klein (p91) The Austrian wine world uncorked.

Best Markets

Karmelitermarkt (p169) Bag fresh produce and do brunch Viennese-style.

Brunnenmarkt (p138) Vienna's longest street market is as buzzing as a Turkish bazaar.

Freyung Market (p144) Organic farm goodies.

Best Antiques & Crafts

feinedinge (p109) Porcelain from the understated to the filigree.

Augarten Wien (p72) Vienna's finest hand-painted porcelain since 1718.

Sports & Activities

Vienna is a cracking city for outdoor activities. The Wienerwald to the west is criss-crossed with hiking and cycling trails, while the Donube, Alte Donau, Donauinsel and Lobau to the east provide ample opportunities for boating, swimming, cycling and inline skating. The city itself has hundreds of kilometres of designated cycle paths and is dotted with parks, some big (the Prater), some small (Stadtpark).

Hiking & Walking

The Viennese are into *Wandern* (walking) and their vast backyard is perfect for hiking in woods, through meadows and along riverside trails. The green belt of the Wienerwald (p171), on the western edge of Vienna, attracts walkers and cyclists, but the likes of the Prater, with its lengthy tree-flanked trails, and the Lainzer Tiergarten (p180), a park to the west of Vienna, where deer roam freely in woods of beech and oak, attract plenty of locals. Bordering the Danube, the Nationalpark Donau-Auen (p171) is a back-to-nature wilderness for walkers, and offers themed excursions such as birdwatching rambles.

The Vienna Forestry Office maintains a number of local hiking paths, all of which are well signposted and accessible by public transport. Many include children's playgrounds, picnic tables and exceptional views en route. For a comprehensive list of local hiking trails in and around the Greater Vienna area, including detailed route descriptions and printable maps, go to www.wien.gv.at/english and type 'hiking' in the search field.

Cycling & Inline Skating

Vienna is easily handled by bicycle. Around 1200km of cycle tracks cover the city, making it a breeze to avoid traffic, but not always pedestrians. Many one-way streets do not apply to cyclists; these are indicated by a bicycle sign with the word *ausgen* alongside it. Cycling routes lead through Vienna's parklands, along its waterways and the 7km path around the Ringstrasse. Popular cycling and inline skating areas include the Donauinsel (Danube Island), the Prater and along the Danube Canal (Donaukanal).

Most bike- and skate-hire places are well informed and give local tips about where to head, including maps. Expect to pay between €25 and €30 per day.

Citybike Wien (www.citybikewien.at; 1st hr free, 2nd/3rd hr €1/2, per hr thereafter €4) bicycle stands are located all over the city; currently there are more than 100. A credit card and €1 registration fee is required to hire bikes; just swipe your card in the machine and follow the instructions (provided in a number of languages). Keep in mind that these bikes are mainly for use as an alternative to transport (they can only be locked up at a bike station, unless you have your own bike chain, of course). A lost bike will set you back €600.

Swimming

Swimming is easily the favoured summer pastime of the Viennese. The Donauinsel, Alte Donau and Lobau are often swamped with urbanites cooling off on hot summer days. Topless sunbathing is quite the norm, as is nude sunbathing, but only in designated areas; much of Lobau and both tips of the Donauinsel are FKK (*Freikörperkultur;* free body culture/naked) areas.

There are also lidos run by the city, which open from early May to early September, with open-air pools for swimming laps and

NEED TO KNOW

Planning Ahead

For most activities in Vienna, just turn up and you're good to go, though you might want to reserve your wheels with a bike rental outlet before you arrive. It's worth pre-booking guided walking, cycling and segway tours (see p28) a week or two in advance, especially in the high summer season, and the same goes for purchasing tickets for spectator sports.

Sporting Events

➡ **Argus Bike Festival** (www.bike festival.at) Trial shows, trick competitions and riders' parties, alongside workshops, exhibitions and other bike-focused fun. Held on Rathausplatz.

➡ **Vienna City Marathon** (www.vienna -marathon.com) Races through town in mid-April, starting at the Reichsbrücke and finishing at Heldenplatz.

➡ **Friday Night Skating** (http://wien. gruene.at/skater) Roll along to Helden-platz at 9pm on Friday from May to September and join the Friday Night Skating team on a tour of the city. Participation is free.

➡ **Wiener Eistraum** (www.wienereis traum.com) From late January to mid-March, you can twirl across the open-air ice rink in front of the *Rathaus*.

Online Resources

➡ **Wein.at** (www.wien.gv.at) A rundown of the main outdoor activities available in Vienna, from inline skating to running, swimming and climbing.

➡ **Tourist Info Wien** (www.wien.info) The inside scoop on activities in Vienna, including climbing halls, ice rinks, open-air swimming pools and jogging trails.

➡ **Fahrrad Wien** (www.fahrradwien.at) Helps plan your cycling route.

lawns for sunbathing. Many also feature picnic areas, volleyball courts and slides for kids. They're open from 9am to around 7pm daily from May to mid-September and entry costs €5/1.70 for adults/children. For a full list of pools, visit www.wien.gv.at /english/leisure/bath.

Ice Skating

Most Viennese have ice skates collecting dust at the back of the wardrobe that are dragged out at least once over winter. Along with specialised ice-skating rinks, a number of outdoor basketball courts are turned into rinks during winter. For as little as €1 you can spend the whole day gliding around one of these temporary rinks: 08, Buch-feldgasse 7a; 16, Gallitzinstrasse 4; and 19, Osterleitengasse 14. When it's cold enough, the Alte Donau is transformed into an ice-skater's paradise, with miles of natural ice.

Boating

The Alte Donau is the main boating and sailing centre in Vienna, but the Neue Donau, a long stretch of water separated from the Danube by the Donauinsel, also provides opportunities for boating, wind-surfing and waterskiing. You can learn to sail or rent a boat at Hofbauer (p172).

Spectator Sports

The **Stadthalle** (Map p260; ☑98 100 200; www. stadthalle.com; 15, Vogelweidplatz 14; Ⓜ Burggasse-Stadthalle) is a major player in hosting sporting events. Tennis tournaments (including the Austrian Open), horse shows and ice-hockey games are just some of the diverse events held here. The swimming pool is a major venue for aquatic events like races, water polo and synchronised swimming.

Krieau (p172) is where Vienna's trotting racing events are held, and you can of course watch Lipizzaner stallions perform at the Spanish Riding School (p61).

Sports & Activities by Neighbourhood

➡ **The Hofburg & Around** Stroll sculpture-dotted parks with palace views.

➡ **Stephansdom & the Historic Centre** Zip past landmarks on a segway or leap into the Badeschiff's pool by the Danube Canal. (p92)

➡ **The Museum District & Neubau** Open-air ice skating in front of the illuminated Rathaus in winter. (p131)

➡ **Schloss Belvedere to the Canal** Park life, ice skating and proximity to Vienna's best day spa. (p161)

➡ **Prater & East of the Danube** Tops for activities in Vienna, with the Danube, lidos and a wildlife-crammed national park to explore. (p170)

Lonely Planet's Top Choices

Donauinsel (p170) Walk, cycle, swim, sail, boat or windsurf on this island in the Danube.

Wienerwald (p171) Tiptoe off the beaten trail to hike or mountain bike in these wooded hills.

Therme Wien (p158) Revive in the whirlpools, waterfalls and grotto-like pools at this thermal water wonderland.

Wiener Eislaufverein (p161) Get your skates on at the world's biggest open-air ice rink.

Prater (p164) Join the Wiener to jog, cycle and stroll in their best-loved park.

Best Hiking & Walking

Lobau (p172) Trails weave across this woody, lake-dotted floodplain, nicknamed Vienna's 'jungle'.

Wienerwald (p171) Don a pair of boots and head into Vienna's forested hills for a scenic day hike.

Nationalpark Donau-Auen (p171) Keep your eyes peeled for deer, kites and kingfishers on a back-to-nature ramble through these wetlands.

Prater (p164) Meadows, pockets of woodland and tree-lined boulevards great for strolling.

Best Cycling

Wienerwald (p171) Roll through dappled woodlands or tear downhill, mountain biking on 46 marked trails.

Donauinsel (p170) Pedal gently along the Danube, pausing for picnics, swims and cityscape views.

Prater (p164) The Prater's die-straight, chestnut-fringed Hauptallee is terrific for a city-centre spin.

Pedal Power (p172) Hook onto a cycling tour to cruise past city landmarks.

Best Adrenalin Rush

Wienerwald (p171) Test your mettle on 1000km of mountain bike trails.

Donauturm (p167) Feel the rush as you bungee jump from 152m, hitting speeds of 90km/h.

Best Lidos & Pools

Badeschiff (p92) Splash around with the cool kids in this shipshape pool on the Danube.

Strandbad Gänsehäufel (p172) Summertime magnet, with a pool, activities and nudist area.

Strandbad Alte Donau (p172) Take a cooling dip in the river at this urban beach.

Therme Wien (p158) The new kid on Vienna's spa scene, with thermal pools, slides, saunas and more.

Best Ice Rinks

Wiener Eislaufverein (p161) Glide across the ice at this gargantuan open-air skating rink.

Wiener Eistraum (p131) DJ beats put a swing in your skate at this open-air rink on Rathausplatz.

GRANT FAINT / GETTY IMAGES ©

Explore Vienna

VIENNA'S TOP SIGHTS

Neighbourhoods at a Glance

❶ The Hofburg & Around p58

With the Hofburg palace complex and streets north to Stephansplatz, this part of the Innere Stadt (city centre) is brimming with museums. The hotel and restaurant scene is fairly limited here, but improves closer to Stephansplatz, and the shopping is excellent. It's easy to skip across Maria-Theresien-Platz from the palace into the MuseumsQuartier.

❷ Stephansdom & the Historic Centre p73

In the oldest part of Vienna, the highlight is indisputably Vienna's towering cathedral. The neighbourhood takes in the medieval Jewish quarter in the northwest, the area down to the southern bank of the Danube Canal and regions northeast and east of Stephansplatz – altogether covering most of the hubs of Vien-

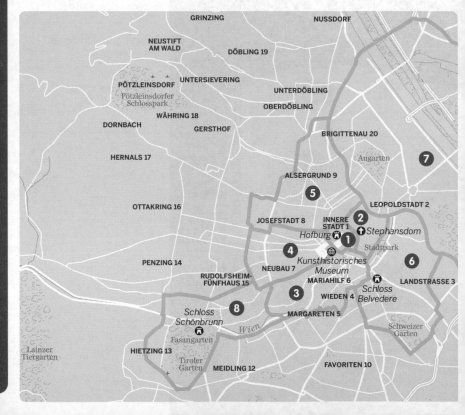

na's eating, drinking, clubbing and sleeping scenes inside the Ringstrasse.

③ Karlsplatz & Around Naschmarkt p93

Fringing the Ringstrasse in the southeast corner of the Innere Stadt, this neighbourhood includes the Opera and extends south beyond Vienna's enormous market and food paradise, Naschmarkt, into some of the city's most interesting *Vorstädte* (inner suburbs): Margareten, Mariahilf and Wieden. There's great eating, drinking and nightlife and a truly Viennese *Vorstadt* character. Its clear highlight is the magnificent Karlskirche.

④ The Museum District & Neubau p111

Beginning on Maria-Theresien-Platz with high-profile Kunsthistorisches Museum and Naturhistorisches Museum, this neighbourhood sweeps west to include the Museums-Quartier and the hip Neubau *Vorstadt* to the Gürtel. Shopping is more offbeat than in the Innere Stadt and it also has some good eating and drinking venues.

⑤ Alsergrund & the University District p132

This neighbourhood includes a small section of the Innere Stadt inside the Ringstrasse, including Freyung and its market, and stretches into the Alsergrund *Vorstadt*, where you find the university campuses. When not residential, it's dominated by business clientele around the stock exchange and uni students.

⑥ Schloss Belvedere to the Canal p145

The absolute highlight of this neighbourhood is Schloss Belvedere and gardens. Restaurants, bars and other sights and places of interest are few and, especially the further out you go, far between.

⑦ Prater & East of the Danube p162

Leopoldstadt, the predominant *Vorstadt* in this neighbourhood, begins directly across the Danube Canal. It's an unusual former Jewish quarter that's sleepy and quiet in many parts, but interesting around Karmelitermarkt and in the famous Prater parkland. Further east is the Danube River and Danube Island recreation area.

⑧ Schloss Schönbrunn & Around p173

The palace dominates this neighbourhood, which otherwise has very limited attractions. The parts around the palace have a relatively suburban feel, and this also goes for an ensemble of suburbs adjoining the neighbourhood to the north – Fünfhaus, Rudolfsheim and Ottakring – which throw up interesting pastiches of suburban life.

The Hofburg & Around

Neighbourhood Top Five

1 Strolling through the **Hofburg palace complex** (p60), exploring courtyards like the Schweizerhof, and admiring the elegant gates, impressive squares, statues of the Habsburg rulers and monumental architecture.

2 Visiting the **Albertina** (p66), with its world-class exhibitions, augmented by luxurious palace rooms and copies from its collection of original graphics by masters.

3 Admiring the **Kaiser-appartements** (p60), the Habsburg imperial apartments, with the Sisi Museum dedicated to Empress Elisabeth.

4 Catching the famous white Lipizzaner stallions during a performance of the **Spanish Riding School** (p61).

5 Revelling in the historical musical instruments and arms and armour exhibited in the **Neue Burg Museums** (p63).

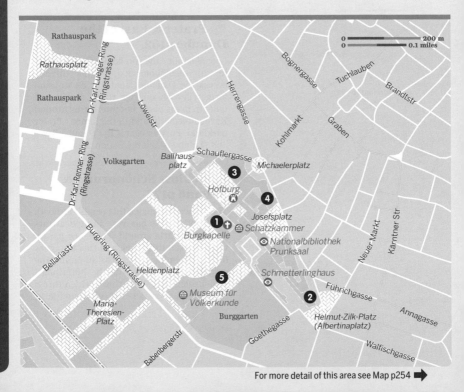

For more detail of this area see Map p254 ➡

Explore the Hofburg & Around

The Hofburg is one of the most impressive and attractive palace complexes in Vienna and should not be missed. Although it can be easily approached from the MuseumsQuartier by crossing Maria-Theresien-Platz, the best place to start is at the gate on Michaelerplatz, which is where the Habsburgs used to enter. From here you can stroll from one end to the other in about an hour, with stops to admire the architecture. If you plan on visiting several museums, block your calendar for much of the day to do these comfortably. Although tourist groups are almost always walking through, it rarely feels crowded. Plan to spend at least another four hours taking in the most important sights around the Hofburg – the Albertina, Kaisergruft and the Jüdisches Museum. The neighbourhood has some good shopping as well as a handful of excellent eating and drinking options, despite its heavily touristed character; also consider ducking out of the neighbourhood into the close-by MuseumsQuartier to eat.

Local Life

Green Spaces This part of town has some of the prettiest parks in Vienna, with the Volksgarten (p68) flanking one side of the Hofburg and the Burggarten (p68) the other. In summer, these are perfect places to sit and relax.

Day or Night Haunts Oddly, a small but legendary collection of places for drinking or clubbing are here, ranging from coffee houses through Loos American Bar (p69) to Volksgarten Pavillon (p70) or Palffy Club (p69).

Getting There & Away

U-Bahn Herrengasse (U3) and Stephansplatz (U1, U3) are closest to the Hofburg, but Museumsquartier (U4) can also be convenient for the Heldenplatz side of Hofburg.

Tram Useful for entering from Ringstrasse (D, 1, 2, 71 Dr-Karl-Renner-Ring, Burgring and Kärntner Ring/ Oper).

Bus Buses 1A and 2A connect Michaelerplatz with Stephansplatz.

Lonely Planet's Top Tip

Although this neighbourhood is full of iconic sights, it's also a part of town that invites aimless strolling to soak up the atmosphere. The Hofburg is most impressive during the quiet hours of early morning or early evening, whereas the streets between the Hofburg and Stephansplatz have lots of private art galleries. Walk, drop into a few and explore the art.

Best Places to Drink

→ Loos American Bar (p69)
→ Villon (p69)
→ Café Leopold Hawelka (p69)
→ Le Bol (p69)

For reviews, see p69 →

Best Places for Free

→ The Hofburg (p60)
→ Dorotheum (p71)
→ Augustinerkirche (p67)
→ Burggarten (p68)

For reviews, see p60 →

Best Places for Children

→ Globenmuseum (p67)
→ Museum für Völkerkunde (p65)
→ Spanish Riding School (p61)
→ Neue Burg Museums (p63)

For reviews, see p66 →

JOHN HAY / GETTY IMAGES ©

TOP SIGHT
THE HOFBURG

The Hofburg palace complex, first built as a fortified castle in the 13th century and which has been continuously revamped and expanded over the years, is the ultimate display of Austria's former imperial power. It was once home to the Habsburg rulers from Rudolph I in 1279 until the Austrian monarchy collapsed under Karl I in 1918. Today, this impressive palace complex includes the offices of the Austrian president, an ensemble of extraordinary museums and public squares as well as picturesque parkland flanking it on both sides.

Kaiserappartements

The **Kaiserappartements** (Imperial Apartments; 01, Michaelerplatz; adult/child €10.50/6.50, with guided tour €13/7.50; ⊘9am-5.30pm; MHerrengasse) were once the official living quarters of Franz Josef I (1830–1916) and Empress Elisabeth (1837–98), or Sisi, as she was affectionately named. The first section, known as the **Sisi Museum** (⊠533 75 70; 01, Michaelerkuppel; adult/child €11.50/7, with guided tour €13.50; ⊘9am-5.30pm Sep-Jun, to 6pm Jul & Aug), is devoted to Austria's most beloved empress. It has a strong focus on the clothing and jewellery of Austria's monarch; if your interest in pretty dresses is limited, you may find the reconstruction of Sisi's luxurious Pullman coach more interesting. Part of this first section also has a replica of her personal fitness room complete with rings and bars, testament to her obsession with keeping slim. Many of the empress's famous portraits are also on show, as is her death mask, made after her assassination in Geneva in 1898.

The adjoining **Silberkammer** (Silver Depot) collection is included in the entry price. The largest silver service here can take care of 140 dinner guests. Audio guides – available

- ➔ Walking through the Hofburg
- ➔ Kaiserappartements
- ➔ Schatzkammer
- ➔ Neue Burg Museums

PRACTICALITIES
- ➔ Imperial Palace
- ➔ Map p254
- ➔ www.hofburg-wien.at
- ➔ 01, Michaelerkuppel
- ➔ ◻1A, 2A Michaelerplatz, MHerrengasse, ◻D, 1, 2, 71, 46, 49 Burgring

in 11 languages – are also included in the admission price. Admission on guided tours includes the Kaiserappartements plus either the Silberkammer or the Sisi Museum.

Kaiserliche Schatzkammer

The **Kaiserliche Schatzkammer** (Imperial Treasury; www.kaiserliche-schatzkammer.at; 01, Schweizerhof; adult/under 19yr €12/free; ☉9am-5.30pm Wed-Mon; ⓂHerrengasse) contains secular and ecclesiastical treasures of priceless value and splendour – the sheer wealth of this collection of crown jewels is staggering. As you walk through the rooms you see a golden rose, diamond-studded Turkish sabres, a 2680-carat Colombian emerald and, the highlight of the treasury, the imperial crown. The wood-panelled **Sacred Treasury** has a collection of rare religious relics, some of which can be taken with a grain of salt: fragments of the True Cross, one of the nails from the Crucifixion, a thorn from Christ's crown and a piece of tablecloth from the Last Supper.

Burgkapelle

The **Burgkapelle** (Royal Chapel; ☑533 99 27; www.hofburgkapelle.at; 01, Schweizer Hof; ☉10am-2pm Mon & Tue, 11am-1pm Fri; ⬜2A Heldenplatz, ⓂHerrengasse, ⬚D, 1, 2 Burgring) originally dates from the 13th century and received a Gothic makeover from 1447 to 1449, but much of this disappeared during the baroque fad. The vaulted wooden statuary survived and is testament to those Gothic days. This is where the Vienna Boys' Choir (p47) Mass takes place every Sunday at 9.15am between September and June. The chapel is sometimes closed to visitors in July and August, so check ahead in those months. For more on ticketing see p47.

Spanish Riding School

The world-famous **Spanish Riding School** (Spanische Hofreitschule; ☑533 90 31; www.srs.at; 01, Michaelerplatz 1; performances €31-173; ⬜1A, 2A Michaelerplatz, ⓂHerrengasse) is a Viennese institution truly reminiscent of the imperial Habsburg era. This unequalled equestrian show is performed by Lipizzaner stallions formerly kept at an imperial stud established at Lipizza (hence 'Lipizzaner').

There are many different ways to see the Lipizzaner stallions. Performances are the top-shelf variant, and for seats at these you will need to book several months in advance. The website has the performance dates and you can order tickets online. As a rule of thumb, performances are at 11am on Sunday from mid-February to June and mid-August to December, with performances frequently on

VISITING THE IMPERIAL APARTMENTS

Entrance to the Kaiserappartements is via the Kaiserstieg staircase, after which you learn about the Habsburgs and the history of the Hofburg and you can look at a model of the complex. You then enter the Sisi Museum and afterwards the restored apartments of Empress Elisabeth and Kaiser Franz Josef I. The Silberkammer occupies another part of the Reichskanzeleitrakt (State Chancery Tract) of the building.

Empress Maria Theresia (1717–80) may cling to her chair in all her robed, operatic glory in the middle of Maria-Theresien-Platz, but Empress Elisabeth, better know as Sisi, is the real darling of the Habsburg show in this part of town. The cult of Sisi knows no bounds in German-speaking countries, due in no small part to the trilogy of films from the 1950s starring Austro-French actress Romy Schneider. Schneider embodied the empress so well that in the popular mind it often seems hard to distinguish between Sisi as art and the empress in reality.

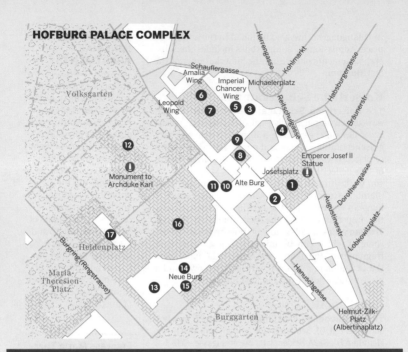

HOFBURG PALACE COMPLEX

🏃 Palace Tour
The Hofburg

LENGTH ONE HOUR TO ONE DAY

The Hofburg is a jigsaw puzzle of monumental buildings. For the full effect, enter from Michaelerplatz, as the monarchs used to. First, though, admire the pretty square just to the south, **1 Josefsplatz**, adorned with the equestrian monument to Emperor Josef II. Josefsplatz also serves as the entrance to the **2 Nationalbibliothek Prunksaal** (p64).

Pass through the **3 Michaelertor** and neo-baroque Michaelertrakt. The Michaelerplatz side of the building is lined with statues of Hercules and evocative fountains depicting the Power of the Land and Power of the Sea. On the left of the hall is the **4 Spanish Riding School** (p61) and its visitor centre, on the right the **5 Kaiserappartements** (p60).

Straight ahead, you reach the large courtyard **6 In der Burg**, with a monument to **7 Emperor Franz I**, the last in a long line of Holy Roman emperors after

Napoleon brought about the collapse of the Reich in 1806.

The oldest part of the Hofburg is the **8 Schweizerhof** (Swiss Courtyard), named after the Swiss guards who used to protect its precincts. This is reached via the Renaissance **9 Swiss Gate**, which dates from 1553. The 13th-century courtyard gives access to the **10 Burgkapelle** (p61) and the **11 Schatzkammer** (p61).

Straight ahead is **12 Heldenplatz** (Hero's Square) and the **13 Neue Burg**, built between the second half of the 19th century and WWI. The Neue Burg houses the **14 Museum für Völkerkunde** (p65) and the three **15 Neue Burg Museums** (p63). The balcony is where Hitler addressed a rally during his triumphant 1938 visit to Vienna after the *Anschluss* (annexation). Facing each other on Heldenplatz are the monuments to **16 Prince Eugene of Savoy** (closest to the Neue Burg) and **17 Archduke Karl** (Charles of Austria). Pass through the Äusseres Burgtor (Outer Palace Gate) to the Ringstrasse.

Nationalbibliothek Prunksaal (p64)

TIPS FOR THE KAISERLICHE SCHATZKAMMER

Multilingual audio guides cost €4 (the shorter highlight audio tour is free) and are very worthwhile. A combined 'Treasures of the Habsburgs' ticket, which includes the Kunsthistorisches Museum, Neue Burg Museums and Schatkammer, costs €20. Allow anything from 30 minutes to two hours for the Schatzkammer.

The Kaislerliche Schatzkammer dates back to the time of Ferdinand I (1503–64), who commissioned an antiquarian to take care of the collection. In the 18th century under Maria Theresia the treasures were separated and reorganised into paintings and other categories, but her good housekeeping is suspected to have been to hide the sale of some treasures to finance the War of the Austrian Succession (1740–48). Under Hitler, all the imperial regalia from the Holy Roman Empire was transferred to Nuremberg, where it had previously been kept for about 400 years from 1424. But this was returned to the Hofburg after WWII.

Saturday and occasionally other days of the week. For standing room, book at least one month in advance. During the summer break, special 'Piber meets Vienna' performances are held for tourists.

Visitors to the **Morgenarbeit sessions** (Morning Training; adult/child €14/7; ⊙10am-noon Tue-Fri Jan-Jun & mid-Aug–Dec, check website for exact dates) can drop in for part of a session and leave whenever they want to. **Guided tours** (adult/child €16/8; ⊙2pm, 3pm & 4pm, closed Mon late Jan & Feb) conducted in English and German take you into the performance hall, stables and other facilities, and a combined **morning training and tour** (adult/child €28/14) is another option. The **visitor centre** (01, Michaelerkuppel; ⊙9am-4pm Tue-Fri, to 7pm Fri on performance days) sells all tickets; morning training tickets can also be bought at Gate 2 on Josefsplatz during training sessions.

Neue Burg Museums

The Neue Burg is home to the three excellent **Neue Burg Museums** (⊘525 240; www.khm.at; 01, Heldenplatz; adult/under 19yr €14/free; ⊙10am-6pm Wed-Sun; ⓜHerrengasse, Museumsquartier, ⓐD, 1, 2, 71 Burgring). The **Sammlung Alter Musik Instrumente** (Collection of Ancient Musical Instruments) contains fascinating musical instruments in all shapes, sizes and tones. The **Ephesos Museum** features artefacts from Ephesos and Samothrace, donated (some say 'lifted') by the sultan in 1900 after a team of Austrian archaeologists excavated Ephesus in Turkey. Last but not least is the **Hofjägd und Rüstkammer**

THE WHITE HORSE IN HISTORY

The Lipizzaner stallion breed dates back to the 1520s, when Ferdinand I imported the first horses from Spain for the imperial palace. His son Maximilian II imported new stock in the 1560s, and in 1580 Archduke Charles II established the imperial stud in Lipizza (Lipica, today in Slovenia), giving the horse its name. Austria's nobility had good reason for looking to Spain for its horses: the Spanish were considered the last word in equine breeding at the time, thanks to Moors from the 7th century who had brought their elegant horses to the Iberian Peninsula. Italian horses were added to the stock around the mid-1700s (these too had Spanish blood) and by the mid-18th century the Lipizzaner had a reputation for being Europe's finest horse.

Over the centuries, natural catastrophe, but more often war, caused the Lipizzaner to be evacuated from their original stud in Slovenia on numerous occasions. One of their periods of exile from the stud in Lipica was in 1915 due to the outbreak of WWI. Some of the horses went to Laxemburg (just outside Vienna), and others to Bohemia in today's Czech Republic (at the time part of the Austro-Hungarian Empire).

When the Austrian monarchy collapsed in 1918, Lipica passed into Italian hands and the horses were divided between Austria and Italy. The Italians ran the stud in Slovenia, while the Austrians transferred their horses to Piber, near Graz, which had been breeding military horses for the empire since 1798 – at that time stallions were mostly crossed with English breeds.

The fortunes of our pirouetting equine friends rose and fell with the collapse of the Habsburg empire and advent of two world wars. When WWII broke out, Hitler's cohorts goose-stepped in and requisitioned the Piber stud in Austria and started breeding military horses and – spare the thought! – pack mules there. They also decided to bring the different studs in their occupied regions together under one roof, and Piber's Lipizzaner wound up in Hostau, situated in Bohemia. Fearing the Lipizzaner would fall into the hands of the Russian army as it advanced towards the region in 1945 (and amid rather odd fears that the stallions would be eaten), American forces seized the Lipizzaner and other horses in Hostau and transferred them back to Austria.

Today, Piber still supplies the Spanish Riding School with its white stallions.

(Arms and Armour) museum, with an exciting collection of ancient armour dating mainly from the 15th and 16th centuries. Admission includes the Kunsthistorisches Museum (p113). An audio guide costs €4.

Nationalbibliothek Prunksaal

The Nationalbibliothek (National Library) was once the imperial library and is now the largest library in Vienna. The real reason to visit these esteemed halls of knowledge is to gaze on the **Nationalbibliothek Prunksaal** (Grand Hall; ☑534 10 394; www.onb.ac.at; 01, Josefsplatz 1; adult/under 19yr €7/free; ☺10am-6pm Tue-Sun, to 9pm Thu; Ⓜ Herrengasse). Commissioned by Charles VI, this baroque hall was the brainchild of Johann Bernhard Fischer von Erlach, who died the year the first brick was laid, and finished by his son Joseph in 1735. Leather-bound scholarly tomes line the walls, and the upper storey of shelves is flanked by an elegantly curved wood balcony. Rare ancient volumes (mostly 15th century) are stored within glass cabinets, with pages opened to beautifully illustrated passages of text. A statue of Charles VI stands guard under the central dome, which itself has a magnificent fresco by Daniel Gran depicting the emperor's apotheosis.

Papyrusmuseum

Part of the Nationalbibliothek museum ensemble, the **Papyrusmuseum** (☑534 10 420; www.onb.ac.at; 01, Heldenplatz; adult/under 19yr €4/free; ☺10am-6pm Tue-Sun, to 9pm Thu; ⓂHerrengasse, Museumsquartier, ⓐD, 1, 2, 71 Burgring) displays a collection of 200 fragments of ancient writing on papyrus. Papyrus was used for writing in ancient Egypt and the museum focuses on this, and cultures that influenced ancient Egypt, as well as fragments of writing on other media such as parchment and clay. Admission to the museum includes the Globenmuseum and Esperantomuseum.

Museum für Völkerkunde

Children will be impressed by the **Museum für Völkerkunde** (Museum of Ethnology; ☑525 240; www.ethno-museum.ac.at; 01, Heldenplatz; adult/under 19yr €8/free; ☺10am-6pm Wed-Mon; ⓂHerrengasse, Museumsquartier, ⓐD, 1, 2 Burgring) – it was revamped a few years ago and exudes a lightness of mood and has a thoughtful use of space that adults will appreciate too. Exhibits are on non-European cultures and divided into regions and nationalities, covering countries such as China, Japan and Korea, and also Polynesian, Native American and Inuit cultures.

Schmetterlinghaus

Sharing the Habsburg's personal *Jugendstil* (art nouveau) glasshouse (1901) with the Palmenhaus bar (p70), the **Schmetterlinghaus** (Butterfly House; ☑533 85 70; www.schmetterlinghaus.at; 01, Burggarten; adult/child €5.50/3; ☺10am-4.45pm Mon-Fri, to 6.15pm Sat & Sun; ⓂKarlsplatz, ⓐD, 1, 2, 72 Burgring) is for the butterfly-mad only. There are hundreds of butterflies and the shop stocks a great range of butterfly paraphernalia, but the air is hot and unbearably humid, the species range is fairly limited and it's quite a small display area. It's located in the Burggarten, directly behind the Neue Burg.

NATIONAL LIBRARY MUSEUMS

Combined tickets for the Nationalbibliothek Prunksaal, Globenmuseum, Esperantomuseum and Papyrusmuseum cost €12, which is €1 more expensive than paying separate admission but is valid for seven days. Admission to the Globenmuseum, Esperantomuseum or Papyrusmuseum (adult/under 19yr €4/free) is valid for the other two museums (but not for the Prunksaal) on the same day.

The Daniel Gran fresco inside the Prunksaal of the Austrian National Library is considered to be the artist's greatest work. Gran's motifs create a transition from war to peace as you move through the hall. The centre of the fresco has an apotheosis of Charles VI, held by Hercules (symbolising strength) and Apollo (order and wisdom). The fresco is designed to be viewed from different perspectives, so move around to literally get the full picture.

◉ SIGHTS

THE HOFBURG
PALACE

See p60.

ALBERTINA
GALLERY

Map p254 (www.albertina.at; 01, Albertinaplatz 3; adult/child €11/free; ☺10am-6pm Thu-Tue, to 9pm Wed; ⓂKarlsplatz, Stephansplatz, ⓐD, 1, 2, 71 Kärntner Ring/Oper) Once used as the Habsburg's imperial apartments for guests (you can walk through these), the Albertina is now a repository for the greatest collection of graphic art in the world. A very small selection of copies is on display, but the permanent Batliner Collection – with paintings covering the period from Monet to Picasso – and the high quality of changing exhibitions are what really make the Albertina so worthwhile visiting.

French Impressionism and post-Impressionism, as well as the works of the Swiss Alberto Giacometti, were the original focus of the Batliner Collection, but over time husband and wife benefactors Herbert and Rita Batliner added a substantial number of Russian avante-garde works to create a who's who of 20th-century and contemporary art: Monet, Picasso, Degas, Cézanne, Matisse, Chagal, Nolde, Jawlensky and many more.

All this is augmented by the top-notch changing exhibitions. Multilingual audio guides (€4) cover all exhibition sections and tell the story behind the apartments and works you see. Tickets (but not the audio guides) are valid for the whole day, so you can retire to lunch somewhere and return later to finish off a visit.

The Österreichisches Filmmuseum (p71) is located in the Albertina.

KAISERGRUFT
CHURCH

Map p254 (Imperial Burial Vault; www.kaisergruft.at; 01, Neuer Markt; adult/child €5/2; ☺10am-6pm; ⓂStephansplatz, Karlsplatz, ⓐD, 1, 2, 71 Kärntner Ring/Oper) The Kaisergruft beneath the **Kapuzinerkirche** (Church of the Capuchin Friars) is the final resting place of most of the Habsburg royal family (the hearts and organs reside in Augustinerkirche and Stephansdom, respectively). Opened in 1633, it was instigated by Empress Anna (1585–1618), and her body and that of her husband, Emperor Matthias (1557–1619), were the first entombed in this impressive vault.

---

❶ MUSEUM TICKETS

There are lots of combined options for visiting the Hofburg and nearby museums. See p232 for information on discounts and concessions.

Sisi Ticket (adult/child €25.50/15) Includes the Imperial Apartments, Sisi Museum and Imperial Silver Collection with audio guide as well as Schloss Schönbrunn and the Imperial Furniture Collection.

Neue Burg Museums (€14) Includes the Kunsthistorisches Museum.

Annual ticket Kunsthistorisches Museum (€34) Includes Kunstkammer, Kunsthistorische Museum, Neue Burg Museums, Schatzkammer, Wagenburg Wien, Schloss Ambras Innsbruck, Museum für Völkerkunde and Theatermuseum.

Schatz der Habsburger (€20) Includes Kunsthistorisches Museum, Neue Burg and Schatzkammer, saving you €6.

Buying Tickets in Advance

Many museums sell admission tickets online. Tickets for the Albertina, Jüdisches Museum, Haus der Musik, Mozarthaus, Kunsthaus Wien and others are sold by **Wien-Ticket** (www.wien-ticket.at) and Wien-Ticket representatives (see 'Vorverkaufsstellen' on the website side menu). This can be useful and save time on visits. Sometimes you can print tickets yourself, while in other cases you can pick them up using the booking confirmation and by showing a passport or ID at the **Wien-Ticket Pavillon** (Map p256; ☎588 85; www.wien-ticket.at; Herbert-von-Karajan-Platz; ☺10am-7pm; ⓂKarlsplatz, ⓐD, 1, 2 Kärntner Ring/Oper), on Herbert von Karajan Platz, outside the Staatsoper. No commission is charged on museum admissions, but there can be a small fee for some events, rising to a maximum of 12%.

Only three Habsburgs are notable through their absence here. The last emperor, Karl I, was buried in exile in Madeira, and Marie Antoinette (daughter of Maria Theresia) still lies in Paris. The third is Duc de Reichstadt, son of Napoleon's second wife, Marie Louise, who was transferred to Paris as a publicity stunt by the Nazis in 1940.

THEATERMUSEUM   MUSEUM

Map p254 (⌨525 24 610; www.theatermuseum. at; 01, Lobkowitzplatz 2; adult/under 19yr incl all exhibitions €8/free; ⊙10am-6pm Wed-Mon; ⓜKarlsplatz, 🚋D, 1, 2, 71 Kärntner Ring/Oper) Housed in the baroque Lobkowitz palace (1694), this museum has a permanent exhibition devoted to Austrian composer Gustav Mahler (1860–1911), and temporary exhibitions on Vienna's theatre history. A small room hidden towards the back of the 1st floor contains an ensemble of puppets from puppeteer Richard Teschner, vaguely reminiscent of Java's Wayang Golek wooden puppets. The ticket desk can tell you about performances.

JÜDISCHES MUSEUM   MUSEUM

Map p254 (Jewish Museum; ⌨535 04 31; www. jmw.at; 01, Dorotheergasse 11; adult/child €10/ free, valid 48hr both Jewish museums; ⊙10am-6pm Sun-Fri; ⓜStephansplatz) Housed inside Palais Eskeles, Vienna's Jüdisches Museum showcases the history of Jews in Vienna, from the first settlements at Judenplatz in the 13th century to the present. A new permanent exhibition on Jewry in the 21st century was due to open in 2013, complementing spaces mostly devoted to changing exhibitions, and the exhibition highlight, a startling collection of ceremonial art on the top floor.

MICHAELERPLATZ (ROMAN RUINS)   RUINS

Map p254 (01, Michaelerplatz; 🚋1A, 2A Michaelerplatz, ⓜHerrengasse) **FREE** Ringed by gorgeous architecture, Michaelerplatz is centred on Roman ruins that are reputed to have been a brothel for soldiers. This cobblestoned circular 'square' is often packed with snap-happy travellers, ticket touts and *Fiaker* (small horse-drawn carriages).

MICHAELERKIRCHE   CHURCH

Map p254 (⌨533 80 00; www.michaelerkirche. at; 01, Michaelerplatz; admission free, tour adult/ child €7/3; ⊙7am-10pm; 🚋1A, 2A Michaeler-

platz, ⓜHerrengasse) The Michaelerkirche dates from the 13th century. Its highlight is the burial crypt which you can see on 40-minute bilingual German/English tours at 11am and 1 pm Monday to Saturday between Easter and October (Thursday to Saturday only from November to Easter). Tours take you past coffins, some revealing occupants preserved by the rarefied air of the crypt.

AUGUSTINERKIRCHE   CHURCH

Map p254 (⌨533 09 470; www.augustinerkirche. at; 01, Augustinerstrasse 3; admission free; ⊙dawn-dusk; 🚋1A, 2A Michaelerplatz, ⓜHerrengasse) The real highlight of the 14th-century Gothic Augustinerkirche (Augustinian Church) is not its pale, vaulted interior but a crypt containing urns with the hearts of 54 Habsburg rulers. The church hosts regular evening classical music concerts, and the 11am Mass on Sunday is celebrated with a full choir and orchestra. The website (www.hochamt.at/augustines_programm. php) has details. Sometimes on a visit you can catch the choir practising. The crypt is open on Sunday after the Mass – turn up around 12.30pm.

LOOS HAUS   BUILDING

Map p254 (01, Michaelerplatz; ⊙9am-5pm Mon-Fri, to 5.30pm Thu; 🚋1A, 2A Michaelerplatz, ⓜHerrengasse) Designed by Adolf Loos, this modernist gem put Franz Josef's nose seriously out of joint when it was completed in 1911. Its intentionally simple facade offended the emperor so deeply that he ordered the curtains to be pulled on all palace windows overlooking the building. Today it houses a bank, with exhibition halls on the upper floors, including displays about this controversial building.

While it was being erected, critics were describing this as a 'house without eyebrows', referring to its lack of window detail, and work had to be stopped until Loos agreed to add the 10 window boxes adorning it today.

GLOBENMUSEUM   MUSEUM

Map p254 (⌨534 10 710; www.onb.ac.at; 01, Herrengasse 9, 1st fl; adult/under 19yr €4/free; ⊙10am-6pm Tue-Sun, to 9pm Thu; 🚋1A, 2A Michaelerplatz, ⓜHerrengasse) Part of the Nationalbibliothek collection of museums, this small museum situated inside a former palace (Palais Mollard) is dedicated to cartography. Among the collection of

19th-century globes and maps are some gems dating from the 16th century. Look for the globe made for Emperor Karl V by Mercator in 1541.

ESPERANTOMUSEUM
MUSEUM

Map p254 (📍534 10 730; www.onb.ac.at; 01, Herrengasse 9, ground fl; adult/under 19yr €4/ free; ⊙10am-6pm Tue-Sun, to 9pm Thu; 🚃1A, 2A Michaelerplatz, Ⓜ Herrengasse) The oft-overlooked Esperantomuseum is mostly devoted to the artificial language created by Dr Ludvik Zamenhof in 1887. The first book in Esperanto, by Dr Zamenhof himself, features among interesting exhibits on artificial languages, such as language used in the *Star Trek* TV series and films. A media terminal briefly explains the language used by the Klingons, reciting lines from Shakespeare's *Hamlet!*

VOLKSGARTEN
GARDENS

Map p254 (www.bundesgaerten.at; 01, Dr-Karl-Renner-Ring; ⊙6am-10pm Apr-Oct, 6.30am-7pm Nov-Mar; Ⓜ Volkstheater, Herrengasse, 🚋D, 1, 2, 71, 46, 49 Dr-Karl-Renner-Ring) FREE Spreading out between the Burgtheater and Heldenplatz, the Volksgarten (People's Garden) is great for relaxing among dignified rose bushes and even more dignified statues. A **monument to Empress Elisabeth** is in the northeast corner, not far from the **Temple of Theseus**, an imitation of the one in Athens (commissioned by Napoleon), and the club Volksgarten.

BURGGARTEN
GARDENS

Map p254 (www.bundesgaerten.at; 01, Burgring; ⊙6am-10pm Apr-Oct, 6.30am-7pm Nov-Mar; Ⓜ Museumsquartier, 🚋D, 1, 2, 71, 46, 49 Burgring) FREE Tucked behind the Hofburg, the Burggarten (Castle Garden) is a leafy oasis amid the hustle and bustle of the Ringstrasse and Innere Stadt. The marble **statue of Mozart** is the park's most famous tenant, but there's also a **statue of Franz Josef** in military garb. Lining the Innere Stadt side of the Burggarten is the Schmetterlinghaus and the ever-popular Palmenhaus bar.

PHANTASTENMUSEUM WIEN
MUSEUM

Map p254 (International Museum of Fantastic Art; www.phantastenmuseum.at; 01, Josefsplatz 6; admission €9; ⊙10am-6pm; 🚃1A, 2A Michaelerplatz, Ⓜ Herrengasse, 🚋D, 1, 2, 71, 46, 49 Burgring) Situated upstairs in Palais Palffy, this newcomer to the museum scene exhibits the works of the Viennese School of Fantastic Realists, which arose in the 1950s. Anyone with a passing or deeper interest in the fantastic painting style with surrealistic (sometimes explicit) edges will enjoy large permanent and frequently changing temporary exhibitions here.

MINORITENKIRCHE
CHURCH

Map p254 (📍533 41 62; www.minoritenkirche-wien.info; 01, Minoritenplatz; admission free; ⊙8am-6pm; 🚃1A, 2A Michaelerplatz, Ⓜ Herrengasse) The Minoritenkirche (Minorite Church) is a 13th-century Gothic church that later received a baroque facelift. If you think the tower looks a little stubby, you're right on the button: it was 'shortened' by the Turks in 1529. The most noteworthy piece inside is a mosaic copy of da Vinci's *Last Supper,* commissioned by Napoleon. The website has details of services and concerts.

Sunday services are held at 8.30am in German and at 11am in Italian. The church is used for occasional classical concerts and choir recitals throughout the year.

HELMUT-ZILK-PLATZ
SQUARE

Map p254 (Albertinaplatz; Ⓜ Stephansplatz, Karlsplatz) This attractive square wedged between the Staatsoper and the Albertina stands out for its **Monument Against War & Fascism**, by Alfred Hrdlicka (1988). The series of pale block-like sculptures has a dark, squat shape wrapped in barbed wire, representing a Jew scrubbing the floor; poignantly, the greyish block originally came from the Mauthausen concentration camp.

✖️ EATING

TRZESNIEWSKI
SANDWICHES €

Map p254 (www.trzesniewski.at; 01, Dorotheergasse 1; bread & spread €1.10, glass of wine €2.10; ⊙8.30am-7.30pm Mon-Fri, 9am-5pm Sat; Ⓜ Stephansplatz) Possibly the finest sandwich shop in Austria, Trzesniewski has been serving spreads and breads to the entire spectrum of munchers (Kafka was a regular here) for over 100 years. Choose from 22 delectably thick spreads. Plan on sampling a few; two bites and they're gone. This branch is one of seven in Vienna.

FRESHII
HEALTH FOOD €

Map p254 (www.freshii.com; 01, Herrengasse 5; €3.50-6.50; ⊗11am-7pm Mon-Fri, 11.30am-7pm Sat & Sun; 🖉; MHerrengasse) 🍃 Affiliated with the small North American wholefood chain, freshii is an eat-in, takeaway place that sells wraps, rice and noodle dishes, burritos, soups and breakfasts based on organic ingredients and a philosophy of environmental as well as bodily health.

BITZINGER WÜRSTELSTAND AM ALBERTINAPLATZ
SAUSAGE STAND €

Map p254 (01, Albertinaplatz; sausages €3.70-4.10; ⊗9.30am-5am, drinks from 8am; MKarlsplatz, Stephansplatz, 🚋Kärntner Ring/Oper) Vienna has many sausage stands but this one located behind the Staatsoper offers the contrasting spectacle of ladies and gents dressed to the nines, sipping beer, wine or champagne while enjoying sausage at outdoor tables or the heated counter after performances. You'll find Joseph Perrier champagne (€19.90 for 0.2L) and, for the less well-heeled, there's house wine (€3.20).

RESTAURANT HERRLICH
AUSTRIAN €€€

Map p254 (🖉53404-920; www.steigenberger. com/wien/restaurants; 01, Herrengasse 10; mains €18-28, menus €56-82, 3-course lunch €29; ⊗lunch & dinner Mon-Fri, dinner Sat; MHerrengasse) Located inside the Steigenberger Hotel Herrenhof, the upmarket Herrlich focuses on a lighter style of Austrian cooking in a modern setting replete with crisp tablecloths. It serves classic dishes on its changing, seasonal menus.

🍷 DRINKING & 🍸 NIGHTLIFE

⭐LOOS AMERICAN BAR
COCKTAIL BAR

Map p254 (www.loosbar.at; 01, Kärntner Durchgang 10; ⊗noon-5am Thu-Sat, to 4am Sun-Wed; MStephansplatz) *The* spot for a classic cocktail in the Innere Stadt, expertly whipped up by talented mixologists. Designed by Adolf Loos in 1908, this tiny box (seating no more than about 20) is bedecked from head to toe in onyx and polished brass; mirrored walls trick the mind into thinking it's a far bigger space.

⭐PALFFY CLUB
CLUB

Map p254 (www.palais-palffy.at; 01, Josefsplatz 6; cover €12; ⊗from 10pm Fri & Sat; 🚋1A, 2A

LOCAL KNOWLEDGE

WHERE TO DRINK WINE

There is no shortage of places to taste the nectar of the gods in Vienna, but one of the most welcoming is **Villon** (Map p254; www.villon.at; 01, Habsburgergasse 4; ⊗6pm-midnight Tue-Fri, 7pm-midnight Sat; MHerrengasse, Stephansplatz), a fully fledged wine cellar sunk deep into the ground of the Innere Stadt (it's the deepest wine cellar in the 1st district). Forget all about your mobile phone working. Although the cellar itself is historic, the interior is smart and modern, with light-coloured woods in the main room where you can order wine by the glass or bottle, accompanied by parmesan cheese, bread, olives and Thun ham (a local speciality) to replenish the palate. Some 20 wines served by the glass and another 100 by the bottle are mostly from small vineyards in Austria or from the Vienna region.

Michaelerplatz; MHerrengasse, 🚋D, 1, 2, 71 Burgring) This 550-sq-metre club occupies two floors (right as you enter) of an illustrious old building used for live-music performances. The 1st-floor lounge bar is set with thousands of miniature glittering gemstones below a 12m chandelier with 80,000 Swarovski crystals. The 1st floor has R&B and '70s and '80s, while the 2nd floor opens at 1am with house and techno beats.

CAFÉ LEOPOLD HAWELKA
COFFEE HOUSE

Map p254 (www.hawelka.at; 01, Dorotheergasse 6; ⊗8am-1am Mon-Sat, 10am-1am Sun; MStephansplatz) This classic coffee house has a relaxed and convivial vibe with orange wallpaper and decorative tones. Nothing much has changed at Hawelka since it opened in the late 1930s. Friedensreich Hundertwasser, Elias Canetti, Arthur Miller and Andy Warhol, just to name a few, are among the artists and writers who have hung out here.

LE BOL
CAFE

Map p254 (www.lebol.at; 01, Neuer Markt 14; ⊗from 8am Mon-Sat, from 10am Sun; MStephansplatz) This French cafe and bistro does wonderful coffee and hot chocolates, a good selection of baguettes (€6.20 to €9.10) as well as inexpensive *tartines* and salads to still a hunger while exploring the area. It has both individual and communal tables.

DEMEL
COFFEE HOUSE

Map p254 (www.demel.at; 01, Kohlmarkt 14; ☺9am-7pm; ☑1A, 2A Michaelerplatz, Ⓜ Herrengasse, Stephansplatz) An elegant and regal cafe within sight of the Hofburg, Demel was once the talk of the town but now mainly caters to tourists. The quality of the cakes hasn't dropped, however, and it wins marks for the sheer creativity of its sweets. Demel's speciality is the Ana Demel Torte, a calorie-bomb of chocolate and nougat.

The window displays an ever-changing array of edible art pieces (ballerinas and manicured bonsai, for example).

PALMENHAUS
BAR, CAFE

Map p254 (www.palmenhaus.at; 01, Burggarten; ☺10am-2am; Ⓜ Karlsplatz, Museumsquartier, ☑D, 1, 2, 71 Burgring) In a beautifully restored Victorian palm house, complete with high arched ceilings, glass walls and steel beams, Palmenhaus occupies one of the most attractive locations in Vienna. The crowd is generally well-to-do, but the ambience is relaxed and welcoming, making it ideal for a glass of wine or cup of coffee. The outdoor seating in summer is a must; it serves food (mains €16.80 to €27) and there are occasional club nights.

CAFÉ GRIENSTEIDL
COFFEE HOUSE

Map p254 (☎535 26 92-0; www.cafegriensteidl. at; 01, Michaelerplatz 2; ☺8am-11pm; ☑1A, 2A Michaelerplatz, Ⓜ Herrengasse) Griensteidl holds a prestigious position between the Hofburg and the Loos Haus, and was once the *Stammlokal* (local haunt) for Vienna's late-19th-century literary set. Expect lots of tourists, *Jugendstil* lamps and huge windows to Michaelerplatz.

CAFÉ TIROLERHOF
COFFEE HOUSE

Map p254 (☎512 78 33; 01, Führichgasse 8; ☺7am-10pm Mon-Sat, 9am-8pm Sun; ☏; Ⓜ Stephansplatz, Karlsplatz, ☑D, 1, 2, 71 Kärntner Ring/Oper) Lovingly renovated *Jugendstil* decor from the 1920s and homemade *Apfelstrudel* help to make Tirolerhof an inviting choice in the Innere Stadt.

ESTERHÁZYKELLER
WINE TAVERN

Map p254 (☎533 34 82; www.esterhazykeller. at; 01, Haarhof 1; ☺11am-11pm; Ⓜ Stephansplatz, Herrengasse) Esterházykeller, tucked away on a quiet courtyard just off Kohlmarkt,

has an enormous cellar – rustic decor, complete with medieval weaponry and farming tools – where excellent wine is served direct from the Esterházy Palace wine estate in Eisenstadt. Unlike most *Heurigen* (wine taverns), Esterházykeller offers beer.

VOLKSGARTEN PAVILLON
BAR

Map p254 (www.volksgarten-pavillon.at; 01, Burgring 1; ☺11am-2am Apr–mid-Sep; ☏; Ⓜ Volkstheater, ☑D, 1, 2, 71 Dr-Karl-Renner-Ring) This lovely 1950s-style pavilion has views of Heldenplatz. During the day and very early evening it's a cafe and restaurant, but its highlight is the legendary Tuesday night Techno Cafe, when its ever-popular garden is packed to the gunnels. Entrance some nights is free; for the Techno Cafe it's around €4.

VOLKSGARTEN CLUBDISKOTHEK
CLUB

Map p254 (www.volksgarten.at; 01, Burgring 1; cover from €6; ☺10pm-4am or later Tue & Thu-Sat ; Ⓜ Museumsquartier, Volkstheater, ☑D, 1, 2, 71 Dr-Karl-Renner-Ring) A hugely popular club superbly located near the Hofburg, Volksgarten serves a clientele eager to see and be seen. The long cocktail bar is perfect for people-watching and the music is an ever-rotating mix of hip-hop, house and hits. Opening hours are variable so check the website. Dress well to glide past the bouncers.

FLEDERMAUS
DISCO

Map p254 (www.fledermaus.at; 01, Spiegelgasse 2; cover about €5 Wed-Mon; ☺from 9pm; Ⓜ Stephansplatz) Fledermaus is not the coolest disco in town but it is among the most relaxed and down-to-earth in terms of decor and club-goers, with a program running the spectrum of musical styles from the 1950s to '90s, each night dedicated to a particular movement or epoch.

PASSAGE
CLUB

Map p254 (☎961 88 00; www.club-passage.at; 01, Burgring 3, Babenberger Passage; cover from €6; ☺from 8pm or 9pm Tue-Sat; Ⓜ Museumsquartier, ☑D, 1, 2, 71 Burgring) Passage is the closest thing to a megaclub for a mostly young crowd in Vienna. Its sleek interior, soothing colours and sweaty atmosphere attract the beautiful people of the city, their entourage and plenty of oglers and barflies. The music is loud (noise from the Ringstrasse traffic directly outside is easily drowned out) and covers anything from early classics to house.

CAFÉ BRÄUNERHOF
COFFEE HOUSE

Map p254 (⌂512 38 93; 01, Stallburggasse 2; ⏲8am-9pm Mon-Fri, 8am-7pm Sat, 10am-7pm Sun; ⓂHerengasse, Stephansplatz) Little has changed in Bräunerhof since the days when Austria's seminal writer Thomas Bernhard frequented the premises: staff can be stand-offish, the mood somewhat stuffy, and the newspaper selection good. For all this, it's a coffee house with traditional Viennese flavour. Classical music features from 3pm to 6pm on weekends.

☆ ENTERTAINMENT

ÖSTERREICHISCHES FILMMUSEUM
CINEMA

Map p254 (⌂533 70 54; www.filmmuseum.at; 01, Augustinerstrasse 1; adult/child €10/5.80; ⓂKarlsplatz, 🚊D, 1, 2, 71 Kärntner Ring/Oper) Situated inside the Albertina, the Austrian Film Museum shows a range of films with and without subtitles in the original language, featuring a director, group of directors or a certain theme from around the world in programs generally lasting a couple of weeks. Screenings are generally at 6.30pm; check the website for other times.

HOFBURG CONCERT HALLS
CLASSICAL MUSIC

Map p254 (⌂587 25 52; www.hofburgorchester.at; 01, Heldenplatz; tickets €42-55; ⓂHerengasse, 🚊D, 1, 2, 71 Burgring) The Neue Hofburg's concert halls, the sumptuous Festsaal and Redoutensaal, are regularly used for Strauss and Mozart concerts, featuring the Hofburg Orchestra and soloists from the Staatsoper and Volksoper. Performances start at 8.30pm and tickets are available online and from travel agents and hotels. Seating isn't allocated, so get in early to secure a good spot.

SHOPPING

ÖSTERREICHISCHE WERKSTÄTTEN
GLASS, CERAMICS

Map p254 (www.austrianarts.com; 01, Kärntner Strasse 6; ⏲10am-6.30pm Mon-Fri, to 6pm Sat; ⓂStephansplatz) Established in 1945, Österreichische Werkstätten is dedicated to selling work made by Austrian companies and designed by Austrian designers. Look out for Kisslinger, a family glassware company since 1946, with Klimt- and Hundertwasser-styled designs; Peter Wolfe's more traditional Tirol-style designed glassware;

and of course the world-renowned Riedel wineglasses.

KABUL SHOP
HANDICRAFTS

Map p254 (01, Herrengasse 6-8; ⏲9am-7pm Mon-Fri, to 6pm Sat; ⓂHerengasse) The name is somewhat misleading as most of this shop is dedicated to Tibetan and Central Asian handicrafts and jewellery, along with silk scarves and other textiles, and some furniture and carpets. It's in fact a treasure trove of oriental handicrafts. Expect to pay about €35 for earrings.

FREYTAG & BERNDT
BOOKS, MAPS

Map p254 (www.freytagberndt.at; 01, Kohlmarkt 9; ⏲9.30am-6.30pm Mon-Fri, to 6pm Sat; 🚇1A, 2A Michaelerplatz, ⓂHerrengasse) There is no better place for maps and travel guides than Freytag & Berndt. There's an exhaustive collection of guides to and maps of Vienna and Austria (including some superbly detailed walking maps) and guides to Europe and the world (many in English).

UNITED NUDE
SHOES

Map p254 (www.unitednude-shop.at; 01, Herrengasse 6-8; ⏲10am-8pm Thu-Sat & Mon, to 7pm Tue & Wed; ⓂHerrengasse) The boots are not Viennese but they are kinky enough to be. This is the Vienna flagship store of some of the most unusual (and postmodern) boots you will ever see. Creative folds cost from €160, and you can expect to pay €200 and upwards for summer and winter boots.

J&L LOBMEYR VIENNA
CERAMICS

Map p254 (www.lobmeyr.at; 01, Kärntner Strasse 26; ⏲9am-5pm Mon-Fri; ⓂStephansplatz) Sweep up the beautifully ornate wrought-iron staircase to one of Vienna's most lavish retail experiences. The collection of Biedermeier pieces, Loos-designed sets, fine/arty glassware and porcelain on display here glitters from the lights of the chandelier-festooned atrium. Lobmeyr has been in business since the early 19th century, when it exclusively supplied the imperial court. Today production is more focused towards pieces inspired by the Wiener Werkstätte artists from the early 20th century. This movement sought to bring a philosophy of artistic craftsmanship into functional design, later helping pave the way for art deco.

AUGARTEN WIEN
GLASS, CERAMICS

Map p254 (www.augarten.at; 01, Spiegelgasse 3; ☺10am-6pm Mon-Sat; Ⓜ Stephansplatz) Wiener Porzellanmanufaktur Augarten makes Vienna's finest porcelain – the most delicate of ornaments, vases and dinnerware with traditional hand-painted designs. Prices start at around €80 for a small vase and go way up. Tours of the factory are available; see the website for details.

LODEN-PLANKL
CLOTHING

Map p254 (www.loden-plankl.at; 01, Michaelerplatz 6; ☺10am-6pm Mon-Sat; 🚇 1A, 2A Michaelerplatz, Ⓜ Herrengasse) Christopher Plummer wannabes alert: kit yourself out Von Trapp-family style at this 180-year-old institution full of handmade embroidered dirndls (women's traditional dress) and blouses, capes, high-collared jackets, and deer-suede and *loden* (a traditional fabric made from boiled and combed wool) coats. Modern variations share racks with traditional designs, but you're likely to find more nostalgic charm in the trad stuff.

MÜHLBAUER
FASHION, ACCESSORIES

Map p254 (www.muehlbauer.at; 01, Seilergasse 10; ☺10am-6.30pm Mon-Fri, to 6pm Sat; Ⓜ Stephansplatz) Adorning Viennese heads since 1903, Mühlbauer embodies the spirit of fun that hat-wearing in the 21st century should be all about: cool without being unapproachable, glamorous without being stuffy. Cloches, pillboxes, caps and even bonnets – designs nod to the traditional but with colours and detailing that are oh so now.

OBERLAA
CONFECTIONERY

Map p254 (www.oberlaa-wien.at; 01, Neuer Markt 16; ☺8am-8pm; Ⓜ Stephansplatz) Some locals swear that Oberlaa sells the best confectionery in Vienna. We're out to lunch on that, but it no doubt offers the most beautifully packaged chocolates, and no other local macaroon measures up to its 'LaaKronen' – brightly coloured in flavours like pistachio, lemon and strawberry, available singly or in gorgeous boxed sets. There are seven other branches around town.

WOLFORD
ACCESSORIES, FASHION

Map p254 (www.wolford.com; 01, Kärntner Strasse 22; ☺10am-7pm Mon-Fri, to 6pm Sat; Ⓜ Stephansplatz) Perhaps the best-known Austrian brand in the fashion world, Wolford (founded in 1949) is renowned for high-quality hosiery. Here you'll find a huge range – including fishnets in all colours of the rainbow and imaginatively patterned tights, stay-ups, stockings and knee-highs – as well as body stockings and swimwear. There are a number of Wolford branches scattered around town.

Stephansdom & the Historic Centre

WEST & NORTH OF STEPHANSPLATZ | SOUTH & EAST OF STEPHANSPLATZ

Neighbourhood Top Five

1 Strolling through **Stephansdom** (p75) and admiring the intricate details of Vienna's famous landmark and Austria's best-known Gothic cathedral.

2 Admiring the highlights of the **cathedral treasures** (p76), currently exhibited inside Stephansdom.

3 Wandering through the **historic centre** (p84) of Vienna and exploring the quiet courtyards and lanes.

4 Discovering all about Wolfgang Amadeus Mozart and his epoch on a visit to **Mozarthaus Vienna** (p82).

5 Conducting your own virtual orchestra and engaging with other exhibits at the **Haus der Musik** (p82).

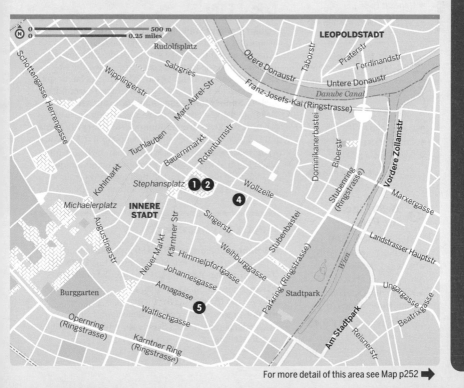

For more detail of this area see Map p252 ➡

Lonely Planet's Top Tip

Although there are lots of quick-eats places in the historic centre, you can often eat very stylishly and relatively inexpensively (for about €15) by choosing one first-course dish (say, a fish soup with bread) and a drink in all but the very top restaurants. The best places are those with the kitchen open all day; otherwise turn up around 1.30pm. Lunch menus are also great value everywhere.

✖ Best Places to Eat

➡ Motto am Fluss (p85)

➡ Griechenbeisl (p85)

➡ Meinl's Restaurant (p87)

➡ Yohm (p85)

➡ Expedit (p86)

For reviews, see p85 ➡

🍷 Best Places to Drink

➡ Kruger's American Bar (p88)

➡ Kleines Café (p88)

➡ Cafe Neko (p90)

➡ Café Prückel (p88)

➡ First Floor (p89)

For reviews, see p88 ➡

◉ Best Places for Free

➡ Stephansdom (p75)

➡ Neidhart-Fresken (p79)

➡ Bawag Contemporary/ Bawag Foundation (p85)

➡ Archiv des Österreichischen Widerstands (p79)

For reviews, see p75 ➡

Explore Stephansdom & the Historic Centre

Vienna's Innere Stadt is compact and easily walked, and this is especially true of the Stephansdom and historic centre. Plan to spend half a day to explore the cathedral properly. The Haus der Musik or Mozarthaus Vienna would fit in better after lunch, especially when it's cold or rainy. The next day would be ideal for a neighbourhood walk, choosing the sights you want to visit along the way or dropping into others close to the route, such as the Museum Judenplatz; none of the sights take more than 30 minutes or one hour to visit. The best place to start is usually Stephansplatz. Simply choose a side of town or series of sights and make a trajectory to it, backtracking or taking different streets to reach the other side of the centre if you wish.

Remember that the historic centre gets very crowded in summer, so early morning or early evening are the best times to stroll around if you don't want to visit specific sights. Late on a warm night can also be a romantic, safe and crowd-free time. One final tip: keep the coffee houses on your radar along the way – these are fine places for resting up.

Local Life

➡**Quiet Corners** Walking the streets of the centre in summer can sometimes give you the feeling of being on an ant trail. Take side lanes like **Blutgasse** and duck into squares and courtyards along the way. Heiligenkreuzerhof may be parked with cars but despite this it's spacious and very attractive. Streets around it, such as **Sonnenfelsgasse**, **Schönlaterngasse** and Dr-Ignaz-Seipel-Platz (p83), are also quieter parts of town, as are areas around Ruprechtskirche (p79), Maria am Gestade (p79) or between Judenplatz and Am Hof.

➡**Night Moves** The historic centre can be beautiful when lit up at night. Soak it up the way the Viennese do – change locations by taking a leisurely stroll between restaurant and bar or club on a night out.

Getting There & Away

➡**U-Bahn** Stephansplatz (U1, U3) and Schwedenplatz (U1, U4) – and to a lesser extent Stubentor (U3), Herrengasse (U3) and Karlsplatz (U1, U2, U4) – are the main stops.

➡**Tram** Schwedenplatz (1, 2) and Kärntner Ring/Oper (1, 2, D, 71) are the most convenient.

➡**Bus** 1A links Stephansplatz, Schottentor and Michaelerplatz; 3A links Stubentor with Stephansplatz and Börsenplatz.

TOP SIGHT
STEPHANSDOM

Vienna's Gothic masterpiece Stephansdom (St Stephan's Cathedral), or Steffl (Little Stephan) as it's locally called, symbolises Vienna like no other building. A visit to the cathedral takes in the spectacular main nave, catacombs, two towers and the cathedral treasures, which are currently housed inside the cathedral itself. An audio guide is useful, especially for exploring the main nave. The side aisle (on the left, facing the altar) is free if you only want to gain a quick impression of the cathedral.

A church has stood on this site since the 12th century, reminders of which today are the Romanesque **Riesentor** (Giant Gate) and **Heidentürme** (Towers of the Heathens) at the entrance and above it. In 1359, at the behest of Habsburg Duke Rudolf IV, Stephansdom began receiving its Gothic makeover and Rudolf earned himself the epithet of 'The Founder' by laying the first stone in the reconstruction.

From outside the cathedral, the first thing that will strike you is the glorious tiled roof, with its dazzling row of chevrons on one end and the Austrian eagle on the other. Inside the cathedral, the magnificent Gothic stone pulpit takes pride of place, fashioned in 1515 by an unknown artisan. The pulpit railing is adorned with salamanders and toads, symbolising the battle of good against evil. The baroque high altar, at the very far end of the main nave, shows the stoning of St Stephan. The chancel to its left has the winged Wiener Neustadt altarpiece, dating from 1447; the right chancel has the Renaissance red marble tomb of Friedrich III. Under his guidance the city became a bishopric (and the church a cathedral) in 1469.

DON'T MISS...

→ Audio guide explaining highlights in main nave

→ Pulpit by unknown artisan

→ High altar

PRACTICALITIES

→ St Stephan's Cathedral

→ Map p252

→ www.stephans kirche.at

→ 01, Stephansplatz

→ ⏱6am-10pm Mon-Sat, 7am-10pm Sun, main nave & Domschatz audio tours 9-11.30am & 1-5.30pm Mon-Sat, 1-5.30pm Sun

→ Ⓜ Stephansplatz

STEPHANSDOM: ANIMAL ELDORADO

Stephansdom is an unlikely eldorado for animal lovers. The Riesentor (Giant Gate) is packed with basilisks as well as ugly dragons and lions. Friedrich III's tomb (1513) has some rather hideous creatures (serpents, ugly eagles, lions and a goat-like creature) on top, but you can't get close enough to see these. The zoological highlight, however, is the pulpit, with salamanders and toads, topped off by the pug-faced Fearless Dog, warding off evil.

The first church built on the site of the cathedral was a Romanesque church consecrated in 1147. This was remodelled completely and consecrated again in 1263. Entering the cathedral today, you pass though the Riesentor, which dates from the early 13th century. The Heidentürme (Towers of the Heathens) rise above this main portal. The name 'Riesentor' has less to do with the size of the gate than its deep, inward-sloping funnel shape (derived from the old German *rīsanan* (rising).

Stephansdom Katakomben

The area around the cathedral was originally a graveyard. But with plague and influenza epidemics striking Europe in the 1730s, Karl VI ordered the graveyard to be closed and henceforth Vienna buried its dead beneath Stephansdom in the **Katakomben** (Catacombs; ☑515 52 3054; tours adult/child €4.50/1.50; ⏰10-11.30am & 1.30-4.30pm Mon-Sat, 1.30-4.30pm Sun). Today, they contain the remains of countless victims, who are kept in a mass grave and a bone house. Also on display are rows of urns containing the internal organs of the Habsburgs. One of the many privileges of being a Habsburg was to be dismembered and dispersed after death: their hearts are in the Augustinerkirche in the Hofburg and the rest of their bodies are in the Kaisergruft. You can only enter on tours.

Cathedral South Tower

When the foundation stone for the **south tower** (Südturm; ☑515 52 3054; adult/child €4/1.50; ⏰9am-5.30pm) was laid in 1359, Rudolf IV is said to have used a trowel and spade made of silver. Two towers were originally envisaged, but the Südturm grew so high that little space remained for the second. In 1433 the tower reached its final height of 136.7m, and today you can ascend the 343 steps to a cramped platform for one of Vienna's most spectacular views over the rooftops of the Innere Stadt.

Cathedral Pummerin

Weighing 21 tonnes, the **Pummerin** (Boomer Bell; ☑515 52 3520; adult/child €5/2; ⏰8.15am-4.30pm mid-Jan–Jun & Sep-Dec, to 6pm Jul & Aug) is Austria's largest bell and was installed in the north tower in 1952. While the rest of the cathedral was rising up in its new Gothic format, work was interrupted on this tower due to a lack of cash and the fading allure of Gothic architecture; it's accessible by lift only today, without a ticket for the main nave.

Domschatz

The highlights of the **Domschatz** (Cathedral Treasures; Domschatz kehrt Zurück; adult/child €4/1.50; ⏰10am-6pm Mon-Sat) are currently on display in Stephansdom. The collection comprises an exhibition called 'Der Domschatz kehrt zurück' ('The cathedral treasure returns'). You can admire the treasures here until they resume their usual space inside the **Dom- & Diözesanmuseum** (☑515 52 3300; 01, Stephansplatz 6; ⏰closed for restoration; ⓂStephansplatz), expected to be sometime in 2015.

 SIGHTS

STEPHANSDOM CATHEDRAL
See p75.

◉ West & North of Stephansplatz

PETERSKIRCHE CHURCH
Map p252 (☎533 64 33; www.peterskirche.at; 01, Petersplatz; ☺7am-8pm Mon-Fri, 9am-9pm Sat & Sun; Ⓜ Stephansplatz) The Peterskirche (Church of St Peter), situated just north of Graben, was built in 1733 according to plans of the celebrated baroque architect Johann Lukas von Hildebrandt. Interior highlights that make a visit highly worthwhile include a fresco on the dome painted by JM Rottmayr and a golden altar depicting the martyrdom of St John of Nepomuk.

This was not the first baroque church built in Vienna (the Dominikanerkirche has that honour), nor is it considered the finest (the Karlskirche, with its glass elevator to the cupola, pips it at the post), but it is one of the most attractive. Free pamphlets inside explain the interior. Regular organ recitals and concerts are also held here.

GRABEN STREET
Map p252 (01; Ⓜ Stephansplatz) Branching off from Stock-im-Eisen-Platz, Graben boasts two very remarkable sights. One of these is the writhing, towering **Pestsäule** (Plague Column; Map p252; 01, Graben), erected in 1693 to commemorate the end of the plague. It was designed by Johann Bernhard Fischer von Erlach. Not to be missed here are also **Adolf Loos' public toilets** (Map p254; 01, Graben), which are in the *Jugendstil* (art nouveau) design.

Graben literally began life as a ditch dug by the Romans to protect Vinodoba. In 1192 Leopold V filled in the ditch and built a defensive city wall that ended in Freyung, using as finance the ransom paid by archrival Richard the Lionheart, who at that time was being kept under lock and key in a castle near Dürnstein, on the Danube.

Other architectural highlights to look out for on Graben include the neo-Renaissance **Equitable Palais** (Map p254; 01, Graben) at No 3; the ornate inner courtyard is tiled with

---

ⓘ GUIDED TOURS & MUSIC IN VIENNA'S CATHEDRAL

The main nave with all the important features described in the audio guides is pay-to-enter. Only the flanking aisle is free of charge. This will give you an impression of the cathedral but is too distant for you to admire or understand details. Entrance to the main nave without an audio guide of any sort costs €3.50/free for an adult/child, with an audio guide adult/child €4.50/1.50. Note that the main nave, catacombs and lift to the north tower are closed to visitors during Mass.

Guided tours in English and German English-language tours of the Dom explain briefly the background of the cathedral and walk you through its main interior features. The 30-minute tours leave at 3.45pm from April to October and cost €4.50 (for those younger than 14 it's €1.50). The same guided tours in German leave at 10.30am and 3pm Monday to Saturday and 3pm Sunday.

Evening tours in German Conducted at 7pm every Saturday from June to September, including a brisk climb to the top of the south tower (€10/4).

All-inclusive tour This is part audio guide, part with a tour guide (adult plus one child under 14 is €16; a senior or student pays €13.50). It takes in the cathedral interior, catacombs, Domschatz (cathedral treasures), south tower and the north tower. Children aren't allowed to do it alone.

Multilingual audio guide tour This is the most common option and costs €8 (including one child), taking in the cathedral interior and Domschatz. You can do this tour from 9am to 11.30am and 1pm to 5.30pm Monday to Saturday, and from 1pm to 5.30pm Sunday.

Special events & Mass The Dom website (www.stephanskirche.at) has a program of special concerts and events, but the 10.15am Mass on Sundays (9.30am during the school holidays around July and August) is something special as it's conducted with full choral accompaniment.

Hungarian Zsolnay ceramics. The blackened and aged stump encased in glass in the building's eastern corner was where apprentice journeyfolk during the Middle Ages would hammer nails into the stump to ensure a safe homeward journey. Also interesting are the neoclassical revivalist **Erste Österreichische Sparkasse** (Map p252; 01, Graben), 1836, on the corner of Tuchlauben, complete with a gilded bee symbolising thrift and industriousness, and the *Jugendstil* **Grabenhof** (Map p254; 01, Graben), 1876, at No 14, built by Otto Wagner using the plans of Otto Thienemann.

MUSEUM JUDENPLATZ   MUSEUM

Map p252 (☑535 04 31; www.jmw.at; 01, Judenplatz 8; adult/child €10/free, valid 48hr both Jewish museums; ⊕10am-6pm Sun-Thu, to 2pm Fri; Ⓜ Stephansplatz, Herrengasse) The main focus of Museum Judenplatz is on the excavated remains of a medieval synagogue that once stood on Judenplatz, with a film and numerous exhibits to elucidate Jewish history. It was built in the Middle Ages, but Duke Albrecht V's 'hatred and misconception' led him to order its destruction in 1421. The basic outline of the synagogue can still be seen here.

After entering the museum you watch an informative 12-minute video on Judaism, the synagogue and the Jewish quarter. Next up are the excavations, after which you can search the databases for lost relatives or friends if you wish. Glass cases containing fragments, such as documents from Jewish history in Vienna, are dotted throughout the museum. An audio guide costs €2 (in German and English, with a special children's version too). Vienna's other Jewish museum (p67) is on Dorotheergasse. Free tours, generally on the first Sunday in the month (in German), are conducted at 3pm from the Jüdisches Museum and 4.30pm from Museum Judenplatz, covering all exhibitions.

HOLOCAUST-DENKMAL   MEMORIAL

Map p252 (01, Judenplatz; Ⓜ Stephansplatz) The Holocaust-Denkmal (2000) is the focal point of Judenplatz and a memorial to the 65,000 Austrian Jews who perished in the Holocaust. Designed by British sculptor Rachel Whiteread, this 'nameless library' depicts books with their spines facing inwards, representing the untold stories of Holocaust victims; it's embellished with the names of Austrian concentration camps.

The northern side of Judenplatz is occupied by the former **Böhmische Hofkanzlei** (Bohemian Court Chancery; Map p252; 01, Judenplatz), with a striking facade by Johann Bernhard Fischer von Erlach. Walk around to Wipplingerstrasse to see this.

STADTTEMPEL   SYNAGOGUE

Map p252 (☑531 041 11; www.jmw.at; 01, Seitenstettengasse 4; tours adult/child €4/free; ⊕guided tours 11.30am & 2pm Mon-Thu; Ⓜ Stephansplatz, Schwedenplatz) Vienna's main synogogue was completed in 1826 after *Toleranzpatent* reforms by Joseph II in the 1780s granted rights to Vienna's Jews to practise their religion. This paved the way for improved standing for Jews and brought a rise in fortunes. Built in an exquisite Biedermeier style, the main prayer room is flanked by 12 ionic columns and is capped by a cupola.

The synagogue seats about 500 people. Visitors of the Jewish faith can phone (Hebrew, English and German spoken) for more information about services. Arrive early to register with security, and bring your passport.

ANKERUHR   CLOCK

Map p252 (Anker Clock; 01, Hoher Markt 10-11; Ⓜ Stephansplatz, Schwedenplatz) Hoher Markt is Vienna's oldest square and was once the centre of the Roman outpost; today it is also home to the Ankeruhr, an art nouveau masterpiece created by Franz von Matsch in 1911 and named after the Anker Insurance Co, which commissioned it. Over a 12-hour period, figures slowly pass across the clock face, indicating the time against a static measure showing the minutes.

Figures range from Marcus Aurelius (the Roman emperor who died in Vienna in AD 180) to Josef Haydn, with Eugene of Savoy, Maria Theresia and many others in between. Details of who's who are on a plaque on the wall below. People flock here at noon, when all the figures trundle past in succession to the tune of organ music.

AM HOF   SQUARE

Map p252 (01; Ⓜ Herrengasse, Schottentor) This large square was where the Babenbergs resided before rulers moved to the site of the Hofburg in the late 13th century. The attractive Mariensäule (Mary's Column; 1667) rises up in the centre, but also look for house No 11, where a gold-painted cannonball is a reminder of the 1683 Turkish siege. The former Jesuit monastery **Kirche Am Hof** (Map p252; ☎533 83 94; admission free; ◌8am-noon & 4-6pm Mon-Sat, 4pm-6pm Sun; ⓂHerrengasse, Schottentor) occupies the southeast side.

Kirche Am Hof has a baroque facade adapted from its fire-damaged Gothic predecessor and a hugely expansive nave lined with white pillars and topped with gold badges. It was here in 1806 that a royal herald announced the end of the Holy Roman Empire, ruled by the Habsburgs for about 500 years.

UHREN MUSEUM   MUSEUM
Map p252 (Clock Museum; ☎533 22 65; www. wienmuseum.at; 01, Schulhof 2; adult/under 19yr €6/free; ◌10am-6pm Tue-Sun; ⊟1A, 3A Renngasse, ⓂHerrengasse) The municipal Uhren Museum loudly ticks away time from its location behind the Kirche Am Hof. Opened in 1921 in the Hafenhaus, one of Vienna's oldest buildings, its three floors are weighed down with an astounding 21,200 clocks and watches, ranging from the 15th century to a 1992 computer clock.

The collection of Biedermeier and belle époque models will, for most, steal the show. The peace and quiet is shattered at the striking of the hour, so those with sensitive ears should avoid these times.

ARCHIV DES ÖSTERREICHISCHEN WIDERSTANDS   MUSEUM
Map p252 (☎228 94 69; www.doew.at; 01, Wipplingerstrasse 8; ◌9am-5pm Mon-Thu; ⓂStephansplatz) FREE Housed in the Altes Rathaus (Old City Hall), the Austrian Resistance Archive has a disturbing but highly worthwhile exhibition that documents with photos and other exhibits the little-known antifascist resistance force that operated during the Nazi regime; some 2700 resistance fighters were executed by the Nazis and thousands more sent to concentration camps.

The exhibition gives in-depth analysis of the Nazi doctrines on homosexuality, 'unworthy' citizens, concentration camps and forced labour, with many of the photos and memorabilia detailing the time before and after the *Anschluss* (annexation).

NEIDHART-FRESKEN   MURAL
Map p252 (☎535 90 65; 01, Tuchlauben 19; ◌10am-1pm & 2-6pm Tue-Sun; ⓂStephansplatz) FREE An unassuming house on Tuchlauben hides quite a remarkable decoration: the oldest extant secular murals in Vienna. The small frescoes, dating from 1398, tell the story of the minstrel Neidhart von Reuental (1180–1240) and life in the Middle Ages in lively and jolly scenes. The frescoes are in superb condition considering their age.

RÖMER MUSEUM   MUSEUM
Map p252 (☎535 56 06; 01, Hoher Markt 3; adult/under 19yr €6/free; ◌9am-6pm Tue-Sun; ⊟1A, 3A Hoher Markt, ⓂStephansplatz) This small expanse of Roman ruins dating from the 1st to the 5th century is thought to be part of the officers' quarters of the Roman legion camp at Vindobona. You can see crumbled walls, tiled floors and a small exhibition of artefacts here. The ruins are part of the 'Wien Museum' municipal museum ensemble of Vienna.

MARIA AM GESTADE   CHURCH
Map p252 (☎533 95 94-0; www.maria-am-gestade.redemptoristen.at; 01, Passauer Platz; ◌8am-7pm; ⓂStephansplatz, ⊟1, 2 Salztorbrücke) Originally a wooden church built by Danube boatmen around 880, Maria am Gestade (Maria on the Riverbank) is today a shapely Gothic beauty of stone assembled from the 14th century. Because of the steep ground, the nave was built narrower than the choir (and with a slight bend). In 1805 Napoleon used it to store weapons and as a stall.

The interior boasts a high vaulted Gothic ceiling and pretty stained glass behind a winged Gothic altar. The church is on a picturesque flight of steps in a quiet corner of town.

RUPRECHTSKIRCHE   CHURCH
Map p252 (St Rupert's Church; ☎535 60 03; www. ruprechtskirche.at; 01, Seitenstettengasse 5; ◌10am-noon & 3-5pm Mon, Wed & Fri, 10am-noon Tue & Thu; ⓂSchwedenplatz, ⊟1, 2 Schwedenplatz) Located a few steps north of Ruprechtsplatz, Ruprechtskirche dates from about 1137 or earlier, giving it the honour of being the oldest church in Vienna. The lower levels of the tower date from the 12th century, the roof from the 15th century and the iron Renaissance door on the west side from the 1530s.

What makes this church attractive in summer is its unusually simple exterior of ivy-clad stone walls in cobblestoned surrounds. The interior is sleek and worth a quick viewing, with a Romanesque nave from the 12th century.

1. Mozarthaus Vienna (p82)
The famed composer spent 2½ years at this residence, now the city's premier Mozart attraction.

2. Haus der Musik (p82)
Learn how music is created at this interactive museum.

3. Stephansplatz
This busy square is host to the spectacular Stephansdom (p75).

MORZINPLATZ   SQUARE

Map p252 (01; MSchwedenplatz, 1, 2 Schwedenplatz) Situated on the Danube Canal between Salztorbrücke and Marienbrücke, Morzinplatz is dominated by the **Monument to the Victims of Fascism** (Map p252), 1985, on the site of the former Gestapo headquarters during the Nazi era. The monument features the Star of David and the pink triangle, representing the Jewish and homosexual victims of the Nazis.

◉ South & East of Stephansplatz

MOZARTHAUS VIENNA   MUSEUM

Map p252 (512 17 91; www.mozarthausvienna.at; 01, Domgasse 5; adult/child €10/3, with Haus der Musik €17/7; 10am-7pm; MStephansplatz) Mozarthaus Vienna, the residence where the great composer spent 2½ happy and productive years, is now the city's premier Mozart attraction. Although the exhibits in themselves are not startling (they tend to be mainly copies of music scores or based around paintings), the free audio guide is indispensable and recreates well the story of Mozart and his time.

Mozart spent a total of 11 years in Vienna, changing residence frequently and sometimes setting up his home outside the Ringstrasse in the cheaper *Vorstädte* (inner suburbs) when he needed to tighten his purse.

The exhibition begins on the top floor of this historic building with a narrow, closed-in inner courtyard. This deals with the society of the late 18th century, providing asides into prominent figures in the court and Mozart's life, such as the Freemasons to whom he dedicated a number of pieces. Mozart's vices – his womanising, gambling and ability to waste excessive amounts of money – lend a spicy edge (you can look through some peepholes). The next floor concentrates on Mozart's music and his musical influences. It was in this house that he penned *The Marriage of Figaro,* which went down like a lead balloon in Vienna but was enthusiastically received in Prague. A surreal holographic performance of scenes from *The Magic Flute* is in another room. The final floor has Mozart's bedroom and a few period pieces of furniture in glass cases to give a feel for the era.

◉ TOP SIGHT
HAUS DER MUSIK

The Haus der Musik brings sound and music close to adults and children alike in an amusing and interactive way (in English and German).

Floor 1 hosts the **Museum of the Vienna Philharmonic**. Find out about the history of the orchestra's famous New Year's concerts, listen to recent concert highlights and even compose your own waltz by rolling dice.

Floor 2, called the Sonosphere, has plenty of engaging instruments, interactive toys and touch screens. Test the limits of your hearing and play around with sampled sounds to record your own CD (€7). One of the highlights for aficionados of everyday audioscapes is a collection of street and subway sounds from New York, Tokyo and other places.

Floor 3 covers Vienna's classical composers and is polished off with an amusing interactive video in which you conduct the Vienna Philharmonic Orchestra.

Floor 4 has the so-called virtostage in which your own body language and movements shape the music to create an opera.

DON'T MISS...

➡ Sonosphere

➡ Virtual conductor

➡ The Vienna Philharmonic Orchestra concert footage

PRACTICALITIES

➡ Map p252

➡ 513 4850

➡ www.hdm.at

➡ 01, Seilerstätte 30

➡ adult/child €12/5.50, with Mozarthaus Vienna €17/7

➡ 10am-10pm

➡ MKarlsplatz, D, 1, 2 Kärntner Ring/Oper

FLEISCHMARKT
STREET

Map p252 (01, Fleischmarkt; ⓂStephansplatz) Greek merchants settled around Fleischmarkt from about 1700, which gradually became known as the Griechenviertel (Greek quarter). Today it has some attractive art nouveau buildings, such as No 14, built by F Dehm and F Olbricht (1899), No 7 (Max Kropf; 1899) – the childhood home of Hollywood film director Billy Wilder from 1914 to 1924 – and Nos 1 and 3 (1910).

The favourite meeting place of the Greek community was the Griechenbeisl (p85), today one of Vienna's most popular (and touristed) *Beisln*. As the they became more established, a few wealthier Greeks spun off towards the Ringstrasse and built larger abodes there, and one immigrant, the industrialist and politician Nikolaus von Dumba, commissioned the building of Palais Dumba in 1866.

GREEK ORTHODOX CHURCH
CHURCH

Map p252 (⌐533 38 89; 01, Fleischmarkt 13; ⏱10am-3pm; ⓂSchwedenplatz, ⌐1, 2 Schwedenplatz) Built in 1861 at the behest of the Greek community, the interior of Vienna's main Greek Orthodox church is a glittering blaze of Byzantine designs. A ceiling fresco depicting the prophets surrounded by swirls of gold is augmented by a high altar of 13 panels, each of which features sparkling gilding, and a doorway to the inner sanctum.

Today, the Greek community in Vienna numbers about 10,000.

FRANZISKANERKIRCHE
CHURCH

Map p252 (⌐512 45 7811; 01, Franziskanerplatz; ⏱7am-8pm; ⓂStephansplatz) This Franciscan church is a glorious architectural deception. Outside it exudes the hallmarks of an early 17th-century Renaissance style, yet inside it is awash with gold and marble decorative features from the baroque era about 100 years later. The high altar takes the form of a triumphal arch and hidden behind this is Vienna's oldest organ (1642), built by Johann Wöckherl.

JESUITENKIRCHE
CHURCH

Map p252 (⌐512 5232-0; www.jesuitenwien1.at; 01, Dr-Ignaz-Seipel-Platz 1; ⏱7am-7pm Mon-Sat, 8am-7pm Sun; ⓂStephansplatz, Stubentor, ⌐2 Stubentor) Opposite Dr-Ignaz-Seipel-Platz is the Jesuitenkirche, formerly the university church, which dates from 1627. In 1703 this church received a baroque makeover

by the Italian architect and painter Andrea Pozzo (1642–1709), who created its startling *trompe-l'œil* dome and other ceiling frescoes. Walk beyond the 'dome' to visually destroy Pozzo's illusion.

DR-IGNAZ-SEIPEL-PLATZ
SQUARE

Map p252 (01; ⓂStephansplatz) Formerly known as Universitätsplatz (University Square), this was once the heart of Vienna's old university quarter. Today, the **Austrian Academy of the Sciences** (Map p252; ⌐515 81-0; www.oeaw.ac.at; Dr-Ignaz-Seipel-Platz 2; ⏱9am-6pm Mon-Fri, Festsaal from 10am; ⓂStubentor, ⌐2 Stubentor) FREE is located inside the Alte-Uni (Old Uni) building. An early university was built here in the 1420s, but the current building has all the hallmarks of the new late-baroque building erected here in the mid-18th century, especially the decorative Festsaal (Festive Hall).

DOMINIKANERKIRCHE
CHURCH

Map p252 (⌐512 91 74; 01, Postgasse 4; ⏱7am-7pm; ⓂStubentor, ⌐2 Stubentor) The Dominican church was the first baroque church built in Vienna and was consecrated in 1634. It was largely the work of Italian architects and artisans and is well worth dropping into for its spacious interior adorned with white stucco and frescoes.

The Dominicans first came to Vienna in 1226, when Leopold VI of Babenberg invited them to settle, but their earliest church burned down less than 50 years later. Its Gothic replacement had the ignominy of being dismantled during the first Turkish siege in 1529 and its stone being used to fortify the city walls, before finally this baroque church was built.

POSTSPARKASSE
BUILDING

Map p252 (⌐534 53 33088; 01, Georg-Coch-Platz 2; museum adult/child €6/free; ⏱9am-5pm Mon-Fri, 10am-5pm Sat; ⓂSchwedenplatz, ⌐1, 2 Schwedenplatz) The marble-cased and metal-'studded' Post Office Savings Bank building is the *Jugendstil* work of Otto Wagner, who oversaw its construction between 1904 and 1906, and again from 1910 to 1912. You can explore the back section of the building, where there's also a small museum with temporary exhibitions on design and a video section on the history of the building.

The *Jugendstil* design and choice of materials were innovative for the time, with the grey marble facade held together by 17,000 metal nails, and an interior filled

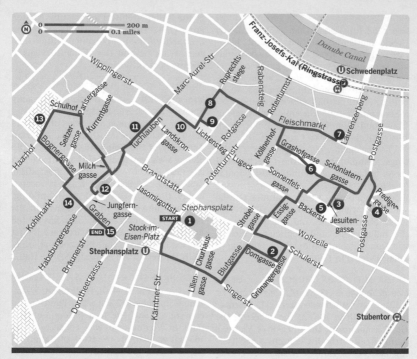

Neighbourhood Walk
The Historic Centre

START STEPHANSPLATZ
FINISH GRABEN
LENGTH 3KM; 90 MINUTES TO FIVE HOURS

Begin at Stephansplatz and Vienna's signature ❶ **Stephansdom**. After following a small section of Kärntner Strasse, the walk leads through the atmospheric backstreets to ❷ **Mozarthaus Vienna** (p82), where the great composer spent almost three years.

A series of narrow lanes leads you down towards two fine baroque churches. The interior of the ❸ **Jesuitenkirche** (p83) is pure deception, with frescoes creating the illusion of a dome, while the 1634 ❹ **Dominikanerkirche** (p83) is Vienna's finest reminder of the early baroque period of church building. The Jesuitenkirche is opposite the ❺ **Austrian Academy of the Sciences** (p83), housed in a university building dating from 1755.

If doing the walk during daylight hours, you can enter ❻ **Heiligenkreuzerhof** from the eastern side (if not, enter it from Grasshofgasse). This is a lovely, tranquil courtyard, and during the Christmas period transforms into one of the popular Christmas markets. Busy ❼ **Fleischmarkt** (p83) is the heart of the traditional Greek quarter of Vienna, where the Greek merchants settled from the 18th century. Climb the stairs and enter the lively but seedy Bermuda Triangle of bars on ❽ **Judengasse**, the centre of the traditional Jewish quarter. Hoher Markt has lost much of its attractiveness these days but the art-nouveau ❾ **Ankeruhr** (p78) and the ❿ **Römer Museum** (p79) are highlights, before you pass the ⓫ **Neidhart-Fresken** (p79) mural and reach the most impressive church this side of Stephansdom, the ⓬ **Peterskirche** (p77).

Northwest of here, ⓭ **Am Hof** (p78) is spiked by an impressive Mariensäule column. As you make your way along Graben back towards Stephansplatz, drop into ⓮ **Adolf Loos' Public Toilets**, and admire the writhing baroque ⓯ **Pestsäule memorial** (1693) to plague victims.

with sci-fi aluminium heating ducts and naked stanchions.

BAWAG CONTEMPORARY/
BAWAG FOUNDATION   GALLERY
Map p252 (☑534 53-0; www.bawag-foundation.at; 01, Franz-Josefs-Kai 3; ☺2pm-8pm; MSchwedenplatz, ☐1, 2 Julius-Raab-Platz) **FREE** This gallery, financed by the Bawag Bank, features contemporary artists from both the international and local scenes, focusing on the generation born in the 1970s. It has a regular influx of excellent temporary exhibitions on display in all media, with works ranging from painting, multimedia and sculpture to photo exhibitions and film.

✖ EATING

★BEIM CZAAK   BISTRO PUB €
Map p252 (☑513 72 15; www.czaak.com; 01, Postgasse 15; midday menus €8, mains €9.20-17; ☺11am-midnight Mon-Sat; MSchwedenplatz, ☐1, 2 Schwedenplatz) In contrast to more heavily touristed *Beisln* in the Innere Stadt, Beim Czaak has a genuine and relatively simple interior. As you would expect, Classic Viennese meat dishes dominate the menu, with long-time favourites such as Wiener Schnitzel, *Tafelspitz* (prime boiled beef), the *Haus Schnitzel* (weighted down with ham, cheese, mushrooms and onions – yum) and Styrian chicken.

★MASCHU MASCHU   MIDDLE EASTERN €
Map p252 (☑533 29 04; www.maschu-maschu. at; 01, Rabensteig 8; mains €3.50-8; ☺11.30am-11.30pm; ☑; MSchwedenplatz, ☐1, 2 Schwedenplatz) Delicious falafels, hummus and salads are the keys to Maschu Maschu's success. This branch on Rabensteig, with its meagre number of tables, is better used as a takeaway joint, while another branch in Neubau (p127) is best for sit-down meals.

FRESH SOUP & SALAD   VEGETARIAN €
Map p252 (01, Wipplingerstrasse 1; soups, salads & curries €3.50; ☺11am-7.30pm Mon-Fri; ☑; MStephansplatz, Schwedenplatz, ☐Schwedenplatz) The name says it all, except Fresh Soup & Salad also does inexpensive curries on top of this.

AKAKIKO   ASIAN €
Map p252 (www.akakiko.at; 01, Rotenturmstrasse 6; most dishes €4.90-10.90, sushi €9.90-18.50;

☺10.30am-11.30pm; MStephansplatz, ☐1, 2 Schwedenplatz) Head for the roomy upstairs area to avoid the bustle in this rambling joint serving inexpensive, off-the-rack noodle dishes, curries, sushi and sashimi, as well as a three-course set-lunch menu that won't break budgets. This is a chain of pan-Asian restaurants, with a better but less central branch on **Heidenschuss** (Map p254; 01, Heidenschuss 3; ☺10.30am-11.30pm).

★MOTTO AM FLUSS   INTERNATIONAL €€
Map p252 (☑25 255; www.motto.at/mottoamfluss; 01, Franz-Josefs-Kai, btwn Marien- and Schwedenbrücke; mains €19-26; ☺11.30am-2.30pm & 6pm-2am, bar 6pm-4am, cafe 8am-2am; ☎; MSchwedenplatz, ☐1, 2 Schwedenplatz) Exuding an inviting glow from inside the Wien-City ferry terminal on the Danube Canal, Motto am Fluss (affiliated with Motto in Margareten) is one of Vienna's better midrange restaurants, exuding a stylish lounge feel throughout the bar and restaurant areas, topped off by a cafe upstairs – all of this is with fantastic views over the Danube Canal. After 10pm smoking is allowed, but it rarely gets smoky.

The restaurant serves Austro-International cuisine with quality organic meats; the bar is a superbly relaxed hangout for pre- and post-dinner drinks (or simply drop by for a drink); and the cafe upstairs rounds off the chic feel throughout with good coffee and a small selection of cakes and pastries for the sweet tooth.

★GRIECHENBEISL   BISTRO PUB €€
Map p252 (☑533 19 77; www.griechenbeisl.at; 01, Fleischmarkt 11; mains €11.60-25; ☺11am-1am; MSchwedenplatz, ☐1, 2 Schwedenplatz) As the oldest guesthouse in Vienna (dating from 1447), and once frequented by the likes of Ludwig van Beethoven, Franz Schubert and Johannes Brahms, Griechenbeisl is a lovely haunt popular among locals and tourists alike, with vaulted rooms, age-old wood panelling and a figure of Augustin trapped at the bottom of a well just inside the front door.

Every classic Viennese dish is on the menu, and in summer the plant-fringed front garden is pole position.

★YOHM   ASIAN €€
Map p252 (☑533 29 00; 01, Petersplatz 3; mains €19.50-34, noodles €14-29.50, 4-/6-course menus €48/65; ☺noon-3pm & 6pm-midnight; ☑; MStephansplatz) A typical scene in Yohm is

LOCAL KNOWLEDGE

THE ART OF VIENNESE LIFE

Tom Venning is a calligrapher and *Lebenskünstler* (artist of life) who has been living in Vienna for over 20 years. He's painted alongside DJs in Roxy and other clubs, and his work has been exhibited in galleries around town. These are some of Tom's favourite bars and eating places in the historic centre.

Café Alt Wien (p88) I like to come here late at night, often after the drinks have run out at exhibition openings. It's a favourite for the art scene of Vienna – a big, bustling cafe-bar and usually full till late.

Palmenhaus (p70) Although I generally don't eat here, this is a place I go in the evening or at night for a cocktail. In summer I especially like sitting outside, looking over the Burggarten.

Viennese Sausage Stand I ride a bike around Vienna so many of my favourite sausage stands are outside the centre. One I go to in the Innere Stadt, however, is the Bitzinger Würstelstand am Albertinaplatz (p69).

Kleines Café (p88) This is on Franziskanerplatz, with good seating in summer on the quiet square. It's a very local place where people living and working in Vienna go for coffee, a drink or a snack. It's got typical Viennese charm – fast and efficient service without the waiters being overly friendly.

of black-clad waiters gliding between tables to refill glasses with celebrated Austrian wines as diners revel in views of Peters-kirche while enjoying contemporary Asian cuisine. Sushi looms large on the menu, but consider ordering one of the kitchen's more unusual offerings in this long-standing and much loved pan-Asian place.

★**EXPEDIT**   ITALIAN €€

Map p252 (℡512 33 1323; www.xpedit.at; 01, Wiesingerstrasse 6; pasta €10.50-12.50, mains €18.50; ⊙11am-2am Mon-Fri, 8pm-2am Sat; ⊠2 Julius-Raab-Platz) Expedit successfully moulds itself on a Ligurian *osteria*. The warehouse decor helps lend an informal atmosphere along with a clean, smart look. Every day brings a new selection of seasonal dishes to the small menu. Reservations are recommended and you can take food away to eat in your hotel if you like.

TIAN   VEGETARIAN €€

Map p252 (℡890 4665; www.tian-vienna.com; 01, Himmelpfortgasse 23; 3-course lunch €12.50-16, 3-6-course evening menu €39-69, mains €18; ⊙noon-4pm & 6pm-midnight Mon-Fri, from 9am Sat; ⊠; Ⓜ Stephansplatz, ⊠2 Weihburggasse) 🌱 Stealthy charm meets urban attitude at this sleek lounge-style restaurant which takes vegetarian cuisine to delicious heights. Lunch menus offer the best value; you can also enjoy a drink in the delightful cocktail bar (Friday and Saturday from 5pm to 3am).

FIGLMÜLLER   BISTRO PUB €€

Map p252 (℡512 61 77; www.figlmueller.at; 01, Wollzeile 5; mains €13-23; ⊙11am-10.30pm, kitchen closes 9.30pm; 🕾; Ⓜ Stephansplatz) The Viennese would simply be at a loss without Figlmüller. This famous *Beisl* has some of the biggest and best schnitzels in the business. The rural decor is contrived for its inner-city location and beer isn't served (wine is from the owner's vineyard), but it's a fun *Beisl* eating experience. The kitchen of the **Bäckerstrasse 6** (Map p252; ℡512 17 60; www.figlmueller.at; 01, Bäckerstrasse 6; ⊙11.45am-midnight) section is open till 11pm.

CAFÉ KORB   AUSTRIAN €€

Map p252 (www.cafekorb.at; 01, Brandstätte 9; mains €6.20-17.80; ⊙8am-midnight Mon-Sat, 10am-11pm Sun; 🕾; Ⓜ Stephansplatz) As the name suggests, Sigmund Freud's favourite hangout of yore is a coffee house, but its menu places it in the realm of a *Beisl* – and if you don't mind the smoke, a very good one at that. The food is classic and the crowd eclectic and offbeat. There's an attractive 'art lounge' downstairs area too, used for events, and toilets designed to impress!

BODEGA MARQUÉS   SPANISH €€

Map p252 (℡533 91 70; www.bodegamarques. at; 01, Parisergasse 1; tapas €4.50-15.50, most mains €12-21.50; ⊙5pm-1am Mon-Sat, to 11pm Sun; Ⓜ Stephansplatz) Calamari specialties, *Gambas* (shrimps) and over 30 different tapas imported from Spain help make Bodega

Marqués an excellent Mediterranean choice in the Innere Stadt. Throw in 120 varieties of wine, vaulted ceilings and subdued lighting and you've got the makings of a romantic atmosphere. Friday and Saturday nights (in winter, until the garden area opens) have live flamenco music.

ALL' ISOLA ITALIAN, SEAFOOD €€
Map p252 (☎513 94 33; www.all-isola.at; 01, Sonnenfelsgasse 5; pasta €11-14.90, mains €11.20-21.90, lunch special €8.90; ☺11.30am-midnight Mon-Sat; ⓂStephansplatz) The kitchen is open throughout the day in this small Italian place with ultra-rustic decor and good pasta and seafood.

ZUM SCHWARZEN KAMEEL INTERNATIONAL €€
Map p252 (☎533 81 25 12; www.kameel.at; 01, Bognergasse 5; sandwiches around €3, soups €6, mains €15-40, 4-/5-course menu €78/90; ☺8.30am-midnight Mon-Sat; ☎; ⓂStephansplatz, Herrengasse) Zum Schwarzen Kameel is an eclectic cross between a deli/sandwich shop and highbrow wine bar. The mostly well-heeled folks who frequent it nibble on sandwiches at the bar while facing the difficult choice of which *Achterl* of wine (0.125L) to select from the lengthy list. Soups are available to go, while more-substantial dishes are served in the wood-panelled dining area upstairs.

WRENKH VEGETARIAN €€
Map p252 (☎533 15 26; www.wiener-kochsalon.at; 01, Bauernmarkt 10; mains €8.80-26.50; ☺noon-10pm Mon-Sat; ☝; ⓂStephansplatz) Wrenkh was long the cutting edge of vegetarian cuisine, but in more recent times owner Christian Wrenkh has begun offering a handful of meat and fish dishes. Choose from the vibrant front section with its glass walls and chatty customers, or the quieter back room with its intimate booths. Vegetarian dishes cost less than €15, the lunch menu about €10.

★MEINL'S RESTAURANT INTERNATIONAL €€€
Map p252 (☎532 33 34 6000; www.meinlam graben.at; 01, Graben 19; mains €26-45, 3–6-course menus €47-93; ☺lunch & dinner Mon-Sat; ☎☝; ⓂStephansplatz) Meinl's combines cuisine of superlative quality with an unrivalled wine list and views of Graben. The freshest of ingredients are used to create inviting dishes, often integrating delicate Mediterranean sauces and sweet aromas. There is a quality providore (p90) on-site,

a cellar **wine bar** (Map p252; ☺11am-midnight Mon-Sat) with good lunch menus (€9.90 to €12.90), as well as a cafe and sushi bar (€8.60 to €18)

KORNAT SEAFOOD €€€
Map p252 (☎535 65 18; www.kornat.at; 01, Marc-Aurel-Strasse 8; soup €5-7.50, mains €19.50-27.50, fish of the day per 100g €8; ☺11.30am-midnight; ⓂStephansplatz, Schwedenplatz, ◫1, 2 Schwedenplatz) Finding a meal in one of the more upmarket restaurants with an all-day kitchen in Vienna's historic old town is not always easy; Dalmatian Kornat serves good seafood all day and evening. If you don't want a fully fledged seafood meal, drop by outside the lunch and dinner hours and just order one of the soups.

Kornat also has an exceptional wine list, which you can peruse while enjoying the olives and capers, fresh bread and delicious olive oil that come with the table setting.

AURELIUS ITALIAN, CROATIAN €€€
Map p252 (☎535 55 24; www.aurelius-wien.at; 01, Marc-Aurel-Strasse 8; antipasti €10-16, mains €20-30; ☺lunch & dinner Mon-Sat; ⓂStephansplatz, Schwedenplatz, ◫1, 2 Schwedenplatz) This stylish Italian and Croatian restaurant has a large, loyal following for its fantastic range of antipasti and main-course seafood, as well as for a couple of dishes based around beef and lamb. The fish of the day costs €6 per 100g and the bar stays open until 1am if you would like to linger.

A SLICE OF ITALY IN THE INNERE STADT

One of the most useful places to know about in the Innere Stadt is **Zanoni & Zanoni** (Map p252; ☎512 79 79; www.zanoni.co.at; 01, Lugeck 7; ice cream from €1.30; ☺7am-midnight; ⓂStephansplatz). This Italian *gelateria* and *pasticceria* has some of the most civilised opening times around (365 days a year) and is just right when you realise you'd like a late-night dessert (about 35 varieties of gelati, with more cream than usual). It does breakfast and some great cakes with cream, but best of all it's a buzzing place on a Sunday where you can mull over a coffee and plan your moves for the day.

HOLLMANN SALON
BISTRO PUB €€€

Map p252 (🎫961 19 60 40; www.hollmann-salon. at; 01, Grashofgasse 3; mains €13-24, 3–4-course menus €38-48; ⊗8am-3pm & 6-10pm Mon-Fri, 9am-10pm Sat; 🐶🍽; MStephansplatz, Stubentor, 🚋2 Stubentor) Situated inside the extraordinarily beautiful Heiligenkreuzerhof, Hollmann Salon combines the rural flavour of a country homestead with urban chic. Its succulent organic meats on a changing menu come from the Waldviertel north of the Danube, while always relying on seasonal produce from local producers. Seating is mostly at communal tables; last orders are at 9pm.

Cakes and breads are homemade and there's outstanding outdoor eating in summer.

RESTAURANT BAUER
FRENCH €€€

Map p252 (🎫512 98 71; 01, Sonnenfelsgasse 17; 5-course menu €79, mains about €25; ⊗dinner Mon, lunch & dinner Tue-Fri; MStephansplatz) This intimate, exquisite restaurant offers a small, seasonal menu and has the relaxed style of a French noble bistro, with broader influences from Mediterranean countries such as Spain. Add €35 to the menu if you choose the wine accompaniment.

🍷 DRINKING & NIGHTLIFE

★KRUGER'S AMERICAN BAR
BAR

Map p252 (www.krugers.at; 01, Krugerstrasse 5; ⊗from 6pm Mon-Sat; MStephansplatz, 🚋D, 1, 2, 71 Kärntner Ring/Oper) This wood-panelled American-style bar is a legend in Vienna, retaining some of its original furnishings

---

LOCAL KNOWLEDGE

VINOTHEKS
···

The Innere Stadt has some great *Vinotheks* (wine bars), but one of best is **Enrico Panigl** (Map p252; www. enrico-panigl.at; 01, Schönlaterngasse 11; ⊗6pm-4am Mon-Sat, to 2am Sun; MStephansplatz, Stubentor, 🚋2 Stubentor), a Mediterranean *Vinothek* (smoking allowed) with enough rustic woods in its interior and style in its selection of mostly Austrian wines to satisfy even the most strident buffs. For a modern ambience, head for Wein & Co (p91).

---

from the 1930s and complete with a separate cigar and smoker's lounge.

SKY BAR
ROOFTOP BAR

Map p252 (www.skybar.at; 01, Kärntner Strasse 19; ⊗9.30am-3am; MStephansplatz) Fans into the kick of glass panorama lifts won't be disappointed by this one, which whisks you up into the Sky Bar on the top floor of the Steffl department store to sip on one (or more) of the 350 cocktails, in Vienna's most spectacular rooftop bar in the Innere Stadt. During the day and early evening it has the flavour of a cafe and restaurant.

CAFÉ ALT WIEN
COFFEE HOUSE

Map p252 (🎫512 52 22; 01, Bäckerstrasse 9; ⊗10am-2am; 🐶; MStephansplatz) Dark, Bohemian and full of character, Alt Wien is a classic dive attracting students and arty types. It's also a one-stop shop for a lowdown on events in the city – every available wall space is plastered with posters advertising shows, concerts and exhibitions. The goulash is legendary and perfectly complemented by dark bread and beer.

KLEINES CAFÉ
CAFE

Map p252 (01, Franziskanerplatz 3; ⊗10am-2am Mon-Sat, 1pm-2am Sun; MStubentor, 🚋2 Weihburggasse) Designed by architect Hermann Czech in the 1970s, Kleines Café exudes a Bohemian atmosphere reminiscent of Vienna's heady *Jugendstil* days. It's tiny inside, but the wonderful summer outdoor seating on Franziskanerplatz is arguably the best in the Innere Stadt.

CAFÉ PRÜCKEL
COFFEE HOUSE

Map p252 (www.prueckel.at; 01, Stubenring 24; ⊗8.30am-10pm; 🐶; MStubentor, 🚋2 Stubentor) Prückel's unique mould is a little different from other Viennese cafes: instead of a sumptuous interior, it features an intact 1950s design. Intimate booths, aloof waiters, strong coffee, diet-destroying cakes and Prückel's speciality, its delicious apple strudel, are all big attractions. Live piano music tinkles across the room from 7pm to 10pm on Monday, Wednesday and Friday.

VIS-À-VIS
WINE BAR

Map p252 (🎫512 93 50; www.weibel.at; 01, Wollzeile 5; ⊗4.30pm-10.30pm Tue-Sat; MStephansplatz) Hidden down a narrow, atmospheric passage is this wee wine bar seating only 10, but it makes up for it with over 350 wines on offer (with a strong emphasis on

BERMUDA TRIANGLE & BEYOND

The old town has lots of in-your-face bars, especially in the quarter of town Viennese called the *Bermudadreieck* (Bermuda Triangle), which extends just northeast of Schwedenplatz/Morzinplatz; the corner of Seitenstettengasse and Judengasse forms the hub of the bars. To explore them it's best just to walk around and poke your nose through doors until you find a place you like. Most places here draw an early-20s crowd. Expect smoke.

One bar not fitting into this category is **First Floor** (Map p252; www.firstfloorbar.at; 01, Seitenstettengasse 5; ⊙8pm-4am; ⓂSchwedenplatz, ⓃN, 1, 2, 21 Schwedenplatz), a small, smoky upstairs American-style joint attracting a 30s-upwards crowd that hangs out and listens to the jazz, blues and eclectic mid- and late-20th century classics.

You'll also find some pub-style places – like most Bermuda Triangle bars – especially popular with Austrians visiting from out of town. One interesting option nearby is **Pickwick's** (Map p252; www.pickwicks.at; 01, Marc-Aural-Strasse 10; ⊙11am-midnight Mon-Thu & Sun, to 2am Fri & Sat; ☎; ⓂSchwedenplatz), a bookshop and pub with video rental and a screen for football. Expat English speakers go here or flock to a handful of pubs and Australian bars located across town near the Opera and Schwarzenbergstrasse. Two of the most popular are **Flanagan's** (Map p252; www.flanagans.at; 01, Schwarzenbergstrasse 1-3; ⊙10am-2am Sun-Thu, to 4am Fri & Sat; ☎; ⓂKarlsplatz, Ⓠ2 Schwarzenbergstrasse) and **1516 Brewing Company** (Map p252; ☎961 15 16; www.1516brewingcompany.com; 01, Schwarzenbergstrasse 2; ⊙11am-2am; ⓂKarlsplatz, Ⓠ2 Schwarzenbergstrasse).

Not fitting any of these moulds is the arty **Wunderbar** (Map p252; www.facebook.com/wunderbarwien; 01, Schönlaterngasse 8; ⊙5pm-2am; ⓂStephansplatz, Stubentor, Ⓠ2 Stubentor), a bar with sofas and a loyal following of young and oldish alternative drinkers.

Austrian faves). It's a perfect spot to escape after a packed day of sightseeing – tapas, antipasto and gourmet olives round out the selection.

AIDA
CAFE
Map p252 (☎512 29 77; www.aida.at; 01, Singerstrasse 1; ⊙7am-9pm Mon-Sat, 9am-9pm Sun; ⓂStephansplatz) An icon of the *Konditorei* (cake shop) scene, Aida is a time warp for coffee lovers. Its pink-and-brown colour scheme – right down to the waiters' socks – matches the 1950s retro decor perfectly. Order a *Melange* (milky coffee) and a slice of cake (there are almost 30 to choose from) and head upstairs for views. Thirty such Aida gems are scattered throughout Vienna.

DIGLAS
COFFEE HOUSE
Map p252 (☎512 57 65; www.diglas.at; 01, Wollzeile 10; ⊙8am-10.30pm; ⓂStephansplatz) Diglas comes straight from the classic coffee-house mould, with swanky red-velvet booths, sharp-tongued waiters, an extensive (and good) coffee range, and old dames dressed to the nines. The reputation of Diglas' cakes precedes it, and the *Apfelstrudel* is unrivalled. Meals are delicate and more like snacks. Live piano music

fills Diglas from 7pm to 10pm Thursday to Saturday.

HAAS & HAAS
CAFE
Map p252 (☎512 26 66; www.haas-haas.at; 01, Stephansplatz 4; ⊙8am-8pm Mon-Sat, 9am-6pm Sun; ⓂStephansplatz) The fragrance of tea from around the world greets customers on entry to Haas & Hass, Vienna's prime tearoom (coffee is also served). Green, herbal, aromatic, Assam, Ceylon, Darjeeling – the selection seems endless. The rear garden is a shaded retreat from the wind, rain, sun and tourist bustle, while the front parlour sports comfy cushioned booths and views of Stephansdom.

ZWÖLF APOSTELKELLER
WINE TAVERN
Map p252 (☎512 67 77; www.zwoelf-apostelkeller.at; 01, Sonnenfelsgasse 3; ⊙11am-midnight; ⓂStephansplatz) Even though Zwölf Apostelkeller (Twelve Apostle Cellar) plays it up for the tourists, it still retains plenty of charm, dignity and authenticity. This is mostly due to the premises themselves: a vast, dimly lit multilevel cellar. The atmosphere is often lively and rowdy, helped along by traditional *Heuriger* (wine tavern) music from 7pm daily.

LOCAL KNOWLEDGE

COOL PLACE FOR CATS

Ishimitsu Takako is the proprietor of **Cafe Neko** (Map p252; www.cafeneko.at; 01, Blumen-stockgasse 5, cnr Ballgasse; hot drinks, Japanese nibbles under €5, nibble for cat €1; MStephans-platz), Vienna's only 'cat cafe'. Here you can stroke and play with feline friends or watch them walk or repose high up on a walkway. Note that dogs are not allowed.

Why open up a cafe with cats? 'To be honest,' Ishimitsu Takako says, 'it was an inexpensive way to open up a cafe, but I'm also active in the local animal protection society. I thought if it doesn't work out, I'll turn it into a normal cafe. The positive reaction was totally unexpected. There are a lot of cat cafes in Japan, but not here.'

Why do guests like it so much? Many of her guests, she says, are people who don't have cats themselves because they're not permitted to keep them in their flats, or they love cats but have a cat allergy. These people drop by and stay until their allergy gets the better of them.

Do the cats have different rhythms? 'Yes,' she laughs, 'and some are petulant, some good-natured, some like small children and others don't.'

WHY NOT? — GAY

Map p252 (www.why-not.at; 01, Tiefer Graben 22; cover after midnight €7; ☺10pm-4am Fri & Sat; ☎; MHerrengasse, ☒1 Salztorbrücke) This is one of the few clubs focusing its attention solely on the gay scene. The small club quickly fills up with mainly young guys out for as much fun as possible.

☆ ENTERTAINMENT

JAZZLAND — JAZZ

Map p252 (☎533 25 75; www.jazzland.at; 01, Franz-Josefs-Kai 29; cover €11-20; ☺from 7pm Mon-Sat, live music from 9pm; MSchwedenplatz, ☒1, 2 Schwedenplatz) Jazzland has been an institution of Vienna's jazz scene for over 30 years. The music covers the whole jazz spectrum, and the brick venue features a grand mixture of both international and local acts.

KAMMEROPER — OPERA

Map p252 (☎Wien Ticket 588 85; www.wienerkammeroper.at; 01, Fleischmarkt 24; tickets €5-48; MSchwedenplatz, ☒1, 2 Schwedenplatz) This ranks as Vienna's third opera house after the Staatsoper and Volksoper. Its small venue is perfect for quirky opera productions and in summer the company is transported to the Schlosstheater Schönbrunn to continue performances in more opulent surroundings. Children under 16 receive 35% discount when accompanied by an adult.

ARTIS INTERNATIONAL — CINEMA

Map p252 (☎535 65 70; www.cineplexx.at; 01, Schultergasse 5; tickets €8.50; MStephansplatz, Schwedenplatz) Artis has six small cinemas in the heart of the Innere Stadt. It only shows English-language films, of the Hollywood blockbuster variety, often in original English without subtitles.

GARTENBAUKINO — CINEMA

Map p252 (☎512 23 54; www.gartenbaukino.at; 01, Parkring 12; tickets €8.50; MStubentor, Stadtpark, ☒2 Stubentor) The interior of the Gartenbaukino has survived since the 1960s, making a trip to the flicks here offbeat and appealing. The actual cinema seats a whopping 750 people, and is often packed during Viennale Film Festival screenings. Its regular screening schedule is full to overflowing with art-house films, normally with subtitles.

PORGY & BESS — JAZZ

Map p252 (☎512 88 11; www.porgy.at; 01, Riemergasse 11; most nights €18; ☺concerts from 7pm or 8pm; MStubentor, ☒2 Stubentor) Quality is the cornerstone of Porgy & Bess' continuing popularity. Its program is loaded with modern jazz acts from around the globe, including many from the USA and nearby Balkan countries. The interior is dim and the vibe velvety and very grown-up.

🛍 SHOPPING

★MEINL AM GRABEN — FOOD, WINE

Map p252 (www.meinlamgraben.at; 01, Graben 19; ☺8am-7.30pm Mon-Fri, 9am-6pm Sat; MStephansplatz, Herrengasse) You've arrived at Vienna's most prestigious providore, part of the famed Meinl's Restaurant. Quality European foodstuffs like chocolate and confectionery dominate the ground floor, and impressive cheese and cold meats beckon upstairs. The top-end wine shop stocks European and Austrian wine and fruit liqueurs, or indulge in a glass at Meinl's Weinbar in a chilled, classy atmosphere.

ART UP
FASHION, ACCESSORIES

Map p252 (www.artup.at; 01, Bauernmarkt 8; ⊗11am-6.30pm Mon-Fri, to 5pm Sat; Ⓜ️Stephansplatz) Take the temperature of Vienna's contemporary design scene at Art Up, offering space for young designers to get a foothold in the fashion world. The model makes for an eclectic collection – elegant fashion pieces rub alongside quirky accessories (Astroturf tie or handbag, anyone?) as well as ceramics and bigger art pieces.

It's a testament to the liveliness of the fashion and design scenes in Vienna, given new vigour by students coming out of the city's fashion schools and driven by a burgeoning confidence in the quality of home-grown talent.

UNGER UND KLEIN
WINE

Map p252 (www.ungerundklein.at; 01, Gölsdorfgasse 2; ⊗3pm-midnight Mon-Fri, 5pm-midnight Sat; Ⓜ️Schwedenplatz, ⛴1 Salztorbrücke) Unger und Klein's small but knowledgeable wine collection spans the globe, but the majority of its labels come from Europe. The best of Austrian wines – from expensive boutique varieties to bargain-bin bottles – are available. It's also a small, laid-back wine bar, with a reasonable selection of wines by the glass, which gets crowded on Friday and Saturday evenings.

WEIN & CO
WINE

Map p252 (www.weinco.at; 01, Jasomirgottstrasse 3-5; ⊗10am-2am Mon-Sat, 3pm-midnight Sun; ☏; Ⓜ️Stephansplatz) With a wide selection of quality European and New World wines, and a huge variety of local bottles, Wein & Co is probably your best bet for wine shopping – you should be able to pick up a bargain, as the specials here are always great. You can also buy cigars, and the wine bar has a terrace with a view of Stephansdom.

ALTMANN & KÜHNE
FOOD

Map p252 (www.altmann-kuehne.at; 01, Graben 30; ⊗9am-6.30pm Mon-Fri, 10am-5pm Sat; Ⓜ️Stephansplatz) This charming small shop has a touch of the Old World about it, part-

ly due to the handmade packaging of its chocolates and sweets, which was designed by Wiener Werkstätte in 1928. Altmann & Kühne have been producing handmade bonbons for more than 100 years using a well-kept secret recipe.

ATELIER NASKE
JEWELLERY

Map p252 (www.goldkunst.at; 01, Wipplingerstrasse 7; ⊗2.30-6.30pm Wed & Thu, 3.30-6.30pm Mon & Tue; Ⓜ️Stephansplatz) Elke Naske's passion for jewellery is intoxicating. Delicate butterfly pendants, perfectly sculpted rings, cufflinks embedded with precious stones and more are all painstakingly hand-tapped. Commission her for a piece and she'll make an initial model of it in (less expensive) silver, just to make sure it fits or hangs correctly and suits you unequivocally.

VIENNA BAG
FASHION, ACCESSORIES

Map p252 (www.viennabag.com; 01, Bäckerstrasse 7; ⊗11am-6pm Mon-Fri, to 5pm Sat; Ⓜ️Stephansplatz) Vienna Bag has been making its funky and practical handbags and satchels since 2001. In both black and brightly coloured varieties, they're not only strong, lightweight and washable but chic as well.

WOKA
HOMEWARES

Map p252 (www.woka.at; 01, Singerstrasse 16; ⊗10am-6pm Mon-Fri, to 5pm Sat; Ⓜ️Stephansplatz) Get a feel for the spectacular Wiener Werkstätte aesthetic and Bauhaus, art deco and Secessionist design, with its accurate reproductions of lamps designed by the likes of Adolf Loos, Kolo Moser and Josef Hoffmann.

AUSTRIAN DELIGHTS
FOOD

Map p252 (www.austriandelights.at; 01, Judengasse 1a; ⊗11am-7pm Mon-Fri, to 6pm Sat; Ⓜ️Stephansplatz) Stocking Austrian-made items by mainly small producers, Austrian Delights has regional specialities – fine confectionery, local wine, schnapps and cognac, jams, jellies, chutneys, honey, vinegars and oils – that you can't find anywhere else in the capital. Check out its sparkling and still Schilcher wines made from Blauer Wildbacher grapes, a fruity and off-pink-coloured tipple rarely found outside Austria.

Most of the wares are manufactured by hand or the kind of items Austrian grandmothers made through the ages. Samples of many food items are available to taste.

STEPHANSDOM & THE HISTORIC CENTRE SHOPPING

MANNER
CONFECTIONERY

Map p252 (www.manner.com; 01, Stephansplatz 7; ⊙10am-9pm; Ⓜ Stephansplatz) Even *Manner* (a glorious concoction of wafers and hazelnut cream), Vienna's favourite sweet since 1898, has its own concept store now decked out in the biscuit's signature peachy pink. Buy the product in every imaginable variety and packaging combination (tip: it's a fab snack to carry around when sightseeing).

SHAKESPEARE & CO
BOOKS

Map p252 (www.shakespeare.co.at; 01, Sterngasse 2; ⊙9am-9pm Mon-Sat; Ⓜ Stephansplatz, Schwedenplatz) This beautifully cluttered bookshop in a charming area just off Judengasse stocks Vienna's best collection of literary and hard-to-find titles in English – history, culture, classic and modern fiction – with a wide range of titles about Austria and by Austrian writers.

🏃 SPORTS & ACTIVITIES

BADESCHIFF
SWIMMING

Map p252 (www.badeschiff.at; 01, Danube Canal; adult/child €5/2.50; ⊙10am-midnight May-Oct; Ⓜ Schwedenplatz, 🚊1 Julius-Raab-Platz) Swim on but not in the Danube. Floating smack on the bank of the canal, between Schwedenplatz and Urania, this pool doubles as a bar at night (in winter the pool closes and the ship is a bar and restaurant only). Multiple decks have lounge chairs, and cocktail and snack bars abound.

Karlsplatz & Around Naschmarkt

Neighbourhood Top Five

1 Being blown away by the baroque splendour of the **Karlskirche** (p95) as you rise up to its oval-shaped cupola for a close-up look at Michael Rottmayr's frescoes.

2 Contemplating the sensuous shapes, gold mosaics and mythological symbolism of Klimt's *Beethoven Frieze* at the **Secession** (p97).

3 Snacking your way from stall to delectable stall at the **Naschmarkt** (p110).

4 Piecing together the tragedies and the triumphs of Vienna's history at the stellar **Wien Museum** (p100).

5 Reliving operatic highs with a guided tour of the **Staatsoper** (p108).

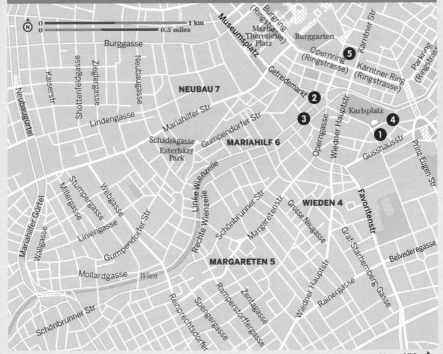

For more detail of this area see Map p256 ➡

Lonely Planet's Top Tip

It is a pleasure simply to wander the backstreets of the Freihausviertel, just south of Naschmarkt. One of the neighbourhood's most elegant streets is Mühlgasse, lined with late-19th-century houses with Juliet balconies and ornate doors in the *Jugendstil* (art nouveau) style. Nos 26 and 28 are fine examples.

✕ Best Places to Eat

➡ Steman (p102)
➡ Ubl (p102)
➡ Motto (p102)
➡ Collio (p104)
➡ Umar (p102)

For reviews, see p102 ➡

♟ Best Places to Drink

➡ Café Sperl (p104)
➡ Phil (p105)
➡ Café Drechsler (p105)
➡ Tanzcafé Jenseits (p105)
➡ Sekt Comptoir (p105)

For reviews, see p104 ➡

🔒 Best Shopping

➡ Blühendes Konfekt (p109)
➡ Dörthe Kaufmann (p109)
➡ Mein Design (p109)
➡ feinedinge (p109)
➡ Gabarage Upcycling Design (p110)

For reviews, see p109 ➡

Explore Karlsplatz & Around Naschmarkt

Spreading south of the Opernring is Vienna's cultured 4th district, Wieden. Here days can be spent gazing upon the baroque frescoes that dance across the Karlskirche, Otto Wagner's art nouveau buildings and Klimt's sensual friezes. Nights lift the curtain on high-calibre opera and classical music in some of the world's finest concert halls. Wander west and within minutes you swing from gilded opulence to the multilingual babble, street-food sizzle and market stall banter of the Naschmarkt. Amble south of here to the easygoing Freihausviertel and Vienna suddenly shrinks to village scale, with arty cafes, ateliers and food shops run by folk with genuine passion.

North of Wieden is 6th-district Mariahilf. Give the high-street throngs on Mariahilfer Strasse the slip and you soon find yourself in quintessentially Viennese backstreets, home to speciality shops and old-school coffee houses. On the cutting edge of the city's nightlife and design scene is Gumpendorfer Strasse.

Wedged between Wieden and Mariahilf in the 5th district is Margareten, with few heavyweight sights but strong local flavour, particularly around the increasingly fashionable Margaretenplatz. Head here to slip off the well-trodden map.

Local Life

➡**Shopping** Follow the hungry Viennese to the Naschmarkt (p110) for a world of street food, and scout out delis, design stores and one-of-a-kind boutiques in the artsy Freihausviertel (p98) and around Margaretenplatz.

➡**Nightlife Haunts** Hang out with a young and up-for-it crowd on Gumpendorfer Strasse, crammed with bars, cafes and lounge-style restaurants, or find a more laid-back scene around Schleifmühlgasse.

➡**Cafes** There are some great ones: from boho Café Jelinek (p106) to starkly contemporary Café Drechsler (p105), open 23 hours a day.

Getting There & Away

➡**U-Bahn** Karlsplatz is well connected to all corners of Vienna, served by lines U1, U2 and U4. The U4 line to Kettenbrückengasse is handy for Naschmarkt and the Freihausviertel, while the U3 line (Zieglergasse, Neubaugasse etc) is useful for reaching Mariahilf. Pilgramgasse (U4) is the most central stop for Margareten, and Taubstummengasse (U1) for Wieden.

➡**Tram** Key tram routes include 1 and 62, which stop at Karlsplatz and pass through Wieden.

TOP SIGHT
KARLSKIRCHE

Rising imperiously above Resselpark is Vienna's baroque magnum opus: the Karlskirche. Crowned by a bulbous, 72m-high copper dome, the church was built between 1716 and 1739 as thanks for deliverance from the 1713 plague. The edifice bears the hallmark of prolific Austrian architect Johann Bernhard Fischer von Erlach, while the interior swirls with the vivid colours of Johann Michael Rottmayr's frescoes.

In the flower-strewn **Resselpark**, a pond centred on a **Henry Moore** sculpture reflects the splendour of the church like a celestial mirror. Your gaze is drawn to the neoclassical portico, the spiralling pillars, which are modelled on Trajan's Column in Rome and embellished with scenes from the life of St Charles Borromeo, as well as a striking pair of cross-bearing angels from the Old and New Testament intricately carved from white marble. The pediment reliefs depict the suffering of Vienna's plague victims.

Inside, a lift soars up into the elliptical cupola for a close-up of Johann Michael Rottmayr's **frescoes** of the glorification of St Charles Borromeo, picked out in bold colours. Look carefully for tongue-in-cheek Counter-Reformation details, such as angels setting fire to Martin Luther's German bible. The **high altar** panel, which shows the ascension of St Charles Borromeo, is a riot of golden sunrays and stucco cherubs clinging playfully to clouds.

Admission includes entry to the **Museo Borremeo**, containing a handful of religious works of art and items of said saint's clothing, including his silk mitre and pontifical shoes. An audio guide costs €2.

DON'T MISS...

➡ Cupola frescoes
➡ High altar panel
➡ Facade from Resselpark

PRACTICALITIES

➡ St Charles Church
➡ Map p256
➡ www.karlskirche.at
➡ Karlsplatz
➡ adult/child €8/4
➡ ⊙9am-5.30pm Mon-Sat, 11.30am-5.30pm Sun
➡ MKarlsplatz

TOP SIGHT
STAATSOPER

Few concert halls can hold a candle to the neo-Renaissance Staatsoper, Vienna's foremost opera and ballet venue. Even if you can't snag tickets (see p45 for ticketing info) to see a tenor hitting the high notes, you can get a taste of the architectural brilliance and musical genius that have shaped this cultural bastion by visiting the museum or taking a guided tour.

Built between 1861 and 1869 by August Siccardsburg and Eduard van der Nüll, the Staatsoper initially revolted the Viennese public and Habsburg royalty and quickly earned the nickname 'stone turtle.' Despite the frosty reception, it went on to house some of the most iconic directors in history, including Gustav Mahler, Richard Strauss and Herbert van Karajan.

The **Staatsopernmuseum** (☑514 44 21 00; museum adult/child €3/2, guided tour €5/2, combined ticket €6.50/3.50; ☺museum 10am-6pm Tue-Sun, tour times vary) presents a 140-year romp through the opera house's illustrious history, with portraits of operatic greats, costumes, stage designs and documents spotlighting premieres and highlights such as Karajan's eight-year reign as director. Opera lovers will enjoy the occasional gem, such as Dame Margot Fonteyn's stubtoed ballet slipper.

Join a 40-minute **guided tour**, which takes in highlights such as the **foyer**, graced with busts of Beethoven, Schubert and Haydn and frescoes of celebrated operas, and the **main staircase**, watched over by marble allegorical statues embodying the liberal arts. The **Tea Salon** dazzles in 22-carat gold leaf, the **Schwind Foyer** captivates with 16 opera-themed oil paintings by Austrian artist Moritz von Schwind, while the Gustav Mahler Hall is hung with tapestries inspired by Mozart's *The Magic Flute*. You'll also get a behind-the-scenes look at the **stage**, which raises the curtain on around 300 performances each year.

DON'T MISS...

→ Staatsopern-museum
→ Foyer
→ Tea Salon
→ Gustav Mahler Hall

PRACTICALITIES

→ Map p256
→ www.wiener
-staatsoper.at
→ 01, Hanuschgasse 3
→ Ⓜ Karlsplatz, 🚊 D, 1, 2 Kärntner Ring/Oper

SIGHTS

KARLSKIRCHE · CHURCH

See p95.

STAATSOPER · CONCERT VENUE

See p96.

OTTO WAGNER BUILDINGS · LANDMARK

Map p256 (06, Linke Wienzeile & Köstlergasse; Ⓜ Kettenbrückengasse) A problem zone due to flooding, the Wien River needed regulating in the late 19th century. At the same time, Otto Wagner had visions of turning the area between Karlsplatz and Schönbrunn into a magnificent boulevard. The vision blurred and the reality is a gushing, concrete-bottomed creek and a couple of attractive Wagner houses on the Linke Wienzeile.

Majolika-Haus at No 40 (1899) is the prettiest as it's completely covered in glazed ceramic to create flowing floral motifs on the facade. The second of these *Jugendstil* masterpieces is a corner house at **No 38**, with reliefs from Kolo Moser and shapely bronze figures from Othmar Schimkowitz. Nearby is a third house, simpler than these, at **Köstlergasse 3** and, finally, you can put Wagner's functionality to the test by descending into his **Kettenbrückengasse U-Bahn station**.

NASCHMARKT · MARKET

Map p256 (www.wienernaschmarkt.eu; 06, Linke Wienzeile/Rechte Wienzeile, btwn Getreidemarkt & Kettenbrückengasse; ⏱ 6am-7.30pm Mon-Fri, to 6pm Sat; Ⓜ Kettenbrückengasse) Vienna's famous market and eating strip began life as a farmers market in the 18th century, when the fruit market on Freyung was moved here. Interestingly, a law passed in 1793 said that fruit and vegetables arriving in town by cart had to be sold on Naschmarkt, while anything brought in by boat could be sold from the decks.

The fruits of the Orient poured in, the predecessors of the modern-day sausage stand were erected and sections were set aside for coal, wood and farming tools and machines. Officially, it became known as Naschmarkt ('munch market') in 1905, a few years after Otto Wagner bedded the Wien River down in its open-topped stone and concrete sarcophagus. This Otto Wagnerian horror was a blessing for Naschmarkt, because it created space to expand. A close shave came in 1965 when there were plans to tear it down – it was saved, and today the

---

⊙ TOP SIGHT
SECESSION

In 1897, 19 progressive artists turned from the mainstream Künstlerhaus artistic establishment to form the Vienna Secession. Among their number were Klimt, Josef Hoffman, Kolo Moser and Joseph M Olbrich. Olbrich designed their new exhibition centre, combining sparse functionality with stylistic motifs. The building's most striking feature is a delicate golden dome of intertwined laurel leaves that deserves better than the description 'golden cabbage' accorded it by some Viennese.

The 14th exhibition (1902) held here featured the *Beethoven Frieze*, by Klimt, based on Richard Wagner's interpretation of Beethoven's ninth symphony. This work was intended as a temporary display, an elaborate poster for the main exhibit, Max Klinger's Beethoven monument. Now the star exhibit, it has occupied the basement since 1983.

Rich in symbolism, the frieze is bewitching. The yearning for happiness finds expression in ethereal, wraithlike female figures floating across the walls, a choir of rapturous, flower-bearing angels, and the arts personified as curvaceous, gold-haired nudes who appear to grow like trees. These are juxtaposed by the hostile forces, whose gorgons and beastly portrayals of sickness, madness and death caused outrage in 1902.

DON'T MISS...

➜ Beethoven Frieze
➜ The facade
➜ Rotating exhibitions of contemporary art

PRACTICALITIES

➜ Map p256
➜ www.secession.at
➜ 01, Friedrichstrasse 12
➜ adult/child €8.50/5, audio guide €3
➜ ⏱ 10am-6pm Tue-Sun
➜ Ⓜ Karlsplatz

KARLSPLATZ & AROUND NASCHMARKT SIGHTS

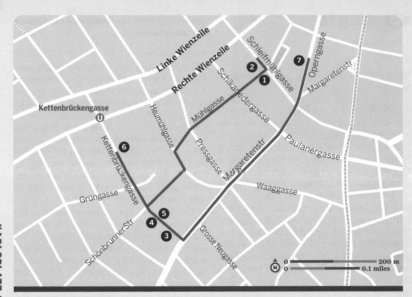

Local Life
Epicure's Tour of the Freihausviertel

Once home to poor artisans, today the Freihausviertel has been revitalised: its attractive lanes harbour boho-flavoured cafes, speciality food stores and some of Vienna's most exciting new galleries and boutiques. After a morning at Naschmarkt, continue your spin of the 4th district with this foodie tour.

❶ Literary Lunch

Spices and books for cooks are what you'll find at **Babettes** (Map p256; www.babettes. at; 04, Schleifmühlgasse 17; ☺10am-7pm Mon-Fri, to 5pm Sat; MKettenbrückengasse). Every day a different lunch special is sizzling in the open kitchen, prepared with own-brand spices and fresh produce from Naschmarkt. Evening cookery classes, with themes from tapas to Tuscan food, are also offered here.

❷ Austrian Bubbly

Toast the start of the afternoon at the Sekt Comptoir (p105) over a glass of Burgenland *Sekt* (sparkling wine). As it's located just a few blocks from the Naschmarkt, shoppers with bulging grocery bags often spill onto the sidewalk here.

❸ Sugar & Spice

If you're lucky you'll see the Henzl family drying, grinding and blending their home-grown and foraged herbs and spices with sugar and salt at delightfully old-school

Henzls Ernte (Map p256; www.henzls.at; 05, Kettenbrückengasse 3; ☺1pm-6pm Tue-Fri, 9am-5pm Sat; MKettenbrückengasse) . Specialities such as sloe-berry salt, lavender sugar, wild garlic pesto and green tomato preserve make tasty gifts.

❹ Farm Fresh

Nip into farmers' store **Helene** (Map p256; www.bauernladenhelene.at; 05, Kettenbrückengasse 7; ☺8am-6pm Tue-Fri, to 3pm Sat; MKettenbrückengasse) for a smorgasbord of top-quality regional produce. Besides super-fresh fruit and veg, cheese and meat, you'll find Joseph Brot von Pheinsten organic loaves from the Waldviertel, chestnut, larch and acacia honeys from Lower Austria, and wine and chilli jam from Burgenland.

❺ Apple of a Needle's Eye

At dinky workshop-store **Näherei Apfel** (Map p256; www.naeherei-apfel.at; Kettenbrückengasse 8; ☺11am-7pm Tue-Fri, 10am-4pm Sat; MKettenbrückengasse), you can learn to sew (a two-hour intro course

Chocolates from Fruth

Naschmarkt is not only the place to shop for food but has an antique market each Saturday.

AKADEMIE DER BILDENDEN KÜNSTE MUSEUM

Map p256 (Academy of Fine Arts; www.akademiegalerie.at; 01, Schillerplatz 3; adult/under 19yr €8/free; ⏱10am-6pm Tue-Sun; ⓂMuseumsquartier, Karlsplatz, ⓭D, 1, 2 Kärntner Ring/Oper) The Akademie der Bildenden Künste is an often underrated art space. Its gallery concentrates on the classic Flemish, Dutch and German painters, and includes important figures such as Hieronymus Bosch, Rembrandt, Van Dyck, Rubens, Titian, Francesco Guardi and Cranach the Elder, to mention a handful.

The supreme highlight is Bosch's impressive and gruesome *Triptych of the Last Judgement* altarpiece (1504–08), with the banishment of Adam and Eve on the left panel and the horror of Hell in the middle and right panels. The building itself has an attractive facade and was designed by Theophil Hansen (1813–91), of Parlament fame. It still operates as an art school and is famous for turning down Adolf Hitler twice and accepting Egon Schiele (though the latter was happy to leave as quickly as possible). Directly in front of the academy is a **statue of Friedrich Schiller**, 18th-century German playwright.

Hour-long tours (€3, in German only) take place at 10.30am every Sunday. Audio guides cost €2.

GENERALI FOUNDATION GALLERY

Map p256 (☎504 98 80; www.gfound.or.at; 04, Wiedner Hauptstrasse 15; adult/child €6/3; ⏱11am-6pm Tue-Sun, to 8pm Thu; ⓂKarlsplatz, Taubstummengasse, ⓭1, 62 Paulanergasse) The Generali Foundation is a fine gallery that picks and chooses exhibition pieces from its vast collection – numbering around 1400 – to create new themes. The majority of its ensemble covers conceptual and performance art from the mid- to late 20th century. The entrance to the exhibition hall is towards the back of a residential passageway.

Guided tours (€3, in German) take place at 6pm on Thursday. Tuesday is free for students, and from 6pm Thursday entry costs €3 for everyone.

HAUS DES MEERES MUSEUM

Map p256 (www.haus-des-meeres.at; 06, Fritz-Grünbaum-Platz 1; adult/child €14.20/6.50;

costs €23), browse Ursula's funky sweaters, jersey dresses and bags, and buy Burgenland apples dried, preserved, chipped, juiced and by the kilo.

❻ Kust Desserts

Viennese locals sing the praises of chocolatier and patisserie **Fruth** (Map p256; www.fruth.at; 04, Kettenbrückengasse 20; ⏱11am-7pm Tue-Fri, 9am-5pm Sat; ⓂKettenbrückengasse), where the inimitable Eduard Fruth creates edible works of art. Strawberry tartlets that crumble just so, rich truffles, feather-light éclairs, chocolate flavoured with chilli, chestnut and cranberry... However will you choose?

❼ Afternoon Tea

What sweeter way to end your tour than at **Süssi** (Map p256; ☎943 13 24; www.suessi.at; 04, Operngasse 30; desserts €3.50-6, afternoon tea €17; ⏱11am-9pm Tue-Sat, 1-9pm Sun; ⓂKarlsplatz), on Operngasse. This boudoir of a French tearoom is a real blast from the past, with ruby-red chairs, striped wallpaper, lace doilies and candelabras. Mariage Frères brews go nicely with the tempting array of macaroons, quiches, fruit tarts and cream cakes.

TOP SIGHT
WIEN MUSEUM

The Wien Museum offers a fascinating romp through Vienna's history, from Neolithic times to the mid-20th century. Exhibits are spread over three floors, including spaces for two temporary exhibitions.

The **ground floor** traces the history of the city from 5600 BC to the late Middle Ages. Standouts include medieval helms with bizarre ornamentation, Celtic gold coins and artefacts from the Roman military camp of Vindobona. The real attention-grabber, though, is the jewel-like stained glass and sculpture retrieved from Stephansdom post-WWII bombing. Of particular note are the 14th-century *Fürstenfiguren*, the princely figures salvaged from the cathedral's west facade.

The **1st floor** takes a brisk trot through the Renaissance and baroque eras and has a fascinating model of the city in its medieval heyday. Both Turkish sieges are well represented. Top billing goes to the **2nd floor**, however, which zooms in on Vienna's fin-de-siécle artistic period. On show is the intact modernist living room that Adolf Loos designed for his nearby apartment in 1903, replete with mahogany and marble, alongside stellar Secessionist works such as Klimt's *Pallas Athene* (1898) and Egon Schiele's *Young Mother* (1914).

DON'T MISS...

➤ The *Fürstenfiguren*
➤ Adolf Loos' living room
➤ Klimt's *Pallas Athene*

PRACTICALITIES

➤ Map p256
➤ www.wien museum.at
➤ 04, Karlsplatz 8
➤ adult/under 19yr €8/free, 1st Sun of each month free
➤ ◷10am-6pm Tue-Sun
➤ Ⓜ Karlsplatz

◷9am-6pm Fri-Wed, to 9pm Thu; ⒨Neubaugasse) What the 'House of the Sea' lacks is the chance for visitors to spring into the shark tank for some thrashing, but a staff member does just that at 6pm on Thursday. While the museum is unlikely to blow you away instantly, it is an interesting glimpse into the world of lizards, sharks, crocodiles, snakes, fish and creepy-crawlies.

The shark and piranha feeding sessions at 3pm Wednesday and Sunday are strong draws, and another is the reptile feeding at 10am Sunday and 7pm Thursday. There's a glass tropical house filled with lithe monkeys and a small rainforest. It occupies the inside of a Flakturm, giving you a chance to see the interior of one of these monoliths.

HAYDNHAUS   HOUSE MUSEUM
Map p256 (www.wienmuseum.at; 06, Haydngasse 19; adult/under 19yr €4/free; ◷10am-1pm & 2-6pm Tue-Sun; ⒨Zieglergasse) Though modest, the exhibition in Haydn's last residence was revamped in 2009 and focuses on Vienna as well as London during the late 18th and early 19th centuries. Haydn lived in Vienna during the heady times of Napoleon's occupation. An Austrian composer promi-

nent in the classical period, he was most celebrated for his 104 symphonies and 68 string quartets. The small garden, open to the public, is modelled on the original.

THIRD MAN PRIVATE COLLECTION   MUSEUM
Map p256 (www.3mpc.net; 04, Pressgasse 25; adult/child €7.50/4; ◷2-6pm Sat; ⒨Kettenbrückengasse) The hours of this private museum may be limited, but fans of the quintessential film about Vienna from 1948 (voted best British film of the 20th century by the British Film Institute) will enjoy perusing the posters, *The Third Man* paraphernalia and the other 3000 or so objects on show here.

Stills on the walls illustrate the work of Australian-born cinematographer Robert Krasker, who received an Oscar for this film. The museum indirectly covers aspects of Vienna before and after 'Harry Lime Time' as well as the film itself.

KUNSTHALLE PROJECT SPACE   GALLERY
Map p256 (www.kunsthallewien.at; 04, Treitlstrasse 2; ◷1pm-midnight Tue-Sat, 1-7pm Sun & Mon; ⒨Karlsplatz) ᖴᖴᖴᕓ Once the Kunsthalle had taken up its new residence in the MuseumsQuartier, this glass cube was built on

the site. Its doors were thrown open in 2001 to temporary exhibitions of up-and-coming artists. The website tells you what's on (and any variation in times). After viewing the exhibition, chill out at the Kunsthallencafé next door.

SCHUBERT STERBEWOHNUNG
HOUSE MUSEUM

Map p256 (www.wienmuseum.at; 04, Kettenbrückengasse 6; adult/under 19yr €4/free; ◎10am-1pm & 2-6pm Wed & Thu; ⓂKettenbrückengasse) Here, in his brother's apartment, Franz Schubert spent his dying days (40 to be precise) in 1828. While dying of either typhoid fever or syphilis he continued to compose, scribbling out a string of piano sonatas and his last work, *Der Hirt auf dem Felsen* (The Shepherd on the Rock).

The apartment (Schubert's Death Apartment) is fairly bereft of personal effects but does document these final days with some interesting Schubi knick-knacks and sounds.

STADTBAHN PAVILLONS
LANDMARK

Map p256 (www.wienmuseum.at; 04, Karlsplatz; adult/under 19yr €4/free; ◎10am-6pm Tue-Sun Apr-Oct; ⓂKarlsplatz) Peeking above the Resselpark at Karlsplatz are two of Otto Wagner's finest designs, the Stadtbahn Pavillons. Built in 1898 at a time when Wagner was assembling Vienna's first public transport system (1893–1902), the pavilions are gorgeous examples of *Jugendstil*, with floral motifs and gold trim on a structure of steel and marble.

The west pavilion now holds an exhibit on Wagner's most famous works, the Kirche am Steinhof (p181) and Postsparkasse, which fans of *Jugendstil* will love. The eastern pavilion is now home to Club U.

✖ EATING

TONGUES
DELI €

Map p256 (www.tongues.at; 06, Theobaldgasse 16; lunch mains €3.60; ◎11am-8pm Mon-Fri, to 6pm Sat; ◪; ⓂMuseumsquartier) ✐ DJs can sometimes be found on the decks at this groovy record-shop–cum-deli, where you can pop in for a healthy organic lunch, electro on vinyl or some locally sourced cheese, salami, honey and wood-oven bread. Wholesome day specials range from homemade pizza to veggie dishes like courgette-feta pasta bakes.

URBANEK
DELI €

Map p256 (04, Naschmarkt 46; ham with bread around €4; ◎9am-6.30pm Mon-Thu, 8am-6.30pm Fri, 7.30am-4pm Sat; ⓂKarlsplatz) ✐ Stepping inside Urbanek is to enter a world of cured meats in all their different varieties – smoked, salted, cooked or raw. The atmosphere is rarefied but relaxed as you squeeze into a corner and enjoy a glass of wine (about €5) and perhaps delicately cut slices of Mangalitza pig – a woolly variety prized for its delicious ham.

The roast beef is organic, as are many other offerings here, and the selection of cheeses is just as good. Although there's scarcely enough room to swing a cat inside, it's well worth finding an empty few square inches to enjoy some of the finest cuts around.

BREAKFAST CLUB
BREAKFAST €

Map p256 (04, Schleifmühlgasse 12-14; breakfasts €5.50-6.50; ◎8am-2pm Mon-Fri, to 3pm Sat & Sun; ◪; ⓂKettenbrückengasse) Mix and match from an international range of breakfasts at this compact New York–style breakfast joint on lively Schleifmühlgasse. The 'Vienna Special' of bread roll, honey, egg, seasonal fruit and *Melange* (milky coffee) is a fine choice, but is completely outdone by the 'BC Royal' (salmon rolls, onions, hard-boiled egg, toast and *Sekt*).

Kids will also love it here: there's a small bar especially designed for the little ones, and a separate menu, too.

CHANG ASIAN NOODLES
ASIAN €

Map p256 (☎961 92 12; www.chang.at; 04, Waaggasse 1; midday menus €6.50-7.50; mains €7.80-15; ◎11.30am-11.30pm Mon-Sat, to 10pm Sun; ◪; ⓂTaubstummengasse) This buzzy Asian diner is bright, open, uncomplicated and highly relaxed, while the service is quick and attentive. Noodles (either fried or in a soup) are the mainstay of a menu spanning the Asian continent (at least from China to Singapore) – expect plenty of chicken, prawns (both baby and tiger) and vegetable choices. Everything is available for takeaway.

CORNS N' POPS
BREAKFAST, CAFE €

Map p256 (www.cornsnpops.com; 06, Gumpendorfer Strasse 37; snacks & light meals €1.50-5.50; ◎7.30am-5pm Mon-Fri, 9am-4pm Sat; ◪; ⓂKettenbrückengasse) This little cafe is a fine pick for a wholesome bite on the hoof. Besides having a great DIY muesli bar, it'll rustle up tasty bagels, soups, smoothies,

KARLSPLATZ & AROUND NASCHMARKT EATING

waffles and muffins, with an emphasis on fair-trade and organic ingredients. Day specials from couscous to curries go for around €5.

DELICIOUS MONSTER FAST FOOD €

Map p256 (✆920 44 54; www.deliciousmonster. at; 04, Gusshausstrasse 12 ; sandwiches & salads €6, mains €8.50; ◷10am-6pm Mon-Fri; MKarlsplatz) There's always a good buzz at this lunchtime snackeria. Art-slung walls and gold banquettes create a funky backdrop for deeply satisfying homemade burgers (try the Styrian beef with pumpkin chutney), wraps, baguettes and salads. Find it tucked behind the Karlskirche.

NASCHMARKT DELI CAFE €

Map p256 (www.naschmarkt-deli.at; 04, Naschmarkt 421; breakfast €7-9, snacks €4-9, mains €8-13.50; ◷8am-midnight Mon-Sat; MKarlsplatz) Among the enticing stands along the Vienna River, Naschmarkt Deli has an edge on the others for its delicious snacks. Sandwiches, falafel, big baguettes and chunky lentil soups fill the menu, but much space is dedicated to a heady array of breakfasts. Come Saturday morning this glass box overflows with punters waiting in anticipation for the Turkish or English breakfast.

STEMAN AUSTRIAN €€

Map p256 (✆597 85 09; www.steman.at; 06, Otto-Bauer-Gasse 7; mains €6-14.50; ◷11am-midnight Mon-Fri; MZieglergasse) Run by the same folk as Café Jelinek, Steman serves good honest Austrian food in a nicely restored, high-ceilinged interior, with a few tables outside in summer. The mood is laidback, the service friendly and the menu packed with classics like goulash and *Käsespätzle* (cheese noodles). The €7.10 two-course lunch is a bargain.

UBL AUSTRIAN €€

Map p256 (✆587 64 37; 04, Pressgasse 26; mains €9.50-18; ◷noon-2pm & 6pm-midnight Wed-Sun; MKettenbrückengasse) This much-loved *Beisl* (bistro pub) is a favourite of the Wieden crowd. Its menu is heavily loaded with Viennese classics, such as *Schinkenfleckerl*, *Schweinsbraten* (roast pork) and four types of schnitzel, and is enhanced with seasonal cuisine throughout the year. You could do worse than finish the hefty meal off with a stomach-settling plum schnapps. The tree-shaded garden is wonderful in summer.

MOTTO FUSION €€

Map p256 (✆587 06 72; www.motto.at; 05, Schönbrunner Strasse 30; mains €9-29; ◷6pm-2am Mon-Thu & Sun, to 4am Fri & Sat; MPilgramgasse) The darling of Margareten's dining scene is this theatrical lounge-style restaurant, which is all clever backlighting, high banquettes and DJ beats. Asian, Austrian and Mediterranean flavours are all in the mix, with well-executed dishes from red Thai curry to the signature fillet steak with chocolate-chilli sauce. Motto is very popular, particularly with the gay crowd; reservations are recommended.

Entrance is through the forbidding chrome door on Rüdigergasse.

UMAR SEAFOOD €€

Map p256 (✆587 04 56; www.umarfisch.at; 04, Naschmarkt 76; midday menu €13, mains €15-32; ◷11am-midnight Mon-Sat; MKarlsplatz) Umar is one of the best fish restaurants in Vienna, serving fresh seafood imported from Italy and Turkey at its large Naschmarkt stall. Choose between whole fish, mussels in white-wine sauce and giant shrimps fried in herb butter. Seriously good wines from the Wachau round off a delicious eating experience.

AMACORD AUSTRIAN, INTERNATIONAL €€

Map p256 (✆587 47 09; 04, Rechte Wienzeile 15; 1-/2-course lunch €7.30/8.80, mains €15-19; ◷10am-2am; ✐; MKettenbrückengasse, Karlsplatz) Friendly staff keep the good vibes and affordable food coming at this cosy, vaulted cafe. Viennese classics are mixed in with a healthy range of Italian pastas, the odd curry and ragout, and an extensive salads selection. Trying to find a seat on a Saturday morning is a fruitless enterprise. Eat off-peak here.

ZUM ALTEN FASSL AUSTRIAN €€

Map p256 (✆544 42 98; www.zum-alten-fassl. at; 05, Ziegelofengasse 37; midday menus €5.70-7.30, mains €7.50-18.50; ◷11.30am-3pm & 5pm-1am Mon-Fri, 5pm-1am Sat, noon-3pm & 5pm-1am Sun; MPilgramgasse) With its private garden amid residential houses and polished wooden interior (typical of a well-kept *Beisl*), Zum Alten Fassl is worth the trip south of the centre just for a drink. But while here sample the Viennese favourites and regional specialities, like *Eierschwammerl* (chanterelles) and *Blunzengröstl* (a potato, bacon, onion and blood sausage fry-up). When it's in season, *Zanderfilet* (fillet of zander) is the chef's favourite.

Between 1974 and 1982 the singer Falco lived upstairs in this building – a plaque marks the spot.

RA'MIEN
ASIAN €€

Map p256 (☑585 47 98; www.ramien.at; 06, Gumpendorfer Strasse 9; mains €7-17.50; ☺11am-midnight Tue-Sun; ☑; ⓂMuseumsquartier) Picture a minimalist grey-white room and lots of bright, young hip things bent over piping-hot Thai, Japanese, Chinese and Vietnamese noodle soups and rice dishes and you have Ra'mien. Ra'mien fills up quickly at night, so it's worth booking ahead; the lounge bar downstairs has regular DJs and stays open until at least 2am.

KOJIRO
JAPANESE €€

Map p256 (☑586 62 33; 04, Kühnplatz 4; sushi sets €8-17; ☺11am-6.15pm Mon-Fri, 10am-2.30pm Sat; ⓂKettenbrückengasse, Karlsplatz) Wiener who are serious about their sushi rave about this tiny nosh spot near the Naschmarkt, which rolls out brilliantly fresh sushi and sashimi. Enough said.

MILL
AUSTRIAN €€

(☑966 40 73; www.mill32.at; 06, Millergasse 32; mains €8-17.50; ☺11.30am-3pm & 5pm-midnight Mon-Fri, 11am-4pm Sun; ⓂWestbahnhof) This bistro, with a hidden courtyard for summer days, still feels like a local secret. Scarlet brick walls and wood floors create a warm backdrop for spot-on seasonal food such as chanterelle cannelloni and Styrian chicken salad drizzled in pumpkin-seed oil. The two-course lunch is a snip at €6.90.

GERGELY'S
STEAKHOUSE €€

Map p256 (☑544 07 67; www.gergelys.at; 05, Schlossgasse 21; steaks €20-32; ☺6pm-1am Tue-Sat; ⓂPilgramgasse) The flagship of the four eateries around Schlossplatz, Gergely's is inside a 14th-century vaulted cellar and focuses exclusively on steaks made from quality beef sourced locally and internationally, served with sauces and accompaniments. The inner courtyard with tables set up under the trees is ideal for summer dining.

TANCREDI
AUSTRIAN €€

Map p256 (☑941 00 48; www.tancredi.at; 04, Grosse Neugasse 5; lunch menus €8.80-16.80, mains €14-20; ☺11.30am-2.30pm Mon, 11.30am-2.30pm & 6pm-midnight Tue-Fri, 6pm-midnight Sat; ☑; ⓂTaubstummengasse) This former

Beisl serves lovingly prepared regional and fish specialities, seasonal fare, organic dishes and an extensive range of Austrian wines. The harmonious surroundings are the icing on the cake: warm, pastel-yellow walls, stripped-back wooden floors, fittings from yesteryear and a tree-shaded garden that fills up quickly in summer. The entrance is on Rubengasse.

AROMAT
INTERNATIONAL €€

Map p256 (☑913 24 53; 04, Margaretenstrasse 52; menus €7.90, mains €10-15; ☺5-11pm Tue-Sun; ⓂKettenbrückengasse) This funky little eatery serves fusion cooking with a strong emphasis on Upper Austrian and Vietnamese cuisine. It has an open kitchen and often caters for those with an intolerance to wheat and gluten. The charming surroundings feature simple formica tables, 1950s fixtures, a blackboard menu and one huge glass frontage. Personable staff help to create a convivial, barlike atmosphere.

PICCINI PICCOLO GOURMET
ITALIAN €€

Map p256 (☑587 52 54; www.piccini.at; 06, Linke Wienzeile 4; mains €8-19; ☺11am-10pm Mon-Sat; ⓂKarlsplatz) 'Gourmet' in the true sense of the word, Piccini has the finest antipasti restaurant in town, with a huge assortment of antipasti rolls, fish treats and stuffed vegetables. It also knows its *Brunello* from its *Vino Nobile*, which, with 60 varieties of wine available, is a good thing. Its shop next door has been selling imported Italian foods since 1856.

From noon to 2pm Monday to Friday, the day pasta special goes for €4 at the bar.

HAAS BEISL
AUSTRIAN €€

Map p256 (☑586 25 52; www.haasbeisl.at; 05, Margaretenstrasse 74; mains €8-16; ☺11am-11pm Mon-Fri, to 10pm Sat, to 9pm Sun; ⓂPilgramgasse) Warm and woody, this traditional Margareten *Beisl* doesn't have the revamped, streamlined culinary edges of a *neo-Beisl*, but Haas is absolutely genuine and a place where you can enjoy decent food and soak up a very local atmosphere. Classics such as offal, sweetmeats, goulash and dumplings are prepared the way your grandmother might have done them.

Above the bar are football (soccer) trophies won by the gentlemen players at Haas who have exceeded their own football prime (but not by much, as the trophies testify). The toilets have an 'art' touch.

SILBERWIRT
AUSTRIAN €€

Map p256 (📞544 49 07; www.silberwirt.at; 05, Schlossgasse 21; mains €8-16.50; ⊙noon-midnight Mon-Sun; 🚲; MPilgramgasse) This atmospheric *neo-Beisl*, another in the four eateries on Schlossplatz, offers traditional Viennese cuisine, mostly using organic and/or local produce. A meal might begin with, say, Waldviertel sheep cheese salad with walnuts and poppy seeds, followed by trout with herby potatoes and almond butter, and *Palatschinken* (pancakes) with homemade apricot jam.

A dedicated kids menu appeals to little appetites. Dine alfresco in the tree-shaded garden in summer.

NENI
MIDDLE EASTERN €€

Map p256 (📞585 20 20; www.neni.at; 06, Naschmarkt 510; breakfasts €5-9, salads & snacks €4.50-10.50, mains €10.50-15; ⊙8am-midnight Mon-Sat; 🚲; MKettenbrückengasse) This industro-cool glass cube combines a cafe, bar and restaurant where food has mostly a Middle Eastern focus. Dishes such as caramelised aubergine with ginger and chilli are served alongside tuna steaks in a seasame-pepper crust with wasabi mash. Tables fill up fast most nights, so reserve ahead or drop by outside prime time. Breakfast is served until 2pm.

SAIGON
ASIAN €€

Map p256 (📞585 63 95; www.saigon.at; 06, Getreidemarkt 7; lunch menus €7.20, mains €9-17.50; ⊙11.30am-11pm Mon-Sun; MKarlsplatz) Saigon was one of the first Asian restaurants in Vienna and remains one of the best. Expect to find a large selection of rice and noodle dishes, including a delicious *Pho Tai Bo* (beef noodle soup). A second Saigon is conveniently located in Ottakring not far from the Brunnenmarkt.

ON
ASIAN €€

Map p256 (📞585 49 00; www.restaurant-on.at; 05, Wehrgasse 8; lunch menus €7.60-8.90, mains €9-16.30; ⊙noon-midnight Mon-Sat, to 10.30pm Sun; MPilgramgasse) The vibe is relaxed and friendly at this colourful Austro-Asian fusion restaurant. Order from a menu that plays up seasonal Chinese flavours and Austrian produce, from tuna tartare with pumpkin-seed oil to trout with ginger and spicy duck expertly matched with Wachau wines. The small, private garden is lovely in summer; reserve in the evening.

VAPIANO
ITALIAN €€

Map p256 (📞581 12 12; 01, Theobaldgasse 19; mains €7.50-9.50; ⊙11am-midnight Mon-Sat, noon-11pm Sun; 🚲 ♿; MMuseumsquartier) This eat-in Italian cafeteria-style chain whips up pizza, homemade pasta and salads right before your eyes. Collect a card at the door, make your choice at one of the counters, then simply pay at the door when you leave. The downside is that the eating is often shoulder-to-shoulder and the noise level can make spaghetti of your nerve endings.

COLLIO
ITALIAN €€€

Map p256 (📞589 18 133; www.dastriest.at; 04, Wiedner Hauptstrasse 12; mains €18-28, 2-course lunch menus €14.80, 5-course menus €49.80; ⊙noon-2.30pm & 6-10pm Mon-Fri, 6-10pm Sat; 🚲; MKettenbrückengasse, Karlsplatz) Tucked inside the Das Triest hotel, this restaurant has a lounge vibe, mellow sounds, a slinky Terence Conran–designed interior and a flower-strewn courtyard for warm-weather dining. Collio's menu is predominantly Italian but wades across a broad and interesting culinary lagoon. Seasonal flavours shine in specialities such as homemade gnocchi with veal and artichokes and roast saddle of venison with parsley roots.

 DRINKING & NIGHTLIFE

★CAFÉ SPERL
COFFEE HOUSE

Map p256 (www.cafesperl.at; 06, Gumpendorfer Strasse 11; ⊙7am-11pm Mon-Sat, 11am-8pm Sun; 🛜; MMuseumsquartier, Kettenbrückengasse) With its gorgeous *Jugendstil* fittings, grand dimensions, cosy booths and unhurried air, Sperl is one of the finest coffee houses in Vienna. And that's to say nothing of a menu that features *Sperl Torte*, a mouth-watering mix of almonds and chocolate cream. Grab a slice and a newspaper, order a strong coffee, and join the rest of the patrons people-watching and daydreaming.

The food is good, too, with snacks and hearty Austrian mains (€7 to €11) staving off hunger.

ALT WIEN
CAFE

Map p256 (www.altwien.at; 04, Schleifmühlgasse 23; ⊙10am-6pm Mon-Fri, to 4pm Sat; MKettenbrückengasse) The enticing aroma of coffee wafts from Alt Wien. This purveyor of freshly roasted and ground beans does a brisk trade in 30 different kinds of coffee, from Brazilian to Nepalese, organic and fair-trade blends. Sip a cup at the little bar out the back.

PHIL
BAR, CAFE

Map p256 (www.phil.info; 06, Gumpendorfer Strasse 10-12; ⊘5pm-1am Mon, 9am-1am Tue-Sun; MMuseumsquartier, Kettenbrückengasse) A retro bar reminiscent of an East Berlin *Lokal*, Phil attracts a Bohemian crowd happy to squat on kitsch furniture your grandma used to own. Half the establishment is store rather than bar; TVs from the '70s, DVDs, records and books are for sale, as is all the furniture. Staff are super-friendly and the vibe is as relaxed as can be.

CAFÉ DRECHSLER
COFFEE HOUSE

Map p256 (www.cafedrechsler.at; Linke Wienzeile 22; ⊘23hr, closed 2-3am; ⊜; MKettenbrückengasse) One of the liveliest coffee houses in town, Drechsler reopened with a smash after extensive renovations (Sir Terence Conran worked his magic with polished marble bar and table tops, Bauhaus light fixtures and whitewashed timber panels – stylish yet still distinctly Viennese). As well as the usual coffee-house suspects, its *Gulasch* (goulash) is legendary.

In the evening, the tunes the DJ spins seemingly change every few hours and always keep the vibe upbeat and hip.

TANZCAFÉ JENSEITS
BAR, CLUB

Map p256 (www.tanzcafe-jenseits.com; 06, Nelkengasse 3; ⊘8pm-4am Tue-Sat; MNeubaugasse) Bordello meets Bohemian at this brothel turned bar, where soft lighting, red velvet and gilt mirrors keep the mood intimate. Jenseits has left its insalubrious past behind and today packs in media and arty types, who jostle for space on its tiny dance floor. The mercurial DJs flick from soul to trashy pop tunes in the blink of an eye.

SEKT COMPTOIR
WINE BAR

Map p256 (www.sektcomptoir.at; 04, Schleifmühlgasse 19; ⊘5-11pm Mon-Fri, noon-6pm Sat; MKettenbrückengasse) Ooooh, sparkly. Szigeti vineyard in Burgenland, which produces a leading Austrian *Sekt* (sparkling wine), serves its own brand only at this tiny, wood-panelled wine bar. As it's located just a few blocks from the Naschmarkt, shoppers with bulging grocery bags often spill onto the sidewalk enjoying a tipple or four.

It rarely offers much elbow room but the, er, bubbly spirit is so intoxicating that most just chuckle and squish with a wide grin. Note the early closing times – and its **shop** (Map p256; Schleifmühlgasse 23; 10.30am-6.30pm Tue-Fri, 10am-5pm Sat) selling bottles a few doors down.

PUFF
BAR

Map p256 (http://puff-bar.at; 06, Giardigasse 10; ⊘6pm-2am Mon-Thu, to 4am Fri & Sat; MMuseumsquartier, Kettenbrückengasse) The name gives the game away: Puff was formerly a brothel. Thanks to TLC from Walking Chair Design Studio, it has been reborn as this uberstylish bar, with bunches of tubular lanterns sprouting from the ceiling and

---

LOCAL KNOWLEDGE

MEET THE OWNER: CAFÉ SPERL

Rainer Staub, the owner and manager of Café Sperl, took time out to speak to us about Vienna's coffee-house scene.

What's special about Vienna's coffee houses? Coffee houses are the cultural calling card of Vienna. I like to think of them as living rooms where you can meet friends, play games or read in peace. Here you are alone but never lonely.

History in a nutshell Not many visitors know that Sperl was the HQ of the Russian army after WWII. They used it as a stable for donkeys! All the furniture was stored in the basement. It was restored according to original plans in 1983.

Easily missed details Look up to the ceiling and you'll see angels showing what customers are entitled to do: eat, drink and play billiards.

Famous past guests This was composer Franz Lehár's favourite haunt. Students from the Academy of Fine Arts also used to frequent Sperl. If they couldn't settle their tab, they would dash off a sketch or two as payment. Freud was also a regular.

Recent claims to fame A scene from *Dangerous Method* (2011) starring Keira Knightley was filmed here over two days – they brought a 200-strong crew!

cocktail machines bring a dash of magic to the mixology. The highballs are terrific, as are proseccos blended with fresh fruit from Naschmarkt.

CAFÉ JELINEK — COFFEE HOUSE

Map p256 (www.steman.at; 06, Otto-Bauer-Gasse 5; ⊙9am-9pm; MZieglergasse) With none of the polish or airs and graces of some other coffee houses, this shabbily grand cafe is Viennese through and through. The wood-burning stove, picture-plastered walls and faded velvet armchairs draw people from all walks of life with their cocoon-like warmth. Take the lead of locals and linger over freshly roasted coffee, cake and the daily papers.

KUNSTHALLENCAFÉ — BAR, CAFE

Map p256 (www.kunsthallencafe.at; 04, Treitlstrasse 2; ⊙10am-2am; MKarlsplatz) The Kunsthallencafé carries plenty of 'cool' clout and attracts a relaxed, arty crowd with its DJs and close proximity to the Kunsthalle Project Space. The big sofas go quickly, but there are plenty of small tables perfect for an intimate evening, and in summer the terrace (with more couches) is one enormous outdoor lounge.

ZWEITBESTER — BAR

Map p256 (www.zweitbester.at; 04, Heumühlgasse 2; ⊙11am-2am; MKettenbrückengasse) This industro-cool bar located bang in the heart of the Freihausviertel hosts DJ nights as well as an original roster of events, from 'concerts in the loo' to 'dish tennis', ping-pong with a party twist. There's a pavement terrace for imbibing on summer nights.

CAFÉ RÜDIGERHOF — COFFEE HOUSE

Map p256 (05, Hamburgerstrasse 20; ⊙9am-2am; MKettenbrückengasse, Pilgramgasse) Rüdigerhof's facade is a glorious example of *Jugendstil* architecture, and the furniture and fittings inside could be straight out of an *I Love Lucy* set. The atmosphere is homely and familiar and the terrace huge and shaded. On Saturday mornings it fills up quickly with Naschmarkt shoppers.

BARFLY'S CLUB — COCKTAIL BAR

Map p256 (www.castillo.at; 06, Esterhazygasse 33 ; ⊙8pm-2am Sun-Thu, to 4am Fri & Sat; MNeubaugasse, Zieglergasse) Bringing a splash of Manhattan-style sophistication to Vienna, Barfly's is a softly lit bar, justly famous for its 500-strong cocktail list and intimate ambience, which attracts a regular crowd of journalists and actors. At around €10 a pop, drinks aren't cheap, but they are among the city's best.

AKRAP — COFFEE

Map p256 (www.akrapcoffee.com; 06, Königslostergasse 7; ⊙9am-5.30pm Mon-Fri, 10am-4pm Sat; MMuseumsquartier) This stylish espresso bar on Theobaldgasse is where Wiener go for freshly roasted coffee, teas, juices and homemade cakes.

CAFÉ SAVOY — GAY

Map p256 (www.savoy.at; 06, Linke Wienzeile 36, ⊙noon-2am Sun-Thu, to 3am Fri & Sat; ☎; MKettenbrückengasse) Café Savoy is an established gay haunt that has a more traditional cafe feel to it. The clientele is generally very mixed on a Saturday – mainly due to the proximity of the Naschmarkt – but at other times it's filled with men of all ages.

EBERT'S COCKTAIL BAR — COCKTAIL BAR

Map p256 (www.eberts.at; 06, Gumpendorfer Strasse 51; ⊙6pm-2am Sun-Thu, 7pm-4am Fri & Sat; MNeubaugasse, Kettenbrückengasse) Expert bartenders shake it up: all the mixologists here double as instructors at the bartending academy next door. The cocktail list is novel-esque, the vibe stylish, modern minimalism, the tunes jazzy to electronic, and on weekends you'll barely squeeze in. Bring your English Cinema Haydn ticket in anytime and receive a cocktail for €5.50.

ELEKTRO GÖNNER — BAR

Map p256 (www.elektro-g.at; 06, Mariahilfer Strasse 101; ⊙7pm-2am Sun-Thu, to 4am Fri & Sat; MZieglergasse) Elektro Gönner is an unpretentious bar opened by architects (and attracting plenty from the profession). Much of the interior is uncomplicated and bare, aside from the occasional art installation in the back room, and DJs spin mostly techno and electro. The bar hides at the back of a courtyard off Mariahilfer Strasse.

LUTZ — BAR, CLUB

Map p256 (www.lutz-bar.at; 06, Mariahilfer Strasse 3; ⊙from 8am Mon-Fri, from 9am Sat, from 10am Sun; ☎; MMuseumsquartier) A cafe and restaurant by day, by night this bar buzzes with cocktail sippers. Caramel leather armchairs and clean lines create a contemporary backdrop for a frozen mojito or lemongrass fizz – try to snag a seat at the floor-to-ceiling windows gazing down to Mariahilfer Strasse. On weekends a subterranean club opens from 9.30pm, playing anything from house to disco.

SCHIKANEDER
BAR

Map p256 (www.schikaneder.at; 04, Margaretenstrasse 22-24; ☺6pm-4am; Ⓜ️Kettenbrückengasse) Most of the colour in Schikaneder comes from the regularly projected movies splayed across one of its white walls – the students and arty crowd who frequent this grungy bar dress predominantly in black. But that's not to detract from the bar's atmosphere, which exudes energy well into the wee small hours of the morning.

MON AMI
BAR

Map p256 (www.monami.at; 06, Theobaldgasse 9; ☺6pm-2am Wed-Sat; Ⓜ️Museumsquartier) Don't let the dog- and cat-grooming sign fool you: this former pet-grooming salon morphed into a lovely '60s-style bar. It mixes excellent cocktails, serves a short but decent beer, wine and snacks list, and attracts a laid-back and unpretentious crowd. DJ Roman Schöny regularly works the decks.

TOP KINO BAR
BAR

Map p256 (www.topkino.at; 06, Rahlgasse 1; ☺3pm-2am; Ⓜ️Museumsquartier) Occupying the foyer of the Top Kino cinema, Top Kino Bar is a pleasantly relaxed place that attracts a fashionable alternative crowd. The decor is highly retro, and there are tunes to match the furniture. Kozel, one of the Czech Republic's better pilsners, is lined up against Austria's finest lagers.

MANGO BAR
GAY

Map p256 (06, Laimgrubengasse 3; ☺9pm-4am; Ⓜ️Kettenbrückengasse) Mango attracts a young, often men-only, gay crowd with good music, friendly staff and plenty of mirrors to check out yourself and others. It usually serves as a kick-start for a big night out on the town.

ROXY
CLUB

Map p256 (www.roxyclub.org; 04, Operngasse 24; ☺11pm-4am Thu-Sat; Ⓜ️Karlsplatz, 🚋D, 1, 2 Kärntner Ring/Oper) A seminal club for years, Roxy still manages to run with the clubbing pack, and sometimes leads the way. DJs from Vienna's electronica scene regularly guest on the turntables and most nights it's hard to find a space on the small dance floor. Expect a crowded, but very good, night out here.

CLUB U
BAR, CLUB

Map p256 (www.club-u.at; 04, Künstlerhauspassage; ☺9pm-4am; Ⓜ️Karlsplatz) Club U occupies one of Otto Wagner's **Stadtbahn Pavillons** on Karlsplatz. It's a small, student-infested bar-club with regular DJs and a wonderful outdoor seating area overlooking the pavilions and park.

WIEDEN BRÄU
MICROBREWERY

Map p256 (www.wieden-braeu.at; 04, Waaggasse 5; ☺11.30am-midnight; 🛜; Ⓜ️Taubstummengasse) *Helles, Märzen* and hemp beers are brewed year-round at this upbeat microbrewery, and there are a few seasonal choices, including a ginger beer. Tipples are matched with Austrian pub grub like schnitzel and goulash. Retreat to the garden in summer.

AUX GAZELLES
CLUB

Map p256 (www.auxgazelles.at; 06, Rahlgasse 5; ☺11pm-5am Thu-Sat; Ⓜ️Museumsquartier) Aux Gazelles' club bar is beautifully Moorish and filled with beautiful people. The music is an eclectic mix of smooth ethnic sounds, and there are plenty of dim corners and low, comfy couches to escape to if so desired. The rest of this gigantic club venue features a restaurant, bar and deli, and there's even a *hammam* (oriental steam bath).

Aux Gazelles is one of the few clubs in town where a dress code is enforced.

ORANGE ONE
BAR

Map p256 (www.orange-one.at; 04, Margaretenstrasse 26; ☺4pm-2am Mon-Fri, 6pm-2am Sat; Ⓜ️Kettenbrückengasse) Once a down-at-heel *Gastehaus* (guesthouse), this place received a complete makeover and reinvented itself as Orange One, a modern bar with a distinct retro feel and grown-up attitude. DJs play most nights and offbeat films are intermittently projected on the back wall.

CAFÉ WILLENDORF
GAY & LESBIAN

Map p256 (http://cafe-willendorf.at; 06, Linke Wienzeile 102; ☺6pm-2am Thu-Sat, to 1am Sun-Wed; Ⓜ️Pilgramgasse) This is one of Vienna's seminal gay and lesbian bars. Housed in the pink **Rosa Lila Villa** (☑586 8150; www.villa.at; Linke Wienzeile 102, 06; Ⓜ️Pilgramgasse), it's a very popular place to meet for a chat, a drink or a meal. The lovely inner courtyard garden opens for the summer months.

GOODMANN
CLUB

Map p256 (www.goodmann.at; 04, Rechte Wienzeile 23; ☺3am-10am Mon-Sat; Ⓜ️Kettenbrückengasse)

A tiny club attracting clubbers who want to boogie before breakfast, Goodmann serves food upstairs (until 8am) and hides its night owls, who are an eclectic mix of old and young (but always in a merry state), downstairs.

TITANIC   CLUB
Map p256 (www.titanic.at; 06, Theobaldgasse 11; ⊙11pm-6am Fri & Sat; Museumsquartier) This club is old school, with door check and bouncers (dress reasonably conservatively), but once you're past these party-poopers it's time to whoop it up. Two large dance floors soon fill with revellers either looking to pull or dance the night away to electro, techno, hip-hop and R&B. Fun, but not to everyone's taste.

☆ ENTERTAINMENT

STAATSOPER   OPERA
Map p256 (☎514 44 7880; www.wiener-staatsoper. at; 01, Opernring 2; Karlsplatz, D 1, 2 Kärntner Ring/Oper) The Staatsoper is *the* premier opera and classical music venue in Vienna. Productions are lavish affairs: the Viennese take their opera very seriously and dress up accordingly. In the interval, be sure to wander around the foyer and refreshment rooms to fully appreciate the gold and crystal interior.

Opera is not performed here in July and August (tours, however, still take place), but its repertoire still includes more than 70 different productions. Tickets can be purchased up to one month in advance (see p45).

MUSIKVEREIN   CONCERT VENUE
Map p256 (☎505 81 90; www.musikverein.at; 01, Bösendorferstrasse 12; Karlsplatz) The Musikverein holds the proud title of the best acoustics of any concert hall in Austria, which the Vienna Philharmonic Orchestra makes excellent use of. The interior is suitably lavish and can be visited on the occasional guided tour. Smaller-scale performances are held in the Brahms Saal.

Tickets are available online, by phone or at the box office, which is open 9am to 8pm Monday to Friday and 9am to 1pm Saturday. Standard tickets range from €25 to €89, though tickets for the famous New Year's Eve concert cost anything from €30 to €950. Standing-room tickets are available up to seven weeks in advance and cost €4 to €6; there are no student tickets.

THEATER AN DER WIEN   THEATRE
Map p256 (☎588 85; www.theater-wien.at; 06, Linke Wienzeile 6; Karlsplatz) The Theater an der Wien has hosted some monumental premiere performances, such as Beethoven's *Fidelo,* Mozart's *Die Zauberflöte* and Strauss Jnr's *Die Fledermaus.* These days, besides staging musicals, dance and concerts, the theatre has re-established its reputation for high-quality opera, playing host to one premiere each month.

All tickets (standard and standing) are available online, by phone or from the box office, which is open 10am to 7pm Monday to Saturday. They range in price from €10 to €160. Discounts include €10 to €15 tickets for students on sale 30 minutes before shows, and €7 standing tickets available one hour before performances.

BURG KINO   CINEMA
Map p256 (☎587 84 06; www.burgkino.at; 01, Opernring 19; Museumsquartier, D, 1, 2 Burgring) The Burg Kino is a central cinema that shows only English-language films. It has regular screenings of the *The Third Man,* Orson Welles' timeless classic set in post-WWII Vienna. See the website for times.

ENGLISH CINEMA HAYDN   CINEMA
Map p256 (☎587 22 62; www.haydnkino.at; 06, Mariahilfer Strasse 57; Neubaugasse) The Haydn is a comfortable cinema screening

---

❶ STANDING ROOM TICKETS

You can get a taste of high culture for next to nothing in Vienna with a little planning. Among the best culture deals are the standing-room tickets at the city's stately 19th-century concert halls. Opera at the Staatsoper? That'll be €3 to €4 for a standing-room ticket, sold 80 minutes before the performance at the venue box office. Or book standing-room tickets (€4 to €6) up to seven weeks ahead to see the Vienna Philharmonic Orchestra perform in the Musikverein's lavishly gilded Grosser Saal. Advance standing-room tickets are also available at the Burgtheater (€2.50).

For more ticketing info, see p45.

mainly mainstream Hollywood-style films in their original language, on three separate screens.

FILMCASINO   CINEMA
Map p256 (☑581 39 00-10; www.filmcasino.at; 05, Margaretenstrasse 78; ⓂKettenbrückengasse) An art-house cinema of some distinction, Filmcasino screens an excellent mix of Asian and European docos and avant-garde short films, along with independent feature-length films from around the world. Its '50s-style foyer is particularly impressive.

SCHIKANEDER   CINEMA
Map p256 (☑585 28 67; www.schikaneder.at; 04, Margaretenstrasse 24; ⓂKettenbrückengasse) Located next to the bar of the same name, Schikaneder is the darling of Vienna's alternative cinema scene. The film subject range is quite broad but also highly selective, and art house through and through.

TOP KINO   CINEMA
Map p256 (☑208 30 00; www.topkino.at; 06, Rahlgasse 1; ⓂMuseumsquartier) Top Kino offers an ever-changing array of European films and documentaries, generally in their original language with German subtitles. It also holds a variety of themed film festivals throughout the year.

 SHOPPING

BLÜHENDES KONFEKT   CONFECTIONERY
Map p256 (www.bluehendes-konfekt.com; 06, Schmalzhofgasse 19; ⊙10am-6.30pm Wed-Fri; ⓂZieglergasse, Westbahnhof) Violets, forest strawberries and cherry blossom, mint and oregano – Michael Diewald makes the most of what grows wild and in his garden to create confectionery that fizzes with seasonal flavour. Peek through to the workshop to see flowers and herbs being deftly transformed into one-of-a-kind bonbons and mini bouquets that are edible works of art.

DÖRTHE KAUFMANN   WOMEN'S CLOTHING
Map p256 (www.doertekaufmann.com; 04, Kettenbrückengasse 6; ⊙11am-7pm Wed-Fri, 10am-4pm Sat; ⓂKettenbrückengasse) Dörthe is the designer behind the biannual collections presented at this little boutique, which might include anything from French-style bolero jackets to dresses inspired by bold Nigerian colours and patterns. These feature alongside a snug assortment of chunky

SHOPPING WITH LUCIE

Former NYC fashion stylist Lucie Lamster-Thury has been running speciality shopping tours in Vienna since 2008. Her three-hour tours, which cover Vienna's shopping districts, cost €35; see www.shoppingwithlucie.com for dates and times. Lucie took time out to tell us her shopping tips.

Why Vienna? I fell in love, moved to the city of music and found a fledgling design and fashion scene just by walking from street to street. Things have come a long way since then. I love the fact that most things are high quality and often have a personal touch.

Best for Boutiques Definitely the Neubau – every time I go something new has opened up, and it's relaxing to wander around the atmospheric lanes. Lindengasse, for example, is chock full of fascinating small shops.

hand-knitted hats, gloves, scarves and booties, all beautifully made with merino, mohair or alpaca wool and coloured with natural pigments.

MEIN DESIGN   ACCESSORIES, FASHION
Map p256 (www.mein-design.org; 04, Kettenbrückengasse 6; ⊙11am-6pm Tue-Thu, 11am-7pm Fri, 10am-4pm Sun; ⓂKettenbrückengasse) Boutique owner and designer Ulrike gives young Austrian creatives and designers a platform for showcasing their fresh, innovative fashion and accessories at this boutique-workshop, where the accent is on quality and sustainability. Though displays change every few months, you might find everything from beautifully made children's clothes to jewellery fashioned from recycled tyres and silk blouses emblazoned with photographs of Vienna icons.

FEINEDINGE   CERAMICS
Map p256 (www.feinedinge.at; 05, Krongasse 20; ⊙11am-6pm Mon-Wed, to 7.30pm Tue-Fri, to 5pm Sat; ⓂKettenbrückengasse) Sandra Haischberger makes exquisite porcelain that reveals a clean modern aesthetic at her atelier shop. Her range of home accessories, tableware and lighting is minimalistic, but often features sublime details, such as crockery in chalky pastels, filigree lamps that cast

NASCHMARKET NIBBLES

The massive **Naschmarkt** (Map p256; 06, Linke & Rechte Wienzeile; ⊘6am-7.30pm Mon-Fri, to 6pm Sat; MKarlsplatz, Kettenbrückengasse), Vienna's food market, extends for more than 500m along Linke Wienzeile between the U4 stops of Kettenbrückengasse and Karlsplatz. The western end near Kettengasse is more fun, with all sorts of meats, fruit and vegetables, spices, wines, cheeses and olives, Indian and Middle Eastern specialities and fabulous kebab and falafel stands. Check out the vinegar and oil place, with 24 varieties of fruit- and veg-flavoured vinegar, 11 balsamics and over 20 types of flavoured oil. The market peters out at the eastern end to stalls selling Indian fabrics and jewellery and trashy trinkets.

exquisite patterns and candle holders embellished with floral and butterfly motifs.

GABARAGE UPCYCLING DESIGN   DESIGN

Map p256 (www.gabarage.at; 06, Schleifmühlgasse 6; ⊘10am-6pm Mon-Thu, 10am-7pm Fri, 11am-5pm Sat; MTaubstummengasse) 🖉 Recycled design, ecology and social responsibility underpin the quirky designs at Gabarage. Old bowling pins become vases, rubbish bins get a new life as tables and chairs, advertising tarpaulins morph into bags, and traffic lights are transformed into funky lights. People also get a second shot at life, with job training in various skills through Gabarage's occupational therapy program.

PICCINI PICCOLO GOURMET   FOOD, WINE

Map p256 (06, Linke Wienzeile 4; ⊘9am-7pm Mon-Fri, to 5pm Sat; MKarlsplatz) Piccini stocks only the finest and freshest goods from Italy, all of which are handled with love and care – wines, multitudes of varieties of dried pasta, 20-odd different types of salami, olives and oil. It's also a superb restaurant.

FLO VINTAGE MODE   VINTAGE

Map p256 (04, Schleifmühlgasse 15a; ⊘10am-6.30pm Mon-Fri, to 3.30pm Sat; MKettenbrückengasse) In a city this enamoured of the glamorous past, it's no less than shocking that there are few true vintage clothing stores in town. The clothes here are fastidiously and beautifully displayed, from pearl-embroidered art nouveau masterpieces to 1950s and '60s New Look pieces and designer wear of the '70s and '80s (alphabetised from Armani to Zegna). Prices (and quality) are high.

GÖTTIN DES GLÜCKS   FASHION

Map p256 (www.goettindesgluecks.com; 04, Operngasse 32; ⊘11am-6pm Wed-Fri, 10am-4pm Sat; MKarlsplatz) Austria's first fair-fashion label conforms to the fair-trade model throughout the production process through relationships with sustainable producers in India, Mauritius and beyond. The result is supple, delicious cotton jerseys, skirts, and shorts for men and women, with the comfort of sleepwear in stylish, casual daywear.

LICHTERLOH   HOMEWARES

Map p256 (www.lichterloh.com; 06, Gumpendorfer Strasse 15-17; ⊘11am-6.30pm Mon-Fri, to 4pm Sat; MMuseumsquartier) This massive, ultra-cool space is filled with iconic furniture from the 1900s to 1970s, by names such as Eames, Thonet and Mies Van Der Rohe. Even if you're not planning to lug home a slick Danish sideboard, it's worth a look at this veritable gallery of modern furniture design.

RAVE UP   MUSIC

Map p256 (06, Hofmühlgasse 1; ⊘10am-6.30pm Mon-Fri, to 5pm Sat; MPilgramgasse) Friendly staff, loads of new vinyl and a massive collection make a trip to Rave Up a real pleasure. The store specialises in indie and alternative imports from the UK and US, but you'll find plenty of electronica, hip-hop and retro tunes, and you can listen before you buy, too.

THALIA   BOOKS

Map p256 (www.thalia.at; 06, Mariahilfer Strasse 99; ⊘9am-7pm Mon-Wed, to 8pm Thu-Fri, to 6pm Sat; MZieglergasse) Vienna's biggest bookshop, spread over four floors including a cafe, Thalia has an 'International Bookshop' at the back of the ground floor, with lots of bestsellers in English and a small selection of books in Spanish, French, Italian and Russian.

The Museum District & Neubau

Neighbourhood Top Five

1 Throwing yourself head first into the artistic vortex of the **Kunsthistorisches Museum** (p113), a whirl of Habsburg treasures from Egyptian tombs to rare breed Raphael, Dürer and Caravaggio masterworks.

2 Checking Vienna's cultural pulse with an art-packed day at the vast **MuseumsQuartier** (p119).

3 Making a date with the dinosaurs and prehistoric divas at the **Naturhistorisches Museum** (p122).

4 Revelling in the neo-Gothic riches of the **Rathaus** (p123) on a free guided tour.

5 Going on a crafty walk through the cobbled backstreets of the Biedermeier **Spittelberg neighbourhood**.

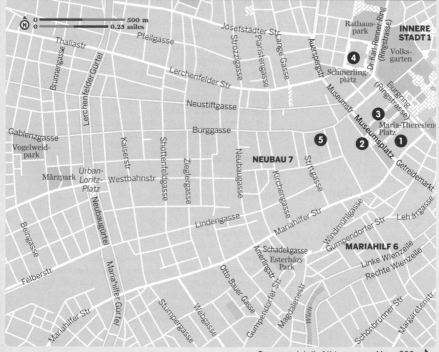

For more detail of this area see Map p260 ➡

Lonely Planet's Top Tip

If you want more of an insight into the neighbourhood's sights, time your visit to catch one of the free guided tours. Gallery tours that won't cost you a cent include those at the Leopold Museum at 3pm on Sunday and the MUMOK at 2pm on Saturday and Sunday and 7pm on Thursday. Best of all are the gratis guided tours of the neo-Gothic Rathaus at 1pm on Monday, Wednesday and Friday.

 Best Places to Eat

➜ Amerlingbeisl (p126)

➜ Pizzeria-Osteria Da Giovanni (p126)

➜ M Lounge (p126)

➜ Gaumenspiel (p128)

For reviews, see p126 ➡

 Best Places to Drink

➜ Dachboden (p128)

➜ Loft (p128)

➜ Café Leopold (p128)

➜ Rote Bar (p128)

➜ Europa (p128)

For reviews, see p128 ➡

 Best Entertainment

➜ Burgtheater (p130)

➜ Volkstheater (p130)

➜ Vienna's English Theatre (p130)

➜ Tanzquartier Wien (p130)

For reviews, see p130 ➡

THE MUSEUM DISTRICT & NEUBAU

Explore the Museum District & Neubau

The Museum District and Neubau walk a fine line between Habsburg history and modernity. The baroque imperial stables have been sent cantering into the 21st century with their transformation into the MuseumsQuartier, a colossal complex of on-the-pulse bars, cafes, boutiques and museums, including the Leopold, the proud holder of the world's largest Schiele collection. Hang out in the courtyards here in summer and you can almost taste the creativity in the air.

Just around the corner on Maria-Theresien-Platz is the Kunsthistorisches Museum, an epic and exhilarating journey through art, where Rubens originals star alongside Giza treasures. Its architectural twin is the neoclassical Naturhistorisches Museum opposite.

When you've had your fill of art and culture, keep tabs on Vienna's ever-evolving fashion and design scene with a mosey around Neubau's backstreet studios and boutiques. After dark, the live-wire clubs and bars tucked under the Gürtel arches, slightly west, are where the young Viennese go to party.

Local Life

➜**Schanigärten** Join the locals to toast summer at a flurry of pavement cafes and courtyard gardens, including Lux (p127) and Amerlingbeisl (p126) in Spittelberg, and Kantine (p126) and Café Leopold (p128) in the MuseumsQuartier.

➜**Neubau Design** Mill around Kirchengasse, Lindengasse, Neubaugasse and Zollergasse, where artists and creatives put a fresh take on Viennese fashion and design.

➜**Nightlife Haunts** Take the lead of locals and go west to the Gürtel to party at happening bars, like Chelsea (p129), Loft (p128) and Rhiz (p129).

Getting There & Away

➜**U-Bahn** Useful U-Bahn stops include Museumsquartier and Volkstheater on the U2 line. The U3 Neubaugasse and Zieglergasse stops, and the U6 stops Burggasse Stadthalle and Thaliastrasse are best for accessing Neubau.

➜**Tram** Trams 1, 2 and D race you around the Ringstrasse, stopping at Rathaus, Dr-Karl-Renner-Ring and Parlament en route. The 49 line trundles from Dr-Karl-Renner-Ring through Neubau, with handy stops including Stiftgasse, Siebensterngasse and Neubaugasse/Westbahnstrasse.

TOP SIGHT
KUNSTHISTORISCHES MUSEUM

The Habsburgs built many a bombastic palace but, artistically speaking, the Kunsthistorisches Museum is their magnum opus. Occupying a neoclassical building as sumptuous as the art it contains, the museum takes you on a time-travel treasure hunt – from classical Rome to Egypt and the Renaissance. If time is an issue, skip straight to the Old Master paintings in the Picture Gallery. There's enough art here to last anyone a lifetime, so all the more reason to return.

Picture Gallery

The Kunsthistorisches Museum's vast Picture Gallery is by far and away the most impressive of its collections. Devote at least an hour or two to exploring its feast of Old Master paintings.

Dutch, Flemish & German Painting

First up is the **German Renaissance**, where Lucas Cranach the Elder stages an appearance with engaging Genesis tableaux such as *Paradise* (1530) and *Adam and Eve* (1520). The key focus, though, is the prized Dürer collection. Dürer's powerful compositions, sophisticated use of light and deep feeling for his subjects shine through in masterful pieces such as *Portrait of a Venetian Lady* (1505), the spirit-soaring *Adoration of the Trinity* (1511) and the macabre *Martyrdom of the Ten Thousand* (1508).

Rubens throws you in the deep end of **Flemish baroque** painting next, with paintings rich in Counter-Reformation themes and mythological symbolism. The monumental *Miracle of St Francis Xavier* (1617), which used to hang in Antwerp's Jesuit church, the celestial *The Annunciation*

DON'T MISS...

➡ Dutch Golden Age paintings
➡ Italian, Spanish & French collection
➡ Kunstkammer
➡ Offering Chapel of Ka-ni-nisut

PRACTICALITIES

➡ Museum of Fine Arts
➡ Map p260
➡ www.khm.at
➡ 01, Maria-Theresien-Platz
➡ adult/under 19yr €14/free
➡ ◷10am-6pm Tue-Sun, to 9pm Thu
➡ Ⓜ Museumsquartier, Volkstheater

GUIDED TOURS

For more insight, pick up a multilingual audio guide (€4) near the entrance. The KHM runs free guided tours in German, from 30-minute lunchtime tours (12.30pm Tuesday and Thursday) to hour-long tours focusing on a particular artist or period (4pm Wednesday, 10.15am Friday). See www.khm. at for more details.

The Habsburgs liked to make an entrance and this is one of their finest. As you climb the ornate main staircase of the Kunsthistorisches Museum, your gaze is drawn to the ever-decreasing circles of the cupola and marble columns guide the eye to delicately frescoed vaults, roaring lions and Antonio Canova's mighty statue of *Theseus Defeating the Centaur* (1805). Austrian legends Hans Makart and the brothers Klimt have left their hallmark between the columns and above the arcades – the former with lunette paintings, the latter with gold-kissed depictions of women inspired by Greco-Roman and Egyptian art.

(1610), the *Miracles of St Ignatius* (1615) and the *Triptych of St Ildefonso* (1630) all reveal the iridescent quality and linear clarity that underscored Rubens' style. Mythological masterworks move from the gory, snake-riddled *Medusa* (1617) to the ecstatic celebration of love *Feast of Venus* (1636).

In 16th- and 17th-century **Dutch Golden Age** paintings, the desire to faithfully represent reality through an attentive eye for detail and compositional chiaroscuro is captured effortlessly in works by Rembrandt, Ruisdael and Vermeer. Rembrandt's perspicuous *Self-Portrait* (1652), showing the artist in a humble painter's smock, Van Ruisdael's palpable vision of nature in *The Large Forest* (1655) and Vermeer's seductively allegorical *The Art of Painting* (1665), showing Clio, Greek muse of history, in the diffused light of an artist's studio, are all emblematic of the age.

The final three rooms are an ode to the art of Flemish baroque master **Van Dyck** and Flemish Renaissance painter **Pieter Bruegel the Elder**. Van Dyck's keenly felt devotional works include the *Vision of the Blessed Herman* (1630), in which the Virgin and kneeling monk are bathed in radiant light, and *Madonna and Child with St Rosalie, Peter and Paul* (1629). An entire room is given over to Pieter Bruegel the Elder's vivid depictions of Flemish life and landscapes, alongside his biblical star attraction – *The Tower of Babel* (1563).

Italian, Spanish & French Painting

The first three rooms here are given over to key exponents of the **16th-century Venetian** style: Titian, Veronese and Tintoretto. High on your artistic agenda here should be Titian's *Nymph and Shepherd* (1570), elevating the pastoral to the mythological in its portrayal of the futile desire of the flute-playing shepherd for the beautiful maiden out of his reach. Veronese's dramatic depiction of the suicidal Roman heroine *Lucretia* (1583), with a dagger drawn to her chest, and Tintoretto's *Susanna at her Bath* (1556), watched by two lustful elders, are other highlights.

Devotion is central to Raphael's *Madonna of the Meadow* (1506) in room 4, one of the true masterpieces of the **High Renaissance**, just as it is to the *Madonna of the Rosary* (1603), a stirring Counter-Reformation altarpiece by **Italian baroque** artist Caravaggio in the next room. Room 7 is also a delight, with compelling works such as Giuseppe Arcimboldo's anthropomorphic paintings inspired by the seasons and elements, including fruit-filled *Summer* (1563), *Winter* (1563) and *Fire* (1566). Look out, too, for Venetian landscape painter Canaletto's *Schönbrunn* (1761), meticulously capturing the palace back in its imperial heyday.

Of the artists represented in the final rooms dedicated to **Spanish, French and English** painting, the undoubted star is Spanish court painter Velázquez. Particularly entrancing is his almost 3D portrait of *Infanta Margarita Teresa in a Blue Dress* (1673), a vision of voluminous silk and eight-year-old innocence. Gainsborough's *Suffolk Landscape* (1748), with its feather-light brushwork and suffused colours, and French baroque painter Nicolas Poussin's turbulent *Destruction of the Temple in Jerusalem* (1639) also demand attention.

Kunstkammer

Imagine the treasures you could buy with brimming coffers and the world at your fingertips. The Habsburgs did just that, filling their *Kunstkammer* (cabinet of art and curiosities) with an encyclopaedic collection of the rare and the precious: from narwhal-tusk cups to table holders encrusted with fossilised shark's teeth. In March 2013 the Kunstkammer reopened to much acclaim, with 20 themed rooms opening a fascinating window on the obsession with collecting curios in royal circles in Renaissance and baroque times.

The biggest crowd-puller here is Benvenuto Cellini's allegorical **Saliera** (salt cellar), commissioned by Francis I of France in 1540, which is exquisitely hand-crafted from rolled gold, ivory and enamel. Among the Kunstkammer's other top-drawer attractions are the wildly expressive early 17th-century ivory sculpture **Furie** (Master of the Furies), the serenely beautiful **Krumauer Madonna** (1400), a masterpiece of the Bohemian Gothic style, and Gasparo Miscroni's lapis lazuli **Dragon Cup** (1570), a fiery beast glittering with gemstones.

Egyptian & Near Eastern Collection

Decipher the mysteries of Egyptian civilisations with a chronological romp through this miniature Giza of a ground-floor collection, beginning with **pre-dynastic** and **Old Kingdom** treasures. Here the exceptionally well-preserved **Offering Chapel of Ka-ni-nisut** spells out the life of the high-ranking 5th dynasty official in reliefs and hieroglyphs. The Egyptian fondness for nature and adornment finds expression in artefacts such as a monkey-shaped kohl container and fish-shaped make-up palette.

Stele, sacrificial altar slabs, jewellery boxes, sphinx busts and pharaoh statues bring to life the **Middle Kingdom** and **New Kingdom**. The Egyptian talent for craftsmanship shines in pieces such as a turquoise ceramic hippo (2000 BC) and the gold seal ring of Ramses X (1120 BC). The **Late Period** dips into the land of the pharaohs, at a time when rule swung from Egypt to Persia. Scout out the 3000-year-old Book of the Dead Chonsu-mes, the polychrome mummy board of Nes-pauti-taui and Canopic jars with lids shaped like monkey, falcon and jackal heads.

Stone sarcophagi, gilded mummy masks and busts of priests and princes transport you back to the **Ptolemaic** and **Greco-Roman** period. In the **Near Eastern** collection, the representation of a prowling lion from Babylon's triumphal Ishtar Gate (604–562 BC) is the big attraction.

Greek & Roman Antiquities

This rich Greek and Roman repository reveals the imperial scope for collecting classical antiquities, with 2500 objects traversing three millennia from the Cypriot Bronze Age to early medieval times.

Cypriot and Mycenaean Art catapults you back to the dawn of western civilisation, 2500 years ago. The big draw here is the precisely carved votive statue of a man wearing a finely pleated tunic. Among the muses, torsos and mythological statuettes in **Greek Art** is a fragment from the Parthenon's northern frieze showing two bearded men. The arts flourished in **Hellenistic** times, evident in

HALF-DAY TOUR OF THE HIGHLIGHTS

The Kunsthistorisches Museum's scale can seem daunting; this half-day itinerary will help you make the most of your visit.

Ascend the grand marble staircase, marvelling at the impact of Antonio Canova's *Theseus Slaying the Centaur*. Turn right into the Egyptian and Near Eastern Collection, where you can decipher the reliefs of the Offering Chapel of Ka-ni-nisut **1** in room II. Skip through millennia to Ancient Rome, where

the intricacy of the Gemma Augustea Cameo **2** in room XVI is captivating. The other wing of this floor is devoted to the Kunstkammer Wien, hiding rarities such as Benvenuto Cellini's golden *Saliera* **3** in room XXIX.

Head up a level to the Picture Gallery, a veritable orgy of Renaissance and baroque art. Bearing to the East Wing brings you to Dutch, Flemish and German Painting, which starts with Dürer's spirit-lifting *Adoration of the Trinity* **4** in room XV, takes in meaty

Gemma Augustea Cameo
Greek & Roman Antiquities, Room XVI
Possibly the handiwork of imperial gem-cutter Dioscurides, this sardonyx cameo from the 1st century AD shows in exquisite bas-relief the deification of Augustus, in the guise of Jupiter, who sits next to Roma. The defeated barbarians occupy the lower tier.

LEEMAGE / GETTY IMAGES ©

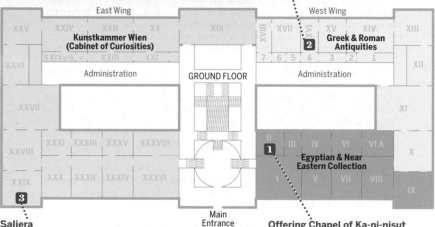

East Wing

West Wing

| XXV | XXIV | XXII | XX | | XIX | XVIII | XVII | | XV | XIV | | XIII |

Kunstkammer Wien (Cabinet of Curiosities)

2 **Greek & Roman Antiquities**

7, 6, 5, 4, 3, 2, 1

| XXVI | XXIVa/b, c | XXIII | XXI | | | | | | | | | XII |

Administration

GROUND FLOOR

Administration

XXVII

XI

| XXVIII | XXXI | XXXIII | XXXV | XXXVIII | | | | **1** | III | IV | VI | VI A | X |

Egyptian & Near Eastern Collection

| XXIX | XXX | XXXII | XXXIV | XXXVI | | | | I | | V | VII | VIII | IX |

3

Main Entrance

Saliera
Kunstkammer, Room XXIX
Benvenuto Cellini's hand-wrought gold salt cellar (1543) is a dazzling allegorical portrayal of Sea and Earth, personified by Tellus and trident-bearing Neptune. They recline on a base showing the four winds, times of day and human activities.

ASABLANCA VIA GETTY IMAGES ©

Offering Chapel of Ka-ni-nisut
Egyptian & Near Eastern Collection, Room II
Reliefs and hieroglyphs depict the life of high-ranking 5th dynasty official Ka-ni-nisut, together with his wife, children and entourage of mortuary priests and servants. This 4500-year-old tomb chamber is a spectacular leap into the afterlife.

Rubens and Rembrandt works en route, and climaxes with Pieter Bruegel the Elder's absorbingly detailed *The Tower of Babel* **5** in room X. Allot equal time to the Italian, Spanish and French masters in the halls opposite. Masterpieces including Raphael's *Madonna of the Meadow* **6** in room 4, Caravaggio's merciful *Madonna of the Rosary* **7** in room V and Giuseppe Arcimboldo's *Summer* **8** in room 7 steal the show.

TOP TIPS

➜ Pick up an audio guide and a floor plan in the entrance hall to orientate yourself.

➜ Skip to the front of the queue by booking your ticket online.

➜ Visit between 6pm and 9pm on Thursday for fewer crowds.

➜ Flash photography is not permitted.

The Tower of Babel
Dutch, Flemish & German Painting, Room X
The futile attempts of industrial souls to reach godly heights are magnified in the painstaking detail of Bruegel's *The Tower of Babel* (1563). Rome's Colosseum provided inspiration.

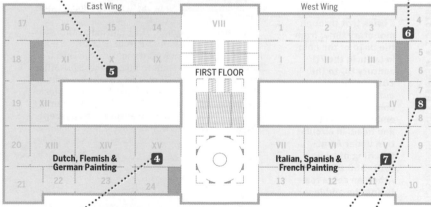

WORLD ILLUSTRATED / F PHOTOSHOT ©

Madonna of the Meadow
Italian, Spanish & French Painting, Room 4
The Virgin Mary, pictured with infants Christ and St John the Baptist, has an almost iridescent quality in Raphael's seminal High Renaissance 1506 masterpiece, set against the backdrop of a Tuscan meadow.

East Wing

17　16　15　14　VIII　1　2　3　4 **6**

18　XI　X　IX　I　II　III　5

6

7

FIRST FLOOR

IV **8**

8

19　XII

5

West Wing

20　XIII　XIV　XV　VII　VI　V **7**　9

Dutch, Flemish & German Painting **4**

Italian, Spanish & French Painting

21　22　23　24　13　12　11　10

Adoration of the Trinity
Dutch, Flemish & German Painting, Room XV
Dürer's magnum opus altarpiece was commissioned by Nuremberg merchant Matthäus Landauer in 1511. Angels, saints and earthly believers surround the Holy Trinity, while Dürer hides in the bottom right-hand corner.

PAINTING / ALAMY ©

Madonna of the Rosary
Italian, Spanish & French Painting, Room V
Caravaggio's trademark chiaroscuro style brings depth, richness and feeling to this 1607 masterpiece. Holding infant Jesus, the Madonna asks St Dominic to distribute rosaries to the barefooted poor who kneel before her.

Summer
Italian, Spanish & French Painting, Room 7
Italian court painter Giuseppe Arcimboldo's *Summer* (1563) was a hit with the Habsburgs. The most striking of his four seasons cycle, this masterwork celebrates seasonal abundance in the form of a portrait composed of fruit and vegetables.

COIN COLLECTION

A piggy bank of gigantic Habsburg proportions, this Coin Collection is one of the world's best. Covering three halls and three millennia on the 3rd floor, the 2000 notes, coins and medallions on display are just a tiny fraction of the Kunsthistorisches Museum's 700,000-piece collection.

The first hall of the coin collection presents medals of honour, first used in Renaissance Italy around 1400, and showcases gold and silver House of Habsburg wonders. The second hall takes a brisk trot through monetary time, from the birth of the coin in Lydia in the 7th century BC to the 20th century. Look out for classical coins, like the stater embellished with a lion head, in circulation under Alyattes, King of Lydia (619–560 BC), and Athenian coins featuring the goddess Athena and her pet owl. The third hall is devoted to one-off exhibitions.

Egyptian & Near Eastern Collection (p115)

exhibits like the *Amazonian Sarcophagus*, engraved with warriors so vivid you can almost hear their battle cries. In **pre-Roman Italy**, look for sculptures of Athena, funerary crowns intricately wrought from gold, and a repoussé showing the Titans doing battle with the Gods.

The sizeable **Roman** stash includes the 4th-century AD *Theseus Mosaic* from Salzburg, a polychrome, geometric marvel recounting the legend of Theseus. You'll also want to take in the captivating 3rd-century AD *Lion Hunt* relief and the 1st-century AD *Gemma Augustea*, a sardonyx bas-relief cameo. Early medieval show-stoppers include the shimmering golden vessels from the **Treasure of Nagyszentmiklós**, unearthed in 1799 in what is now Romania.

<table>
<tr><td>👁</td><td>TOP SIGHT
MUSEUMSQUARTIER</td></tr>
</table>

One of the world's most ambitious cultural spaces, the MuseumsQuartier (MQ) is where baroque heritage spectacularly collides with the avant-garde. Spanning 90,000 sq metres, this remarkable ensemble of museums, cafes, restaurants, shops, bars and performing arts venues occupies the former imperial stables designed by Fischer von Erlach in 1725. You can't see it all in a day, so selectively is the way to go. Here is a taste of what is in store.

Leopold Museum

The **Leopold Museum** (www.leopoldmuseum.org; adult/child €12/7, audio guide €3; ⏰10am-6pm Wed-Mon, to 9pm Thu, guided tours in German 3pm Sun) is named after Rudolf Leopold, a Viennese ophthalmologist who, on buying his first Egon Schiele (1890–1918) for a song as a young student in 1950, started to amass a huge private collection of mainly 19th-century and modernist Austrian artworks. In 1994 he sold the lot – 5266 paintings – to the Austrian government for €160 million (sold individually, the paintings would have made him €574 million), and the Leopold Museum was born. Café Leopold (p128) is located on the top floor.

The Leopold has a white limestone exterior, open space (the 21m-high glass-covered atrium is lovely) and natural light flooding most rooms. Considering Rudolf Leopold's love of Schiele, it's no surprise the museum contains the world's largest collection of the painter's work: 41 paintings and 188 drawings and graphics. Among the standouts are the ghostly *Self Seer II Death and Man* (1911), the mournful *Mother with Two Children* (1915) and the caught-in-the-act *Cardinal and Nun* (1912).

DON'T MISS...

→ Schiele collection at the Leopold Museum

→ Viennese Actionism at the MUMOK

→ Cafe life in the courtyard in summer

PRACTICALITIES

→ Museum Quarter

→ Map p260

→ www.mqw.at

→ 07, Museumsplatz

→ combined ticket €25

→ ⏰info & ticket centre 10am-7pm

→ Ⓜ Museumsquartier, Volkstheater; 🚋49 Volkstheater

CHILDREN'S THEATRE

Dschungel Wien
(☑522 07 2020; www.
dschungelwien.at; adult/
child €14/8.50; ☻box
office 2.30-6.30pm Mon-
Fri, 4.30-6.30pm Sat &
Sun) covers the entire
spectrum, from drama
and puppetry through
to music, dance and
narrative theatre. There
are generally several
performances daily in
German and occasion-
ally in English; see the
website for details.
Adults pay children's
prices for matinee
performances.

**The MQ's courtyards
host a winter and
summer program of
events, from film fes-
tivals to Christmas
markets, and from
literary readings to
DJ nights; see the
website www.mqw.at
for details. They
are also a popular
hangout in the sum-
mer months when the
cafe terraces hum
with life.**

Other artists well represented include Albin Egger-Lienz, with his unforgiving depictions of pastoral life, Richard Gerstl and Austria's third-greatest expressionist, Kokoschka. Of the handful of works on display by Klimt, the unmissable is the allegorical *Death and Life* (1910), a swirling amalgam of people juxtaposed by a skeletal grim reaper. Works by Loos, Hoffmann, Otto Wagner, Waldmüller and Romako are also on display.

MUMOK

The dark basalt edifice and sharp corners of the **Museum moderner Kunst** (Museum of Modern Art; www.mumok.at; adult/child €10/free, 1hr tours free; ☻2-7pm Mon, 10am-7pm Tue-Sun, to 9pm Thu, free guided tours 1pm Fri, 2pm & 4pm Sat & Sun, 7pm Thu) are a complete contrast to the MQ's historical sleeve. Inside, MUMOK is crawling with Vienna's finest collection of 20th-century art, centred on Fluxus, nouveau realism, pop art and photo-realism. The best of expressionism, cubism, minimal art and Viennese Actionism is represented in a collection of 9000 works that are rotated and exhibited by theme – but take note that sometimes all this Actionism is packed away to make room for temporary exhibitions. Viennese Actionism evolved in the 1960s as a radical leap away from mainstream art in what some artists considered to be a restrictive cultural and political climate. Artists such as Günter Brus, Otto Mühl, Hermann Nitsch and Rudolf Schwarzkogler aimed to shock with their violent, stomach-churning performance and action art, which often involved using the human body as a canvas. They were successful: not only did their work shock, some artists were even imprisoned for outraging public decency. Other well-known artists represented throughout the museum – Picasso, Paul Klee, René Magritte, Max Ernst and Alberto Giacometti – are positively tame in comparison.

Kunsthalle

The **Kunsthalle** (Arts Hall; ☑521 890; www.kunsthalle-wien.at; adult/child €8/2; ☻10am-7pm Fri-Wed, to 9pm Thu) is a collection of exhibition halls used to showcase local and international contemporary art. Its high ceilings, open planning and functionality have helped the venue leapfrog into the ranks of the top exhibition spaces in Europe. Programs, which run for three to six months, rely heavily on photography, video, film, installations and new media. Weekend visits cost €1 more, but German-language guided tours are included. The Saturday tours (Halle 1 at 3pm, Halle 2 at 4pm) focus on a theme, while Sunday tours (same times) give an overview.

MUSEUMSQUARTIER COMPLEX

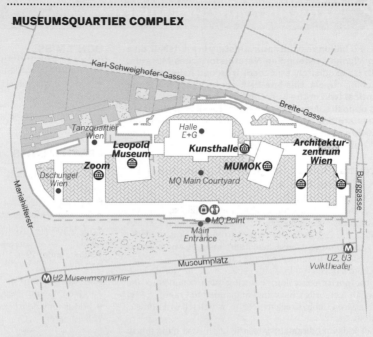

Architekturzentrum Wien

The **Architekturzentrum Wien** (Vienna Architecture Centre; ☎522 31 15; www.azw.at; adult/child 1 exhibition €7/4.50, 2 exhibitions €9/6.50; ☻10am-7pm) takes up much of the MQ north of MUMOK, encompassing three halls used for temporary exhibitions, a library and a cafe. Exhibitions focus on international architectural developments, and change on a regular basis. The library is open to the public from 10am to 5.30pm Monday, Wednesday and Friday and until 7pm on Saturday and Sunday. The centre also organises walking tours (in German) through Vienna on Sunday, covering various architectural themes. You need to book ahead; see the website for information.

Zoom

Kids love this hands-on **children's museum** (☎524 79 08; www.kindermuseum.at; exhibition adult/child €4/free, activities child €4-€6, accompanying adult free; ☻8.45am-4pm Tue-Fri, 9.45am-4pm Sat & Sun, activity times vary), an arts and crafts session with lots of play thrown in. Budding Picassos have the chance to make, break, draw, explore and be creative in the 'Atelier.' 'Exhibition' stages a new exhibition every six months, while 'Ocean' appeals to tots with its mirrored tunnels, grottos and ship deck for adventure play that stimulates coordination. For children aged eight to 14, there is an animated film studio and the future-focused Lab Club.

MQ TICKETS & INFORMATION

Planning on visiting several museums? Combined tickets are available from the **MQ Point** (Map p260; ☎523 58 81-17 31, in Austria 0820 600 600; www.mqw.at; 07, Museumsplatz 1; ☻10am-7pm; Ⓜ Museumsquartier, Volkstheater).

TOP SIGHT
NATURHISTORISCHES MUSEUM

For four billion years of natural history in a nutshell, dive into Vienna's astounding Naturhistorisches Museum. With its exquisitely stuccoed, frescoed halls and eye-catching cupola, this late-19th-century building is the identical twin of the Kunsthistorisches Museum which sits opposite. Among its minerals, fossils and dinosaur bones are one-of-a-kind finds such as the miniscule, 25,000-year-old Venus von Willendorf and a peerless 1100-piece meteorite collection.

Ground Floor: Meteorites, Dinosaurs & Prehistoric Finds

The ground floor leads in with a treasure chest of minerals, fossils and gemstones, with star exhibits such as the 115kg chunk of smoky quartz from Switzerland's Tiefen glacier, a 6.2kg platinum nugget from the Urals and the dazzling 'Blumenstrauss' gemstone bouquet which Maria Theresia gave to Emperor Franz I in 1760.

Room 5 blasts you into outer space with the world's largest **meteorite** collection, featuring such beauties as the Martian meteorite Chassigny that landed in France in 1815 and the iron Cabin Creek meteorite, which fell in Arkansas in 1886.

For kids and **dinosaur** fans, the big-hitters hang out in room 10 on the ground floor. On a raised platform loom the skeletons of a diplodocus, iguanodon and a 6m-tall animatronic replica of an allosaurus. Keep an eye out, too, for the skeleton of an archelonischyros, the largest turtle ever.

Rooms 11 to 13 spell out **prehistory** in artefacts, with curiosities such as the coat of a woolly mammoth and Neanderthal tools. Two of the museum's tiniest stunners vie for attention here: the buxom Stone Age starlet the Venus of Willendorf, just 11cm tall, and her curvy, 32,000-year-old rival Fanny of Galgenberg, one of the world's oldest female statuettes, named after famous Viennese dancer Fanny Elster (1810–84).

Occupying rooms 14 to 15, the **anthropological collection**, which reopened in January 2013, brings to life hominid evolution and themes such as bipedalism and brain development at hands-on stations. You can determine the gender, age and cause of death of a virtual skeleton at the CSI table, take and email a prehistoric photo of yourself and spot the difference between Neanderthals and Homo sapiens by touching skulls.

First Floor: Zoology

The 1st floor is a taxidermist's dream. Spotlighting zoology and entomology, the collection slithers, rattles, crawls, swims and swings with common, endangered and extinct species, from single-cell organisms to large mammals. Show-stoppers include a 1.4m-long giant clam in room 23, a 5.5m Amazonian anaconda in room 27, a Galapagos giant tortoise in room 28 and two-toed sloths, found in 1831 in Brazil, in room 33.

DON'T MISS...

➡ Meteorite collection
➡ Venus of Willendorf and Fanny of Galgenberg
➡ Dinosaurs in room 10

PRACTICALITIES

➡ Museum of Natural History
➡ Map p260
➡ www.nhm-wien.ac.at
➡ 01, Maria-Theresien-Platz
➡ adult/under 19yr €10/free
➡ ⏱9am-6.30pm Thu-Mon, to 9pm Wed
➡ Ⓜ Museumsquartier, Volkstheater

👁 SIGHTS

KUNSTHISTORISCHES MUSEUM MUSEUM
See p113.

MUSEUMSQUARTIER MUSEUM
See p119.

NATURHISTORISCHES MUSEUM MUSEUM
See p122.

HOFMOBILIENDEPOT MUSEUM
Map p260 (www.hofmobiliendepot.at; 07, Andreas-gasse 7; adult/child €8.50/6; ⏰10am-6pm Tue-Sun; Ⓜ Neubaugasse) The Habsburgs stashed away the furniture not displayed in the Hofburg, Schönbrunn, Schloss Belvedere or their other palaces at the Hofmobiliendepot. A romp through this regal attic of a museum, covering four floors, gives a fascinating insight into furniture design, with highlights such as a display of imperial travelling thrones, Emperor Maximilian's coffin and Empress Elisabeth's neo-Renaissance bed from Gödöllő Castle.

Biedermeier aficionados will gravitate to the 2nd floor, where over a dozen rooms are beautifully laid out in the early 19th-century style, and a few dozen chairs from the era can be tested by visitors. In all, it's the most comprehensive collection of Biedermeier furniture in the world. The 4th floor displays *Jugendstil* (art nouveau) furniture from the likes of Otto Wagner, Loos and Hoffmann.

This, one of the more underrated museums in the city, is included in the Sisi Ticket.

BURGTHEATER THEATRE
Map p260 (🗘514 44 4140; www.burgtheater.at; 01, Dr-Karl-Lueger-Ring; tours adult/child €5.50/2; ⏰tours 3pm Sep-Jun; Ⓜ Rathaus, 🚋 D, 1, 2 Rathaus) This stately Renaissance-style theatre sits with aplomb on the Ringstrasse. Designed by Gottfried Semper and Karl Hasenauer in 1888, it was restored to its pre-WWII glory in 1955. The company dates to 1741, making it Europe's second oldest. If walls could speak, these would tell of musical milestones like the premiere of Mozart's *Marriage of Figaro* (1786) and Beethoven's 1st Symphony (1800).

For a behind-the-scenes look at this magnificent theatre, join one of the regular **guided tours**, which zip through its history, architecture and technological wizardry. Besides taking in portraits of famous Austrian actors and busts of well-known playwrights, you'll get to appreciate

👁 TOP SIGHT
RATHAUS

The crowning glory of the Ringstrasse boulevard's 19th-century architectural ensemble, Vienna's neo-Gothic City Hall was completed in 1883 by Friedrich von Schmidt of Cologne Cathedral fame and modelled on Flemish city halls. From **Rathauspark**, you get the full-on effect of its facade of lacy stonework, pointed-arch windows and spindly turrets. The main spire is 102m high if you include the pennant held by the **Rathaus-mann** (medieval knight) guarding its tip.

For an insight into the Rathaus' history, take the free guided tour that leads through the **Arkadenhof**, one of Europe's biggest arcaded inner courtyards, and the barrel-vaulted **Festsaal** (Festival Hall), which hosts the Concordia Ball in June. Look for the reliefs of composers Mozart, Haydn, Gluck and Schubert in the orchestra niches. In the **Stadtsitzungssaal** (Council Chamber), a 3200kg flower-shaped chandelier dangles from a coffered ceiling encrusted with gold-leaf rosettes and frescoes depicting historic events such as the foundation of the university in 1365. Other tour highlights include the **Stadtsenatssitzungssaal** (Senate Chamber), the **Wappensäle** (Coat of Arms Halls) and the **Steinsäle** (Stone Halls).

DON'T MISS...
➡ Rathauspark
➡ Arkadenhof
➡ Festsaal
➡ Stadtsitzungssaal

PRACTICALITIES
➡ City Hall
➡ Map p260
➡ 🗘525 50
➡ www.wien.gv.at
➡ 01, Rathausplatz 1
➡ ⏰guided tours 1pm Mon, Wed & Fri
➡ Ⓜ Rathaus, 🚋 D, 1, 2 Rathaus

THE MUSEUM DISTRICT & NEUBAU SIGHTS

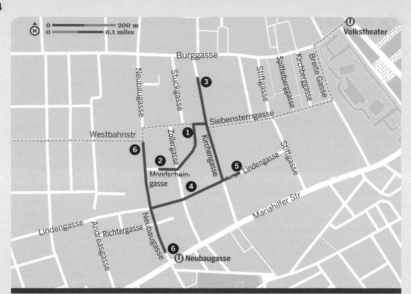

Local Life
Neubau's Design Scene

There's no better place to tap into Vienna's burgeoning fashion and design scene than the happening 7th district, Neubau. This half-day stroll takes you to boutiques showcasing creations by the pick of the city's designers, ateliers and fashion-focused cafes. For the inside scoop, visit www.7tm.at.

❶ Siebensterngasse Stroll

Schauraum (Map p260; www.schauraum. co.at; 07, Siebensterngasse 33; ⊙11am-6pm Mon-Thu; Ⓜ Volkstheater, ☒49 Siebensterngasse) zooms in on unusual applied arts. Besides cutting-edge tableware and accessories, you'll find Karin Merkl's clever, versatile jumpers, scarves and jackets made from merino wool or silk.

❷ Catwalk Trends

Around the corner on Mondscheingasse is **Park** (Map p260; www.park.co.at; 07, Mondscheingasse 20; ⊙10am-7pm Mon-Fri, to 6pm Sat; Ⓜ Neubaugasse), a serious designer store in a snow-white 500-sq-metre space. Here you can swoon over fashion from emerging designers alongside accessories and labels from such catwalk royalty as Ann Demeulemeester and Raf Simons.

❸ Kirchengasse Cool

Retrace your steps to Kirchengasse and graphic-design-studio-cum-gift-store **Le**

Shop (Map p260; http://le-shop.at; 07, Kirchengasse 40; ⊙11am-7pm Tue-Fri, to 6pm Sat; Ⓜ Volkstheater, ☒49 Siebensterngasse) ✎ for fresh-faced, ecofriendly homewares and accessories. Next door at the **Schmuckladen** (Map p260; www.schmuckladen.org; 07, Kirchengasse 40; ⊙1-7pm Wed, 10am-7pm Tue-Fri, 10am-5pm Sat; Ⓜ Volkstheater, ☒49 Siebensterngasse) workshop, goldsmith Ilga puts her own imaginative spin on jewellery, from fragile silver leaf necklaces to quirky button rings.

❹ Zollergasse Creatives

Go to **Freaks & Icons** (Map p260; www. freaksandicons.com; 07, Zollergasse 12; ⊙11am-7pm Tue-Fri, to 5pm Sat; Ⓜ Neubaugasse) for individually tailored, figure-hugging women's clothing. Smooth lines and quality fabrics (raw silk, delicate wool, flowing-yet-structured cotton) dominate, yet most items sell for less than €200. Mandarina, designer and owner, is nearly always at the tiny table sewing her latest creation.

BRUNO KLOMFAR ©

Art Point

⑤ Lindengasse Styles

Top billing for fashion on Lindengasse goes to design maven **Elke Freytag** (Map p260; www.elkefreytag.com; 07, Lindengasse 14; ⊙noon-6pm Tue-Fri, 10am-3pm Sat; MNeubaugasse, ⓐ49 Siebensterngasse), whose silky, curve-enhancing creations regularly grace catwalks. Slightly further along is **Ina Kent**, whose understated clutch, shoulder and tote bags, crafted from vegetable-tanned leather, are much-coveted by locals.

⑥ New Design on Neubaugasse

On your design radar here should be **ebenBERG** (Map p256; http://ebenberg.at; 07, Neubaugasse 4; ⊙10am-7pm Mon-Fri, 11am-5pm Sat; MNeubaugasse), for fair-trade and organic fashion, and **Art Point** (Map p260; www.artpoint.eu; 07, Neubaugasse 35; ⊙11am-7pm Mon-Fri, to 5pm Sat; MNeubaugasse, ⓐ49 Neubaugasse/West-bahnstrasse). The latter is a boutique-design platform presenting Lena Kvadrat's latest Austrian-Russian collection. Versy is the hallmark, with pieces often layering fabrics so that they can be worn in different ways to create a look that is urban, playful and three-dimensional.

the full-on effect of the foyer ceiling frescoes painted by the Klimt brothers. English tours run Friday to Sunday only; otherwise they are in German with English summary.

PARLAMENT — LANDMARK

Map p260 (☑401 10 2400; www.parlament.gv.at; 01, Dr-Karl-Renner-Ring 3; tours adult/under 19yr €5/free, visitor centre admission free; ⊙guided tours hourly 11am-4pm Mon-Sat, visitor centre 8.30am-6.30pm Mon-Fri, 9.30am-4.30pm Sat; MRathaus, Volkstheater, ⓐD, 1, 2 Rathaus/Parlament) The Parlament building opposite the Volksgarten strikes a governing pose over the Ringstrasse. Its neoclassical facade and Greek pillars, designed by Theophil Hansen in 1883, are striking, and the beautiful **Athena Fountain**, sculpted by Karl Kundmann, which guards the building, offsets it magnificently.

The **visitor centre** directly behind Athena is where you can find out about the history of Austrian politics and how parliament runs, from a multimedia show of video clips and interactive screens. A 55-minute **guided tour**, available in German or English, gives insight into the inner workings of this political powerhouse.

PALAIS EPSTEIN — LANDMARK

Map p260 (☑401 10 2400; www.palaisepstein.at; 01, Dr-Karl-Renner-Ring 1; tours adult/child €4/2, combined Parlament €7/3; ⊙tours 11am & 2pm Sat mid-Sep–mid-Jul; MVolkstheater, ⓐD, 1, 2 Dr-Karl-Renner-Ring) Designed by Theophil von Hansen, the same architect who created the plans for Austria's national Parlament, Palais Epstein houses part of the Austrian national parliament and you can take tours (in German) through its hallowed halls (the glass atrium rises an impressive four floors) and visit its *bel étage* rooms. The only way to see inside is by taking a tour.

With a filigree ceiling of gold lacework and circular frescoes (Hansen based it on detail in the Santa Maria dei Miracoli in Venice), the *Spielzimmer* (play room) is one highlight. There are no tours when the parliament is in session.

JUSTIZPALAST — LANDMARK

Map p260 (☑521 52-0; www.ogh.gv.at; 01, Schmerlingplatz 11; ⊙7.30am-4pm Mon-Fri; MVolkstheater, ⓐD, 1, 2 Burgring) Completed in 1881, the Justizpalast is home to the supreme court. It's an impressive neo-Renaissance building that – as long as you're not being dragged in wearing handcuffs – is also

THE MUSEUM DISTRICT & NEUBAU SIGHTS

interesting inside. The 23m-high central hall is a majestic ensemble of staircase, arcades, glass roofing and a statue of Justitia poised with her sword and law book.

The canteen on the top floor is open to the general public and has great views across the Hofburg. To enter, you pass through airport-type security.

HAUPTBÜCHEREI WIEN LIBRARY

Map p260 (www.buechereien.wien.at; 07, Urban-Loritz-Platz; ⊙11am-7pm Mon-Fri, to 5pm Sat; MBurggasse Stadthalle) Vienna's central city library straddles the U6 line, its pyramid like steps leading up to the enormous main doors, which are two storeys tall. At the top of the library is the Café Oben (p129), which has far-reaching views to the south.

✕ EATING

Spittelberg's warren of narrow lanes and the streets fanning west of the MuseumsQuartier, between Burggasse and Mariahilfer Strasse, are packed with restaurants, cafes and bars, many of which offer inexpensive lunch menus.

PIZZERIA-OSTERIA DA GIOVANNI ITALIAN €

Map p260 (2523 77 78; www.giovanniwien.com; 07, Sigmundsgasse 14; pizza €4.60-10.70, mains €16-19; ⊙6-11.30pm Mon-Thu, noon-3pm & 6-11.30pm Fri & Sat; ⚑; MVolkstheater, ⏛49 Stiftgasse) A slice of the south in the cobbled heart of Spittelberg, this homely Italian job rolls out pizzas just as they ought to be: thin, crisp and topped with mozzarella. The pasta is homemade, the fish grilled to a T and the panna cotta dreamily smooth. The handful of tables fills in a flash, so it's worth booking.

KANTINE CAFE €

Map p260 (2523 82 39; www.mq-kantine.at; 07, Museumsplatz 1; mains €7-10; ⊙9am-2am Mon-Sun; ⚑⚑; MMuseumsquartier) This upbeat cafe-bar housed in the former stables of the emperor's personal steeds is the most laid-back spot to eat in the MuseumsQuartier.

Lit by a disco ball, the vaulted interior has comfy chairs for lounging, surfing and refuelling over a salad, pita wrap or cocktail. In summer, folk spill out onto the patio on MuseumsQuartier's main square.

ST JOSEF VEGETARIAN €

Map p260 (2526 68 18; 07, Mondscheingasse 10; plate small/large €6.80/8.20; ⊙8am-5pm Mon-Fri, to 4pm Sat; ⚑; MNeubaugasse, ⏛49 Siebensterngasse) St Josef is a canteen-like vegetarian place that cooks to a theme each day (Indian, for instance) and gives you the choice of a small or large plate filled with the various delights. It has a sparse, industrial character, which is part of its charm, a young and arty vibe, and super-friendly staff.

DIE BURGERMACHER BURGERS €

Map p260 (www.dieburgermacher.at; 07, Burggasse 12; burgers €8.50-10; ⊙5.30-10.30pm Tue-Fri, 12.30-10.30pm Sat; ⚑; MVolkstheater) The burgers at this small, alternative joint are made using organic ingredients and served in meat and vegetarian varieties, from halloumi cheese to Mexican varieties. If you can't get a table, grab a spot at the side bench or get takeaway.

AMERLINGBEISL AUSTRIAN €€

Map p260 (2526 16 60; www.amerlingbeisl.at; 07, Stiftgasse 8; mains €7-14; ⊙9am-2am; ⚑; MVolkstheater, ⏛49 Stiftgasse) Wiener whisper quietly about this tucked-away Spittelberg *Beisl* (bistro pub), an enchanting summer choice for its cobbled, lantern-lit courtyard swathed in ivy and vines. The seasonally inspired food hits the mark, too, whether you opt for pasta such as fettuccine with wild garlic or light mains like salad with smoked trout filet. Sunday brunch (€10.90) is popular, as is the weekly cocktail special (€4.10).

M LOUNGE INTERNATIONAL €€

Map p260 (2524 93 16; http://hackl-gastro.at; 07, Hermanngasse 31; tapas €3-4.50; ⊙4pm-1am Mon-Thu, to 2am Fri & Sat; MNeubaugasse) This contemporary lounge-style restaurant is quite the gourmet globetrotter, whisking you around the world in mini portions. The inventive tapas-style concept means you can try the likes of Thai tom yum soup, potato puree with veal schnitzel, Indian butter chicken and risotto with pesto all in the same sitting. Bartenders mix up a mean cocktail at the strikingly lit bar.

GLACIS BEISL — BISTRO PUB €€

Map p260 (☑526 56 60; www.glacisbeisl.at; 07, Breite Gasse 4; mains €7.50-17.50; ☺11am-2am Mon-Sun; ☑; ⓂVolkstheater) Hidden downstairs along Breite Strasse (follow the signs from MUMOK) in the MuseumsQuartier, Glacis Beisl does an authentic goulash, an accomplished Wiener Schnitzel and some other very decent Austrian classics, which you can wash down with excellent Austrian reds and whites. If you're staying immediately in the area, the chances are high this one will evolve into your regular *Beisl*.

HALLE — INTERNATIONAL €€

Map p260 (☑523 70 01; ww2.diehalle.at; 07, Museumsplatz 1; midday menus €8.50-9.50, mains €9-20; ☺10am-2am Mon-Sun; ☏☑; ⓂMuseumsquartier) Halle is the versatile resident eatery of the Kunsthalle, with a good buzz and optical tricks like cylindrical lamps and low tables. The chefs churn out antipasti, risottos, pastas, salads, plus several Austrian all-rounders such as goulash and pan-Asian dishes. On steamy summer days it's usually a fight for an outside table between the Kunsthalle and MUMOK.

LUX — BISTRO PUB €€

Map p260 (☑526 94 91; www.luxwien.at; 07, Schrankgasse 4; lunch menu €8.40, mains €10-20; ☺5pm-1am Wed-Sat, 10am-1am Sun; ☏☑; ⓂVolkstheater, ◻49 Stiftgasse) Lux combines a cafe-bar and a modern bistro in the French mould, with wood floors and cheek-by-jowl tables. Slow food is the watchword in the kitchen, which plays up seasonal and organic ingredients in dishes such as catfish fillet with porcini mushrooms and truffle ravioli with parsnip puree. Wine starts at a reasonable €1.90 per glass. There's alfresco seating in summer.

MASCHU MASCHU II — MIDDLE EASTERN €€

Map p260 (☑990 47 13; www.maschu-maschu.at; 07, Neubaugasse 20; falafel €4.50-7, mains €9.80-18.20; ☺10.30am-midnight; ☑; ⓂNeubaugasse) This branch of the Maschu Maschu takeaway in the Innere Stadt is a fully fledged restaurant, with sunny streetside seating –

TOP LUNCH SPOTS

We've combed the backstreets of Neubau to find the best spots for a light bite or lunch. Rest your shop- or museum-weary feet at the following places.

Liebling (Map p260; ☑0699-1147 8004; 07, Zollergasse 6; lunch specials €3-5; ☺11am-2am Mon-Sat; ☑; ⓂNeubaugasse) There's no sign hanging above the door at Liebling, where distressed walls and a mishmash of flea-market furniture create a funkily shabby backdrop. Come to read the papers, sip fresh-squeezed juices and lunch on wholesome day specials such as spinach and feta strudel, polished off with a slice of chocolate and lavender cake.

Bizzo (Map p260; 07, Zollergasse 4; mains €7-11; ☺9am-9pm Mon-Sat; ☑⊞; ⓂNeubaugasse) ✔ Next door to Liebling, this pared-down, kid-friendly cafe whips up tasty lunches in an open kitchen using all-organic produce. Homemade pasta is always a good bet, as are the organic beers and juices. There's always a vegetarian option.

Gradwohl (07, Zieglergasse 1; snacks €1-3; ☺7am-6pm Mon-Fri, to noon Sat; ⓂZieglergasse) ✔ Organic wholegrain bread is what this bakery is known for. It's a quick, healthy snack spot for a freshly prepared sandwich or baguette, just off Mariahilfer Strasse.

Tart'a Tata (Map p260; 07, Lindengasse 35; snacks €3-6; ☺8am-7pm Mon-Sat, 9am-2pm Sun; ⓂNeubaugasse) This retro-cool French cafe wouldn't look out of place in the Marais. It does a delectable line in quiches, crêpes, pure-butter croissants and patisserie, including a superb *tarte aux fraises* (strawberry tart).

Spirali (Map p260; ☑890 21 26; ww.spirali.at; 07, Kirchengasse 22; lunch mains €6.80-8.60 ; ☺10am-5pm Mon-Sat; ☑; ⓂNeubaugasse) High ceilings and bursts of lime green define this modern cafe. Lunch menus are appetising and inexpensive, moving from Greek antipasti to herby homemade pasta. Vegetarians are well catered for.

when the weather's playing along – and a menu loaded with lamb dishes. Punters looking out for Vienna's best falafel should drop by here first for some of the best around.

KONOBA
DALMATIAN €€

Map p260 (☎929 41 11; www.konoba.at; 08, Lerchenfelder Strasse 66-68; mains €11.50-19; ⏰5pm-midnight Mon-Sun; ☑; Ⓜ Thaliastrasse) Few restaurants in the city come close to Konoba's expertise with fish. The Dalmatian chefs know their product inside out and serve some of the freshest catch in town. Zander and *Goldbrasse* (sea bream) are often on the menu, but expect to find a healthy array of seasonal dishes too. The open-plan interior creates a convivial atmosphere.

GAUMENSPIEL
INTERNATIONAL €€€

Map p260 (☎526 11 08; www.gaumenspiel.at; 07, Zieglergasse 54; menus €38-48, mains €19.50-25; ⏰6pm-midnight Mon-Sat; ☑; Ⓜ Burggasse Stadthalle, 🚃49 Westbahnstrasse/Zieglergasse) There's a real neighbourly feel to this *Beisl*, where a red-walled, wood-floored interior and tiny courtyard garden create a pleasantly low-key backdrop for fine dining. The menu changes regularly and Mediterranean-Austrian specialities reveal an attentive eye for quality, detail and presentation – be it goat's cheese soufflé with dates or wild duck with rose-hip–red cabbage and mandarin polenta.

VESTIBÜL
INTERNATIONAL €€€

Map p260 (☎532 49 99; www.vestibuel.at; 01, Dr-Karl-Lueger-Ring 2; evening menus €49-59, mains €15-41; ⏰noon-midnight Mon-Fri, 6pm-midnight Sat; ☑; Ⓜ Rathaus, 🚃D, 1, 2 Rathaus, Stadiongasse) Vestibül, which takes pride of place in the southern wing of the Burgtheater, is a heady mix of marble columns and stucco topped off with a glorious sparkling mirrored bar. The menu has a strong regional and seasonal focus, so expect such dishes as black truffle with beef marrow and saffron-poached catfish with root vegetables and meadow herbs. Reservations are recommended.

🍷 DRINKING & NIGHTLIFE

★DACHBODEN
BAR

Map p260 (http://25hours-hotels.com; 07, 25hours Hotel, Lerchenfelder Strasse 1-3; ⏰2pm-1am Tue-Sat, to 10pm Sun; 📶; Ⓜ Volkstheater)

Housed in the circus-themed 25hours Hotel, Dachboden has big-top views of Vienna's skyline from its decked terrace. Inside, the decor is retro-playful, with a suspended bicycle, purple pouffes and pod-shaped rugs, as well as a kids' corner. Besides Fritz cola and an array of wines, beers and speciality teas, there are tapas-style snacks in case you get the munchies.

DJ Hermes spins jazz, soul and funk on Wednesday night.

LOFT
BAR, CLUB

Map p262 (www.theloft.at; 07, Lerchenfelder Gürtel 37; ⏰7pm-2am Tue-Thu, 8pm-4am Fri & Sat; Ⓜ Thaliastrasse) 'Working hard for better parties in Vienna' is the catchphrase of this young live wire of a Gürtel hangout and you can believe the hype. Nearly all events are free and there's something happening every night: Tuesday art-house film screenings, Wednesday acoustic gigs, Thursday table football tournaments, Friday and Saturday clubbing to DJs with a playlist jumping from electro to old school.

CAFÉ LEOPOLD
BAR, CAFE

Map p260 (www.cafe-leopold.at; 07, Museumsplatz 1; ⏰10am-2am Sun-Wed, to 4am Thu-Sat; 📶; Ⓜ Museumsquartier, Volkstheater) The pick of the MuseumsQuartier bars, Café Leopold sits high at the top of the Leopold Museum. Its design is sleek, with spacey lighting and a conservatory overlooking the action on MuseumsQuartier's square, and the atmosphere is more club than bar – DJs feature Thursday to Saturday and Sundays are given over to swing.

ROTE BAR
BAR

Map p260 (www.rotebar.at; 07, Neustiftgasse 1; ⏰10pm-2am; Ⓜ Volkstheater) This marble-, chandelier- and thick-red-velvet-curtain-bedecked space in the nether regions of the Volkstheater is a gorgeous space for cocktails or a glass of wine with antipasti. It hosts regular events, from Wednesday-night performance art sessions to Saturday dance nights with DJs, plus one-offs like Milonga nights when you can try to tango.

EUROPA
BAR, CAFE

Map p260 (07, Zollergasse 8; ⏰9am-5am; 📶; Ⓜ Neubaugasse) A long-standing fixture of the 7th district, Europa is a chilled spot any time day or night. During the sunny hours, join the relaxed set at a window table for coffee and food, and in the evening take a pew at the bar and enjoy the DJ's tunes. Breakfast, served between 9am and 3pm daily, caters to a hungover clientele; Sunday features a sumptuous breakfast buffet.

WIRR
BAR

Map p260 (www.wirr.at; 07, Burggasse 70; ⊚10am-2am Sun-Wed, to 4am Thu-Sat; Ⓜ️Volkstheater, Burggasse) On weekends it's often hard to find a seat on the vintage sofas at this colourful alternative bar. Its rooms are spacious and open, the walls are covered in local artists' work, and light snacks are available. Eclectic club nights – which range from '60s pop to Balkan rhythms – are well attended in the downstairs club.

SIEBENSTERNBRÄU
MICROBREWERY

Map p260 (www.7stern.at; 07, Siebensterngasse 19; ⊚11am-midnight; Ⓜ️Neubaugasse) You can guzzle some of Vienna's finest microbrews at this lively, no-nonsense brewpub. Besides hoppy lagers and malty ales, there are unusual varieties like hemp, chilli and wood-smoked beer. Try them with pretzels or meaty pub grub such as schnitzel, goulash and pork knuckles (mains €9 to €16.50). The courtyard garden fills quickly with Wiener beer-lovers in the warmer months.

DONAU
CLUB

Map p260 (www.donautechno.com; 07, Karl-Schweighofer-Gasse 10; ⊚8pm-4am Mon-Thu, to 6am Fri & Sat, to 2am Sun; Ⓜ️Museumsquartier) DJs spin techno to a friendly, cocktail-sipping crowd at this columned, strikingly illuminated club. It's easily missed – look for the grey metal door.

BLUE BOX
BAR

Map p260 (http://bluebox.at; 07, Richtergasse 8; ⊚10am-2am Sun-Thu, to 4am Fri & Sat; Ⓜ️Neubaugasse) Don't let the run-down appearance of Blue Box put you off. These trademarks, which seem to have been around for generations, are an integral part of the Blue Box experience. It's too small to afford dance-floor space so most guests groove to the regular DJ beats in their seats. Superb breakfasts are available from 10am to 5pm Tuesday to Sunday.

CAFÉ OBEN
CAFE

Map p260 (www.oben.at; 07, Urban-Loritz-Platz 2a; ⊚10am-11pm Mon-Thu, 9am-11pm Fri & Sat, 10am-3pm Sun; Ⓜ️Burggasse Stadthalle) Oben means 'up' and that is precisely where this

cafe is. Perched on top of the Hauptbücherei Wien, its rooftop terrace provides a sweeping vista of Vienna to the south. Come for a quiet coffee, a cocktail with a view or a good-value, two-course lunch (€6.90 to €9.80). Sunday brunch (€16.20) is extremely popular.

CHELSEA
BAR, CLUB

Map p262 (www.chelsea.co.at; 08, Lerchenfelder Gürtel 29-32; ⊚6pm-4am; Ⓜ️Josefstädter Strasse, Thaliastrasse, 🚊2 Josefstädter Strasse) Chelsea is the old, ratty dog on the Gürtel and is very much a favourite of the student/alternative scene. Posters and underground paraphernalia adorn walls, and DJs spin loud sounds (usually indie, sometimes techno) when live acts aren't playing. British and Irish beers are on tap, quite the crowd-pleaser when English Premier League and Champions League football games are broadcast.

RHIZ
BAR, CLUB

Map p262 (www.rhiz.org; 08, U-Bahnbogen (Lerchenfelder Gürtel) 37; ⊚6pm-4am Mon-Sat, to 2am Sun; 🌐; Ⓜ️Josefstädter Strasse, 🚊2 Josefstädter Strasse) Rhiz's brick arches and glass walls are reminiscent of many bars beneath the U6 line, but its status as a stalwart of the city's electronica scene gives it the edge over the competition. Black-clad boozers and an alternative set cram the interior to hear DJs and live acts year-round, while in summer the large outdoor seating area fills to overflowing.

RAUCH
JUICE BAR

Map p260 (07, Neubaugasse 13; ⊚8am-8pm Mon-Fri, 9am-7pm Sat; Ⓜ️Neubaugasse) This laid-back juice bar is the go-to place in Neubau for freshly squeezed vitamin bombs. Shakes and smoothies costing around €4 to €5 a pop include inventive concoctions like 'yoga relax' (watermelon, apple, passionfruit) and 'happy hangover' (beetroot, lime, basil and apple).

FRAUENCAFÉ
CAFE

Map p260 (http://frauencafe.com; 08, Lange Gasse 11; ⊚6pm-midnight Thu & Fri, plus special events; Ⓜ️Rathaus, Volkstheater) A strictly women-, lesbian- and transgendered-only cafe-bar, Frauencafé has long been a favourite of Vienna's lesbian scene. It has a homely, relaxed feel and is located away from the hub of gay and lesbian bars around the Rosa Lila Villa.

⭐ ENTERTAINMENT

★BURGTHEATER
THEATRE

Map p260 (National Theatre; ☑514 44 4440; www.
burgtheater.at; 01, Universitätsring 2; ☻box office
9am-5pm Mon-Fri; Ⓜ Rathaus, 🚋D, 1, 2 Rathaus)
The Burgtheater hasn't lost its touch over
the years – this is one of the foremost theatres in the German-speaking world, staging some 800 performances a year, which
reach from Shakespeare to Woody Allen
plays. The theatre also runs the 500-seater
Akademietheater, which was built between
1911 and 1913.

Tickets at the Burgtheater and Akademietheater range in price from €5 to €51, and
sell for 75% of their face value an hour before performances. Students can purchase
tickets for €8. Standing places are €2.50.
Advance bookings are recommended,
though, depending on the performance,
some last-minute tickets may be available.

VOLKSTHEATER
THEATRE

Map p260 (☑521 11-400; www.volkstheater.at; 07,
Neustiftgasse 1; ☻box office 10am-7.30pm Mon-
Sat; Ⓜ Volkstheater) With a seating capacity
close to 1000, this is one of Vienna's largest
theatres. Built in 1889, its interior is suitably grand. While most performances are
translations (anything from Woody Allen to
Ingmar Bergman to Molière), only German-
language shows are produced. Tickets range
from €11 (balcony) to €50 (stalls). Students
can buy unsold tickets for €4.60 one hour
before performances start. Advanced bookings are necessary, especially for the most
popular performances.

VIENNA'S ENGLISH THEATRE
THEATRE

Map p260 (☑402 12 60; www.englishtheatre.at;
08, Josefsgasse 12; ☻box office 10am-7.30pm
Mon-Fri, 5-7.30pm Sat performance days;
Ⓜ Rathaus, 🚋2 Rathaus/Josefstädter Strasse)
Founded in 1963, Vienna's English Theatre
is the oldest foreign-language theatre in Vienna (with the occasional show in French
or Italian). Productions range from timeless pieces, such as Shakespeare, through
to contemporary works and comedies.
Tickets are priced from €22 to €42; students receive a 20% discount and standby
tickets for €9 go on sale 15 minutes before
showtime.

TANZQUARTIER WIEN
DANCE

Map p260 (☑581 35 91; www.tqw.at; 07, Museumsplatz 1; ☻box office 9am-8pm Mon-Fri,
10am-8pm Sat; Ⓜ Museumsquartier, Volkstheater) Tanzquartier Wien, located in the
MuseumsQuartier, is Vienna's first dance
institution. It hosts an array of local and
international performances with a strong
experimental nature. Tickets range in price
from €11 to €62. Students receive advance
tickets at 30% or €7 for unsold seats 15 minutes before showtime.

🛍 SHOPPING

DIRNDLHERZ
WOMEN'S CLOTHING

Map p260 (www.dirndlherz.at; 07, Lerchenfelder
Strasse 55; ☻noon-7pm Wed-Fri, to 5pm Sat;
Ⓜ Volkstheater) Who says Heidi can't be hip?
Putting its own spin on Alpine fashion, this
boutique is crammed with one-of-a-kind
dirndls, from sassy purple-velvet bosom-
lifters to cheeky 1950s-style numbers in
gingham and dirndls emblazoned with
quirky motifs such as dogs, gauchos and
clocks. Oktoberfest-inspired accessories are
also available.

LOMOSHOP
PHOTOGRAPHY

Map p260 (www.lomography.com; 07, Museumsplatz 1; ☻11am-7pm; Ⓜ Museumsquartier,
Volkstheater) The Lomographic Society's
first ever Lomography shop is in Museums-
Quartier. Lomo is a worldwide cult and the
Lomoshop is considered its heart. There's
all manner of Lomo cameras, gadgets and
accessories for sale; an original Russian-
made Lomo will set you back around €160,
and you can get a single-use disposable
Lomo camera for €14.

DAS MÖBEL
HOMEWARES

Map p260 (http://dasmoebel.at; 07, Burggasse 10;
☻10am-midnight Mon-Sun; Ⓜ Volkstheater) Das
Möbel is more of a bar than a shop, but it
showcases some of the funkiest and most
original furniture in Vienna. Local artists
and designers fill the place with their latest creations, and it's all for sale. The bags
hanging just inside the door, also locally
designed and produced, are truly special
creations.

SCHOKOV
CHOCOLATE

Map p260 (www.schokov.com; 07, Siebensterngasse 20; ☻noon-6.30pm Mon-Fri, 10am-6pm
Sat; Ⓜ Volkstheater, 🚋49 Stiftgasse) Thomas
Kovazh turned his chocolate-making
dream into reality a few years back when he

opened this sleek gallery-style shop. Today, Schokov sells some of Vienna's best pralines and truffles, alongside top Austrian brands like Zotter and Berger. Chilli, lavender, sea-salt, potato and even pepper chocolate – you'll find them all in bar form here.

BE A GOOD GIRL   FASHION

Map p260 (www.beagoodgirl.com; 07, Westbahn-strasse 5a; ⊘10am-7pm Tue-Fri, to 4pm Sat; Ⓜ Neubaugasse, 🚋 49 Neubaugasse) You can revamp your wardrobe and get a hair cut in one fell swoop at this boutique/hair salon hybrid. Cutting-edge fashion comes in the shape of the latest collections of sassy urban labels, such as Lick My Legs and Don't Shoot the Messengers, and features alongside one-off bags, accessories, jewellery and shoes.

HOLZER GALERIE   ANTIQUES

Map p260 (www.galerieholzer.at; 07, Siebenstern-gasse 32; ⊘10am-noon & 2-6pm Mon-Fri, to 5pm Sat; Ⓜ Neubaugasse, 🚋 49 Siebensterngasse) This is the place for high-quality, highly polished furniture, ornaments, lighting and art mainly from the art deco and Bau-haus periods. If you simply must have that Josef Hoffman sideboard, shipping can be arranged. You'll also find some easier-to-transport art deco–inspired jewellery here.

SHU!   SHOES

Map p260 (www.shu.at; 07, Neubaugasse 34; ⊘noon-7pm Tue-Fri, to 5pm Sat; Ⓜ Neubaugasse) Shoe fanatics flock to this store in droves, for the latest styles by INK, Vic Matie, Gidi-gio, Flip Flop and more. In this spot for over a decade, Shu! does a fine line in men's and women's shoes.

MOT MOT   FASHION

Map p260 (www.motmotshop.com; 07, Kirchen-gasse 36; ⊘noon-6pm Tue-Fri, to 5pm Sat; Ⓜ Volks-theater, Neubaugasse) This husband-and-wife team (both former graphic designers) creates custom clothes with fun flair – each piece is screenprinted by hand on American Apparel T-shirts and sweatshirts; choose from the 20-plus designs (imagine a comic book come to life) and colours. They also sell mugs, but-tons, posters and art books.

Their creations have caught the eyes of celebrities: recent projects include printing posters for The Kills and the Black Eyed Peas.

BUCHHANDLUNG WALTHER KÖNIG   BOOKS

Map p260 (www.buchhandlung-walther-koenig.de; 07, Museumsplatz 1; ⊘10am-7pm Mon-Sat, 1-7pm Sun; Ⓜ Volkstheater, Museumsquartier) A must for coffee-table connoisseurs, this lofty 250-sq-metre space, with zinc shelves (to reflect light) and baroque touches, hosts a serious collection of books on art, photog-raphy, fashion and design theory, including a great range on the history of Austrian and Viennese art and design.

🏃 SPORTS & ACTIVITIES

WIENER EISTRAUM   SKATING

Map p260 (www.wienereistraum.at; 01, Rathaus-platz; adult/child from €4, boot hire €6.50/4; ⊘9am-10pm daily late Jan–early Mar; Ⓜ Rathaus, 🚋 D, 1, 2 Rathaus) This is not your ordinary ice-skating rink: Rathausplatz is trans-formed into two connected ice rinks in the heart of winter. It's a bit of a mecca for the city's ice-skaters, and the rinks are comple-mented by food stands, special events and *Glühwein* (mulled wine) bars. The path zig-zags through the nearby park and around the entire square and you boogie your way along to music from live DJs.

Alsergrund & the University District

Neighbourhood Top Five

1 Feeling the Freud as you explore the elegant rooms of his former **home** (p135), with exhibits providing a tantalising insight into the life and cognitive workings of the psychoanalysis godfather.

2 Tiptoeing through the baroque apartments and landscaped gardens of the **Palais Liechtenstein** (p134) on a guided tour.

3 Going for an erudite wander through the arcades and courtyards of Vienna's 650-year-old **university** (p134).

4 Taking a romp through the one-time abodes of two classical giants: **Beethoven** (p134) and **Schubert** (p134).

5 Listening to a pianist play in the vaulted, marble-columned grandeur of **Café Central** (p141).

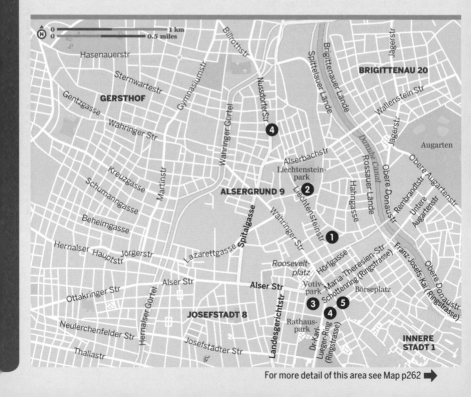

For more detail of this area see Map p262 ➡

Explore Alsergrund & the University District

Book-ended by one of Europe's biggest universities, Alsergrund in the 9th district can hold its own in the world's hall of intellectual fame, counting Mahler and Karl Kraus among its alumni. In these elegant streets, Schubert first saw the light of day and Sigmund Freud navigated the unconscious mind's murky depths. The gravitas of such history still seeps through artily shabby cafes and cavern-like bars, where students contemplate life with beer-glass-clinking conviction. University life sits neatly within the framework of this cultured neighbourhood of churches, leafy squares and gardens, such as those framing the baroque Palais Liechtenstein.

Alsergrund spills south into the 8th district, Josefstadt, which moves to a similar cool-but-not-contrived groove and is scattered with boutiques run by nascent designers, cafes and shops. On the western periphery, you slam into the bass-thumping bars and upbeat music haunts hidden under the Gürtel's railway arches. Further west still lies the 16th district, Ottakring, with its ethnically mixed markets breathing new-found trendiness into Brunnengasse and Yppenplatz.

Local Life

→ **Street Markets** Feel Vienna's multi-ethnic pulse while snacking and strolling around Brunnenmarkt (p138), and find farm-fresh produce at the Bauernmarkt (p138) and Freyung Market (p144).

→ **Backstreets** This is a terrific neighbourhood for getting off the beaten track. Slip down quiet, tree-lined backstreets to find little-known sights, like the Museum für Volkskunde (p137) and Servitenkirche (p137).

→ **Cafes** Laid-back Café Florianihof (p142), studenty Café Stein (p142) and Tunnel (p141) all have a loyal local following.

Getting There & Away

→ **U-Bahn** The closest stops to the centre for reaching Alsergrund and the university district are Schottentor and Rathaus on the U2 line. The U6 line follows the Gürtel further west, with useful stops including Alser Strasse, Josefstädter Strasse and Währingerstrasse-Volksoper.

→ **Tram** Schottentor is a handy stop on the Ring. Other tram lines serving this neighbourhood include 44, which runs from Schottentor along Alser Strasse to the Hernalser Gürtel, and 5 and 33 which trundle along Josefstädter Strasse.

Lonely Planet's Top Tip

This neighbourhood throws itself into a festive vortex from May to September when it plays host to the **Summer Stage**, with food pavilions and stages strung along the banks of the Danube Canal. The mood is incredibly upbeat, and there are regular concerts – some of which are free – reaching from jazz to tango, rock to pop. It's located on Rossauer Lände and is open in the evening between 5pm and 1am from May to September (take the U4 to Rossauer Lände). Visit the website www.summerstage.at for the inside scoop.

✕ Best Places to Eat

→ Brezl Gwölb (p138)
→ Schnattl (p140)
→ La Tavolozza (p138)
→ Kim Kocht (p141)

For reviews, see p138 ➡

🍺 Best Places to Drink

→ Café Central (p141)
→ Flex (p141)
→ Tunnel (p141)
→ Weinstube Josefstadt (p141)

For reviews, see p141 ➡

☆ Best Entertainment

→ Volksoper (p142)
→ Theater in der Josefstadt (p142)
→ B72 (p142)
→ Miles Smiles (p143)

For reviews, see p142 ➡

ALSERGRUND & THE UNIVERSITY DISTRICT

◉ SIGHTS

PALAIS LIECHTENSTEIN   PALACE

Map p262 (☏319 57 67; www.liechtensteinmu-seum.at; 09, Fürstengasse 1; tours €20; ⊘guided tours 3pm 1st & 3rd Friday of each month; MRossauer Lände, ☐D, 1 Seegasse) Once the muse of Italian landscape painter Canaletto, Palais Liechtenstein is a sublime baroque palace that sits in beautifully landscaped, sculpture-dotted grounds. The palace, containing the private collection of Prince Hans-Adam II of Liechtenstein, with around 200 paintings and 50 sculptures dating from 1500 to 1700, can be visited twice monthly on hour-long guided tours (in German only). Book ahead.

On the ground floor, the unmissable **Gentlemen's Apartment Library** is a magnificent neoclassical hall containing about 100,000 books and frescoes by Johann Michael Rottmayr. Upstairs is the **Herkulessaal** (Hercules Hall) – so named for the Hercules motifs within its ceiling frescoes by renowned Roman painter Andrea Pozzo (1642–1709). Surrounding the hall are seven **galleries** providing a trip through 200 years of art history, including such stunners as Raphael's *Portrait of a Man* (1503) and Rubens' intensely perceptive *Portrait of Clara Serena Rubens* (1616), alongside masterpieces of the Van Dyck and Frans Hals ilk. Keep an eye out for the world's most valuable piece of furniture, the **Florentine Badminton Cabinet**, made for the British nobleman Henry Somerset, the Third Duke of Beaufort, in the 1720s.

Until 1938 the royal family of Liechtenstein resided in Vienna, but after the *Anschluss* (annexation) they bid a hasty retreat to their small country squeezed between Austria and Switzerland. They didn't manage to take everything with them, and it was only near the end of WWII that they transferred their collection of baroque masterpieces to Vaduz.

UNIVERSITY MAIN BUILDING   UNIVERSITY

Map p262 (☏4277-0, tours 427 71 7525; www.univie.ac.at; 01, Dr-Karl-Lueger-Ring 1; admission free, tours adult/child €5/3; ⊘7am-10pm Mon-Fri, to 7pm Sat, tours in English 11.30am Sat; MSchottentor, ☐D, 1, 2 Schottentor) Founded in 1365, Vienna's venerable university was the first in the German-speaking countries. Today it has about 92,500 students. Grand Duke Rudolph IV (1339–65) used Paris' Sorbonne as his inspiration, and it was just as well he wasn't around in 1520 during the Reforma-

tion, because in that year his 'Sorbonne' was shoe-horned into the Church.

In fact, occasional head-clinching between Church and secular institutions over the centuries is a feature of Vienna's university history. When Maria Theresia squeezed the Church out of Austrian universities during the Enlightenment in the mid-18th century, she almost made the uni trim and fit for the modern age. 'Almost' because ironically the first woman was admitted only in 1897. During the Nazi era about half the professors and tutors had to pack their bags, because of either their politics or 'race'.

One-hour **tours** take you through the late-19th-century neo-Renaissance and neo-baroque arcades, reading room and, when possible, decorative main ceremonial chamber. They leave from the porter's office in the entrance hall.

Directly opposite the university is the **Votivkirche**, and also the **Mölker Bastei**, one of the couple of remaining sections of the old city walls.

BEETHOVEN
PASQUALATIHAUS   HOUSE MUSEUM

Map p262 (www.wienmuseum.at; 01, Mölker Bastei 8; adult/under 19yr €4/free; ⊘10am-1pm & 2-6pm Tue-Sun; MSchottentor, ☐D, 1, 2 Schottentor) Beethoven made the 4th floor of this house his residence from 1804 to 1814 (he apparently occupied around 80 places in his 35 years in Vienna, but thankfully not all of them are museums!) and during that time composed Symphonies 4, 5 and 7 and the opera *Fidelio*, among other works.

His two rooms (plus another two from a neighbouring apartment) have been converted into a museum, which is lightly filled with photos, articles and a handful of his personal belongings. The house is named after its long-time owner Josef Benedikt Freiherr von Pasqualati.

SCHUBERT GEBURTSHAUS   HOUSE MUSEUM

Map p262 (www.wienmuseum.at; 09, Nussdorfer Strasse 54; adult/under 19yr €4/free; ⊘10am-1pm & 2-6pm Tue-Sun; MWähringer Strasse, ☐37, 38 Canisiusgasse) The house where Schubert was born in 1797, in the kitchen, was known at that time as *Zum roten Krebsen* (The Red Crab), but Schubert probably didn't remember much about that – he and his family toddled off to greater things when he was five.

Apart from his trademark glasses, the house is rather short on objects. But 'Schubertologists' might like to trek here, especially to catch the occasional concert. Bizarrely, a couple of rooms of the house are given over to Adalbert Stifter (1805–68) and his Biedermeier paintings. Apart from being born into the same epoch (more an achievement of their mothers than the men of arts), the two men had absolutely nothing to do with each other.

PALAIS DAUN-KINSKY LANDMARK

Map p262 (www.palaisevents.at; 01, Freyung 4; ⊘10am-6pm Mon-Fri; MHerrengasse, Schottentor) Built by Hildebrandt in 1716, Palais Kinsky has a classic baroque facade and its highlight is an elaborate three-storey stairway off to the left of the first inner courtyard, with elegant bannisters graced with statues at every turn. The ceiling fresco is a fanciful creation filled with podgy cherubs, bare-breasted beauties and the occasional strongman.

The palace now contains art shops and upmarket restaurants.

SCHOTTENKIRCHE CHURCH

Map p262 (01, Freyung; church admission free, museum adult/child €5/1; ⊘11am-5pm Tue-Sat, church shop 10am-6pm Mon-Fri, 10am-5pm Sat;

MHerrengasse, Schottentor) At the northern end of Herrengasse, the Schottenkirche (Church of the Scots) was founded by Benedictine monks probably originating from Scotia Maior (Ireland); the present facade dates from the 19th century. The interior has a beautifully frescoed ceiling and terracotta-red touches.

Although the main nave can only be entered during services, at noon and 6pm to 7pm daily, it's possible to peek through the gates. A small art and artefacts museum in the adjoining monastery displays religious pieces from the church and monastery, but of more interest is the church shop, which stocks homemade schnapps, honey and jams.

KUNSTFORUM GALLERY

Map p262 (www.bankaustria-kunstforum.at; 01, Freyung 8; adult/child €9/4; ⊘10am-7pm Sat-Thu, to 9pm Fri; MHerrengasse) The private Kunstforum museum gets about 300,000 visitors each year, and for good reason: it stages an exciting program of changing exhibitions, often (but not always) with a modern and postmodern skew. The work of Spanish abstract artist Miquel Barceló, Colombian figurative artist Botero and Mexican painter

ALSERGRUND & THE UNIVERSITY DISTRICT SIGHTS

TOP SIGHT
SIGMUND FREUD MUSEUM

This is where Freud spent his most prolific years and developed groundbreaking theories. He moved here with his family in 1891 and stayed until he was forced into exile by the Nazis in 1938. Freud's youngest daughter, Anna, helped to transform the apartment into this museum in 1971.

Exploring the rooms, you can almost picture Freud puffing on a cigar as he pondered the unconscious mind. Pivotal to the permanent collection is the waiting room, where the Wednesday Psychological Society first met in 1902, the consulting room that once contained Freud's famous couch (now in London) and Freud's study. An audio guide gives background on exhibits and interview excerpts, including one in which Freud talks about psychoanalytic theory.

There are also original editions of books, typescripts and cabinets devoted to Freud's hobbies (travelling, smoking and collecting ancient art), as well as screenings of black-and-white Edison movies, including *An Artist's Dream*. Another room is devoted to Anna Freud, born here in 1895, who became a leading light in the field of child psychoanalysis.

DON'T MISS...

➜ The waiting room
➜ The consulting room
➜ Freud's study

PRACTICALITIES

➜ Map p262
➜ www.freud -museum.at
➜ 09, Berggasse 19
➜ adult/child €8/3.50
➜ ⊘9am-6pm
➜ MSchottentor, Schottenring, 🚊D Schlickgasse

Frida Kahlo have all featured in exhibitions in recent years.

PIARISTENKIRCHE   CHURCH
Map p262 (Maria Treu Church; www.mariatreu. at; 08, Jodok-Fink-Platz; ⊗8am-6pm; MRathaus) FREE The Piaristenkirche (Church of the Piarist Order) is notable for two interior features: its ceiling frescoes and its organ. The stunning frescoes, completed by Franz Anton Maulbertsch in 1753, depict various stories from the Bible, while the organ holds the distinction of being used by Anton Bruckner for his entry examination into the Music Academy.

BETHAUS   JEWISH
Map p262 (09, Spitalgasse 2, Courtyard 6, Altes AKH; MSchottentor) FREE This tiny Jewish prayer house, replete with an atrium roof, is a moving aspect of the Altes AKH university campus. It was built in 1903 for Jewish patients of the hospital and in 1938 the Nazis unleashed their terror upon it. The building was completely revamped in the 1970s, and today it has been resurrected as art and a memorial.

The transparent floor chronicles the fate of the prayer house; one level depicts Max Fleischer's original design from 1903; above that is a text from the Gestapo about the pogroms of 1938 against Vienna's Jews; the third layer is a plan of the transformer station. The atrium roof is a glass version of Fleischer's original roof. Bulgarian-born artist Minna Antova was responsible for these artistic features, which successfully capture a mood of vulnerability. Mostly it's locked, but you can see inside.

JOSEPHINUM   MUSEUM
Map p262 (www.josephinum.meduniwien.ac.at; 09, Währinger Strasse 25; adult/child €2/1, guided tours €3; ⊗10am-6pm Fri-Sat, tour 11am Fri; ♿; MWähringer Strasse/Volksoper) The prime exhibits of the Museum of Medical History on the 1st floor of the building are ceroplastic and wax specimen models of the human frame, created more than 200 years ago. They were used in the Academy of Medico-Surgery, an institution instigated by Joseph II in 1785 to improve the skills of army surgeons who lacked medical qualifications.

Three rooms of this gory lot will make you feel like you've wandered onto the set of a horror movie. A book is open at 'The Common Causes of Sadism,' another de-picts common positions of those who hang themselves. Hold down your breakfast and take a wander through this intriguing exhibition. It includes a large collection of medical instruments (plus a first aid kit more likely to be a last resort), photos and an interesting collection of paintings depicting operations.

PATHOLOGISCH-ANATOMISCHE
SAMMLUNG IM NARRENTURM   MUSEUM
Map p262 (www.narrenturm.at; 09, Spitalgasse 2; adult/under 19yr €2/free, tours €6/4; ⊗10am-6pm Wed, 10am-1pm Sat, tours 1pm & 2pm Wed, 10am & 11am Sat; MSchottentor) Housed in the **Narrenturm** (Fool's Tower), which served as an insane asylum from 1784 to 1866, the Pathological Anatomy collection is not for the weak of heart. Filled with medical oddities and abnormalities preserved in jars of formaldehyde, plus the odd wax model with one grisly disease or another, the museum will take your breakfast to the edge.

Guided **tours** of the museum's highlights last 45 minutes. The Narrenturm itself dates from 1784 and is a delightfully circular, neoclassical design by the Franco-Austrian Isidore Canevale (1730–86).

ROSSAUER KASERNE   LANDMARK
Map p262 (09, Rossauer Lände 1; MSchottenring, ⌂D, 1, 2 Schottenring) This huge red-brick complex, today housing the police, Defence Department and Vienna's traffic office, has an impeccable pedigree. It was originally built as barracks after the 1848 revolution. It's a rather fanciful affair replete with pseudo-Medieval turrets and massive entranceways and has been restored after being damaged in bombing during WWII.

VOTIVKIRCHE   CHURCH
Map p262 (www.votivkirche.at; 09, Roosevelt-platz; ⊗9am-1pm & 4-6pm Tue-Sat, to 1pm Sun; MSchottentor, ⌂D, 1, 2 Schottentor) In 1853 Franz Josef I survived an assassination attempt when a knife-wielding Hungarian failed to find the emperor's neck through his collar. The Votivkirche (Votive Church) was commissioned in thanks for his lucky escape; in stepped Heinrich von Ferstel with a twin-towered, mosaic-roofed neo-Gothic construction, completed in 1879.

The rather bleak interior is bedecked with frescoes and bulbous chandeliers, and the tomb of Count Niklas Salm, one of the architects of the successful defence against the Turks in 1529, is in the Baptismal Chapel.

The prize exhibit of a small church museum is the Antwerp Altar from 1460.

MUSEUM FÜR VOLKSKUNDE   MUSEUM

Map p262 (www.volkskundemuseum.at; 08, Laudongasse 15-19; adult/under 19yr €5/free; ◷10am-5pm Tue-Sun; MRathaus, 5, 33 Laudongasse) Housed in turn-of-the-18th-century Palais Schönborn, this folklore museum gives a taste of 18th- and 19th-century rural dwellings, and is stocked with handcrafted sculptures, paintings and furniture from throughout Austria and its neighbouring countries. Many of the pieces have a religious or rural theme, and telltale floral motifs are everywhere. Temporary exhibitions regularly feature.

SERVITENKIRCHE   CHURCH

Map p262 (www.rossau.at; 09, Servitengasse 9; ◷Mass only; MRossauer Lände) Dominating the Serviten quarter – a small confluence of cobblestone streets lined with bars, restaurants and shops a few blocks from the Ringstrasse – the Servitenkirche was built in 1677 and is the only church outside the Innere Stadt to survive the second Turkish siege of 1683.

Its baroque interior and oval nave were inspired by the Karlskirche, but unfortunately it's only open for Mass (see the website); outside of this time you'll have to make do with peering through iron railings. The adjoining monastery is an oasis of calm, in particular its inner courtyard (entry is through the door on the left).

✕ EATING

HIDDEN KITCHEN   DELI €

Map p252 (www.hiddenkitchen.at; 01, Färbergasse 3; light meals €5-8, 3-course lunch €10; ◷11am-4pm Mon, 8am-4pm Tue-Fri; ; MHerrengasse, Schottentor) This slick, white-walled deli raises salads to a new level. Combinations like couscous with tarragon, cranberries and goat's cheese, fennel-mushroom carpaccio, and bulgur wheat with tomatoes, rocket and feta are brilliantly fresh and healthy. It also does a fine line in quiches, soups and juices. Get there before the midday crowds do for the richest pickings.

CUPCAKES WIEN   DESSERTS €

Map p262 (www.cupcakes-wien.at; 08, Josefstädter Strasse 17; cupcake €3.90; ◷10am-7.30pm Mon-Fri, to 6pm Sat; ; MRathaus) This cupcake parlour is a little girl's dream, its pink-kissed walls, flowers and polka-dot crockery. The feather-light cupcakes with mascarpone toppings are made with local ingredients, from organic eggs to Waldviertel poppy seeds. Besides year-round flavours such as caramel, berry and white chocolate, look out for seasonal cupcakes like pumpkin-chestnut and mulled-wine-plum, as well as savoury and sorbet varieties.

WIENER DEEWAN   INTERNATIONAL €

Map p262 (925 11 85; www.deewan.at; 09, Liechtensteinstrasse 10; ◷11am-11pm Mon-Sat; ; MSchottentor) Pakistani cuisine, cooked under the maxim 'eat what you like, pay as you wish', is the speciality of this super-relaxed restaurant. Three vegetarian and three meat dishes, accompanied by one dessert, are prepared daily and served in a buffet-style set-up; prices aren't set, and you can eat all five if you like.

Most people are generous with payment, as the likes of the lamb karah (diced-lamb curry), tinda (pumpkin curry) and dhal masur (red lentil dhal) are excellent and full of subtle flavours.

KENT   TURKISH €

Map p262 (405 91 73; www.kent-restaurant.at; 16, Brunnengasse 67; mains €7-13; ◷6am-2am; ; MJosefstädter Strasse) Kent means 'small town' in Turkish, an appropriate name considering the hordes that frequent this ever-expanding restaurant. In summer the tree-shaded garden is one of the prettiest in the city, and the food is consistently top-notch. Menu highlights include shish kebab and *Ispanakli Pide* (long Turkish pizza with sheep's cheese, egg and spinach). Everything is available as takeaway.

SUPPENWIRTSCHAFT   SOUP €

Map p262 (www.suppenwirtschaft.at; 09, Servitengasse 6; soups, salads & curries €4.80-5.80; ◷11.30am-6pm Mon-Fri; ; MRossauer Lände) This chic little eat-in and takeaway kitchen focuses mainly on soups and a few curries and salads from a weekly menu. All are made fresh each day using ingredients foraged at the Naschmarkt. It fits in well with the genteel style and flair of Servitengasse. All dishes are half price from 5pm to 6pm.

SOUPKULTUR   SOUP €

Map p262 (01, Wipplingerstrasse 32; soups €2.30-4.70, salads €4.20-9; ◷11.30am-3.30pm Mon-

Thu, to 3pm Fri; ✐; MSchottentor, ☐D, 1 Wipplin-gerstrasse) Organic produce and aromatic spices are whipped into an assortment of different soups and salads each week, ranging from red-lentil soup to traditional Hungarian goulash, Caesar salad to Thai papaya salad. There's token seating, but count on taking it away (a leafy park is just around the corner).

CAFÉ HUMMEL   COFFEE €

Map p262 (http://cafehummel.at; 08, Josef-städter Strasse 66; mains €8-17; ⊘7am-midnight Mon-Sat, 8am-midnight Sun; ☎; MJosefstädter Strasse 66, ☐2 Albertgasse) Unpretentious and classic, Hummel is a large *Kaffeehaus* (coffee house) catering to a regular crowd. The coffee is rich, the cakes are baked on the premises, and mains, such as goulash and schnitzel, are satisfying. In summer, it's easy to spend a few hours sitting outside, mulling over the international papers and watching the world go by.

★BREZL GWÖLB   AUSTRIAN €€

Map p252 (✆533 88 11; www.brezl.at; 01, Led-ererhof 9; mains €9-16; ⊘11.30am-1am; ✐; MSchottentor, Herrengasse) Hidden down an alley near Freyung, Brezl Gwölb has won a loyal following for its winningly fresh Austrian home-cooking, served with smiles and a generous dollop of Gothic charm. Atmospherically lit by candles, the crypt-like cellar magics you back in time with its carvings, brick arches, wrought-iron lanterns and alcoves. No wonder the place overflows with regulars.

As the name suggests, the *Brezl* (pretzels) here are precisely as they should be: chewy, fluffy and fresh from the oven. Heart-warming dishes such as beef broth with noodles, schnitzel and cheesy *Pinzgauer Kasnocken* dumplings are matched with some terrific wines from Lower Austria.

LA TAVOLOZZA   ITALIAN €€

Map p262 (✆406 37 57; www.latavolozza.at; 08, Florianigasse 37; pizza €7-13.50, mains €12.50-22; ⊘5pm-midnight Mon-Fri, noon-midnight Sat & Sun; MRathaus, ☐2 Lederergasse) You'll feel part of the *famiglia* at this friendly neigh-bourhood Italian, where tightly packed tables are lit by candlelight. The food is superb: bread crisp from a wood oven is fol-lowed by generous, well-seasoned portions of grilled fish and meat, washed down with beefy chianti reds. Seasonal specialities like truffles often star on the menu.

🏃 Local Life
Stroll from Brunnenmarkt to Yppenplatz

This Saturday morning stroll dipping into Vienna's 16th district, Ottakring, takes you off-piste for a ramble around the city's liveliest and longest street market, Brunnenmarkt. Once an overlooked backwater, this edgy, ethnically diverse neighbourhood is just starting to appear on the city's radar of cool. Go now to discover its independent boutiques, delis and cafes before the crowds catch on.

❶ Street Market
Begin Saturday Viennese-style with a mooch around **Brunnenmarkt** (Map p262; 16, Brunnengasse; MJosefstädter Strasse). Haphazard mountains of fab-rics, clothing, fruit and veg, spices and coffee, cheese and meat – this market has the lot. Most stall owners are Turk-ish or Balkan, and Brunnengasse itself is lined with grocery stores, cafes and bakeries, where you can find authentic pide (Turkish pizza), flat bread, halva and baklava.

❷ Farm Fresh
The delis and boutiques on tree-dotted Yppenplatz open most days, but the square is at its lively best at the **Bau-ernmarkt** (Map p262; 16, Yppenplatz; ⊘9am-1pm Sat; MJosefstädter Strasse, ☐2 Neulerchenfelder Strasse), when farmers from Vienna's rural fringes sell their fruit and veg, meat, honey, preserves, wine and dairy goods. In summer the cafe crowds spill out onto pavement terraces and the square fills with chatter and street entertainers.

❸ Brunch Break
With an open kitchen and a creative menu playing up seasonal organic pro-duce, **Rasouli** (Map p262; ✆403 13 47; www.rasouli.at; 16, Payergasse 12; mains €8-14.50, breakfast €4-12, lunch specials €4-9; ⊘9.30am-midnight Tue-Fri, 9am-midnight Sat, 9.30am-6pm Sun; MJosefstädter-strasse, ☐2 Neulerchenfelder Strasse) is understandably one of the most popular hangouts on Yppenplatz. When the sun's

Kent (p137), a Turkish restaurant on Brunnengasse

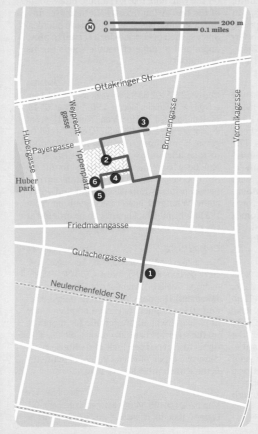

out, snag a spot on the pavement terrace.

❹ Austrian Preserves

Ask the Viennese who makes Austria's best jam and **Staud's** (Map p262; http://stauds.com; 16, Yppenplatz; ⊙8am-12.30pm Tue-Sat, 3.30-6pm Fri; ⓂJosefstädter Strasse, 🚃2 Neulerchenfelder Strasse) 🍃 will invariably make the grade. Hans Staud is rigorous about sourcing the finest ingredients for his sweet and savoury preserves. This pavilion store stocks vegetables with pickled oomph, chutneys, wine jellies, horse-radishes, jams and compotes such as tangy greengage, apricot and wild lingonberry.

❺ Eco Wear

One of a growing crop of cool bou-tiques on Yppenplatz, **Y5** (Map p262; http://y5vienna.wordpress.com; 16, Yppenplatz 5; ⊙10am-3pm Sat; ⓂJosef-städterstrasse, 🚃2 Neulerchenfelder Strasse) 🍃 plays host to a different Viennese designer in residence every few months. Earthy tones, high-quality workmanship, wearable styles and a commitment to sustainability are its hallmarks. Recent labels have included Goodbye Midnight and Milch.

❻ Deli Delight

Just across the way, deli **La Salvia** (Map p262; www.lasalvia.at; 16, Yppen-platz ; ⊙4-10pm Tue-Thu, 10am-10pm Fri, 9am-4pm Sat; ⓂJosefstädter-strasse, 🚃2 Neulerchenfelder Strasse) attracts gourmands with its picnic antipasti, fine wines, prosecco, olive and truffle oil and *dolci* (sweets), as well as specialities such as Sardinian pecorino and wild boar salami. Re-vive over a properly frothy cappuc-cino in the the bistro-cafe.

ALSERGRUND & THE UNIVERSITY DISTRICT EATING

GASTHAUS FLOSZ
AUSTRIAN €€

Map p262 (☎533 89 58; www.flosz.at; 01, Börseplatz 3; mains €15-20; ⊙11am-midnight Mon-Fri, 5pm-midnight Sat; Ⓜ Schottenring, ⓐ1 Börsegasse) The chef uses a minimum of excellent locally sourced ingredients to produce regional food with real depth of flavour at this high-ceilinged brasserie. The season-driven menu might include dishes such as risotto with chanterelles and butter-soft organic Styrian beef with dill sauce, and there are 100 different Austrian wines to choose from. The three-course lunch is a snip at €10.90.

GASTHAUS WICKERL
AUSTRIAN €€

Map p262 (☎317 74 89; 09, Porzellangasse 24a; mains €8-16; ⊙9am-midnight Mon-Fri, 10am-midnight Sat, 10am-4pm Sun; Ⓜ Rossauer Lände) Wickerl is a beautiful *Beisl* (bistro pub) with an all-wood finish and a warm, welcoming mood. Seasonal fare, such as *Kürbisgulasch* (pumpkin goulash) in autumn, *Marillenknödel* (apricot dumplings) in summer and *Spargel* (asparagus) in spring, are mixed in with the usual Viennese offerings of *Tafelspitz* (prime boiled beef), *Zwiebelrostbraten* (steak with onions) and veal and pork schnitzel.

STOMACH
AUSTRIAN €€

Map p262 (☎310 20 99; 09, Seegasse 26; mains €10-18; ⊙4pm-midnight Wed-Sat, 10am-10pm Sun; Ⓜ Rossauer Lände) Stomach has been serving seriously good food for years. The menu brims with meat and vegetarian delights, such as Styrian roast beef, cream-of-pumpkin soup, and, when in season, wild boar and venison. The interior is authentically rural Austrian, and the overgrown garden pretty. The name 'Stomach' comes from the rearrangement of the word Tomaschek, the butcher's shop originally located here.

AN-DO
SEAFOOD €€

Map p262 (☎308 75 76; www.andofisch.at; 16, Brunnenmarkt 161; mains €14-24; ⊙11am-11pm Mon-Sat; Ⓜ Josefstädter Strasse) The Viennese swim across to An-Do for one thing: fish. Start with a fish soup and you'll feel like you're eating your way through the Atlantic. When you resurface, dive into mains such as grilled calamari with rosemary potatoes, scallops with olive risotto or sea bass – all cooked to perfection. Quality is superb and the staff relaxed and efficient.

EN
JAPANESE €€

Map p262 (☎532 44 90; www.restaurant-en.at; 01, Werdertorgasse 8; lunch menus €8.50-9.70, mains €9-25.50; ⊙11.30am-2.30pm & 5.30-10.30pm Mon-Sat; ☒; Ⓜ Schottenring) A Tokyo chef and Hokkaido staff banded together to create this exceptionally relaxed Japanese restaurant in a quiet corner of the Innere Stadt. The many different varieties of sushi (including octopus and sweet shrimp) are among the best in Vienna. The *gyoza* is delightful and warm sake or *genmaicha* (green tea with roasted rice) makes a perfect accompaniment.

SAIGON
ASIAN €€

Map p262 (☎408 74 36; 16, Neulerchenfelder Strasse 37; mains €8-16; ⊙11.30am-11pm; Ⓜ Josefstädter Strasse, ⓐ2 Neulerchenfelder Strasse/Brunnengasse) The second of the Saigon restaurants (the other is in Mariahilf), this branch has an enormous, kitsch mural on the wall and, like its sibling, offers some of the best Asian (mostly Vietnamese) dining in Vienna, based on homemade noodles. Spicy grilled beef, fried duck served in pineapple and a range of noodle soups are its hallmarks.

GU
ASIAN €€

Map p262 (☎402 63 33; www.gu-asia.at; 08, Ledererergasse 16; mains lunch €4.90-7, dinner €9-18; ⊙11am-3pm & 5.30-11pm Mon-Fri, noon-11pm Sat & Sun; ☒; Ⓜ Josefstädter Strasse, ⓐ2 Ledererergasse) If you choose carefully in the evening or take advantage of the lunch dishes, Gu can be a very inexpensive way to fill up on noodles, rice and pan-Asian curries between forays into Alsergrund and Josefstadt. Whatever hasn't been sold out from the lunchtime blackboard can be ordered at the day price in the evening.

CURRYINSEL
INTERNATIONAL €€

Map p262 (☎406 92 33; 08, Lenaugasse 4; curry portions €3.20-5, mains €7-13.50; ⊙5pm-midnight Tue-Fri, 11am-midnight Sat & Sun; ☒; Ⓜ Rathaus) Hoppers (made from baked rice) and string hoppers (steamed noodles made of rice and wheat) are terrific for mopping up the spicy Sri Lankan curries, pickles and dhals at Curryinsel. Pick and choose from different types of curry. A menu mainstay is the €13.50 mixed curry plate.

SCHNATTL
INTERNATIONAL €€€

Map p262 (☎405 34 00; www.schnattl.com; 08, Lange Gasse 40; mains €21-26, 3-course menus

€33-38; ⊘6pm-midnight Mon-Fri; ⚟; ⓂRathaus, 🚋2 Rathaus, Josefstädter Strasse) Despite its weekday-only opening hours, Schnattl is a culinary institution in Josefstadt, particularly beloved of actors and arty types. The inner courtyard is perfect for summer dining, while bottle-green wood panelling creates a cosy mood inside. The chef plays up seasonal specialities like creamy chestnut soup and meltingly tender organic beef, matured on the bone and served with green-pepper gnocchi.

KIM KOCHT   ASIAN €€€

Map p262 (🖉319 02 42; www.kimkocht.at; 09, Lustkandlgasse 4; lunch mains €8.90, 5-course evening menus €67; ⊘noon-3pm & 7pm-midnight Tue-Fri; ⓂWähringer Strasse) 🍴 Kim puts her own creative spin on Korean and Japanese cuisine at this understatedly stylish restaurant. Her menus are constantly changing but often feature fish dishes, such as lemongrass-chilli tuna with rice noodles, as the main. The food is winningly fresh, making best use of organic produce. It's advisable to book well ahead. Kim Kocht also offers cooking courses.

🍷 DRINKING & ⚲ NIGHTLIFE

★CAFÉ CENTRAL   COFFEE HOUSE

Map p262 (www.palaisevents.at; 01, Herrengasse 14; ⊘7.30am-10pm Mon-Sat, 10am-10pm Sun; 📶; ⓂHerrengasse) Grand Café Central has a rich history: Trotsky came here to play chess, and turn-of-the-century literary greats such as Karl Kraus and Hermann Bahr regularly met here for coffee. Its impressive interior of marble pillars, arched ceilings and glittering chandeliers now plays host mostly to tourists, but it remains a decadent setting for a *Melange* (milky coffee) and a slice of chocolate-truffle *Altenbergtorte*.

There's live piano music daily from 5pm to 10pm, and the plaster patron with the walrus moustache near the door is a model of the poet Peter Altenberg.

FLEX   CLUB

Map p262 (www.flex.at; 01, Augartenbrücke; ⊘9pm-6am Mon-Sat; ⓂSchottenring, 🚋1, 2 Schottenring) Flex has been attracting a more mainstream crowd than it did in its early days but it still manages to retain a semblance of its former edginess. The sound system is without equal in Vienna, entry price generally reasonable and dress code unheard of. The monthly DJ line-up features local legends and international names, and live acts are commonplace.

'THAT SHxT' on Monday (the night to catch electro and techno) and 'London Calling' (underground rock) on Friday are among the most popular nights. In summer the picnic tables lining the canal overflow with happy partygoers.

TUNNEL   CAFE

Map p262 (www.tunnel-vienna-live.at; 08, Floriani-gasse 39; ⊘10am-1am, to 2am Fri & Sat; 📶👶; ⓂRathaus, 🚋2 Lederergasse) This laid-back, boho-flavoured cafe attracts students, arty types and all-comers. By day it's a relaxed spot to grab one of the worn wooden tables and flick through the papers over a coffee or €5 lunch special. By night the mood cranks up a notch with (mostly free) gigs at 9pm, skipping from rock to indie and Latin to contemporary jazz.

The full line-up is posted online. Budding stars have a whale of a time at the kids' jam sessions from 3pm to 6pm on Sundays.

WEINSTUBE JOSEFSTADT   WINE BAR

Map p262 (08, Piaristengasse 27; ⊘4pm-midnight, closed Jan-Mar; ⓂRathaus) Weinstube Josefstadt is one of the loveliest *Stadttheurigen* (city wine taverns) in the city. Its garden is a barely controlled green oasis among concrete residential blocks, and tables are squeezed in between the trees and shrubs. Food is typical, with a buffet-style selection and plenty of cheap meats. The friendly, well-liquored locals come free of charge.

The location is not well signposted; the only sign of its existence is a metal Busch'n hanging from a doorway.

CAFÉ CI   CAFE

Map p262 (www.ci.or.at; 16, Payergasse 14; mains €6.50-9, snacks €4-6; ⊘8am-2am Mon-Sat, 10am-2am Sun; ⓂJosefstädterstrasse, 🚋2 Neulerchenfelder Strasse/Brunnengasse) There's always something happening at this cafe on the square, be it a reading, an exhibition, a language course or Greek dance lessons. Come summer, its terrace throngs with locals sipping organic beers and juices, while in winter they retreat inside to browse the daily papers and dig into heart-warming specials such as goulash and *ćevapčići* (spicy Serbian sausages).

ALSERGRUND & THE UNIVERSITY DISTRICT DRINKING & NIGHTLIFE

CAFÉ LANDTMANN
COFFEE HOUSE

Map p262 (www.landtmann.at; 01, Dr-Karl-Lueger-Ring 4; ⏰7.30am-midnight; 🛜; Ⓜ Rathaus, 🚋D, 1, 2 Rathausplatz) Freud, Mahler and Marlene Dietrich all had a soft spot for this coffee house, which opened its doors in 1873. Today, it attracts both politicians and theatregoers with its elegant interior and close proximity to the Burgtheater, Rathaus and Parlament. The list of coffee specialities is formidable and the dessert menu features *Sacher Torte* (chocolate cake) and *Apfelstrudel* (apple strudel).

There's free live piano music from 8pm to 11pm on Sunday to Tuesday.

HALBESTADT BAR
COCKTAIL BAR

Map p262 (www.halbestadt.at; 09, Stadtbogen 155; ⏰7pm-2am Mon-Thu, to 3am Fri & Sat; Ⓜ Nussdorferstrasse) It starts when you can't open the glass door. The host swings it forth, escorts you in and offers to advise you on what to order – impeccable hospitality, no trace of snobbery. More than 500 bottles grace the walls of the tiny space under the *Bogen* (railway arch) and mixologists hold court creating enticing cocktails, shaken and poured into exquisite receptacles.

CAFÉ BERG
CAFE

Map p262 (www.cafe-berg.at; 09, Berggasse 8; ⏰10am-midnight Mon-Sat, to 11pm Sun; 🛜; Ⓜ Schottentor, 🚋D, 1 Schottentor) Café Berg is Vienna's leading gay bar, although it's welcoming to all walks of life. Its staff are some of the nicest in town, the layout sleek and smart, and the vibe chilled. Its bookshop, **Löwenherz** (⏰10am-7pm Mon-Fri, to 5pm Sat), stocks a grand collection of gay magazines and books.

CAFÉ FLORIANIHOF
CAFE

Map p262 (www.florianihof.at; 08, Florianigasse 45; ⏰7.30am-10.30pm Mon-Fri, 9am-7pm Sat & Sun; 🛜🍴; Ⓜ Josefstädter Strasse, 🚋5, 33 Florianigasse) 🚼 This child-friendly cafe in Josefstadt serves food heavily laden with organic produce and a remarkable array of fruit juices. Paintings by local artists add a splash of colour to the clean white walls, and in summer the streetside seating fills quickly.

MAS!
BAR

Map p262 (www.restaurante-mas.at; 08, Laudongasse 36; ⏰5pm-midnight Mon-Wed, 5pm-2am Thu-Sat, 10am-midnight Sun; Ⓜ Alser Strasse, 🚋5, 33 Laudongasse) A designer bar specialising

in cocktails and Mexican food, Mas! attracts an affluent and well-groomed set. Choose from a high, wobbly stool at the long, shimmering bar backed by an enormous light installation, or, for a more intimate evening, a low, dimly lit table. The Mexican brunch (€18) on Sunday is legendary.

CAFÉ STEIN
CAFE

Map p262 (www.cafe-stein.com; 09, Währinger Strasse 6-8; ⏰8am-1am Mon-Sat, 9am-1am Sun; 🛜; Ⓜ Schottentor, 🚋D, 1, 2 Schottentor) During the day this three-level cafe is a popular haunt of students from the nearby university; come evening the clientele metamorphoses into city workers with a lot more money to spend. DJs control the decks in the evenings, and the all-day menu is extensive. During the summer there is outside seating, which enjoys superb views of the Votivkirche.

☆ ENTERTAINMENT

VOLKSOPER
CONCERT VENUE

Map p262 (People's Opera; 📞514 44 3670; www.volksoper.at; 09, Währinger Strasse 78; Ⓜ Währinger Strasse) Offering a more intimate experience than the Staatsoper, this venue specialises in operettas, dance performances, musicals and a handful of standard, heavier operas. Standing tickets go for €2 to €7 and, as at many venues, there is a plethora of discounts and reduced tickets for sale 30 minutes before performances. The Volksoper closes for July and August.

THEATER IN DER JOSEFSTADT
THEATRE

Map p262 (📞427 00 300; www.josefstadt.org; 08, Josefstädter Strasse 26; ⏰box office 10am-performance time Mon-Fri, 1pm-performance time Sat & Sun; Ⓜ Rathaus, 🚋2 Stadiongasse) Theater in der Josefstadt is another theatre in the Volkstheater mould, with an ornate interior and traditional German productions. One hour before performances tickets are available to students and school children for €5; same-day standing-room tickets are available for €4 at 1pm for afternoon productions, and at 3pm for evening productions.

B72
LIVE MUSIC

Map p262 (www.b72.at; 08, Hernalser Gürtel 72; ⏰8pm-4am Sun-Thu, to 6am Fri & Sat; Ⓜ Alser Strasse, 🚋44 Hernalser Gürtel) Fringe live acts, alternative beats and album launches are the mainstay of B72's entertainment line-up, which collectively attracts a predominantly youthful crowd. Its tall glass walls and arched brick interior are typical of most bars along the Gürtel, as is the grungy appearance. Its name comes from its location, *Bogen* 72.

MILES SMILES LIVE MUSIC
Map p262 (www.miles-smiles.at; 08, Lange Gasse 51; ☺8pm-2am Sun-Thu, to 4am Fri & Sat; ⓂRathaus) One of two bars in town named after legend Miles Davis, Miles Smiles is for the discerning jazz fan who likes to see the whites of the artist's eyes. Live acts are irregular but always enthralling, and the atmosphere enthusiastic and energetic.

WUK CULTURAL CENTRE
Map p262 (Workshop & Culture House; ☑401 21-0; www.wuk.at; 09, Währinger Strasse 59; ☺performance times vary; ⓂWähringer Strasse) WUK is many things to many people. Basically a space for art, it hosts plenty of events in its concert hall. International and local rock acts vie with clubbing nights, classical concerts, film evenings, theatre and even children's shows. Women's groups, temporary exhibitions and practical skills workshops are also on-site, along with a cafe with a fabulous cobbled courtyard.

CAFÉ CONCERTO LIVE MUSIC
Map p262 (www.cafeconcerto.at; 16, Lerchenfelder Gürtel 53; ☺7pm-4am Tue-Sat; ☎; ⓂJosefstädter Strasse) Concerto is another of the bars on the Gürtel that hosts local live acts. Jazz features heavily on the program (which is also peppered with DJs) and both the cellar and ground-level bar are used for concerts, although the acoustics of the former may leave a little to be desired. Entry is often free.

CAFÉ CARINA LIVE MUSIC
Map p262 (www.cafe-carina.at; 08, Josefstädter Strasse 84; ☺6pm-2am Mon-Thu, to 4am Fri & Sat; ⓂJosefstädter Strasse) Small, alternative and pleasantly dingy, Carina is a muso's and drinker's bar. Local bands perform most nights, only a few feet from a normally enthusiastic audience, and the music is invariably folk, jazz or country.

DE FRANCE CINEMA
Map p262 (☑317 52 36; www.defrance.at; 01, Schottenring 5; ⓂSchottentor, ☑D, 1, 2 Schottentor) De France screens films in their original language, with subtitles, in its two small cinemas. The schedule includes a healthy

dose of English-language films. Every Saturday afternoon is 'Film & Wein' day, when you get a matinée and a quality glass of wine (usually an Austrian varietal) for €15.

VOTIVKINO CINEMA
Map p262 (☑317 35 71; www.votivkino.at; 09, Währinger Strasse 12; ☑; ⓂSchottentor) Built in 1912, the Votiv is one of the oldest cinemas in Vienna. It's been extensively updated since then and is now among the best cinemas in the city. Its three screens feature a mix of Hollywood's more quirky ventures and arthouse films in their original language.

The 11am Tuesday screening is reserved for mothers, fathers and babies, and weekend afternoons feature special matinées for kids.

SCHAUSPIELHAUS THEATRE
Map p262 (☑317 01 0111; www.schauspielhaus.at; 09, Porzellangasse 19; tickets €19; ☺box office 4-6pm Mon-Sat, 2hr before performance; ⓂRossauer Lände) The Schauspielhaus pushes the boundaries of theatre in Vienna with unconventional productions. Whatever the theme, you can guarantee it will be contemporary and thought-provoking. The adjacent building also features readings by cutting-edge writers. Student tickets cost €10.

🛍 SHOPPING

XOCOLAT CONFECTIONERY
Map p262 (http://xocolat.at; 09, Servitengasse 5; ☺10am-6pm Mon-Fri, 9am-1pm Sat; ⓂRossauer Lände) This upmarket *Konditorei* (cake

IMPERIAL ARCADE
With its hexagonal skylight, allegorical sculptures and beautifully lit arcades in Italian Renaissance style, **Palais Ferstel** (Map p262; 01, Strauchgasse 4; ☺10am-6.30pm Mon-Fri, to 6pm Sat; ⓂHerrengasse) races you back to a more glamorous age of shopping. Opened in 1860, it sidles up to the ever-grand Café Central and likewise bears the hallmark of architect Heinrich von Ferstel, the Habsburgs' blue-eyed boy in the mid-19th century. Today, it shelters upmarket delis, jewellers and chocolatiers, but it's worth a visit even if you have no intention of buying.

shop) offers 40-odd varieties of beautifully decorated handmade chocolates, pralines and truffles – some of which qualify as tiny edible works of art. You can also visit the factory where the chocolates are made.

K&K SCHMUCKHANDELS JEWELLERY
Map p262 (08, Josefstädter Strasse 5; ⓣ10am-6pm Mon-Fri, to 2pm Sat; ⓜRathaus, ⓠ2 Stadiongasse) This is one giant treasure chest, with strings of semiprecious stones heaped over every surface, as well as Chinoiserie, polished coral, shell and wooden beads.

Bangles, bracelets, necklaces and earrings are on display. Or you can get the trinket of your dreams custom-made from the gems of your choice.

FREYUNG MARKET MARKET
Map p262 (01, Freyung; ⓣ9am-6pm Fri & Sat; ⓜHerrengasse, Schottentor) Great for picnic fixings, this low-key market exclusively sells organic produce from farmers. Find everything from wood-oven bread to fruit, fish, meat, honey, cheese, wine and pumpkin-seed oil here.

Schloss Belvedere to the Canal

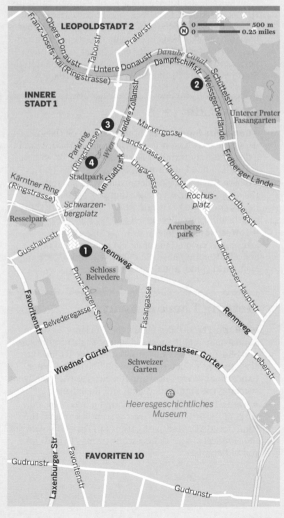

Neighbourhood Top Five

1 Draw breath as you ramble through **Schloss Belvedere** (p147), taking in lavishly frescoed apartments, sculpture-strewn gardens and a gallery home to the ultimate embrace: Klimt's *The Kiss*.

2 Be dazzled by Hundertwasser's wonky floors, madcap mosaics and hallucinatory colours at **KunstHausWien** (p154).

3 Rewind a century to the dawn of a modernist age exploring the **Museum für Angewandte Kunst.** (p153)

4 Hum *The Blue Danube* as you waltz across the **Stadtpark** (p158) to glimpse Strauss' golden statue.

5 Let stress evaporate as you plunge into **Therme Wien** (p158), one of Europe's biggest spa complexes.

For more detail of this area see Map p268 ➡

Lonely Planet's Top Tip

Time your visit right and you can save on sight admissions. The Museum für Angewandte Kunst is free from 6pm to 10pm on Tuesday, tickets for KunstHausWien are half-price on Monday, while the Heeresgeschichtliches Museum won't cost you a cent on the first Sunday of the month.

Best Places to Eat

➡ Steirereck im Stadtpark (p159)

➡ Meierei im Stadtpark (p158)

➡ Österreicher im MAK (p159)

➡ Gasthaus Wild (p159)

➡ That's Amore (p159)

For reviews, see p158 ➡

Best Places to Drink

➡ Strandbar Herrmann (p160)

➡ Café am Heumarkt (p160)

➡ Café Zartl (p160)

➡ Urania (p161)

For reviews, see p160 ➡

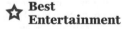 Best Entertainment

➡ Radiokulturhaus (p161)

➡ Konzerthaus (p161)

➡ Kursalon (p161)

➡ Arnold Schönberg Center (p161)

For reviews, see p161 ➡

Explore Schloss Belvedere to the Canal

If you only see one palace in Vienna, make it Schloss Belvedere. What giddy romance is evoked in its sumptuously frescoed baroque halls, replete with Klimt, Schiele and Kokoschka artworks; what stories are conjured wandering its landscaped gardens, which drop like the sudden fall of a theatre curtain to reveal Vienna's skyline. Belvedere is overwhelming in both scale and substance: a day-long marathon of a sight that engrosses from start to finish.

As compelling as Belvedere is, it can be rewarding to explore lesser-known corners of Vienna's third district, Landstrasse, too. Here elegant backstreets lead to art-nouveau cafes, low-key market squares and houses bearing the psychedelic imprint of artistic wild child Hundertwasser. The spirits of classical greats linger in parks and cemeteries, from Strauss on a pedestal in the Stadtpark to Mozart buried at St Marxer Friedhof.

Local Life

➡**Canalside Summer** Embrace summer on the Costa del Danube with your feet in the sand and your bum in a deckchair at Strandbar Herrmann (p160) or with a cocktail in hand at Urania (p161).

➡**Green Spaces** Seek quiet respite with a wander in the dappled leafiness of the Stadtpark (p158) or the headstone-dotted Zentralfriedhof (p154), where the ghosts of Strauss, Beethoven and Brahms hold court.

➡**Coffee Houses** Hone your inner *Wiener* with afternoons devoted to coffee, cake and drawn-out conversations at old-world Café Zartl (p160), Café am Heumarkt (p160) and Café Goldegg (p159).

Getting There & Away

➡**U-Bahn** The U-Bahn makes the quick hop between Landstrasse and the rest of Vienna. Taubstummengasse and Südtiroler Platz stations, both on the U1 line, are close to Schloss Belvedere. The U3 line to Stubentor, Landstrasse-Wien Mitte and Rochusgasse are handy for reaching the Stadtpark, Canal and Rochusplatz.

➡**Trams** Trams trump the U-Bahn for access to some parts of the 3rd district. Tram 2 trundles around the Ring (for MAK, Stadtpark), tram 1 to Radetzkyplatz (for the Hundertwasser sights), while trams 71 and D take you to Belvedere.

TOP SIGHT
SCHLOSS BELVEDERE & GARDENS

A masterpiece of total art, Belvedere is one of the world's finest baroque palaces. Designed by Johann Lukas von Hildebrandt (1668–1745), it was built as a summer residence for the brilliant military strategist Prince Eugene of Savoy, conqueror of the Turks in 1718. Eugene had grown up around the court of Louis XIV and it shows – this is a chateau to rival Versailles.

Oberes Belvedere

Rising splendidly above the gardens and commanding sweeping views of Vienna's skyline, the **Oberes Belvedere** (Upper Belvedere; 03, Prinz-Eugen-Strasse 27; adult/child €11/free; ☺10am-6pm) is one of Vienna's unmissable sights. Built between 1717 and 1723, its peerless art collection, showcased in rooms replete with marble, frescoes and stucco, attest to the unfathomable wealth and cultured tastes of the Habsburg Empire.

Ground Floor: Medieval & Modern Art

The **Sala Terrena** is a grand prelude to the ground floor, with four colossal Atlas pillars supporting the weight of its delicately stuccoed vault. Spread across four beautifully frescoed rooms, **Medieval Art** leads you through the artistic development of the age, with an exceptional portfolio of Gothic sculpture and altarpieces, many from Austrian abbeys and monasteries. Top billing goes to the Master of Grosslobming's sculptural group, whose fluid, expressive works embodied the figurative ideal; among them is the faceless *St George with Dragon* (1395), with a rather tame-looking dragon at his feet. Other heavenly treasures include Joachim's polyptych *Albrechtsaltar* (1435), one of the foremost examples of Gothic realism, and the *Znaim Altar* (1445), a gilded glorification of faith showing the Passion of Christ.

DON'T MISS...

→ The Klimt collection
→ Sala Terrena
→ The gardens
→ The impressionist collection
→ Marmorsaal

PRACTICALITIES

→ Map p268
→ www.belvedere.at
→ Ⓜ Taubstummengasse, Südtiroler Platz, 🚊 D, 71 Schwarzenbergplatz

COMBINED TICKETS

Ordering printable tickets online saves time, but they can't be exchanged or refunded. Several money-saving combined ticket options are available, including one covering the Upper Belvedere, Lower Belvedere and 21er Haus (adult/under 19yr €23/free) and another covering the Upper and Lower Belvedere (adult/under 19yr €19/free). Combined tickets are valid for two weeks after the first visit.

The Nazis seized the property of the wealthy Jewish Bloch-Bauer family following the 1938 *Anschluss*. Among their substantial collection were five Klimt originals, including the *Portrait of Adele Bloch-Bauer I* (1907). The stolen paintings hung in the Oberes Belvedere until 2006, when a US Supreme Court ruled the Austrian government must return the paintings to their rightful owner, Adele Bloch-Bauer's niece and heir Maria Altmann. The portrait alone fetched US$135 million at auction, at the time the highest price ever paid for a painting, and today hangs in the New York Neue Galerie.

Modern Art & Interwar Period is particularly strong on Austrian expressionism. Attention-grabbers here include Oskar Kokoschka's richly animated portrait of art-nouveau painter *Carl Moll* (1913). Egon Schiele is represented by works both haunting and beguiling, such as *Death and the Maiden* (1915) and his portrait of six-year-old *Herbert Rainer* (1910). Other standouts include Oskar Laske's staggeringly detailed *Ship of Fools* (1923) and Max Oppenheimer's musical masterpiece *The Philharmonic* (1935), with a baton-swinging Gustav Mahler.

First Floor: From Klimt to Baroque

The first-floor **Vienna 1880–1914** collection is a holy grail for Klimt fans, with an entire room devoted to erotic golden wonders like *Judith* (1901), *Salome* (1909), *Adam and Eve* (1917) and *The Kiss* (1908). Works by German symbolist painter Max Klinger (1857–1920), as well as portraits by Secessionist Koloman Moser and Norwegian expressionist Edvard Munch also feature. The centrepiece is the **Marmorsaal**, a chandelier-lit marble, stucco, and trompe l'œil confection, crowned by Carlo Innocenzo Carlone's ceiling fresco (1721–23) celebrating the glorification of Prince Eugène. **Baroque & Early 19th-Century Art** pays tribute to Austrian masters of the age, endowed with highlights such as Johann Michael Rottmayr's lucid *Susanna and the Elders* (1692) and Paul Troger's chiaroscuro *Christ on the Mount of Olives* (1750).

Second Floor: Impressionists & Romantics

In **Neoclassicism, Romanticism & Biedermeier Art**, you'll find outstanding works such as Georg Waldmüller's *Corpus Christi Morning* (1857), a joyous snapshot of impish lads and flower girls bathed in honeyed light. Representative of the neoclassical period are clearer, more emotionally restrained pieces like Jacques-Louis David's gallant *Napoleon on Great St Bernard Pass* (1801) and François Gérard's portrait *Count Moritz Christian Fries and Family* (1804). The romantic period is headlined by the wistful, brooding landscapes and seascapes of 19th-century German painter Caspar David Friedrich.

French masters share the limelight with their Austrian and German contemporaries in **Realism & Impressionism**, where you'll feel the artistic pull of Renoir's softly evocative *Woman after the Bath* (1876), Monet's sun-dappled *Garden at Giverny* (1902) and Van Gogh's *Plain at Auvers* (1890), where wheat fields ripple under a billowing sky. Lovis Corinth's tranquil *Woman Reading Near a Goldfish*

Tank (1911) and Max Liebermann's *Hunter in the Dunes* (1913) epitomise the German impressionist style.

Gardens

Belvedere: 'beautiful view.' The reason for this name becomes apparent in the baroque **garden** (03, Rennweg/Prinz-Eugen-Strasse; 🚋D) linking the upper and lower palace, which was laid out around 1700 in classical French style by Dominique Girard, a pupil of André le Nôtre of Versailles fame. Set along a central axis, the gently sloping garden commands a broad view of Vienna's skyline, with the Stephansdom and the Hofburg punctuating the horizon.

The three-tiered garden is lined by clipped box hedges and flanked by ornamental parterres. As you stroll to the **Lower Cascade**, with its frolicking water nymphs, look out for Greco-Roman statues of the eight muses and cherubic putti embodying the 12 months of the year. Mythical beasts squirt water across the **Upper Cascade**, which spills down five steps into the basin below. Guarding the approach to the Oberes Belvedere are winged sphinxes, symbols of power and wisdom, which look as though they are about to take flight any minute.

South of the Oberes Belvedere is the **Alpengarten** (www.bundesgaerten.at; 03, Prinz-Eugen-Strasse 27; adult/child €3.50/2.50; ⊙10am-6pm late Mar-early Aug; Ⓜ Südtiroler Platz, 🚋D, O, 18), a Japanese-style garden nurturing Alpine species, at its fragrant best from spring to summer, when clematis, rhododendrons, roses and peonies are in bloom. North from here is the larger **Botanischer Garten** (www.botanik. univie.ac.at; 03, Rennweg 14; ⊙10am-1hr before dusk; 🚋71, O) **FREE**, belonging to the Vienna University, with tropical glasshouses and 11,500 botanical species, including Chinese dwarf bamboo and Japanese plum yews.

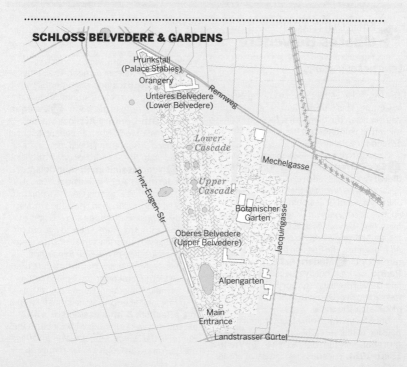

SCHLOSS BELVEDERE & GARDENS

Prunkstall
(Palace Stables)
Orangery
Unteres Belvedere
(Lower Belvedere)
Rennweg
Lower Cascade
Mechelgasse
Prinz-Eugen-Str
Upper Cascade
Botanischer Garten
Jacquingasse
Oberes Belvedere
(Upper Belvedere)
Alpengarten
Main Entrance
Landstrasser Gürtel

OBERES BELVEDERE

Second Floor

First Floor

Ground Floor

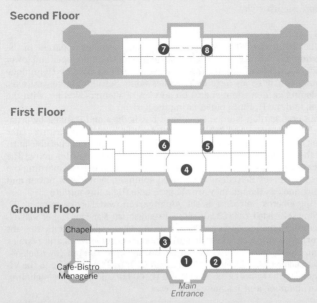

Chapel

Cafe-Bistro
Menagerie

*Main
Entrance*

🏃 Museum Tour
Oberes Belvedere

LENGTH FOUR HOURS

The Upper Belvedere's scale can be overwhelming. This half-day itinerary will help you pin down the highlights, though bear in mind that paintings are frequently shifted around for exhibitions.

Gaze up to the Atlas pillars supporting the ❶ **Sala Terrena** and turn right into ❷ **Medieval Art**, displayed in exuberantly frescoed halls. You'll be drawn to the Gothic brilliance of the Master of Grosslobming's sculptures, such as *St George with Dragon* and *Kneeling Mary*. High on your wish list, too, should be the soul-stirring *Albrechtsaltar* and the *Znaim Altar* depicting the Passion of Christ. Exit and turn left into ❸ **Modern Art & Interwar Period**, where evocative pieces like Schiele's intensely expressionistic portrait of *Herbert Rainer* and Max Oppenheimer's *The Philharmonic* steal the show.

Saunter up the Prunkstiege staircase, pausing to marvel at the opulence of ❹ **Marmorsaal**. Now turn right to reach ❺ **Vienna 1880–1914**, a peerless repository of fin-de-siècle and Secessionist art, to which you'll want to devote at least an hour. The Klimt collection is second to none, shimmering with entrancing golden period stunners like *Judith* and *The Kiss*. Across the way in ❻ **Baroque & Early 19th-Century Art**, look out for light-fantastic works such as Johann Michael Rottmayr's *Susanna and the Elders*.

Head up to the second floor and turn left into ❼ **Neoclassicism, Romanticism & Biedermeier Art**. Notice neoclassical wonders such as François Gérard's portrait of *Count Moritz Christian Fries*, then move swiftly on past landscapes and still lifes to the Romantic era. Here, keep an eye out for Caspar David Friedrich's mist-enshrouded *Rocky Landscape of the Elbe Sandstone Heights*. Georg Waldmüller's mirthful *Corpus Christi Morning* takes pride of place in the Biedermeier collection. Round out with a lingering look at impressionist masterworks in ❽ **Realism & Impressionism**, where exceptional works include Max Liebermann's *Hunter in the Dunes*, Monet's *Woman after the Bath* and Van Gogh's *Plain at Auvers*.

Unteres Belvedere

Built between 1712 and 1716, **Unteres Belvedere** (Lower Belvedere; 03, Rennweg 6; adult/child €11/free; ⊘10am-6pm Thu-Tue, to 9pm Wed; ⌷D) is a baroque feast of state apartments and ceremonial rooms. Most lavish of all is the red marble **Marmorsaal**, an ode to Prince Eugène's military victories, with stucco trophies, medallions and Martino Altomonte's ceiling fresco showing the glorification of the prince and Apollo surrounded by muses. At eye level are sculptures taken from Georg Raphael Donner's mid-18th-century **fountain** on Neuer Markt. Snake-bearing Providentia (Prudence) rises above four putti grappling with fish, each of which symbolises a tributary of the Danube.

In the **Groteskensaal**, foliage intertwines with fruit, birds and mythological beasts in the fanciful grotesque style that was all the rage in baroque times. This leads through to the **Marmorgalerie**, a vision of frilly white stucco and marble, encrusted with cherubs and war trophies. The niches originally displayed three classical statues from Herculaneum (now in Dresden), which inspired baroque sculptor Domenico Parodito to create the neoclassical statues you see today. Maria Theresia put her stamp on the palace in the adjacent **Goldkabinett**, a mirrored cabinet dripping in gold.

Temporary exhibitions are held in the **Orangery** (Österreichishe Galerie), with a walkway gazing grandly over Prince Eugène's private garden. Attached to the Orangery is the **Prunkstall**, the former royal stables, where you can now trot through a 150-piece collection of Austrian medieval art, including religious scenes, altarpieces, sculpture and Gothic triptychs.

21er Haus

The modernist, glass-and-steel **Austria Pavilion** designed by Karl Schwanzer for Expo 58 in Brussels was reborn as the **21er Haus** (www.21erhaus.at; 03, Arsenalstrasse 1; adult/under 18yr €7/free; ⊘10am-6pm Thu-Sun, to 9pm Wed; ⓂSüdtiroler Platz, ⌷D, O, 18) in 2011, with exhibitions devoted to 20th and 21st century art, predominantly with an Austrian focus. Adolf Krischanitz left his clean aesthetic imprint on the open-plan gallery, which sits just south of the Oberes Belvedere in the **Schweizergarten**.

The gallery's dynamic approach embraces an artist in residence scheme and a changing rota of contemporary exhibitions. On permanent display is a peerless collection of sculptures by Viennese artist **Fritz Wotruba** (1907–75), many of which deconstruct the human form into a series of abstract, geometric shapes that have more than an element of cubism about them.

TOP SIGHT
HEERESGESCHICHTLICHES MUSEUM

More riveting than it sounds, the Heeresgeschichtliches Museum presents a fascinating romp through 400 years of Austro-European military history. In the wake of the 1848 rebellion, Franz Josef I strengthened his defences by ordering the building of the fortress-like Arsenal. This large collection of barracks and a munitions depot, completed in 1856, harbours Vienna's oldest public museum.

The museum's whimsical red-brick **arsenal**, with its dome, crenellations, vaulted ceilings, frescos and columns is a potpourri of Byzantine, Hispano-Moorish and neo-Gothic styles. Spread over two floors, the permanent collection takes a deep breath and plunges headfirst into military history, from the *Thirty Years' War* (1618–48) to WWII.

On the **ground floor**, the room dedicated to the assassination of Archduke Franz Ferdinand in Sarajevo in 1914 – which triggered a chain of events culminating in the start of WWI – steals the show. The car he was shot in (complete with bullet holes), the sofa he bled to death on and his grisly blood-stained coat are on show. You can also bone up on Austria's 200-year history as a naval power. Among the displays are balloon bombs that were used during the Siege of Venice in 1849, figureheads, and model ships such as that of the frigate *Novara,* the first Austrian warship to circumnavigate the globe from 1857 to 1859.

Still on the ground floor, the hall devoted to WWI and the end of the Habsburg monarchy showcases Austro-Hungarian uniforms, flags and weapons, including a 38cm calibre howitzer. Leading on from here is an exhibition on the republic years after WWI until the end of WWII in 1945; the excellent displays include propaganda posters and Nazi paraphernalia such as Wehrmacht uniforms and weapons, plus video footage of Hitler hypnotising the masses. Anyone with an interest in tanks and cannons should factor in a spin of the **Panzergarten** and the **Artillery Halls**.

Moving up a level, the **first floor** races you back to the *Thirty Years' War*, with muskets, pikes, uniforms and Belgian artist Peeter Snayers' evocative battle paintings. Weapons, insignia, uniforms and paintings recall the Ottoman Wars in the 16th and 17th centuries and the Napoleonic Wars between 1789 and 1815. In the former, the biggest crowd-puller is a monumental painting showing the 1683 Battle of Vienna.

Other halls are given over to Habsburg military heroes such as **Prince Eugene of Savoy** (1663–1736), celebrated for his crushing victories against the Turks, shrewd ruler **Maria Theresia** (1717–80) and her military reforms, and hallowed Austrian field marshal **Radetzky** (1766–1858).

DON'T MISS...

➡ Archduke Franz Ferdinand's car

➡ WWI and WWII halls

➡ Peeter Snayers' Thirty Years' War paintings

PRACTICALITIES

➡ Museum of Military History

➡ Map p268

➡ www.hgm.or.at

➡ 03, Arsenal

➡ adult/under 19yr €5/free, 1st Sun of each month free

➡ ⊙9am-5pm

➡ Ⓜ Südtiroler Platz

TOP SIGHT
MUSEUM FÜR ANGEWANDTE KUNST

Housed in a stately neo-Renaissance pile on the Ring, Vienna's Museum für Angewandte Kunst (MAK) is a stunning tribute to applied arts and crafts across the ages, gathered around an arcaded, sky-lit courtyard.

On the **ground floor**, each exhibition hall is devoted to a different style. The 'orient,' for instance, is hung with a bazaar's worth of elaborately patterned 16th- and 17th-century Persian, Indian, Turkish and Egyptian carpets, while another hall spotlights mid-19th century bentwood Thonet chairs – now a fixture in Viennese coffee houses.

In the baroque, rococo and classical collection, the star attraction is the 1740 porcelain room from the **Palais Dubský** in Brno. Italian Renaissance needlepoint lace, jewel-coloured Biedermeier *Steingläser* glasses and medieval liturgical vestments from Styria – all unfathomably intricate – are other treasures.

The **first floor** whisks you into Vienna's artistic golden age, from 1890 to 1938. The prized **Wiener Werkstätte** collection, the world's most comprehensive, collates postcards, furniture, fabric patterns, ceramics and distinctive metalwork by modernism pioneers Josef Hoffmann and Koloman Moser and their contemporaries. Unmissable is Klimt's nine-part sketch for the **Palais Stoclet** frieze in Brussels, which depicts the tree of life and a pair of lovers embracing.

The **basement** Study Collection zooms in on materials: glass and ceramics, metal, wood and textiles. Here you'll find anything from exquisite Japanese lacquerware to unusual furniture (note the red-lips sofa).

DON'T MISS...

➡ Palais Dubský porcelain room

➡ Thonet chairs

➡ Wiener Werkstätte collection

➡ Klimt's sketch for the Palais Stoclet frieze

PRACTICALITIES

➡ MAK | Museum of Applied Arts

➡ Map p268

➡ www.mak.at

➡ 01, Stubenring 5

➡ adult/under 19yr €8/free, 6-10pm Tue free, tours €2

➡ ⊙10am-6pm Wed-Sun, to 10pm Tue, tours in English noon Sun

➡ Ⓜ Stubentor, 🚋2 Stubentor

◉ SIGHTS

SCHLOSS BELVEDERE   PALACE, GALLERY
See p147.

HEERESGESCHICHTLICHES
MUSEUM   MUSEUM
See p152.

MUSEUM FÜR
ANGEWANDTE KUNST   MUSEUM
See p153.

KUNSTHAUSWIEN   MUSEUM
Map p268 (Art House Vienna; www.kunsthaus
wien.com; 03, Untere Weissgerberstrasse 13;
adult/child €10/5; ⊙10am-7pm; ⓜ1, Ⓞ Radetzkyplatz) The KunstHausWien, with its bulging
ceramics, wonky surfaces, checkerboard
facade, Technicolour mosaic tilework and
rooftop sprouting plants and trees, bears
the inimitable hallmark of eccentric Viennese artist and ecowarrior Hundertwasser
(1928–2000), who famously called the
straight line 'godless.' It is an ode to his
playful, boldly creative work, as well as to
his green politics.

Besides quality temporary exhibitions
featuring other artists, the gallery is something of a paean in honour of the artist, il-
lustrating his paintings, graphics, tapestry,
philosophy, ecology and architecture. On
two floors you can contemplate how the
artist's style evolved over the years – from
early watercolours and portraits to brightly
hued, more abstract paintings inspired by
his travels from 1949 onwards. Works such
as *The Miraculous Drought* (1950) and the
Land of Men, Trees, Birds and Ships (1949)
reveal childlike forms, intense colours and
a fascination with water, while the high-
rises in *Bleeding Houses* evoke his dislike
of urban conformity. Among Hundertwasser's later works are a tapestry of the
Krka waterfalls and a model of a utopian
city, the rooftops overgrown with trees and
meadows.

Monday is half-price day (unless it's a
holiday) and guided tours in German of the
permanent exhibition leave at noon on Sundays and are included in the price. Audio
guides cost €3.

FÄLSCHERMUSEUM   MUSEUM
Map p268 (Museum of Art Fakes; www.faelsch
ermuseum.com; 03, Löwengasse 28; adult/
child €4.90/2.20; ⊙10am-5pm Tue-Sun; ⓐ1
Hetzgasse) Wow, a museum with Schiele,
Raphael, Rembrandt and Marc Chagall
paintings that nobody knows about? Well,
that's because they are all fakes, though
spotting the difference is a near impossibil-
ity for the untrained eye. The tiny, privately
run Fälschermuseum opens a fascinating
window on the world of art forgeries. Besides giving background on the who, how,

---

WORTH A DETOUR

ZENTRALFRIEDHOF

When a Wiener says, *'Er hat den 71er genommen'* ('He took the No 71'), they are,
metaphorically speaking, referring to the end of the line: **Zentralfriedhof** (www.
friedhoefewien.at; 11, Simmeringer Hauptstrasse 232-244; ⊙7am-8pm; ⓐ6, 71 Zentralfriedhof) **FREE**. The cemetery's mammoth scale (2.4 sq km, more than three million
resting residents) has made its tram line a euphemism for death. One of Europe's
biggest cemeteries, this is where rich and poor, Buddhists and Jews, Catholics and
Protestants lie side by side in eternal slumber under ash and maple trees. With leafy
avenues and overgrown monuments, it is a remarkably calming place to wander.

The cemetery has three gates: the first leads to the old Jewish graves; the second,
the main gate, directs you to the tombs of honour and the **Dr Karl Lueger Kirche**,
the cemetery's perkily domed art nouveau church, which bears the hallmark of
Austrian architect Max Hegele. The third is closer to the Protestant and new Jewish
graves. The **information centre** and map of the cemetery are at Gate Two.

Just beyond Gate Two are the all-star **Ehrengräber** (Tombs of Honour). Besides
the clump of big-name composers such as Beethoven, Brahms, Johann Strauss
Father and Son and Schubert, lie Austrian luminaries including artist Hans Makart,
sculptor Fritz Wotruba, architect Adolf Loos and 1980s pop icon, Falco. Mozart
may have a monument here, but he is buried in an unmarked grave in the St Marxer
Friedhof (p158).

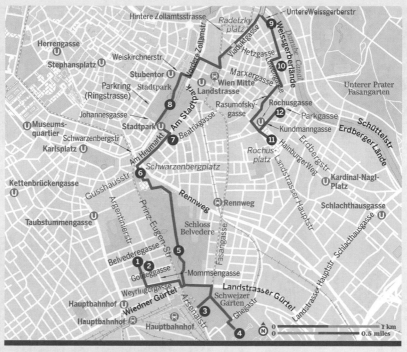

🏃 Neighbourhood Walk
Grand Designs in Landstrasse

START SANKT-ELISABETH-PLATZ
FINISH WITTGENSTEINHAUS
LENGTH 8KM; TWO TO FOUR HOURS

Begin by soaking up the neighbourly vibe of Sankt-Elisabeth-Platz, dwarfed by the neo-Gothic **1** **Sankt-Elisabeth-Kirche**, then nip around the corner to **2** **Café Goldegg** (p159) for coffee with a dash of art-nouveau flair.

Wandering south through the sculpture-dotted Schweizergarten, you'll glimpse the cubical **3** **21er Haus** (p151), Belvedere's repository for contemporary art. Nearby sits the architecturally imposing **4** **Arsenal**, built in the wake of the 1848 rebellion, which harbours the Heeresgeschichtliches Museum.

Backtrack to the **5** **Belvedere gardens**, a ribbon of greenery linking the two sections of the baroque palace. A brisk 30-minute walk takes in their cascading waterfalls, winged sphinx sculptures and ornamental parterres.

You'll emerge at **6** **Schwarzenbergplatz**, a grand square flanked to the north by a statue of Karl von Schwarzenberg, who led Austrian and Bohemian troops in the Battle of Leipzig (1813).

Rest over a drink in nearby **7** **Café am Heumarkt** (p160) before tracing the Wien River north through the **8** **Stadtpark** (p158), pausing for golden snapshots of the Johann Strauss memorial. Walk 10 minutes north to spy the chessboard-like facade of **9** **KunstHausWien** (p154), a mini forest of foliage sprouting from its roof. A five-minute mosey south reveals another of Hundertwasser's creations: the trippy, rainbow-bright **10** **Hundertwasserhaus** (p158).

Head to the **11** **Rochusmarkt**, where market stalls sell flowers, fruit, meat and cheese. Visit the Rochuskirche, then sidle east to the **12** **Wittgensteinhaus** at Park gasse 18. Designed by Paul Engelmann and the philosopher Ludwig Wittgenstein, this building has strict lines and a design reminiscent of the Bauhaus style. It's now occupied by the Bulgarian embassy.

Klimt in Vienna

The shining star of Austria's *Jugendstil* (art-nouveau) age, the works of Gustav Klimt (1862–1918) are as resonant and alluring today as they were when he sent ripples of scandal through the rigid artistic establishment in fin-de-siècle Vienna with his exotic, erotic style. For total immersion, your first port of call should be the Belvedere, which is home to the world's largest Klimt collection.

The Kiss

(1908; Upper Belvedere) 'All art is erotic,' Klimt said, and gazing upon this most sensual of artworks, who can disagree? A couple draped in elaborate robes are shown entwined in an embrace in a flower meadow. Rumours suggest this to be Klimt and his lifelong lover, Emilie Flöge, a porcelain-skinned, red-headed beauty. A sinuous waterfall of gold-leaf and elaborate patterning set against a stardust backdrop, the couple appear to transgress the canvas with their dreamlike, rapturous state.

Adam and Eve

(1918; Upper Belvedere) Klimt was working on this biblical wonder when he suddenly died of a stroke on 6 February 1918. The painting is an ode to the female form Klimt so adored. Adam is less prominent in the background, while in the foreground stands Eve, a vision of radiant skin, voluptuous curves and a cascade of golden hair, with anemones scattered at her feet.

Judith

(1901; Upper Belvedere) One of Klimt's seminal art works, this is an entrancing evocation of the Old Testament heroine Judith, a rich widow who charms and decapitates Holofernes (look for the severed head in the right-hand corner of the canvas). Here Judith is presented as

1. *Beethoven Frieze*
2. *The Kiss* 3. *Judith*

a femme fatale: a pouting, bare-breasted Assyrian goddess with a halo of dark hair and a glimmer of ecstatic desire in her eye. The use of gold-leaf and mosaic-like detail is typical of Klimt's golden period, which was inspired by the Byzantine imagery he saw on his travels to Venice.

The Beethoven Frieze

(1902; Secession) This monumental frieze is a phantasmagorical depiction of Beethoven's ninth symphony, anchored in mythological symbolism and the conflict of good and evil. Klimt's golden touch and love of mosaics give a decadent flourish to nymph-like creatures that drift across the walls and choirs of flower-bearing angels. The trio of gorgons, symbolising sickness, madness and death, and the three women embodying lasciviousness, wantonness and intemperance caused widespread outrage. The latter were considered obscene.

THE FEMALE FORM

Klimt's fascination with women is a common thread in many of his paintings. The artist was most at ease in women's company and lived with his mother and two sisters even at the height of his career. Despite his long-term relationship with the fashion designer Emilie Flöge, Klimt was a philanderer who had countless affairs with his models – in his studio, he apparently wore nothing under his artist's smock – and he fathered around 14 illegitimate children. Though of humble origins, Klimt rapidly climbed the social ladder and was sought out by high-society ladies wishing to have their portraits done.

WORTH A DETOUR

THERME WIEN

Rest museum-weary feet or escape the city for a day at **Therme Wien** (☏680 09; www.thermewien.at; 11, Kurbadstrasse 14; adult/child 3-hour ticket €16/10, day ticket €23.50/13.50; ☺9am-10pm Mon-Sat, 8am-10pm Sun; ☐67 Oberlaa-Therme Wien). Austria's largest thermal baths, the water here bubbles at a pleasant 27°C to 36°C and jets, whirlpools, waterfalls and grotto-like pools pummel and swirl you into relaxation. Besides a jigsaw of indoor and outdoor pools, there is an area where kids can splash, dive and rocket down flumes, a sauna complex where grown-ups can detox in herb-scented steam rooms with names like 'morning sun' and 'rainbow,' as well as gardens with sun loungers, outdoor massage and games like volleyball and boules for warm-weather days.

The best way to reach the thermal baths is by taking U1 to Reumannplatz, then catching tram 67 to Oberlaa-Therme Wien. It's around a 10-minute tram ride from Reumannplatz.

when and what, the museum recounts some incredible stories about master forgers who briefly managed to pull the wool over the experts eyes.

STADTPARK
PARK

Map p268 (City Park; 01, 03; ⓂStadtpark, ☐2 Weihburggasse) Opened in 1862, the Stadtpark is a tranquil pocket of greenery, with winding paths and willow tree–rimmed duck ponds. It's great for strolling or relaxing in the sun and a favourite lunchtime escape for Innere Stadt workers. The park spans the Wien River, which empties into the Danube Canal.

The most famous of the several statues inhabiting the park (including Schindler, Bruckner and Schubert) is the much-photographed **Johann Strauss Denkmal**, a golden statue of a violin-playing Johann Strauss the Younger under a white arch.

HUNDERTWASSERHAUS
LANDMARK

Map p268 (03, cnr Löwengasse & Kegelgasse; ☐1 Hetzgasse) This residential block of flats bears all the wackily creative hallmarks of Hundertwasser, Vienna's radical architect and lover of uneven surfaces, with its curvy lines, crayon-bright colours and mosaic detail.

It's not possible to see inside, but you can cross the road to visit the **Kalke Village** (Map p268; www.kalke-village.at; Kegelgasse 37-39, 03; ☺9am-6pm; ☐1 Hetzgasse) **FREE**, also the handiwork of Hundertwasser, created from an old Michelin factory. It contains pricey cafes, souvenir shops and art shops, all in typical Hundertwasser fashion with colourful ceramics and a distinct absence of straight lines.

ST MARXER FRIEDHOF
CEMETERY

Map p268 (Cemetery of St Marx; www.friedhoefewien.at; 03, Leberstrasse 6-8; ☺7am-7pm Jun-Aug, to 5pm May & Sep, to 5pm Apr & Oct, to dusk Nov-Mar; ⓂZippererstrasse) Also known as the Biedermeier cemetery, after the period in which all 6000 graves were laid out, St Marxer Friedhof is a pilgrimage site for Mozart aficionados. In December 1791 Mozart was buried in an unmarked grave with none of his family present. Over time the site was forgotten and his wife's search for the exact location was in vain.

The search did, however, bear one fruit: a poignant memorial, **Mozartgrab**, made from a broken pillar and a discarded stone angel was erected in the area where he was most likely buried. In May the cemetery is blanketed in lilies and is a sight to behold.

 **EATING**

ROCHUSMARKT
MARKET €

Map p268 (03, Landstrasser Hauptstrasse; ☺6am-7.30pm Mon-Fri, to 5pm Sat; ⓂRochusgasse) The stalls are piled high with olives, flowers, farm-fresh meat and cheese at this market. There are a handful of cafes, takeaway joints and bakeries located on the square.

THAT'S AMORE
PIZZERIA €

Map p268 (☏343 95 18; www.thatsamore.at; 03, Messenhausergasse 13; pizza €6-11; ☺11.30am-3pm & 5.30-11pm Mon-Sat, 5.30-11pm Sun; ⓂKardinal-Nagl-Platz, Rochusgasse) The authentically Neopolitan pizzas are love at first bite for many at That's Amore – soft, chewy and with tangy-sweet tomato toppings. A relaxed atmosphere, chipper staff and wallet-friendly prices make this a winner.

CAFÉ GOLDEGG
CAFE €

Map p268 (www.cafegoldegg.at; 04, Argentinierstrasse 49; snacks €3.50-6, mains €9-13; ⊘8am-9pm; ☎🖉; MSüdtiroler Platz) Goldegg is a coffee house in the classic Viennese mould, with its green velvet booths, wood panelling, billiard tables and art-nouveau sheen – but with a twist. Staff are refreshingly attentive, and alongside menu stalwarts like goulash, you'll find lighter dishes such as toasted paninis with homemade basil pesto and Ayurvedic vegetable curries.

TRZESNIEWSKI
SANDWICHES €

Map p268 (www.trzesniewski.at; 03, Rochusmarkt 8-9; bread with spread €1.10; ⊘8.30am-7pm Mon-Fri, 9am-2pm Sat; 🖉; MRochusgasse) This branch of Vienna's famous open-sandwich shop in the Rochusmarkt is one of many stands where you can buy eat-in or takeaway on the hop. The quality and prices are the same as those of the Innere Stadt branch (p68).

DENN'S BIOMARKT
SUPERMARKET €

Map p268 (03, Landstrasser Hauptstrasse 37; ⊘8am-7pm Mon-Thu; MRochusgasse) Has organic produce, food products and cosmetics.

★MEIEREI IM STADTPARK
AUSTRIAN €€

Map p268 (🖉713 31 68; http://steirereck.at; 03, Am Heumarkt 2a; set breakfasts €19.50-24, mains €10.50-19; ⊘8am-11pm Mon-Fri, 9am-7pm Sat & Sun; 🖉; MStadtpark) Attached to Steirereck im Stadtpark, Meierei im Stadtpark serves a bountiful breakfast until noon, with gastronomic showstoppers such as poached egg with parsnip and Périgord truffle, gammon with fresh horseradish and panini, and warm curd-cheese strudel with elderberry compote. It also rolls out Viennese classic fare with unusual twists, along the lines of veal with chive dumplings.

It's most famous, though, for its goulash served with leek roulade (€17.50) and selection of 120 types of cheese.

ÖSTERREICHER IM MAK
AUSTRIAN €€

Map p268 (🖉714 01 21; www.oesterreicherimmak. at; 01, Stubenring 5; 2-course lunch €10, mains €16-22; ⊘10am-1am; MStubentor, 🚋2 Stubentor) Located in the MAK, Österreicher im MAK is the brainchild of Helmut Österreicher, one of the country's leading chefs and a force behind the movement towards back-to-the-roots Austrian flavours. Using strictly seasonal, high-quality ingredients, the menu see-saws between classic and contemporary, with dishes like *Tafelspitz* (prime boiled beef) and sea bass on rocket noodles and beetroot.

Sleek architectural lines contrast with a coffered ceiling in the restaurant and the lounge-bar is strikingly lit by a wine-glass chandelier.

GASTHAUS WILD
AUSTRIAN €€

Map p268 (🖉920 94 77; 03, Radetzkyplatz 1; 2-course lunch menus €7.50-8.50, mains €9-17.50; ⊘9am-1am; 🖉; 🚋1, O Radetzkyplatz) Gasthaus Wild, formerly a dive of a *Beisl*, has in recent years morphed into a great *neo-Beisl*. Its dark, wood-panelled interior retains a traditional look, and the menu includes flavoursome favourites like goulash, schnitzel with potato salad and paprika chicken with *Spätzle* (egg noodles). The menu changes regularly, the vibe is relaxed, the staff welcoming and the wine selection good.

KIANG
ASIAN €€

Map p268 (🖉715 34 70; www.kiang.at; 03, Landstrasser Hauptstrasse 50; mains €11-14; ⊘11.30am-3pm & 6pm-midnight, 🖉; MRochusgasse) This ultra-modern pan-Asian restaurant near Rochusplatz is a relaxed and slick affair where you can enjoy brilliantly fresh sushi and sashimi. As well as nicely spiced dishes like Singapore noodles and Peking duck, Mongolian, Thai and Japanese staples figure on the menu. In summer there's outdoor seating.

RESTAURANT INDUS
INDIAN €€

Map p268 (🖉713 43 44; www.restaurantindus. at; 03, Radetzkystrasse 20; mains €11.50-15; ⊘11.30am-2pm Mon-Fri & Sun, 6-11pm Mon-Sun; 🖉; 🚋1, O Radetzkyplatz) Subtle back-lighting, clean lines and scatter cushions in zingy colours create a warm yet modern aesthetic at Indus. The mood is laid-back and the biryanis, tandooris, curries and dhals are spot on.

★STEIRERECK IM STADTPARK
GASTRONOMIC €€€

Map p268 (🖉713 31 68; http://steirereck.at; 03, Am Heumarkt 2A; mains €44-48, lunch mains €21-39, 6-/7-course menus €125/135; ⊘11.30am-2.30pm & 6.30pm-midnight Mon-Fri; MStadtpark) Heinz Reitbauer is at the culinary helm of this two-starred Michelin restaurant, beautifully lodged in a 20th-century former dairy building in the leafy Stadtpark. His tasting menus are an exuberant feast, fizzing with natural, integral flavours that speak of a chef with exacting standards. Wine pairing is an additional €69/75 (six/ seven courses).

The seasons play a definitive role, but you might begin with pan-fried grayling with sesame, baby artichokes and rose mallow, followed by barbecued Alpine beef with salsify, Viennese figs and celery. Be sure to save an inch for the legendary cheese trolley, with hundreds of delectable cheeses to choose from. Service is predictably flawless, reservations are essential.

🍷 DRINKING & 🍸 NIGHTLIFE

⭐STRANDBAR HERRMANN   BAR

Map p268 (www.strandbarherrmann.at; 03, Herrmannpark; ⊙10am-2am Apr-early Oct; 🛜; Ⓜ︎Schwedenplatz, 🚃O Hintere Zollamtsstrasse) You'd swear you're by the sea at this hopping canalside beach bar, with beach chairs, sand, DJ beats and hordes of Vien-

nese livin' it up on hot summer evenings. Films occasionally feature, blankets are available and if you get bored of lounging, you can have a go at a game of boules.

Cool trivia: it's located on Herrmannpark, named after picture postcard inventor Emanuel Herrmann (1839–1902).

CAFÉ AM HEUMARKT   COFFEE HOUSE

Map p268 (03, Am Heumarkt 15; ⊙9am-11pm Mon-Fri; Ⓜ︎Stadtpark) Look for the house number, not the name, as there's no sign at this old-school charmer of a coffee house. Inside, it's a 1950s time-warp – all shiny parquet, leather banquettes and marble tables. Do as the locals do: grab a newspaper, play billiards and unwind over coffee and no-nonsense Viennese grub.

CAFÉ ZARTL   COFFEE HOUSE

Map p268 (03, Rasumofskygasse 7; ⊙8am-midnight; 🛜; Ⓜ︎Rochusgasse, 🚃1 Rasumofskygasse) A withered beauty of a coffee house, Zartl pings you back to when it opened in 1883, with its striped banquettes, cocoon-like warmth and, at times, somnambulant staff. Come for lazy breakfasts, people-watching and coffee with delightfully flaky strudel.

VIENNA'S COFFEEHOUSE CONVERSATIONS

Eugene Quinn, radio producer, teacher and co-founder of Vienna Coffeehouse Conversations, which can be booked online at www.vienna-unwrapped.com, filled us in on the importance of rekindling the art of conversation in the city's coffee houses.

What's special about Vienna's coffee houses? They're still so civilised, with their coat hangers and velvet banquettes. And each one has a different mood. You can sit for hours, read the papers and listen to locals engaged in lively conversation with just one coffee – there's no pressure. It's good for the soul.

Tell us about Coffeehouse Conversations In some coffee houses, it used to be tradition to sit with a stranger. Barbara Cacao at Vienna Unwrapped and I decided to revive this. Vienna Coffeehouse Conversations are evenings where Viennese locals get the chance to talk to visitors over a three-course dinner and drinks.

What can people expect? To be surprised – you might have more in common with someone from Rwanda than you realise. So that dinner guests don't just end up talking about the weather and schnitzel, they're given a 25-question conversation menu, based on those in Theodore Zeldin's *An Intimate History of Humanity*.

What questions are on the menu? That would be telling [laughs]. Which different kinds of love have you known? What are the limits of your compassion? They are a couple of examples. You can choose a question for each course or spend two hours on the same subject – it's entirely up to you.

What are your favourite coffee houses? I really like Heumarkt. It's like Warsaw in 1970. There's no sign and it's completely uncommercial, with lots of space and good food. The waiters have that grumpy Viennese thing – you need to click into their groove.

You'll be mostly among regulars. The €6.50 lunch is a bargain.

URANIA
BAR

Map p268 (www.barurania.com; 01, Uraniastrasse 1; ☺9am-midnight Mon-Sat, to 6pm Sun; ⓂSchwedenplatz, ☐2 Julius-Raab-Platz) Another addition to the canal's ever-increasing stock of bars, Urania occupies the first floor of a rejuvenated cinema and observatory complex. Its slick, clean decor, elevated position overlooking the canal and extensive cocktail selection are all big pluses.

SALM BRÄU
MICROBREWERY

Map p268 (www.salmbraeu.com; 03, Rennweg 8; ☺11am-midnight; ⓂKarlsplatz, ☐71 Unteres Belvedere) Salm Bräu brews its own *Helles*, *Pils* (pilsner), *Märzen* (red-coloured beer with a strong malt taste), *G'mischt* (half *Helles* and half *Dunkel* – dark) and *Weizen* (full-bodied wheat beer, slightly sweet in taste). Smack next to Schloss Belvedere and hugely popular, with a happy hour from 3pm to 5pm Monday to Friday and noon to 4pm Saturday.

☆ ENTERTAINMENT

RADIOKULTURHAUS
CONCERT VENUE

Map p268 (✆501 70 377; http://radiokulturhaus.orf.at; 04, Argentinierstrasse 30a; ticket prices vary; ☺box office 4-7pm Mon-Fri; ⓂTaubstummengasse, ☐D Plösslgasse) Expect anything from odes to Sinatra and R.E.M. or an evening dedicated to Beethoven and Mozart at the Radiokulturhaus. Housed in several performance venues including the Grosser Sendesaal – home to the Vienna Radio Symphony Orchestra and the Klangtheater (used primarily for radio plays) – this is one of Vienna's cultural hot spots.

The venue also presents dance, lectures and literary readings as well as low-key performances in its cafe.

KONZERTHAUS
CONCERT VENUE

Map p268 (✆242 002; www.konzerthaus.at; 03, Lothringerstrasse 20; ☺box office 9am-7.45pm Mon-Fri, to 1pm Sat, plus 45 mins before performance; ⓂStadtpark, ☐D Gusshausstrasse) The Konzerthaus is a major venue in classical-music circles, but throughout the year ethnic music, rock, pop or jazz can also be heard in its hallowed halls. Up to three simultaneous performances – in the Grosser Saal, the Mozart Saal and the Schubert Saal – can be staged; this massive complex also features another four concert halls.

Students can pick up €14 tickets 30 minutes before performances; children receive 50% discount.

KURSALON
CLASSICAL MUSIC

Map p268 (✆512 57 90; www.strauss-konzerte.at; 01, Johannesgasse 33; tickets €40-92, concert with 3-course dinner €70-122, with 4-course dinner €75-127; ⓂStadtpark, ☐2 Weihburggasse) Fans of Strauss and Mozart will love the performances at Kursalon, which holds daily evening concerts at 8.15pm devoted to the two masters of music in a splendid, refurbished Renaissance building. Also popular is the concert and dinner package (three- or four-course meal – not including drinks – at 6pm, followed by the concert) in the equally palatial on-site restaurant.

ARNOLD SCHÖNBERG CENTER
CULTURAL CENTRE

Map p268 (✆712 18 88; www.schoenberg.at; 03, Schwarzenbergplatz 6, entrance at Zaunergasse 1; ☺10am-5pm Mon-Fri; ⓂStadtpark, ☐D Schwarzenbergplatz) This brilliant repository of Arnold Schönberg's archival legacy is a cultural centre and celebration of the Viennese school of the early 20th century honouring the Viennese-born composer, painter, teacher, theoretician and innovator known for his 'Method of composing with 12 tones which are related only with one another.' The exhibition hall hosts intimate classical concerts, which in-the-know Wiener flock to.

🏃 SPORTS & ACTIVITIES

WIENER EISLAUFVEREIN
SKATING

Map p268 (www.wev.or.at; 03, Lothringerstrasse 22; adult/child €6.50/5.50, boot hire €6; ☺9am-8pm Sat-Mon, to 9pm Tue-Fri; ⓂStadtpark, ☐D Schwarzenbergplatz) Fancy a twirl? At 6000 sq metres, the Wiener Eislaufverein is the world's largest open-air skating rink. It's close to the Ringstrasse and Stadtpark. Remember to bring mittens and a hat.

Prater & East of the Danube

LEOPOLDSTADT | DONAUSTADT

Neighbourhood Top Five

1 Enjoying a slice of Viennese park life in the **Prater** (p164), with boulevards for strolling, woods for roaming and a funfair. Take a nostalgic twirl above the capital in the **Riesenrad** (p164), at its twinkling best after dark.

2 Waltzing over to the **Johann Strauss Residence** (p166), where ball chart-topper 'The Blue Danube' was composed.

3 Seeing banquet-worthy porcelain in the making behind the scenes at the **Porzellanmuseum im Augarten** (p166).

4 Meeting Freud, Klimt, Falco and a host of other Austrian waxwork wonders at **Madame Tussauds Vienna** (p166).

5 Relaxing Viennese-style at a riverside beach or bar on the **Donauinsel** (p170) in summer.

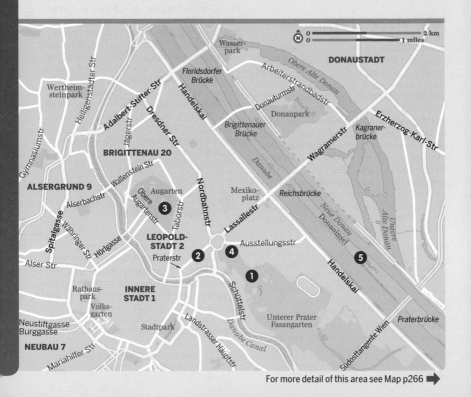

For more detail of this area see Map p266 ➡

Explore Prater & East of the Danube

Between the bends of the Danube Canal and the Danube, Leopoldstadt in Vienna's 2nd district is just a couple of U-Bahn stops from the Innere Stadt, but feels light years away in spirit at times. Here, you can easily tiptoe off the beaten track; not least in the 4.5km ribbon of greenery that is the Prater. The Riesenrad rises above it all, rotating slowly to maximise on the skyline views. To the west unfurl the manicured baroque gardens of the Augarten, home to a world-famous porcelain maker.

Leopoldstadt itself is worth more than a cursory glance, with boutiques, delis and cafes continuing to pop up on and around Karmelitermarkt, bringing a dash of gentrification to a once decidedly working class area. The market, at its vibrant best on a Saturday morning, was once the centre of a flourishing Jewish quarter, which was all but extinguished during WWII. Yet a glimmer of that legacy is still visible in the district's sprinkling of kosher shops and men wearing wide-brimmed fedoras.

Strung along the banks of the Danube further north is Donaustadt, the 22nd district, whose personality swings between the forests of glass-and-steel skyscrapers in the UNO-City and the serene, deer-dotted woodlands of the Nationalpark Donau-Auen. The long slither of an island called Donauinsel is a much-loved summertime hangout of the Wiener for its bars, water-based action and urban beaches.

Local Life

→**Walks** Ah, what could be more Viennese than a languid bike ride through the chestnut-filled Prater (p164) or a saunter through the Augarten (p166).

→**Views** Riesenrad not your scene? Join locals to play 'I Spy' with the city's iconic landmarks at Le Loft (p169).

→**Markets** Scoot through the Karmelitermarkt (p169) Wiener-style on a Saturday morning for farm-fresh, organic grub, followed by brunch at a curbside deli.

Getting There & Away

→**U-Bahn** Praterstern (U1 and U2) is the main public transport link through Leopoldstadt to the Prater, with the U1 continuing on to the Donauinsel. Other handy stops include Nestroyplatz (U1) and Taborstrasse (U2) for the Karmelitermarkt.

→**Tram** Tram No 1 is a useful link between the southern portions of the Prater and the Ringstrasse.

Lonely Planet's Top Tip

For a truly Viennese experience, visit the 2nd district on a Saturday. Begin with a morning's mooch around the farmers market at Karmelitermarkt, stopping for brunch at one of the deli-cafes, then head southeast for a lazy stroll around the Prater or northwest to the baroque gardens of the Augarten.

Best Places to Eat

→ Skopik & Lohn (p168)
→ Tempel (p168)
→ Restaurant Vincent (p168)
→ Pizza Mari' (p167)
→ Restaurant Mraz & Sohn (p169)

For reviews, see p167

Best Places to Drink

→ Le Loft (p169)
→ Sperlhof (p169)
→ Pratersauna (p170)
→ Fluc (p170)
→ Tachles (p169)

For reviews, see p169 ➡

Best Places for Children

→ Riesenrad (p164)
→ Planetarium (p165)
→ Alte Donau (p171)
→ Donauinsel (p170)

For reviews, see p164

PRATER & EAST OF THE DANUBE

TOP SIGHT
PRATER

The Prater describes two distinct areas of parkland, which together comprise the city's favourite outdoor playground. First up, as you enter, is the Würstelprater, with all the roller-coaster-looping, dodgem-bashing fun of the fair, where the iconic Riesenrad turns. The Unterer Prater is a vast swath of woodland park where Habsburgs once went hunting. Today, it is perfect for gentle bike rides, walks and warm-day picnics.

DON'T MISS...

➡ The Riesenrad
➡ Hauptallee
➡ Lusthaus
➡ Planetarium
➡ Prater Museum

PRACTICALITIES

➡ Map p266
➡ www.wiener-prater.at
➡ Ⓜ Praterstern

Würstelprater

No matter how old you are, you're forever 10 years old with money burning a hole in your pocket at the **Würstelprater** (rides €1-5). Come summer, this funfair throngs with excitable tots and big kids, gorging on doughnuts and lugging around hoopla-won teddies. The fairground's 250 attractions reach from old-school ghost trains and merry-go-rounds to g-force, human cannon-like rides.

Several recent white-knuckle additions to the funfair have cranked up the fear factor, including the **Turbo Boost** that spins at 100km/h, the **Ejection Seat**, a ball that dangles daredevils 90m above the ground, and the **Space Shot**, which shoots thrill-seekers like bullets at up to 80km/h. The 4km **Liliputbahn** (mini railway) trundles between the Würstelprater and the Ernst-Happel-Stadion.

Riesenrad

Top of every Volksprater wish-list is the **Riesenrad** (www.wienerriesenrad.com; 02, Prater 90; adult/child €9/4; ⊙9am-11.45pm, shorter hrs in winter); at least for anyone of an age to recall Orson Welles' cuckoo clock speech in British film noir *The Third Man* (1949), set in a shadowy postwar Vienna. This icon also achieved celluloid fame in the James Bond flick *The Living Daylights,* and *Before Sunrise,* directed by Richard Linklater.

Built in 1897 by Englishman Walter B Basset to celebrate the Golden Jubilee of Emperor Franz Josef I, the Ferris wheel rises to 65m and takes about 20 minutes to rotate its 430-tonne weight one complete circle – giving you ample time to snap some fantastic shots of the city spread out at your feet. It survived bombing in 1945 and has had dramatic lighting and a cafe at its base added.

Planetarium

The **Planetarium** (www.planetarium-wien.at; 02, Oswald-Thomas-Platz 1; adult/child €8/6; ⊙shows from 9.30am), Vienna's extraterrestrial and interstellar viewfinder, is located on the edge of the Würstelprater behind the Riesenrad. Shows change on a regular basis, but usually focus on how the earth fits into the cosmological scheme of things. Shows are in German.

Pratermuseum

Sharing the same building as the Planetarium, this **municipal museum** (www.wienmuseum.at; 02, Oswald-Thomas-Platz 1; adult/under 19yr €4/free; ⊙10am-1pm & 2-6pm Fri-Sun) traces the history of the Würstelprater and its woodland neighbour. For all the life and splendour the Prater has seen, unfortunately its museum has only a rather dull mix of photos and stories, mainly from the 19th century. The antique slot machines, some of which are still functioning, are the museum's saving grace.

Unterer Prater

Few places in Vienna can match the Unterer Prater for fresh air, exercise and a burst of seasonal colour. Spread across 60 sq km, central Vienna's biggest park comprises woodlands of poplar and chestnut, meadows and tree-lined boulevards, as well as children's playgrounds, a swimming pool, golf course and race track.

Fringed by statuesque chestnut trees that are ablaze with russet and gold in autumn and billowing with delicate white blossom in late spring, the **Hauptallee** avenue is the Unterer Prater's central 4.5km vein, running as straight as a die from the Praterstern to the **Lusthaus** (☏728 95 65; 02, Freudenau 254; mains €9-16; ⊙noon-11pm Mon-Fri, to 6pm Sat & Sun, shorter hrs winter; ☎; ☐77A). Originally erected as a 16th-century hunting lodge, the Lusthaus pavilion was rebuilt in 1783 to host imperial festivities and the like. Today, it shelters a chandelier-lit cafe and restaurant.

UNTERER PRATER IN SUMMER

While the Unterer Prater can be virtually empty save for the odd horse-drawn carriage and jogger on a monochrome winter's day, warmer weather brings out the Viennese in droves. Hand-holding couples, families, cyclists, inline skaters, BMX bikers, horse riders and dog walkers all gravitate towards this patch of greenery to stretch their legs and find cool respite under thickets of trees. In mid-April, crowds and runners descend on the park for the Vienna Marathon.

Colourful, bizarre, deformed statues of people and creatures are located in the centre of the parkland as well as on and around Rondeau and Calafattiplatz.

JESUITENWIESE

Kids can swing, slide and climb to their hearts' content at the Jesuitenwiese playground, Vienna's biggest, in the Unterer Prater. This meadow is also where friends and families convene to picnic, play beach volleyball or toss a frisbee.

PRATER & EAST OF THE DANUBE PRATER

⊙ SIGHTS

⊙ Leopoldstadt

PRATER   PARK
See p164.

PORZELLANMUSEUM
IM AUGARTEN   MUSEUM
Map p266 (Augarten Porcelain Museum; www.
augarten.at; 02, Obere Augartenstrasse 1; adult/
child €6/4, incl guided tour €12/10; ⊘10am-
6pm Mon-Sat; MTaborstrasse) Restored to its
former glory and reopened in 2011, this
imperial pleasure palace harbours a new
museum dedicated to exquisite Augarten
porcelain. Founded in 1718, Augarten is the
second-oldest porcelain manufacturer in
Europe. A chronological spin of the museum takes in lavish rococo creations, boldly
coloured Biedermeier pieces, Spanish Riding School equestrian figures and the simpler porcelain fashionable in the 1950s.

One-hour tours of the premises are available daily at 10.15am and 11.30am, when
you can learn about the process of turning white kaolin, feldspar and quartz into
delicate creations through the process
of moulding, casting, luting, glazing and
painting. It's free to get a glimpse of some
of Augarten's fabulously detailed creations
in the **shop**, open during the same hours.

AUGARTEN   PARK
Map p266 (www.kultur.park.augarten.org; 03,
Obere Augartenstrasse; ⊘6am-dusk; MTaborstrasse) This landscaped park from 1775
is dotted with open meadows and criss-
crossed by tree-lined paths. You can kick

ⓘ RIESENRAD COMBINED TICKETS

The various combination tickets for
the giant **Ferris wheel**, a magic show
on Riesenradplatz known as Miracu-
lum, Donauturm (p167), **Liliputbahn**
and Schönbrunn's Tiergarten (p176)
can be good value, especially if you
have kids. The Riesenrad plus Miracu-
lum show costs adult/child €11.50/7,
Riesenrad plus Liliputbahn costs
€10/4.20, Riesenrad plus Tiergarten
costs €16.50/7, and Riesenrad plus
Donauturm costs €11/6.

---

a ball in one section, let the kids stage
a riot in a playground in another, or visit
the porcelain museum. Among the park's
most eye-catching features are the austere
Flaktürme (flak towers) in its northern and
western corners.

WIENER KRIMINALMUSEUM   MUSEUM
Map p266 (www.kriminalmuseum.at; 02, Grosse
Sperlgasse 24; adult/child €6/2; ⊘10am-5pm
Thu-Sun; MTaborstrasse) The Vienna Crime
Museum is another gruesome chapter in
the Viennese obsession with death. It takes
a tabloid-style look at crimes and criminals
in Austria and dwells on murders in the
last 100 years or so with particularly grisly
relish; there are skulls of earlier criminals,
and even an 18th-century head pickled in
a jar.

MADAME TUSSAUDS VIENNA   MUSEUM
Map p266 (www.madametussauds.com/wien;
02, Riesenradplatz 1; adult/child €18.50/14.50;
⊘10am-6pm; MPraterstern) Opened in 2011,
this waxwork wonderland in the Würstelprater is a stage for a host of sculpted celebrities – Nicole Kidman, Michael Jackson
and Johnny Depp star among them. Other
figures such as Emperor Franz Joseph and
his beloved Sisi, Klimt, Freud and Falco give
the experience a distinctly Austrian edge.

There are hands-on exhibits that let
you interact with the wax, from taking an
IQ test with Albert Einstein to composing
with Mozart and Beethoven.

JOHANN STRAUSS RESIDENCE   MUSEUM
Map p266 (www.wienmuseum.at; 02, Praterstrasse 54; adult/under 19yr €4/free; ⊘10am-
1pm & 2-6pm Tue-Sun; MNestroyplatz) Strauss
the Younger called Praterstrasse 54 home
from 1863 to 1878 and composed *the* waltz,
'The Blue Danube,' under its high ceilings. Inside you'll find an above-average
collection of Strauss and ballroom memorabilia, including an Amati violin said to have
belonged to him and oil paintings from his
last apartment, which was destroyed during WWII.

The rooms are bedecked in period furniture from Strauss' era. The residence is a
municipal museum.

⊙ Donaustadt

The largest of Vienna's districts, Donaustadt (the 22nd), features the straightened

LEOPOLDSTADT'S JEWISH HERITAGE

Leopoldstadt started life as a walled Jewish ghetto in 1624 under the watchful eye of Ferdinand II, but the district gained its name from Leopold I, the notoriously anti-Semitic Habsburg who dispelled Jews from a ghetto in the area in 1670, destroyed their synagogue and replaced it with the **Leopoldkirche** (Map p266).

Long the scapegoats of the city, Jews had gradually been moving back after their expulsion in the 15th century and resettling the area. By the 18th and 19th centuries, the city was experiencing an influx of immigrant Jews, particularly from Eastern Europe. The area saw overcrowding and some of the worst conditions in the city. The barbaric treatment later meted out under the Nazis, who expelled all Jews and left behind a desolate district.

The beginning of the 21st century has seen a new influx, and Jews now share Leopoldstadt with immigrants from Turkey and the Balkans, who have arrived in recent decades; Karmelitermarkt (p169), the district's busy food market, is the place to find kosher and halal food and a healthy ethnic diversity.

Danube River, the elongated Donauinsel and the Danube's arcing backwaters, now used as recreational areas. Otherwise it is characterised by seemingly endless blocks of residential housing and the modern UNO-City, where the UN bases some of its institutions.

DONAUTURM TOWER
Map p266 (www.donauturm.at; 22, Donauturmstrasse 4; adult/child €7.50/5, combined ticket incl Riesenrad €13/7.50; ⊙10am-midnight; MKaisermühlen Vienna International Centre) At 252m the Danube Tower in Donaupark is Vienna's tallest structure. Its revolving restaurant at 170m allows fantastic panoramic views of the city and beyond – the food tends to be tried and trusted Viennese favourites. The adventurous can bungee jump off the side of the tower; see the website for details.

UNO-CITY CULTURAL BUILDING
Map p266 (☑260 60 3328; www.unvienna.org; 22, Wagramer Strasse 5; adult/child €6/3; ⊙11am & 2pm Mon-Fri; MKaisermühlen Vienna International Centre) UNO-City, or Vienna International Centre as it is officially known, is home to a variety of international organisations, but mainly houses the UN's third-largest office in the world. Multilingual guided tours lasting about one hour take you through conference rooms and exhibitions on UN activities and give you an insight into what goes on behind usually closed doors.

The complex was the picture of modernism way back in 1979 when it was built; today it looks less than fab. It does have a rather glamorous extraterritorial sta-

tus, though, so bring your passport when visiting.

EATING

PIZZA MARI' PIZZERIA €
Map p266 (☑0676-687 49 94; www.pizzamari.at; 02, Leopoldgasse 23a; pizzas €6-9; ⊙noon-midnight Tue-Sat, to 11pm Sun; ☑; MTaborstrasse) The kitchen closes between 3pm and 6pm, the choice of pizza isn't enormous and (oddly for a pizza restaurant) it *never* uses anchovies – they're the downsides. The rest is good: Pizza Mari' serves some of the best pizzas this side of the canal, the inexpensive salads as side dishes are fresh and Mari' has a friendly, comfortable atmosphere that makes you feel at home.

SCHÖNE PERLE BISTRO €
Map p266 (☑0664-243 35 93; www.schoene-perle.at; 02, Grosse Pfarrgasse 2; midday menus €7-8.50, mains €6-16; ⊙noon-11pm Mon-Fri, 10am-11pm Sat & Sun; ☑⏸; MTaborstrasse) UFO-shaped lights cast a contemporary glow over minimalist Schöne Perle (beautiful pearl), which serves everything from lentil soups through *Tafelspitz* (prime boiled beef) to vegetarian and fish mains, all of which are created with organic produce. Wines are from Austria, as are the large array of juices.

STEWART CAFE €
Map p266 (02, Praterstrasse 11; soups €4, lunch mains €6.50; ⊙11am-3pm Mon-Fri; ☑; MSchwedenplatz, ⏹2 Gredlerstrasse) Come lunchtime this small, modern cafe buzzes with hungry

locals, who come to slurp comforting soups and fill up on good-value day specials such as yellow chicken curry, dhal and spinach-feta quiche. Everything is homemade and brilliantly fresh. There's plenty of choice for vegetarians, and many dishes are lactose and gluten free.

FETT+ZUCKER   CAFE €

Map p266 (www.fettundzucker.at; 02, Holland-strasse 16; cakes & snacks €2.50-6; ⊗1-9pm Wed-Fri, 11am-9pm Sat & Sun; ⚲; Ⓜ Taborstrasse, ⓠ2 Karmeliterplatz) The cheesecakes, stru-dels and brownies at this relaxed retro cafe don't skimp on the fat and sugar. Whole-some vegetarian snacks like lentil salad and bean strudel are more of an afterthought – cake is the big deal here. There are lactose and gluten free options.

SPEZEREI   ITALIAN €€

Map p266 (⚎0699-1720 0071; www.spezerei.at; 02, Karmeliterplatz 2; antipasti €7.50-14, lunch special €9; ⊗11.30am-11pm Mon-Sat; ⚲; Ⓜ Ta-borstrasse, ⓠ2 Karmeliterplatz) Wine bottles line the walls of this intimate and friendly *Vinothek* (wine bar). Top quality wines are matched with a tempting array of anti-pasti and freshly made pasta – from *mor-tadella* (Italian sausage) with fig mustard to homemade *fusilli* (spiral-shaped pasta) in tomato-vanilla sauce. The pavement ter-race bubbles with life in summer.

★ SKOPIK & LOHN   MODERN EUROPEAN €€

Map p266 (⚎219 89 77; www.skopikundlohn.at; 02, Leopoldsgasse 17; mains €11-26; ⊗6pm-1am Tue-Sat; Ⓜ Taborstrasse) The spidery web of scrawl that creeps across the ceiling at Skopik & Lohn gives avant-garde edge to an otherwise French-style brasserie – all wainscoting, globe lights, cheek-by-jowl tables and white-jacketed waiters. The menu is modern European, but sways heavily towards French, with spot-on dishes like entrecôte with skinny frites and Béarnaise sauce and slow-braised rabbit with candied lemons.

TEMPEL   INTERNATIONAL €€

Map p266 (⚎214 01 79; www.restaurant-tem pel.at; 02, Praterstrasse 56; mains €15-22, 2-/3-course lunch €12.50/16; ⊗noon-3pm & 6pm-midnight Tue-Fri; Ⓜ Nestroyplatz) Rudi runs a tight ship at this intimate bistro, hid-den in a courtyard off Praterstrasse. Pre-sented with an eye for detail, dishes such as braised veal shank with caper-lemon sauce and chilli polenta reveal true depth of flavour and creativity. The selection of Aus-trian wines is excellent, as is the outdoor seating on warm summer evenings.

RESTAURANT VINCENT   INTERNATIONAL €€€

Map p266 (⚎214 15 16; www.restaurant-vincent. at; 02, Grosse Pfarrgasse 7; 10-course menu €110, mains €20-30; ⊗5.30pm-midnight Tue-Sat; Ⓜ Ta-borstrasse) Art-slung walls and candlelight set the scene in Vincent, which has evolved from a humble student place into its higher calling as one of Vienna's top gourmet ad-dresses. Courses vary with the seasons but the focus is on classic produce, such as lamb, beef and pheasant prepared expertly, but locally produced snails also feature.

FLAKTÜRME

It can be quite a shock – and a little unnerving – to walk around a corner and be con-fronted with a gigantic relic from WWII, a *Flakturm* (flak tower). Built from 1943 to 1944 as a defence against air attacks, these bare, monolithic blocks stand like sleep-ing giants among the residential districts of Vienna. Apart from their air-defence ca-pabilities, they were built to house up to 30,000 troops, had an underground hospital and munitions factory and could control their own water and power supplies. They were built to last too: with 5m-thick walls of reinforced concrete, they are almost im-possible to pull down. So they remain standing as an uncomfortable reminder of the Nazi era, featureless but for four circular gun bases at the top corners (these protru-sions are strangely reminiscent of Mickey Mouse's ears).

Six flak towers still exist: two in Augarten (p166); one just off Mariahilfer Strasse in Esterházypark, which houses the Haus des Meeres (p99); and another behind the MuseumsQuartier in the **Stiftskaserne**. Of the last two WWII dinosaurs in **Aren-bergpark**, one was used by MAK for temporary exhibitions, but is now closed for the foreseeable future due to unanticipated renovation works.

KARMELITERMARKT FOR FOODIES

Set in an architecturally picturesque square, the **Karmelitermarkt** (Map p266; 02, Karmelitermarkt; ☺6am-7.30pm Mon-Fri, to 5pm Sat; MTaborstrasse, 🚋2 Karmeliterplatz) reflects the ethnic diversity of its neighbourhood; you're sure to see Hasidic Jews on bikes shopping for kosher goods here. On Saturday the square features a **Bauern-markt**, where farmers set up stalls brimming with seasonal goods from fruit and veg to cheese, freshly baked bread, speciality salamis and organic herbs. The Viennese fill their bags here in the morning before doing brunch or lunch in one of the deli-cafes, many with outdoor seating. Take their lead and rest your shop-weary feet at one of these five favourites:

Kaas am Markt (Map p266; www.kaasammarkt.at; 02, Karmelitermarkt 33-36; light meals & mains €5-9; ☺9am-6pm Tue-Fri, 8am-2pm Sat; 🍴; MTaborstrasse, 🚋2 Karmeliterplatz) 🌿 Deli-restaurant making the most of farm-fresh and organic produce. Sells picnic goodies like cheeses, salamis, preserves and apricot liqueur.

Zimmer 37 (Map p266; 02, Karmelitermarkt 37-39; lunch mains €7-8; ☺9am-5.30pm Mon-Fri, to 5pm Sat; 🍴; MTaborstrasse, 🚋2 Karmeliterplatz) 🌿 Cosy, oft-candlelit cafe rustling up wholesome lunches like white bean chilli and homemade pasta.

Madiani (Map p266; http://madiani.com; 02, Karmelitermarkt 21-24; snacks €4-7, menus €8.50; ☺8.30am-10pm Mon-Fri, 8am-2pm Sat; 🍴; MTaborstrasse, 🚋2 Karmeliterplatz) Relaxed boho cafe serving Georgian dishes like *chikhirtma* (chicken-coriander soup) and lamb kebabs.

Einfahrt (Map p266; www.einfahrt.at; 02, Haidgasse 3; breakfast €3.80-8, snacks €2.50-5; ☺11am-1am Mon-Fri, 10am-5pm Sat; MTaborstrasse) Arty cafe with generous breakfasts, appetising snacks and occasional gigs in the evening.

Tewa (Map p266; http://tewa-karmelitermarkt.at; 02, Karmelitermarkt 26-32; breakfast €5.50-9.50, lunch €7-8; ☺7am-11pm Mon-Sat; MTaborstrasse, 🚋2 Karmeliterplatz) Great bagels, wraps, salads and breakfasts. The terrace is packed when the sun's out.

RESTAURANT
MRAZ & SOHN   INTERNATIONAL €€€

Map p266 (☎330 45 94; www.mraz-sohn.at; 20, Wallenstein Strasse 59; mains €40-48, set course menus €49-99; ☺7pm-midnight Mon-Fri; MJägerstrasse, 🚋5 Rauscherstrasse) Mraz & Sohn is not only a snappy name, it really is a family-owned-and-run restaurant. The *chef de cuisine,* Markus Mraz, is the creative force behind the Michelin star, chef hats and other accolades awarded for innovative dishes. The menu changes frequently, but in winter you might find expertly prepared saddle of venison with chicory, tonka beans and black salsify.

🍷 DRINKING & NIGHTLIFE

★LE LOFT   BAR

Map p266 (02, Praterstrasse 1; ☺10am-2am; MSchwedenplatz, 🚋2 Gredlerstrasse) Wow, what a view! Take the lift to Le Loft on the 18th floor of the Sofitel to reduce Vienna to toy-town scale in an instant. From this slinky, glass-walled lounge, you can pick out landmarks such as the Stephansdom and the Hofburg over a pomegranate martini or mojito. By night, the backlit ceiling swirls with an impressionist painter's palette of colours.

SPERLHOF   COFFEE HOUSE

Map p266 (02, Grosse Sperlgasse 41; ☺4pm-1.30am Mon-Sun; MTaborstrasse) Every Viennese coffee house ought to be just like the wood-panelled, poster-plastered, fantastically eccentric Sperlhof, which opened in 1923. It still attracts a motley crowd of coffee sippers, daydreamers, billiard and ping-pong players and chess whizzes today. If you're looking for a novel, check out the table of secondhand books.

TACHLES   BAR, CAFE

Map p266 (www.cafe-tachles.at; 02, Karmeliterplatz 1; ☺4pm-1am Sun-Thu, to 2am Fri & Sat; 🎵; MTaborstrasse, 🚋2 Karmeliterplatz) Smack on the main square in up-and-coming Leopoldstadt, this Bohemian cafe-bar attracts an intellectual and laid-back crowd of locals in relaxed, wood-panelled surrounds. Small bites with a Slavic slant (such as pierogi) are on offer and it hosts occasional live music and readings; the last Thursday of each month features young musicians in its vast cellar space.

★ ENTERTAINMENT

★MUTH
CONCERT VENUE

Map p266 (☑347 80 80; www.muth.at; 02, Obere Augartenstrasse 1e; tickets for Vienna Boys' Choir Fri afternoon performances €39-89; ☺4-6pm Mon-Fri & 1hr before performances; MTaborstrasse) Opened to much acclaim in December 2012, this striking baroque meets contemporary concert hall is the new home of the Wiener Sängerknaben, or Vienna Boys' Choir, which previously only performed at the Hofburg. Besides Friday afternoon choral sessions with the angelic-voiced lads, the venue also stages a top-drawer roster of dance, drama, opera, classical, rock and jazz performances.

The acoustics are second to none in the 400-seat auditorium and there's a cafe where you can grab a drink before or after a show.

PRATERSAUNA
CLUB

Map p266 (www.pratersauna.tv; 02, Waldsteingartenstrasse 135; ☺club 9pm-6am Wed-Sun, pool 1-9pm Fri & Sat Jun-Sep; MMesse-Prater) Pool, cafe, bistro and club converge in a former sauna – these days, you'll sweat it up on the dance floor any given night. Pratersauna hosts light installations and performance art to check out before or after you groove to electronica played by international DJs. On warm nights it all spills out onto the terrace, gardens and illuminated pool.

FLUC
CLUB

Map p266 (www.fluc.at; 02, Praterstern 5; ☺6pm-4am; MPraterstern) Located on the wrong side of the tracks (Praterstern can be rough around the edges at times) and looking for all the world like a prefab schoolroom, Fluc is the closest that Vienna's nightlife scene comes to anarchy – without the fear of physical violence.

Black-clad students, alcoholics and the occasional TV celebrity all share the stripped-back venue without any hassle,

and DJs or live acts play every night (electronica features heavily).

ODEON
CONCERT VENUE

Map p266 (☑216 51 27; www.odeon-theater.at; 02, Taborstrasse 10; ☺6pm-performance time; MSchwedenplatz, ☐2 Gredlerstrasse) This oft-forgotten performance venue looks suitably grand from the outside but the interior doesn't impress as much – come for the performance versus a palatial theatre experience. Anything from classical concerts to raves are held within its walls.

🛍 SHOPPING

NAGY STRICKDESIGN
FASHION

Map p266 (02, Krummbaumgasse 2-4; ☺2-6pm Tue-Fri, 11am-1pm Sat; MTaborstrasse) The stripy cotton and viscose knitwear here is both classic and up-to-the-minute, with flattering shapes and vivid colours, and designs for hot and cold weather. There are also linen pants and skirts in a refreshing range of bright colours and casual styles.

SONG
FASHION

Map p266 (www.song.at; 02, Praterstrasse 11-13; ☺1-7pm Mon, 10am-7pm Tue-Fri, 10am-6pm Sat; MSchwedenplatz, ☐2 Marienbrücke) A holy grail for style-seekers, this industrial-minimalist gallery and boutique hosts rotating exhibitions of modern art and is a showcase for designer furnishings, jewellery, accessories and fashion from the revered likes of Dries van Noten and Paul Harnden.

STILWERK WIEN
DESIGN STORE

Map p266 (www.stilwerk.de/wien; 02, Praterstrasse 1; ☺10am-7pm Mon-Fri, to 6pm Sat; MSchwedenplatz, ☐2 Marienbrücke) Plug into Vienna's contemporary design scene at this cluster of concept and interior stores in the glass-clad Design Tower.

🏃 SPORTS & ACTIVITIES

★DONAUINSEL
ISLAND

Map p266 (Danube Island 22; MDonauinsel) The svelte Danube Island stretches some 21.5km from opposite Klosterneuburg in the north to the Nationalpark Donau-Auen in the south and splits the Danube in two, creating a separate arm known as the Neue

WORTH A DETOUR

INTO THE WOODS: THE WIENERWALD

If you really want to get into the great outdoors, scamper across to the **Wienerwald** (Vienna Woods; www.wienerwald.info). The Austrian capital's rural escape vault, this 45km swath of forested hills, fringing the capital from the northwest to the southeast, was immortalised in 'Tales from the Vienna Woods,' the concert waltz by Johann Strauss Junior in 1868.

These woods are made for walking and the city council website (www.wien.gv.at/english/leisure/hiking/paths) details nine walks, a couple of which take you into the forest. You'll need about three hours to complete the 7.2km trail No 4, which threads up to the **Jubiläumswarte**. Rising above the Wienerwald's green canopy, this lookout tower offers sweeping views from the uppermost platform that take in most of Vienna and reach as far as the 2076m hump of Schneeberg. On a breezy day the climb to the top is exhilarating. Grab some picnic supplies, jump on tram 49 to Bahnhofstrasse and walk in the direction of the tram to Rosentalgasse, then follow the signs. From the Jubiläumswarte the trail is mainly through suburbs, so it's nicer to return the way you came.

A slightly longer alternative is trail No 1, an 11km loop, which starts in Nussdorf (take tram D from the Ring) and climbs **Kahlenberg** (484m), a vine-streaked hill commanding fine city views. On your return to Nussdorf you can undo all that exercise by imbibing at a *Heuriger* (wine tavern). You can spare yourself the leg work by taking the Nussdorf–Kahlenberg 38A bus in one or both directions.

Another way of exploring the Wienerwald on your own is in one of the 46 marked mountain-bike trails, covering 1000km of terrain. These are signposted and graded according to difficulty, from 'Family' (easy) to 'Power' (tough). The website www.mbike.at has routes listed and mapped.

In winter, the **Hohe Wand** (☑979 10 57; Mauerbachstrasse 172-174; day pass adult/child €13/6; ☺9am-9pm Dec-Mar; ☐249, 250, Ⓜ Wien Hütteldorf) ski slopes in the Wienerwald can be used only when there is enough natural snow on the ground to bond with daily layers of artificial snow. It offers rides down the Rodelbahn (like a bobsled on wheels).

PRATER & EAST OF THE DANUBE SPORTS & ACTIVITIES

Donau (New Danube). Created in 1970, it is Vienna's aquatic playground, with sections of beach (don't expect much sand) for swimming, boating and a little water skiing.

The tips of the island are designated FKK (*Freikörperkultur*; free body culture) zones reserved for nudist bathers, who also enjoy dining, drinking, walking, biking and in-line skating *au naturel* – it's quite a sight. Concrete paths run the entire length of the island, and there are bicycle and inline-skate rental stores. Restaurants and snack bars are dotted along the paths, but the highest concentration of bars – collectively known as Sunken City and Copa Cagrana – is near Reichsbrücke and the U1 Donauinsel stop. In late June the island hosts the **Donauinselfest** (www.donauinselfest.at).

ALTE DONAU　　　　　WATER SPORTS

Map p266 (22, Untere Alte Donau; Ⓜ Alte Donau) The Alte Donau, a landlocked arm of the Danube, is separated from the Neue Donau by a sliver of land. It carried the main flow of the river until 1875. Now the 160-hectare water expanse is a favourite of Viennese sailing and boating enthusiasts, and also attracts swimmers, walkers, fishermen and, in winter (if it's cold enough), ice skaters.

NATIONALPARK DONAU-AUEN　　OUTDOORS

(☑400 04 9495; www.donauauen.at; 22, Dechantweg 8; ☺10am-6pm Wed-Sun late Feb-late Oct; ☐91A, 92A, 93A, ☒S80) A vast ribbon of greenery looping along the Danube from the fringes of Vienna to the Slovakian border, the 9300-hectare Donau-Auen National Park is one of the last remaining major wetlands in Europe. Established in 1996, the park comprises around 65% forest, 20% lakes and waterways and 15% meadows, which nurture some 700 species of fern and flowering plants.

The park's quieter reaches attract abundant birdlife and wildlife, such as red deer, beavers, fire-bellied toads, eagles, kites and a high density of kingfishers. The **wien-lobAU National Park House**, located at the northern entrance to the park, offers a series of themed guided tours, ranging from winter walks to birdwatching rambles, most of which cost around €10/5 for adults/children. **Boat tours** into the national park leave from Salztorbrücke and last 4½ hours; booking is necessary. See the website for further details.

LOBAU
OUTDOORS

(🚌91A, 92A, 93A, 🚈S80) This one is for those who want to go off-piste in summer. The Lobau, at the southern extremes of Donaustadt, is an area of dense scrub and woodland home to the western extension of the Nationalpark Donau-Auen, with an abundance of small lakes, walking and cycling trails. In summer, Vienna's alternative crowd flock to the Lobau for skinny-dipping.

PEDAL POWER
CYCLING

Map p266 (📞729 72 34; www.pedalpower.at; 02, Ausstellungsstrasse 3; per hr/half-/full-day €5/17/27; ⏰8am-7pm Apr-Oct; 🚇Praterstern) Pick up city and mountain bikes here or, for an extra €5, arrange for the two wheels to be conveniently dropped off and picked up at your hotel. Pedal Power also offers 'City Segway' and guided bike tours, which start at €70/29 respectively for a three-hour spin; visit the website for further details.

Child seats and helmets are €4 extra a piece.

COPA CAGRANA RAD UND SKATERVERLEIH
BICYCLE RENTAL

Map p266 (📞263 52 42; www.fahrradverleih.at; 22, Am Kaisermühlendamm 1; per hr/half-/full-day from €5/15/25; ⏰9am-6pm Mar-Oct, to 9pm May-Aug; 🚇Kaisermühlen Vienna International Centre) All manner of bikes are on offer here – city, mountain, trekking, tandem, kid's and more. Also has rollerblades for hire (from €6 per hour).

KRIEAU
HORSE RACING

Map p266 (📞728 00 46; www.krieau.at; 02, Nordportalstrasse 247; 🚇Krieau, Stadion) Sidling up to the Ernst-Happel-Stadion in the Prater is Krieau, the track where Vienna's trotting meets (tickets from €6) are held. Visit the website for a timetable of race days. An open-air cinema operates here in July and August.

STRANDBAD ALTE DONAU
SWIMMING

Map p266 (22, Arbeiterstrandbadstrasse 91; adult/child €5/1.70; ⏰9am-7pm May-mid-Sep; 🚇Alte Donau) This bathing area makes great use of the Alte Donau during the summer months. It's a favourite of Viennese locals and gets extremely crowded at weekends during summer. Facilities include a restaurant, beach-volleyball court, playing field, slides and plenty of tree shade.

STRANDBAD GÄNSEHÄUFEL
SWIMMING

Map p266 (www.gaensehaeufel.at; 22, Moissigasse 21; adult/child €5/1.70; ⏰9am-7pm May-mid-Sep; 🚇Kaisermühlen) Gänsehäufel occupies half an island in the Alte Donau. It does get crowded in summer, but there's normally enough space to escape the mob. There's a swimming pool and FKK (read: nudist) area. The playground, slides, splash areas and mini golf keep kids amused for hours. Besides swimming, Gänsehäufel offers activities like tennis, volleyball and a climbing zone.

SAILING SCHOOL HOFBAUER
BOATING

Map p266 (📞204 34 35; www.hofbauer.at; 22, An der Obere Alte Donau 191; ⏰Apr-Oct; 🚇Alte Donau) Hofbauer rents sailing boats (from €14.80 per hour) and row boats (€8.50 per hour) on the eastern bank of the Alte Donau and can provide lessons (in English) for those wishing to learn or brush up on their skills. Pedal boats (€12 per hour) are also available for hire.

Schloss Schönbrunn & Around

Neighbourhood Top Five

1 Living a day in the life of a Habsburg saunter-ing around the gloriously over-the-top baroque state apartments and fountain-dotted gardens of **Schloss Schönbrunn** (p175).

2 Diving into the sensual, colour-charged imagination of Klimt at his last studio, the **Klimt Villa** (p179).

3 Wandering in Empress Elisabeth's footsteps at the **Hermesvilla** (p180), a 19th-century mansion romanti-cally nestled in woodland.

4 Being amazed by the art-nouveau grace of gold-topped **Kirche am Steinhof** (p181), Otto Wagner's mag-num opus.

5 Enjoying the rousing melodies of Strauss and Mozart in the **Orangery** (p181), Schönbrunn's former imperial greenhouse.

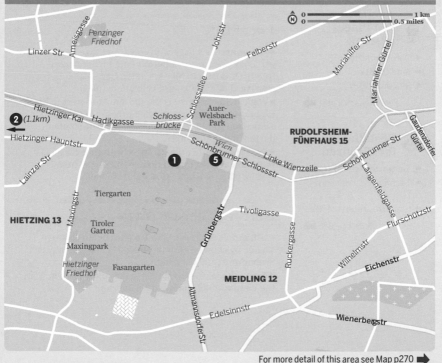

For more detail of this area see Map p270 ➡

Lonely Planet's Top Tip

Because of the popularity of the palace, tickets are stamped with a departure time, and there may be a time lag before you're allowed to set off in summer, so buy your ticket straight away and explore the gardens while you wait. Or skip to the front of the queue by buying your ticket in advance online (www.schoenbrunn.at). Simply print the ticket yourself and present it when you enter.

SCHLOSS SCHÖNBRUNN & AROUND

Best Places to Eat

➡ Pure Living Bakery (p180)

➡ Quell (p180)

➡ Hollerei (p180)

For reviews, see p180 ➡

Best Places to Drink

➡ Café Gloriette (p181)

➡ Aida (p181)

➡ Reigen (p182)

For reviews, see p181 ➡

Best Places for Children

➡ Tiergarten (p176)

➡ Technisches Museum (p179)

➡ Kindermuseum (p178)

For reviews, see p176 ➡

Explore Schloss Schönbrunn & Around

Few sights in Vienna enthral like Schloss Schönbrunn. The vision of its imposing baroque facade, glowing like warm butter up on a sunny afternoon, is not one you are likely to forget in a hurry. You can almost picture the Habsburgs swanning around the fragrant rose beds and mythological fountains in the French-style formal gardens, which provide a harmonious backdrop for the baroque palace, a Unesco World Heritage site.

Once a hunting lodge for parties of rambunctious deer-shooting royals, Schönbrunn was destroyed during the Turkish siege of Vienna in 1683. Three years later, Emperor Leopold I enlisted the baroque whiz-kid of the age, Johann Fischer von Erlach, to restore it to its former glory. During Maria Theresia's 40-year rule from 1740 to 1780, Schönbrunn became the centre of court life. The empress' fondness for rococo extravagance still glitters in the palace interiors today.

Schönnbrunn is the star attraction and merits at least half a day of your time. The palace is situated in Hietzing, a laid-back neighbourhood with a village feel, which tapers out to the rambling woodland of the Lainzer Tiergarten to the west. The Klimt Villa and Otto Wagner's gracefully domed Hofpavillon are among the district's lesser-known treasures.

Local Life

➡**Hangouts** Kick back with coffee and cake in the garden of the cute-as-a-button Pure Living Bakery (p180). Or quaff microbrews in the tree-shaded courtyard of Brandauers Schlossbräu (p181).

➡**Walks** Give the crowds the slip and head west to hike, jog or cycle in the vast, wooded expanse of the Lainzer Tiergarten (p180), where deer can often be spotted darting out of the forest.

➡**Quiet Moments** Calm the pace with time for quiet reflection at Hietzinger Friedhof (p180), the final resting place of Klimt, Moser and Wagner.

Getting There & Away

➡**U-Bahn** Schönbrunn is well connected to central Vienna by subway, with the green U4 line stopping at Schönbrunn and Hietzing.

➡**Tram** Alternatively, tram 58 makes the short hop from the Westbahnhof station to Schönbrunn.

GÜNTER LENZ / IMAGEBROKER ©

TOP SIGHT
SCHLOSS SCHÖNBRUNN

The pomp and ceremony of the Habsburg Empire is revealed in all its frescoed, gilded, chandelier-lit glory in the wondrously ornate apartments of Schloss Schönbrunn, which are among Europe's best-preserved baroque interiors. Audio guides give you the inside scoop on the palace's history, with titbits about Empress Elisabeth's slim-fast regimes and the first public performance of wunderkind Mozart. Of the 1441 rooms within the palace, 40 are open to the public.

State Apartments

The frescoed **Blue Staircase** makes a regal ascent to the palace's upper level. First up are the 19th-century apartments of Emperor Franz Joseph I and his beloved wife Elisabeth, a beauty praised for her size-zero waist and cascading tresses. The tour whisks you through lavishly stuccoed, chandelier-lit apartments such as the **Billiard Room** where army officials would pot a few balls while waiting to attend an audience, and Franz Joseph's **study**, where the emperor worked tirelessly from 5am. The iron bedstead and washstand for morning ablutions in his bedroom reveal his devout, highly disciplined nature.

Empress Elisabeth, or 'Sisi' as she is fondly nicknamed, whiled away many an hour penning poetry in the ruby-red **Stairs Cabinet**, and brushing her ankle-length locks in her **dressing room**. Blue-and-white silk wall hangings adorn the **imperial bedroom** that Franz and Sisi shared. The neo-rococo **Empress' Salon** features portraits of some of Maria Theresia's 16 children, including Marie Antoinette in hunting garb, then oblivious to her ending at the guillotine in

DON'T MISS...

➡ Great Gallery
➡ Neptunbrunnen
➡ Gloriette
➡ Wagenburg
➡ Palmenhaus
➡ Tiergarten

PRACTICALITIES

➡ Map p270
➡ www.schoenbrunn.at
➡ 13, Schönbrunner Schlossstrasse 47
➡ Imperial Tour with audio guide adult/child €11.50/8.50, Grand Tour adult/child €14.50/9.50, gardens admission free
➡ ⏱8.30am-5.30pm, gardens 6am-dusk, maze 9am-6pm

SCHÖNBRUNN ZOO

Founded in 1752 as a menagerie by Franz Stephan, the Schönbrunn **Tiergarten** (www.zoovienna.at) is the world's oldest zoo. Open between 9am and 6.30pm, adult/ child entry is €15/7. It houses some 750 animals, including giant pandas, emus, armadillos and Siberian tigers. Feeding times are staggered throughout the day – maps on display tell you who's dining when. The zoo's layout is reminiscent of a bicycle wheel, with pathways as spokes and an octagonal pavilion at its centre. The pavilion dates from 1759 and was used as the imperial breakfast room.

The Wüstenhaus (Desert House) at 13, Maxingstrasse 13b is open from 9am to 6pm May to September (to 5pm October to April) and costs adult/child €4/2.50. It makes good use of the once disused Sonnenuhrhaus (Sundial House) to recreate arid desert scenes. There are four sections – Northern Africa and the Middle East, Africa, the Americas and Madagascar – with rare cacti and live desert animals, such as the naked mole rat from East Africa.

1793. Laid with leaded crystal and fragile porcelain, the table in the **Marie Antoinette Room** is where Franz Joseph used to dig into hearty meals of goulash and schnitzel; figure-watching Sisi used to skip most family meals.

More portraits of Maria Theresia's brood fill the **Children's Room** and the **Balcony Room**, graced with works by court painter Martin van Meytens. Keep an eye out for the one of ill-fated daughter Maria Elisabeth, considered a rare beauty before she contracted smallpox. The disease left her so disfigured that all hope of finding a husband vanished, and she entered convent life.

In the exquisite white-and-gold **Mirror Room**, a six-year-old Mozart performed for a rapturous Maria Theresia in 1762. According to his father Leopold, 'Wolferl leapt onto Her Majesty's lap, threw his arms around her neck and planted kisses on her face.' Fairest of all, however, is the 40m-long **Great Gallery**, where the Habsburgs threw balls and banquets, a frothy vision of stucco, mirrors and gilt chandeliers, topped with a fresco by Italian artist Gregorio Guglielmi showing the glorification of Maria Theresia's reign. Decor aside, this was where the famous meeting between John F Kennedy and Soviet leader Nikita Khrushchev took place in 1961.

Wandering through the porcelain-crammed **Chinese Cabinets** brings you to the equestrian fanfare of the **Carousel Room** and the **Hall of Ceremonies**, with five monumental paintings showing the marriage of Joseph, heir to the throne, to Isabella of Parma in 1760. Mozart, only four at the time of the wedding, was added as an afterthought by the artist, who took several years to complete the picture, by which time the virtuoso was a rising star.

If you have a Grand Tour ticket, you can continue through to the palace's **east wing**. Franz Stephan's apartments begin in the sublime **Blue Chinese Salon**, where the intricate floral wall paintings are done on Chinese rice paper. The jewel-box *pietra dura* tables, inlaid with semi-precious stones, are stellar examples of Florentine craftsmanship. The negotiations that led to the collapse of the Austro-Hungarian Empire in 1918 were held here. Napoleon chose Schönbrunn as his HQ when he occupied Vienna in 1805 and 1809 and the **Napoleon Room** was most likely where he dreamed about which country to conquer next. Look for the portrait of his only legitimate son, the Duke of Reichstadt, shown as a cherubic lad in the park at Laxenburg Palace.

Passing through the exquisite rosewood **Millions Room**, the **Gobelin Salon**, filled with Flemish tapestries, and the **Red Salon** brimming with Habsburg portraits, you reach Maria Theresia's **bedroom**, with a throne-like red velvet and gold embroidered four-poster bed. This is where Franz Joseph was born in 1830. Gilt-framed portraits of the Habsburgs hang on the red-damask walls of Archduke Franz Karl's **study**, and the tour concludes in the **Hunting Room**, with paintings noting Schönbrunn's origins as a hunting lodge.

Schloss Schönbrunn Gardens

The beautifully tended formal **gardens** (⊙6am-dusk Apr-Oct, 6.30am-dusk Nov-Mar) **FREE** of the palace, arranged in the French style, are a symphony of colour in the summer and a combination of greys and browns in winter; all seasons are appealing in their own right. The grounds, which were opened to the public by Joseph II in 1779, hide a number of attractions in the tree-lined avenues that were arranged according to a grid and star-shaped system between 1750 and 1755. From 1772 to 1780 Ferdinand Hetzendorf added some of the final touches to the park under the instructions of Joseph II: fake **Roman ruins** in 1778; the **Neptunbrunnen** (Neptune Fountain), a riotous ensemble from Greek mythology, in 1781; and the crowning glory, the **Gloriette** (adult/child €3/2.20; ⊙9am-btwn 4pm & 7pm, closed early Nov-late Mar) in 1775. The view from the Gloriette, looking back towards the palace with Vienna shimmering in the distance, ranks among the best in Vienna. It's possible to venture onto its roof, but the view is only marginally superior.

The original **Schöner Brunnen**, from which the palace gained its name, now pours through the stone pitcher of a nymph near the Roman ruins. The garden's 630m-long **Irrgarten** (Maze; adult/child €4.50/2.50; ⊙9am-btwn 5pm & 7pm, closed early Nov-late Mar) is a classic hedge design based on the original maze that occupied its place from 1720 to 1892; adjoining this is the **Labyrinth**, a playground with games, climbing equipment and a giant mirror kaleidoscope.

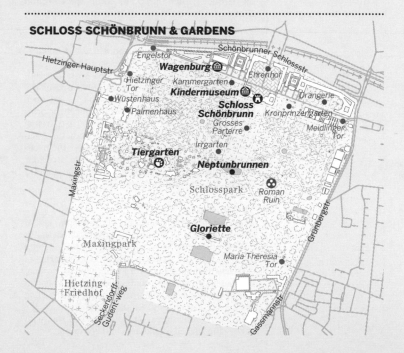

SCHLOSS SCHÖNBRUNN & GARDENS

PALMENHAUS

Travellers from London or fresh from a London spell may think they're experiencing déjà vu on sighting the **Palm House**. This was built in 1882 by Franz Segenschmid as a replica of the one in London's Kew Gardens. Inside is a veritable jungle of tropical plants from around the world. The Palmenhouse is at 13, Maxingstrasse 13b and is open from 9.30am to 6pm May to September (to 5pm October to April) and entry costs €4. A combined ticket for the Palmenhaus and Wüstenhaus costs €6 per person.

Palmenhouse

To the east of the palace is the **Kronprinzengarten** (Crown Prince Garden; adult/child €3/2.20; ⊗9am-btwn 4pm & 6pm, closed early Nov-late Mar), a replica of the baroque garden that occupied the space around 1750.

Kindermuseum

Schönbrunn's **Children's Museum** (www.schoenbrunn.at; 13, Schloss Schönbrunn; adult/child €7/5.50; ⊗10am-5pm Sat & Sun; ﷽) does what it knows best: imperialism. Activities and displays help kids discover the day-to-day life of the Habsburg court, and once they've got the idea, they can don princely or princessly outfits and start ordering the serfs (parents) around. Other rooms devoted to toys, natural science and archaeology all help to keep them entertained. **Guided tours** in German are a regular feature, departing at 10.30am, 1.30pm and 3pm (in English by appointment only).

Wagenburg

The **Wagenburg** (Imperial Coach Collection; www.kaiserliche-wagenburg.at; 13, Schloss Schönbrunn; adult/under 19yr €6/free; ⊗9am-6pm Apr-Oct, 10am-4pm Nov-Mar) is *Pimp My Ride* imperial style. On display is a vast array of carriages, including Emperor Franz Stephan's coronation carriage, with its ornate gold plating, Venetian glass panes and painted cherubs. The whole thing weighs an astonishing 4000kg. Also look for the dainty child's carriage built for Napoleon's son, with eagle-wing-shaped mudguards and bee motifs.

👁 SIGHTS

SCHLOSS SCHÖNBRUNN PALACE
See p175.

★KLIMT VILLA HOUSE MUSEUM
(www.klimtvilla.at; 13, Feldmühlgasse 11; adult/child €10/8, guided tour €2; ☺10am-6pm Tue, Fri & Sat Feb–mid-Jul & mid-Aug–Oct; ⓂUnter St Veit) The Klimt Villa immerses you in the sensual world of Vienna's most famous Secessionist. Set in landscaped grounds in a leafy corner of Hietzing, the 1920s neobaroque villa was built on and around the site of the artist's last studio (1911 to 1918), which opened to the public in September 2012 following a complete makeover.

Standouts include Moritz Nähr's original photos of the studio and garden, carefully reproduced furnishings, carpets, prints and paintings, as well as Klimt's sketches of models. Just as special is the intimate atmosphere of strolling through the painter's one-time house and gardens. With a little imagination you can still picture gorgeous dames swanning around here draped in flowing robes, as depicted in portraits such as *Adele Bloch-Bauer II* and *Frederike Beer,* which Klimt painted here. Guided tours take place at 2pm on Saturdays.

TECHNISCHES MUSEUM MUSEUM
Map p270 (www.technischesmuseum.at; 14, Mariahilfer Strasse 212; adult/under 19yr €10/free; ☺9am-6pm Mon-Fri, 10am-6pm Sat & Sun; ⓓ; ⓂSchönbrunn, ⓑ52, 58 Winckelmannstrasse)

Opened in 1918, the Technical Museum is dedicated to advances in the fields of science and technology. There are loads of hands-on gadgets allowing you to conduct experiments, but the most interesting aspect of the museum is its displays from past ages. A Mercedes Silver Arrow from 1950, a model-T Ford from 1923 and penny-farthing bicycles to name a few.

Its musical instrument collection is small and focuses mainly on keyboard instruments, so if this is your main interest, head for the Neue Burg museums instead. The permanent exhibition is complemented by temporary ones, and overall it's an interesting museum for the average visitor, but of course anyone with an engineering mind will absolutely love it. Das Mini section has loads of kids toys and activities and is specifically aimed at two- to six-year-olds.

HOFPAVILLON HIETZING LANDMARK
Map p270 (www.wienmuseum.at; 13, Schönbrunner Strasse; ⓂHietzing) Built between 1898 and 1899 by Otto Wagner as part of the public transport system, the Hofpavillon Hietzing was originally designed as a private station for the imperial court. The regal wood-panelled interior was designed by Wagner in conjunction with Josef Olbrich. Its white facade, decorated with wrought ironwork, is easily spotted just east of the U4 Hietzing stop.

It is in poor shape and was closed for renovation at the time of writing.

ℹ TICKETS FOR SCHLOSS SCHÖNBRUNN

If you plan to see several sights at Schönbrunn, it's worth purchasing one of the combined tickets. Prices vary according to whether it's summer season (April to October) or winter. The best way to get a ticket is to buy it in advance online. Print the ticket yourself and present it when you enter.

The summer season **Classic Pass** (adult/under 19yr €18/11) is valid for a grand tour of Schloss Schönbrunn and visits to the Kronprinzengarten (Crown Prince Garden), Irrgarten (Maze) & Labyrinth, Gloriette with viewing terrace, and **Hofbackstube Schönbrunn** (Court Bakery Schönbrunn; Map p270; ☎24 100-300; per person €8.90; ☺10am-5pm, shows on the hr, mid-Mar–Oct) with the chance to watch apple strudel being made and the opportunity to enjoy the result with a cup of coffee. A **Classic Pass 'light'** (adult/under 19yr €14/9.50) excludes the Apple Strudel Show. The Court Bakery Schönbrunn can be viewed separately (it's inside Café Residenz).

The summer **Gold Pass** (adult/under 19yr €36/18) includes the Grand Tour, Crown Prince Garden, Tiergarten, Palmenhaus, Wüstenhaus, Wagenburg, Gloriette, Maze & Labyrinth and Court Bakery Schönbrunn.

The **Winter Pass** (adult/under 19yr €25/12) includes the Grand Tour, Tiergarten, Palmenhaus, Wüstenhaus, Wagenburg, Gloriette and Maze & Labyrinth.

WORTH A DETOUR

LAINZER TIERGARTEN

At 25 sq km, the **Lainzer Tiergarten** (www.lainzer-tiergarten.at; 13, Hermesstrasse; ⊙8am-dusk; 🚌60B Hermesstrasse, 🚌60 Hermesstrasse) **FREE** is the largest (and wildest) of Vienna's city parks. The 'zoo' refers to the abundant wild boar, deer, woodpeckers and squirrels that freely inhabit the densely forested park, and the famous Lipizzaner horses that summer here. Opened by Emperor Ferdinand I in 1561, the park was once the hunting ground of Habsburg royalty. Today it offers extensive walking possibilities through lush woodlands of beech and oak, as well as attractions like the **Hubertus-Warte** (508m), a viewing platform on top of Kaltbründlberg.

On the eastern edge of the park sits the stately **Hermesvilla** (www.wienmuseum.at; 13, Lainzer Tiergarten; adult/under 19yr €6/free; ⊙10am-6pm Tue-Sun mid-Mar–early Nov; 🚌60B Hermesstrasse, 🚌60 Hermesstrasse), commissioned by Franz Josef I and presented to his wife as a gift. It is named after the white marble statue of Hermes, which guards the garden in front of the palace. Built by Karl von Hasenauer between 1882 and 1886, with Klimt and Makart on board as interior decorators, the villa is plush – it's more a mansion than simply a 'villa.' Empress Elisabeth's bedroom is totally over the top, with the walls and ceiling covered in motifs from Shakespeare's *A Midsummer Night's Dream*. A visit also takes in the room where Elisabeth, or 'Sisi', used to exercise rigorously in order to keep her famous 16-inch waist.

HIETZINGER FRIEDHOF CEMETERY

Map p270 (www.friedhoefewien.at; 13, Maxingstrasse 15; ⊙8am-dusk; MHietzing) **FREE** Aficionados of Vienna's Secessionist movement will want to make the pilgrimage to the Hietzinger cemetery to pay homage to some of its greatest members. Klimt, Moser and Wagner are all buried here. Others buried in the cemetery include Engelbert Dollfuss, leader of the Austro-Fascists, assassinated in 1934, and composer Alban Berg.

EATING

★ PURE LIVING BAKERY CAFE €

Map p270 (www.purelivingbakery.com; 13, Altgasse 12; cakes & snacks €3.50-6.50; ⊙9.30am-7pm Mon-Fri, 10am-7pm Sat & Sun; 🍴; MHietzing) Inspired by her time in the USA, sweet-toothed traveller Kirsten has brought the laid-back mood and food of a NYC deli to Vienna. Decked out with surfboards and coffee sacks, wicker chairs and holiday snapshots, this living room of a cafe is the place to unwind over a freshly toasted bagel and chocolate-drizzled cinnamon roll.

Pot plants and pink and blue deckchairs lend a personal touch to the pretty garden, where you can easily while away a sunny afternoon reading a magazine, sipping a shake and nibbling on locally baked goodies like deep-filled apple pie, banana bread and giant cookies.

MAFIOSI PIZZERIA €

Map p270 (☎892 72 28; www.pizzeria-mafiosi.at; 15, Reindorfgasse 15; pizza €3.20-5.50; ⊙11am-midnight; MGumpendorfer Strasse) According to its strapline, Mafiosi rustles up 'Vienna's best, biggest and cheapest pizzas.' While it's a tall claim, you can believe some of the hype. The woody Naples-meets-Alpine-chalet interior is an inviting setting for authentic pizzas, which start at a wallet-friendly €3.20. Add that to cheap booze (€2 for a beer) and you can see why students love the place.

QUELL AUSTRIAN €€

Map p270 (☎893 24 07; www.gasthausquell.at; 15, Reindorfgasse 19; mains €7-15; ⊙11am-midnight Mon-Fri; 🍴; MGumpendorfer Strasse) Time stands still at Quell, a traditional *Beisl* in suburban Rudolfsheim-Fünfhaus. The wood-panelled interior looks untouched for years, the archaic wooden chandeliers and ceramic stoves wouldn't be out of place in a folklore museum, and some guests look as though they've been frequenting the place for decades. The menu is thoroughly Viennese, with goulash, pork cutlets and schnitzel featuring heavily.

That said, there is also a surprising number of fish and vegetarian options. Genial staff and quiet streetside seating add to the attractions.

HOLLEREI VEGETARIAN €€

Map p270 (☎892 33 56; www.hollerei.at; 15, Hollergasse 9; lunch menus €7.50-11, mains €14-15.50;

⏲11.30am-3pm & 6-11pm Mon-Sat, 11.30am-3pm Sun; 🅿; ⓂMeidling Hauptstrasse, Schönbrunn) Located a 10-minute walk from Schloss Schönbrunn, this wood-panelled, all-vegetarian bistro does a fine line in seasonal salads, soups and pasta dishes. Whether you go for dhal, homemade spinach gnocchi with sun-dried tomatoes or red Thai curry with almond rice, the wholesome food here bursts with freshness. See the website for details on the monthly cookery course (€25).

BRANDAUERS SCHLOSSBRÄU AUSTRIAN €€
Map p270 (☎879 59 70; www.bierig.at; 13, Am Platz 5; mains €9-16; ⏲10am-1am; 🅿🖶; ⓂHietzing) This microbrewery in the Viennese mould rolls out hoppy house brews, speciality beers (including an organic one) and decent pub grub. Famous spare ribs served with lashings of potatoes feature alongside vegetarian options and the usual hearty suspects like goulash, cheese-laden dumplings and schnitzel. The €8.50 lunch buffet represents great value. Sit in the leafy courtyard when the sun's out.

🍷 DRINKING & NIGHTLIFE

CAFÉ GLORIETTE COFFEE
Map p270 (www.gloriette-cafe.at; 13, Gloriette; ⏲9am-dusk; ⓂSchönbrunn, Hietzing) Café Gloriette occupies the neoclassical Gloriette, high on a hill behind Schloss Schönbrunn, built for the pleasure of Maria Theresia in 1775. With sweeping views of the Schloss, its magnificent gardens and the districts to the north, Gloriette has arguably one of the best vistas in all of Vienna. It's a welcome pit stop after the short climb up the hill.

AIDA CAFE
Map p270 (13, Maxingstrasse 1; ⏲9am-7pm; ⓂHietzing) Just a short amble from the Hietzing Gate to Schloss Schönbrunn, this cafe is a fine spot to escape the crowds, sip a *Melange* and dig into delectable pastries, tortes and cakes after a visit to the palace.

LOSCH GAY
Map p270 (www.club-losch.at; 15, Fünfhausgasse 1; ⏲10pm-2am Fri & Sat; ⓂGumpendorfer Strasse) This leather-fetish bar is normally strictly men only, but occasionally it hosts unisex parties on Saturday nights. Lo:sch sometimes opens during the week for special events.

U4 CLUB
Map p270 (www.u-4.at; 12, Schönbrunner Strasse 222; ⏲8pm-late Mon, 10pm-late Tue-Sun; ⓂMeidling Hauptstrasse) U4 was the birthplace of techno clubbing in Vienna way back when, and its longevity is a testament to its ability to roll with the times. A fairly young, studenty crowd are its current regulars, and while the music isn't as cutting edge as it used to be, it still manages to please the masses.

☆ ENTERTAINMENT

ORANGERY CONCERT VENUE
Map p270 (☎812 50 04; www.imagevienna.com; 13, Schloss Schönbrunn; tickets €39-89; ⓂSchönbrunn) Schönbrunn's lovely former imperial greenhouse is the location for year-round Mozart and Strauss concerts. Performances

---

WORTH A DETOUR

AMAZING ART NOUVEAU GRACE

Perched on the crest of the Baumgartner Höhe in Vienna's 14th district, **Kirche am Steinhof** (☎910 60-11 204; 14, Baumgartner Höhe 1; admission €2, tours €8; ⏲4-5pm Sat, noon-4pm Sun, tours 3-4pm Sat, 4-5pm Sun; 🚌47A, 48A Baumgartner Höhe), built from 1904 to 1907, is the crowning glory of Otto Wagner. It's a steepish walk up to the church, nestled in the grounds of the Psychiatric Hospital of the City of Vienna and commanding fine views of the city.

Kolo Moser chipped in with the mosaic windows, and the roof is topped by a copper-covered dome that earned the nickname *Limoniberg* (Lemon Mountain) from its original golden colour. It's a bold statement in an asylum that has other art nouveau buildings, and it could only be pushed through by Wagner because the grounds were far from the public gaze. The church interior can only be visited by guided tour.

last around two hours and begin at 8.30pm daily.

MARIONETTEN THEATER PUPPET THEATRE

Map p270 (☑817 32 47; www.marionettentheater. at; 13, Schloss Schönbrunn; tickets full performances adult €11-35, child €8-22; ☺box office on performance days from 11am; ⓂSchönbrunn) This small theatre in Schloss Schönbrunn puts on marionette performances of the much-loved productions *The Magic Flute* (2½ hours) and *Aladdin* (1¼ hours). They're a delight for kids young, old and in between. The puppet costumes are exceptionally ornate and eye-catching.

REIGEN LIVE MUSIC

Map p270 (☑894 00 94; www.reigen.at; 14, Hadikgasse 62; ☺6pm-late; ⓂHietzing) Reigen's tiny stage is the setting for jazz, blues, Latin and world music in a simple space housing rotating art and photography exhibits, so you can groove while perusing art.

 SHOPPING

GOLD N' GUITARS MUSIC

Map p270 (13, Maxingstrasse 2; ☺10am-12.30pm & 2-6pm Mon-Fri, 9am-12.30pm Sat; ⓂHietzing) This is one of a kind in Vienna: owner and guitar craftsman Michael Eipeldauer restores and sells contraguitars, also known as a *Schrammelguitar*, used for folk music, jazz and other styles – they have a standard neck and a second fretless one for bass notes. A prize piece is a Biedermeier model from the 1840s.

Expect to pay between €1600 (used) and €3500 (new). Stylish secondhand East German guitars such as models from Musima, as well as Arthur Lang jazz guitar classics, glisten on stands around the store.

Day Trips from Vienna

Salzburg p184

Mozart's birthplace, Maria von Trapp's spiritual home and the former hangout of lordly prince-archbishops – Salzburg will make you yodel out loud with its baroque beauty and high-on-a-hill fortress.

Krems an der Donau p190

Gateway to the Wachau, quaint Krems plies its visitors with wine and apricot schnapps then sends them out to explore its eye-catching historical core by the Danube.

Melk & Around p192

Easily reachable from the capital, must-see Stift Melk and nearby Schallaburg castle make up an architectural duo you won't want to miss.

Znojmo p194

With its wine-producing traditions, pretty historical centre and dramatic location, this easygoing Czech town is the gateway to the Podyjí National Park.

Bratislava (Slovakia) p195

Straddling the Danube, the Slovak capital offers an intriguing insight into the Austro-Hungarian and more recent socialist past.

Salzburg

Explore

Visiting Salzburg from Vienna is doable in two days, but consider tagging on a third day to explore at a more leisurely pace. High on your itinerary for day one should be the Unesco-listed baroque *Altstadt* (old town), which is burrowed below steep hills, with the main trophy sights clustering on the left bank of the Salzach River. You can walk everywhere in this compact, largely pedestrianised city.

On your second day, whiz up to medieval clifftop fortress Festung Hohensalzburg for sublime city and mountain views, or take a spin around the galleries and Mozart museums. With an extra day, you could head for kitsch-country on a *Sound of Music* bicycle or Segway tour.

Base yourself centrally to see Salzburg beautifully illuminated by night. Classical music performances and beer gardens are the big draws after dark.

The Best...

➡ **Sight** Old Town
➡ **Place to Eat** Bärenwirt (p188)
➡ **Place to Drink** Augustiner Bräustübl (p188)

Top Tip

The **Salzburg Card** (1-/2-/3-day card €26/35/41) includes entry to the major sights and attractions, a river cruise, unlimited use of public transport plus discounts on tours and events.

Getting There & Away

Car & Motorcycle The A1 motorway links Vienna to Salzburg; it's approximately a three-hour drive. The largest car park in the centre is the Altstadt Garage under Mönchsberg (€18 per day).

Train There are at least two trains hourly from Vienna's Westbahnhof to Salzburg (€100, 2½ to three hours). Discounted ÖBB SparSchiene (www.oebb.at/en/tickets/SparSchiene) tickets can be booked online in advance and can cost as little as a third of the standard train fare.

Need to Know

➡ **Area Code** 🖉0662
➡ **Location** 296km west of Vienna
➡ **Tourist Office** (🖉889 87-330; www.salzburg.info; Mozartplatz 5; ☺9am-7pm)

⊙ SIGHTS

OLD TOWN   HISTORIC QUARTER
A Unesco World Heritage site, Salzburg's Old Town centre is equally entrancing whether viewed from ground level or the hills above.

The grand **Residenzplatz**, with its horse-drawn carriages and mythical fountain, is a good starting point for a wander. The overwhelmingly baroque **Dom** (Cathedral; Domplatz; ☺8am-7pm Mon-Sat, 1-7pm Sun), slightly south, is entered via bronze doors symbolising faith, hope and charity. The adjacent **Dommuseum** (adult/child €5/1.50; ☺10am-5pm Mon-Sat, 11am-6pm Sun May-Oct) is a treasure-trove of ecclesiastical art.

From here, head west along Franziskanergasse and turn left into a courtyard for **Stiftskirche St Peter** (St Peter's Abbey Church; St Peter Bezirk 1-2; catacombs adult/child €1.50/1; ☺church 8.30am-noon & 2.30-6.30pm, cemetery 6.30am-7pm, catacombs 10.30am-5pm Tue-Sun), an abbey church founded around 700. Among the lovingly tended graves in the grounds you'll find the **Katakomben** (catacombs; admission €1.50; ☺10.30am-5pm Tue-Sun), cavelike chapels and crypts hewn out of the Mönchsberg cliff face.

The western end of Franziskanergasse opens out into Max Reinhardt Platz, where you'll see the back of Fisher von Erlach's **Kollegienkirche** (Universitätsplatz; ☺8am-6pm), another outstanding example of baroque architecture. The **Stift Nonnberg** (Nonnberg Convent; Nonnberggasse 2; ☺7am-dusk), where Maria first appears in *The Sound of Music*, is back in the other direction, a short climb up the hill to the east of the Festung Hohensalzburg.

⭐**FESTUNG HOHENSALZBURG**   FORT
(www.salzburg-burgen.at; Mönchsberg 34; adult/child/family €7.80/4.40/17.70, with Festungsbahn funicular €11/6.30/25.50; ☺9am-7pm) Salzburg's most visible icon is this mighty clifftop fortress, one of the best preserved in Europe. Built in 1077, it was home to many prince-archbishops who ruled Salzburg from 798.

Inside are the impressively ornate state-rooms, torture chambers and two museums.

It takes 15 minutes to walk up the hill to the fortress, or you can catch the **Festungsbahn funicular** (Festungsgasse 4).

MOZARTS GEBURTSHAUS · MUSEUM

(Mozart's Birthplace; www.mozarteum.at; Getreidegasse 9; adult/child/family €10/3.50/21; ☺9am-5.30pm) Mozart was born in this bright-yellow town house in 1756 and spent the first 17 years of his life here. The museum today harbours a collection of memorabilia, including the miniature violin the child prodigy played, plus a lock of his hair and buttons from his jacket.

MOZART-WOHNHAUS · MUSEUM

(Mozart's Residence; www.mozarteum.at; Makartplatz 8; adult/child €10/3.50, incl Mozarts Geburtshaus €17/5; ☺9am-5.30pm) The Mozart family moved to this more spacious abode in 1773, where a prolific Mozart composed works such as the *Shepherd King* and *Idomeneo*. Alongside family portraits and documents, you'll find Mozart's original fortepiano.

Under the same roof and included in your ticket is the **Mozart Ton-und Filmmuseum** (☺9am-1pm Mon, Tue & Fri, 1-5pm Wed & Thu), a film and music archive for the ultra-enthusiast.

SALZBURG MUSEUM · MUSEUM

(www.salzburgmuseum.at; Mozartplatz 1; adult/child €7/3; ☺9am-5pm Tue-Sun, to 8pm Thu) Housed in the Neue Residenz palace, this flagship museum takes you on a romp through Salzburg past and present. Ornate rooms showcase medieval sacred art, prince-archbishop portraits and highlights such as Carl Spitzweg's renowned *Sonntagsspaziergang* (Sunday Stroll; 1841) painting. There are free guided tours at 6pm on Thursday. Salzburg's famous 35-bell glockenspiel, which chimes daily at 7am, 11am and 6pm, is on the palace's western flank.

SCHLOSS MIRABELL · PALACE

(Mirabellplatz 4; ☺palace 8am-4pm Mon, Wed & Thu, 1-4pm Tue & Fri, gardens dawn-dusk) **FREE** Prince-Archbishop Wolf Dietrich built this splendid palace in 1606 for his beloved mistress Salome Alt. Its lavish baroque interior, replete with stucco, marble and frescoes, is free to visit. The **Marmorsaal** (Marble Hall) provides a sublime backdrop for evening chamber concerts.

WANT MORE?
••
Head to **Lonely Planet** (www.lonely planet.com/austria) for planning advice, author recommendations, traveller reviews and insider tips.

For stellar fortress views, take a stroll in the manicured, fountain-dotted **gardens**. *The Sound of Music* fans will of course recognise the Pegasus statue, the gnomes and the steps where the mini von Trapps practised 'Do-Re-Mi'.

RESIDENZ · PALACE

(www.residenzgalerie.at; Residenzplatz 1; combined ticket state rooms & gallery adult/child €9/3; ☺10am-5pm) This baroque palace is where the prince-archbishops held court until the 19th century. You can visit their opulently frescoed staterooms, while the gallery spotlights Dutch and Flemish masters of the Rubens and Rembrandt ilk.

MUSEUM DER MODERNE · GALLERY

(www.museumdermoderne.at; Mönchsberg 32; adult/child €8/6; ☺10am-6pm Tue-Sun, to 8pm Wed) Straddling Mönchsberg's cliffs, this contemporary gallery shows first-class exhibitions of 20th- and 21st-century art. The works of Alex Katz, Emil Nolde and John Cage have previously featured. There's a free guided tour of the gallery at 6.30pm on Wednesday.

The **Mönchsberg Lift** (Gstättengasse 13; one-way/return €2.10/3.40, incl gallery ticket €9.70/6.80; ☺8am-7pm Thu-Tue, to 9pm Wed) whizzes up to the gallery year-round.

FRIEDHOF ST SEBASTIAN · CEMETERY

(Linzer Gasse 41; ☺9am-6.30pm) Tucked away behind the baroque St Sebastian's Church, this peaceful cemetery is the final resting place of Mozart family members and 16th-century physician Paracelsus. Out pomping them all, though, is Prince-Archbishop Wolf Dietrich von Raitenau's mosaic-tiled mausoleum, an elaborate memorial to himself.

 EATING

Self-caterers can find picnic fixings at the **Grüner Markt** (Green Market; Universitätsplatz; ☺Mon-Sat).

Salzburg

0 200 m
0 0.1 miles

Sterneckstr

Rupertgasse

Bayerhamerstr

Auerspergstr

Schallmooser Hauptstr

Glockengasse

33

Steinhamerstr

Vierthalerstr

Franz-Josef-Str

Lasserstr

Wolf-Dietrich-Str

31

35

Paracelsusstr

17

Linzer Gasse

4

Kapuzinerberg

Auerspergstr

Franz-Josef-Str

Pars-Lodron-Str

Bergstr

Kapuzinerberg
Viewpoint

Weiserstr

Hubert-Sattler-Gasse

Schrannengasse

Priesterhausgasse

21

Auerspergstr

Mirabellplatz

Dreifaltigkeitsgasse

Makartplatz

Right

32

Bank Bus
Departures

8

Theatergasse

Rainerstr

28

30

Mirabellgarten

14

25

26

Markus Sittikus Str

Schwarzstr

Elisabethkai

Makartsteg

Schwarzstr

Müllner Steg

Bärenwirt (100m);
Augustiner
Bräustübl (300m)

Müllner Hauptstr Ursulinenplatz

Gstätten

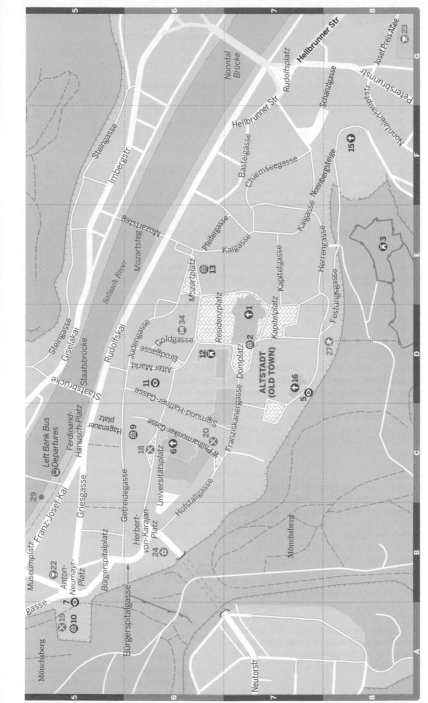

Salzburg

BÄRENWIRT
AUSTRIAN €€

(☑42 24 04; www.baerenwirt-salzburg.at; Müllner Hauptstrasse 8; mains €9-18; ☉11am-11pm) Sizzling and stirring since 1663, Bärenwirt combines a woody, hunting-lodge-style interior with a river-facing terrace. Go for hearty *Bierbraten* (beer roast) with dumplings, locally caught trout or organic wild-boar bratwurst.

ALTER FUCHS
AUSTRIAN €€

(☑88 20 22; Linzer Gasse 47-49; mains €10-17; ☉noon-midnight Mon-Sat; ☑◈) This old fox prides itself on serving up old-fashioned Austrian fare, such as schnitzels fried to golden perfection. Foxes clad in bandanas guard the bar in the vaulted interior and there's a courtyard for good-weather dining.

ZUM FIDELEN AFFEN
AUSTRIAN €€

(☑87 73 61; www.fideleraffe.at; Priesterhausgasse 8; mains €10.50-19.50; ☉5pm-midnight Mon-Sat) At the jovial monkey you'll dine heartily on Austrian classics like goulash and sweet curd dumplings in the vaulted interior or on the pavement terrace. Reservations are recommended.

M32
FUSION €€

(☑84 10 00; www.m32.at; Mönchsberg 32; 2-course lunch €14, 5-course dinner €68-70, mains €14-23; ☉9am-1am Tue-Sun; ☑◈) Bold colours and a forest of stag antlers reveal architect Matteo Thun's imprint at Museum der Moderne's glass-walled restaurant. The seasonal food and views are fantastic.

TRIANGEL
AUSTRIAN €€

(☑84 22 29; Wiener-Philharmoniker-Gasse 7; lunch €4.90, mains €9-30; ☉noon-midnight Mon-Sat) The menu is market-fresh at this arty bistro. It does gourmet salads, a mean Hungarian goulash with organic beef, and delicious homemade ice cream.

 DRINKING

You'll find the biggest concentration of bars along both banks of the Salzach and the hippest around Gstättengasse and Anton-Neumayr-Platz.

AUGUSTINER BRÄUSTÜBL
BREWERY

(www.augustinerbier.at; Augustinergasse 4-6; ☉3-11pm Mon-Fri, 2.30-11pm Sat & Sun) Who says monks can't enjoy themselves? Since

1621 this cheery monastery-run brewery has been serving potent home brews in the vaulted hall and beneath the chestnut trees in the 1000-seat beer garden.

REPUBLIC   BAR
(www.republic-cafe.at; Anton-Neumayr-Platz 2; ⊘8am-1am Sun-Thu, to 4am Fri & Sat) One of Salzburg's most happening haunts, with regular DJs and free events, from jazz breakfasts to Tuesday salsa nights.

UNIKUM SKY   CAFE
(Unipark Nonntal; ⊘10am-7pm Mon-Fri, 9.30am-6pm Sat) For knockout fortress views, drinks and inexpensive snacks, head up to this sun-kissed terrace atop the new Unipark Nonntal campus.

☆ ENTERTAINMENT

Some of the high-brow venues include the **Schlosskonzerte** (✆84 85 86; www.salzburger-schlosskonzerte.at; Theatergasse 2; ⊘8pm), chamber music concerts in Schloss Mirabell's sublime baroque Marble Hall, and the Mozart-focused **Mozarteum** (✆889 40; www.mozarteum.at; Schwarzstrasse 26-28). Marionettes bring *The Sound of Music* and Mozart's operas magically to life at **Salzburger Marionettentheater** (✆87 24 06; www.marionetten.at; Schwarzstrasse 24; ⊘May-Sep, Christmas, Easter;).

Austria's most renowned classical music festival, the **Salzburg Festival** (www.salzburgerfestspiele.at) attracts international stars from late July to late August. Book on its website, or ask the **ticket office** (✆80 45-500; info@salzburgfestival.at; Herbert-von-Karajan-Platz 11; ⊘9.30am-1pm & 2-5pm Mon-Sat) about cancellations during the festival.

🏃 SPORTS & ACTIVITIES

The tourist office has iGuide audiovisual city tours (€9), which take in big-hitters like the Residenz, Mirabellgarten and Mozartplatz, for those who want to go it alone.

FRÄULEIN MARIA'S BICYCLE TOURS   BIKE TOUR
(www.mariasbicycletours.com; Mirabellplatz 4; adult/child €26/18; ⊘9.30am May-Sep, plus 4.30pm Jun-Aug) Belt out *The Sound of Music*

faves as you pedal on one of these 3½-hour bike tours of the film locations. No booking is required; just turn up at the Mirabellplatz meeting point.

SEGWAY TOURS   TOUR
(www.segway-salzburg.at; Wolf-Dietrich-Strasse 3; city/Sound of Music tour €33/65; ⊘tours 9am, noon, 3pm & 5pm Mar-Oct) These guided Segway tours take in the big sights by zippy battery-powered scooter.

SALZBURG SIGHTSEEING TOURS   BUS TOUR
(✆88 16 16; www.salzburg-sightseeingtours.at; Mirabellplatz 2; ⊘office 8am-6pm) Sells a 24-hour ticket for a multilingual hop-on, hop-off bus tour of the city and *The Sound of Music* locations.

SALZBURG SCHIFFSFAHRT   BOAT TOUR
(www.salzburghighlights.at; Makartsteg; adult/child €15/7; ⊘Apr-Oct) Hour-long cruises depart from Makartsteg bridge, with some chugging on to Schloss Hellbrunn (the ticket price does not cover entry to the palace).

🛏 SLEEPING

Ask for the tourist office's hotel brochure, which gives prices for hotels, pensions, hostels and camping grounds. Beds are like gold dust during the Salzburg Festival from mid-July to August.

YOHO SALZBURG   HOSTEL €
(✆879 649; www.yoho.at; Paracelsusstrasse 9; dm €15-23, d €45-75; @⊛) Comfy bunks, free wi-fi, plenty of cheap beer – what more could a backpacker ask for? Except, perhaps, a merry sing-along with *The Sound of Music* screened daily (yes, every day). The friendly crew can arrange tours, adventure sports and bike hire.

ARTE VIDA   GUESTHOUSE €€
(✆87 31 85; www.artevida.at; Dreifaltigkeitsgasse 9; s €55-140, d €80-152; ⊛) Arte Vida has the boho-chic feel of a Marrakesh *riad* (traditional house), with its lantern-lit salon, communal kitchen and individually designed rooms done out in rich colours and fabrics. Reinhold arranges yoga sessions in the quiet garden, and outdoor activities.

HOTEL AM DOM   BOUTIQUE HOTEL €€
(✆84 27 65; www.hotelamdom.at; Goldgasse 17; s €90-160, d €130-280; ❋⊛) Antique meets

boutique at this *Altstadt* hotel, where the original vaults and beams of the 800-year-old building contrast with razor-sharp design features. Artworks inspired by the Salzburg Festival grace the strikingly lit rooms.

**HOTEL & VILLA
AUERSPERG**   BOUTIQUE HOTEL €€

(✆88 94 40; www.auersperg.at; Auerspergstrasse 61; s €129-155, d €165-205, ste €235-310; P @ �) ✎ This charismatic villa-hotel hybrid fuses late-19th-century flair with contemporary design. Relax by the lily pond in the garden or in the rooftop wellness area with mountain views. Free bike hire is a bonus.

Krems an der Donau

Explore

Krems, as its known to its friends, is the prettiest of the larger towns on the Danube and marks the beginning of the Wachau. Enjoyable eating and drinking, an atmospheric historical centre, rivers of top-quality wine from local vineyards and a couple of unexpected museums attract the summer tourist crowds, but the rest of the year things can be pretty quiet. Aimless wandering is the best plan of attack, dipping into churches and museums, strolling the banks of the Danube and sampling the local tipples as you go.

Krems has three parts: Krems to the east, the small settlement of Stein (formerly a separate town) to the west, and the connecting suburb of Und. Hence the local witticism: *Krems und Stein sind drei Städte* (Krems and Stein are three towns). A day is ample time to explore the trio.

The Best...

➡ **Sight** Kunsthalle
➡ **Place to Eat** Jell
➡ **Place to Drink** Stadtcafe Ulrich (p192)

Top Tip

A walk through the cobblestone streets of Krems and Stein, especially after dark, is a real highlight. The tourist office hands out a useful walk-by-numbers guide to the town.

Getting There & Away

Boat DDSG Blue Danube (Map p266; ✆58 880; www.ddsg-blue-danube.at; Handelskai 265) runs a Sunday service between Vienna and Dürnstein. Boats leave from near the DDSG office at Quay 5 (Handelskai 265) alongside the Wien/Reichsbrücke at 8.30am, stopping at Krems at 2pm and returning from Krems at 5pm (arriving back in Vienna at 9pm). The return fare is €32. The river station in Krems is just off Donaustrasse, 1.5km west of the train station.

Car From Vienna take the A22 north towards Stockerau, then the S5 west to Krems. The 76km journey takes around an hour.

Train & Bus Hourly direct trains connect Krems with Vienna's Franz-Josefs-Bahnhof (€15.20, one hour).

Need to Know

➡ **Area Code** ✆02732
➡ **Location** 60km northwest of Vienna
➡ **Tourist Office Krems Tourismus** (✆82 676; www.krems.info; Utzstrasse 1; ☺9am-6pm Mon-Fri)

◉ SIGHTS

KUNSTHALLE   GALLERY

(www.kunsthalle.at; Franz-Zeller-Platz 3; admission €10; ☺10am-6pm) The flagship of Krems' **Kunstmeile** (www.kunstmeile-krems.at), an eclectic collection of galleries and museums, the Kunsthalle has a program of small but excellent changing exhibitions which can home in on anything from mid-19th-century landscapes to today's concept art. Guided tours run on Sunday at 2pm.

KARIKATURMUSEUM   MUSEUM

(www.karikaturmuseum.at; Steiner Landstrasse 3a; admission €10; ☺10am-6pm) Austria's only caricature museum occupies a suitably tongue-in-cheek chunk of purpose-built architecture opposite the Kunsthalle. Changing exhibitions and a large permanent collection of caricatures of prominent Austrian and international figures make for a fun diversion.

MUSEUM KREMS   MUSEUM

(www.museumkrems.at; Körnermarkt 14; adult/child €5/3; ☺11am-6pm Wed-Sun Apr & May, daily Jun-Oct) Housed in a former Dominican

Krems an der Donau

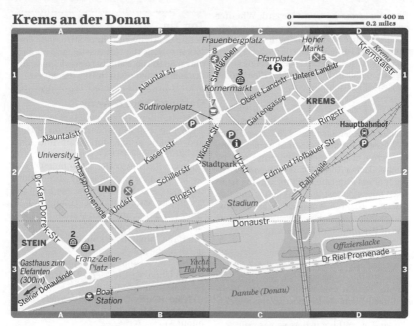

monastery, the town's museum has collections of religious and modern art (including works by Kremser Schmidt, who painted the frescoes in Pfarrkirche St Veit), as well as winemaking artefacts and a section on the famous Krems mustard.

PFARRKIRCHE ST VEIT   CHURCH
(Pfarrplatz 5; ☉dawn-dusk) Known as the 'Cathedral of the Wachau', the large baroque parish church boasts colourful frescoes by Martin Johann Schmidt, an 18th-century local artist who was also known as Kremser Schmidt and occupied a house from 1756 near the Linzer Tor in Stein.

WEINGUT DER STADT KREMS   WINE TASTING
(www.weingutstadtkrems.at; Stadtgraben 11; ☉9am-noon & 1-5pm Mon-Fri, 9am-noon Sat) A city-owned vineyard yielding 200,000 bottles per year (90% is Grüner Veltliner and Riesling), some of which you can sample and buy.

✖ EATING & DRINKING

GASTHAUS ZUM ELEFANTEN   AUSTRIAN €
(www.zum-elefanten.at; Schürerplatz 10; mains €9.50-16.50; ☉lunch & dinner Mon-Sat) Bag a seat indoors or out on the pretty baroque

square to enjoy a reassuringly brief menu of local treats with an upmarket kink. The crayfish in spicy apricot sauce and gourmet Elefanten-Burger (contains no pachyderm we were assured) are best helped along with a shot of the homemade schnapps.

★JELL   AUSTRIAN €€
(www.amon-jell.at; Hoher Markt 8-9; mains €12-22; ☉lunch & dinner Tue-Fri, lunch Sat & Sun) Occupying a gorgeous stone house, Jell is hard to beat for a rustic atmosphere and

fine wine from its own vineyard. Whether you go for the braised veal with potato mash flavoured with pumpkin-seed oil or the smoked salmon gnocchi with crayfish-and-lime sauce, be sure to leave some room for the delightfully fluffy *Marillenknödel* (apricot-filled dumplings).

MÖRWALD KLOSTER UND   AUSTRIAN €€€
(📞70 493; www.moerwald.at; Undstrasse 6; mains €35-39, 5-course menu €75, 3-course lunch €29; ⊘lunch & dinner Tue-Sat) Mörwald is one of a crop of gourmet restaurants run by kitchen kaiser Toni Mörwald outside Vienna. It offers exquisite delights ranging from roast pigeon breast to beef, poultry and fish dishes with French angles. A lovely yard and an impressive wine selection round off one of Wachau's best restaurants.

STADTCAFE ULRICH   CAFE
(www.stadtcafe-ulrich.at; Südtirolerplatz 7; ⊘7am-11pm Mon-Thu, to midnight Sat, 9am-11pm Sun) Krems' busiest cafe is this elegantly high-ceilinged Viennese job next to the Steinertor, good for your first and last cuppa of the day, and everything in between as well.

Melk & Around

Explore

With its sparklingly majestic abbey-fortress, Melk is a highlight of any visit to the Danube Valley. Separated from the river by a stretch of woodland, this pretty town makes for an easy and rewarding day trip from the capital. Combine a visit with nearby Schloss Schallaburg and you have yourself a day packed with architectural bliss.

Melk is one of the most popular destinations in Austria so you certainly won't be alone on its cobbled streets. It's also one of the few places in the Wachau that has a pulse in winter, making it a year-round excursion option.

The Best...
→ **Sight** Stift Melk
→ **Place to Eat** Zur Post (p194)

Top Tip
Before or after your tour of Stift Melk, don't forget to visit the Nordbastei guarding the entrance to the complex, always home to a fascinating and often quirky exhibition.

Getting There & Away
Boat An interesting way to tackle Melk as a day trip is to use a combination of train and Danube cruise ship. From mid-April to late October DDSG Blue Danube and Austrian Railways offer a combined train/boat/train ticket for one-way connections to Krems and Melk and the boat trip between the two. Purchase tickets (adult/child €57/16) at any train station or DDSG Blue Danube booking office. Boats leave from the canal by Pionierstrasse, 400m north of the abbey.

Car The A1 motorway runs all the way from Vienna west to Melk. The 87km journey takes around 90 minutes.

Train Hourly trains link Vienna's Westbahnhof with Melk (€15.90, one hour 20 minutes).

Need to Know
→ **Area code** 📞02752
→ **Location** 77km west of Vienna
→ **Tourist Office** (📞51160; www.nieder-oesterreich.at/melk; Babenbergerstrasse 1; ⊘9.30am-6pm Mon-Sat, to 4pm Sun Apr-Oct, 9am-5pm Mon-Thu, to 2.30pm Fri Nov-Mar)

◉ SIGHTS

STIFT MELK   ABBEY
(Benedictine Abbey of Melk; 📞5550; www.stift-melk.at; Abt Berthold Dietmayr Strasse 1; adult/child €9.50/5, with guided tour €11.50/7; ⊘9am-5.30pm May-Sep, tours at 11am & 2pm only Oct-Apr) The Danube Valley's most popular sight was once the residence of the Babenberg family. Benedictine monks transformed Melk's top piece of real estate into a monastery in 1089, but the building you see today is mostly the result of a rebuild commissioned by Abbot Berthold Dietmayr and executed in ostentatious baroque style by Jakob Prandtauer.

It's said nine million bricks were used in the reconstruction work, and the Stift has almost 500 rooms. Most of these are taken

DRIVING TOUR: THE DANUBE VALLEY

This tour mostly follows the Danube, taking in towns and sights on a circuit between Krems an der Donau and Maria Taferl on the north bank, and Melk and several castles and ruins on the south bank. You'll finish at Stift Göttweig after 150km and a long day.

From the **Krems-Stein roundabout** take the B3 southwest towards Spitz. About 3km from Krems-Stein you approach the small settlement of Unterloiben, where on the right you'll see the **Franzosendenkmal** (French Monument), erected to celebrate the victory of Austrian and Russian troops over Napoleon here in 1805. Continuing on, you'll reach **Dürnstein**, 6km from Krems, where the blue-towered Chorherrenstift is backed by Kuenringerburg, the castle where Richard the Lionheart was imprisoned in 1192.

Much of the valley is hemmed by picturesque terraced vineyards as you enter the heart of the Wachau. In **Weissenkirchen**, 12km from Krems, you'll find a striking fortified parish church on the hilltop. The Wachau Museum here houses work by artists of the Danube school. A couple of kilometres on, just after Wösendorf, you arrive at the church of **St Michael** with seven terracotta hares adorning the roof.

Some 17km from Krems, the town of **Spitz** occupies a ledge between the Danube and the terraced vineyards behind. The old centre is made up of quiet, cobblestone streets and there are some good trails leading out of town up into the hills.

Turn right at Spitz onto the B217 (Ottenschläger Strasse). The terraced hill on your right is **1000-Eimer-Berg**, so-named for its reputed ability to yield 1000 buckets of wine each season. On your left, high above the valley opening, is the castle ruin **Burgruine Hinterhaus**. Continue along the B217 and turn right towards **Burg Oberranna** (☏8221; www.burg-oberranna.at; s/d €88/148; Ⓟ), 6km west of Spitz in Mühldorf. This castle and old-world hotel overlooking the valley is furnished with antiques. From here, backtrack down to the B3 and continue the circuit. The valley opens up and on the left, across the Danube, you glimpse the ruins of Burg Aggstein.

Willendorf, 21km from Krems, is where a 25,000-year-old figurine of Venus was discovered. The original is housed in the Naturhistorisches Museum (p122) in Vienna. As you continue along the B3, the majestic Stift Melk rises up across the river.

At Klein Pöchlarn a sign indicates a first turn-off on Artstettner Strasse (L7255), which you can follow for 5km to **Artstetten**, unusual for its many onion domes. From here, the minor road L7257 winds 6.5km through a verdant landscape to **Maria Taferl** high above the Danube Valley. The main attraction here is the **Pfarr- und Wallfahrtskirche Maria Taferl** (Parish & Pilgrimage Church; www.basilika.at; Maria Taferl 1; ⊘7am-8pm), a magnificent baroque church created by Jakob Prandtauer.

Backtrack 6km down towards the B3. Turn left at the B3 towards Krems and follow the ramp veering off to the left and across the river at the Klein Pöchlarn bridge. Follow the road straight ahead to the B1 and turn left onto this towards Melk. This first section along the south bank is uninteresting, but it soon improves. Across the river you should be able to make out Artstetten in the distance, and before long Stift Melk (p192), one of Austria's top sights, rises up ahead.

From Stift Melk, a 7km detour leads south to the Renaissance castle of Schloss Schallaburg (p194). To reach the castle from the abbey in Melk, follow the signs to the *Bahnhof* (train station) and Lindestrasse east, turn right into Hummelstrasse/Kirschengraben (L5340) and follow the signs to the castle. Just beyond the entrance is the castle's architectural centrepiece, a two-storey arcaded Renaissance courtyard.

Return to the B33. Be careful here that you stay on the south side of the river. When you reach the corner of Abt-Karl-Strasse and Bahnhofstrasse, go right and right again at the river. Follow the B1 for 4km to **Schloss Schönbühel**, a 12th-century castle perched right on the river bank 5km northeast of Melk. Continue along this lovely stretch of the B33 in the direction of Krems. About 10km from Schloss Schönbühel the ruins of **Burg Aggstein** (www.ruineaggstein.at; Aggsbach Dorf; adult/child €6.50/4.50; ⊘9am-7pm) should be your next stop.

About 27km from Melk some imposing cliffs rise up above the road. When you reach the roundabout near the bridge to Krems follow the road right from the B33 to Mautern and right again immediately afterwards towards Fürth. **Stift Göttweig** is signposted at the next roundabout on the L7071. From there it's a short drive back to Krems.

up by Melk's top school, monks' quarters and offices, leaving visitors to marvel at the Marble Hall with its 3D ceiling frescoes, the ornately decorated library and the church boasting Lower Austria's most over-the-top interior. Guided tours take around an hour; count on around two hours without a guide.

SCHLOSS SCHALLABURG
PALACE

(☎02754-6317; www.schallaburg.at; Schallaburg 1; adult/child €10/3.50, combined ticket with Stift Melk €17.50; ⊙9am-5pm Mon-Fri, 9am-6pm Sat Apr-early Nov) This Renaissance palace set in lovely gardens is famous not only for its stunning architecture but also for the innovative exhibitions it houses. Architecturally, it boasts some 400 terracotta sculptures, completed between 1572 and 1573, the largest of which support the upper-storey arches of the palace. Every year the building hosts a prestigious exhibition based on a chosen cultural theme; shows in recent years have focused on the Beatles, Venice and Byzantium. Combined tickets with Stift Melk cost €15. To reach Schallaburg, take the shuttle bus (€4), which leaves Melk train station at 10.40am, 1.15pm and 4.45pm.

 EATING

ZUM FÜRSTEN
INTERNATIONAL €

(☎523 43; Rathausplatz 3; mains €3.70-9.60; ⊙10.30am-11pm) Right at the foot of the Stift, relax after a tour on faux-velvet 1970s seating at this popular cafe serving pastas, strudel, chilli con carne and other international staples.

ZUR POST
AUSTRIAN €€

(☎523 45; Linzer Strasse 1; mains €7.20-20.50; ⊙lunch & dinner Mon-Sat ; ☑) A traditional, understated restaurant in the hotel of the same name on Melk's main drag. Waldviertel carp, Wiener Schnitzel, Danube catfish and organic lamb populate the menu, which also features several vegetarian options.

Znojmo

Explore

Known as Znaim to the Austrians, picturesque Znojmo (pronounced *znoy*-moh) perches (very) high above the Dyje River on the border between southern Moravia in the Czech Republic and Austria. Quiet even at the height of summer, the old centre makes for an easygoing day trip from Vienna, and if you've never been on the 'wrong' side of the former Iron Curtain, this is a gentle introduction to post-communist Europe.

Znojmo's stellar sight is the Romanesque Rotunda of Our Lady & St Catherine, one of the oldest surviving churches in the country. Outside of town the main draw in these parts is the Podyjí National Park (Nationalpark Thayatal on the Austrian side), which straddles the border and offers some vista-rich day hiking.

The Best...

➡ **Sight** Rotunda of Our Lady & St Catherine
➡ **Place to Eat** Na Věčnosti
➡ **View** Dyje Gorge

Top Tip

Some 76km of well-marked hiking trails start from the Church of St Nicholas – the tourist office sells very detailed maps of the Podyjí National Park through which they pass.

Getting There & Away

Car Take the A22 north out of Vienna towards Prague, change to the B303 and (in the Czech Republic) follow the 38. The journey should take no more than 90 minutes.

Train At least six direct trains daily link Znojmo with Wien-Hauptbahnhof (return EURegio ticket €18, 1¾ hours).

Need to Know

➡ **Area Code** ☎+420 515
➡ **Location** 74km north of Vienna, in the Czech Republic
➡ **Tourist Office** (☎216 111; www.znojmocity.cz; Obroková 1/12; ⊙8am-6pm Mon-Fri, 9am-5pm Sat, 10am-5pm Sun May, Jun, Sep & Oct, slightly longer hrs Jul & Aug)

⊙ SIGHTS

ROTUNDA OF OUR LADY & ST CATHERINE
CHURCH

(Rotunda Panny Marie a sv Kateřiny; ☎515 222 311; www.znojmuz.cz; Castle grounds 90Kč; ⊙9.15am-5pm Tue-Sun May-Sep, Sat & Sun only Apr) In the grounds of Znojmo castle, the town's top sight is this 11th-century church, one of the Czech Republic's oldest Romanesque structures containing a beautiful series of 12th-century frescoes. These depict biblical scenes, figures from Czech legends and, most significantly, 19 rulers from the Přemyslid dynasty, all astonishingly well preserved after nine centuries. Due to the sensitive nature of the frescoes, visitors are limited to groups of 10 or fewer, and are allowed in for 15 minutes at a time once per hour.

ZNOJMO UNDERGROUND   UNDERGROUND
(Znojemské podzemí; ☑515 221 342; Slepičí trh 2; ticket 95Kč; ⊗9am-6pm Jul-Aug, to 4pm May, Jun & Sep, 10am-4pm Mon-Sat Apr, 10am-4pm Sat Oct) One of Znojmo's most popular attractions is this tour through the labyrinthine 14th-century tunnels and cellars below the old town. Dress warmly and expect lots of animated trolls and animatronic skeletons.

 **EATING**

NA VĚČNOSTI   VEGETARIAN €
(☑776 856 650; www.navecnosti.cz; Velká Miku-lášská 11; mains 60-130Kč, lunch 69Kč; ⊗10.30am-1am Mon-Thu, to 2am Fri & Sat, 11am-1am Sun; ⊛☑) Take a break from central Europe's meat-heavy diet at this hip, atmospheric vegetarian restaurant-pub buried deep in the old town. Fried cheese is a major player on the menu alongside Slovak halušky (small dumplings in cheese sauce), curries (nothing hot), pastas and a nod to the local vintners in the form of tofu in wine sauce.

U ZLATÉ KONVE   CZECH €
(Nám TGM 9; mains 50-130Kč; ⊗10am-10pm) Take curvaceous vaulting leaps over diners as they recline on Chesterfield-style sofas with views of Znojmo's main square. The menu of sirloin in cream sauce, Moravian cabbage soup, apple strudel and pork in mushroom sauce is pure Czech comfort food.

Bratislava (Slovakia)

Explore
Just over an hour from Vienna by train, Slovakia's diminutive capital is a quietly

energetic city, laced with Slavic spice but still bearing the intriguing hallmarks of 40 years of communism. Its low-rise historical centre is small, easy to explore on foot and crammed with restored historical buildings, churches and museums. Throw in a bunch of friendly locals and some delicious Carpathian food and you have yourself one fascinating cross-border excursion.

The Best...
➜ **Sight** Municipal Museum
➜ **Place to Eat** Modrá Hviezda (p197)
➜ **Place to Drink** Bratislavský Meštiansky Pivovar (p197)

Getting There & Away
Boat Daily **LOD** (www.lod.sk; single/return €23/38) hydrofoils link Vienna with Bratislava. Boats leave from quay 6 at Reichsbrücke.

Bus Slovak Lines (www.slovaklines.sk) run hourly buses (return €14.30, 1½ hours) between Südtirolerplatz and Bratislava's main bus station.

Car Head east on the A4 from Vienna until the Fischamend junction, where you continue on Bundesbahn 9, which crosses the border just south of Bratislava.

Train From the Hauptbahnhof, hourly trains (return EURegio ticket €15, one hour) travel to both Bratislava's main train station (Hlavná Stanica) and Petržalka station, 3km south of the old town. From the latter, take bus 80 (€0.90) across the Danube into the centre.

Need to Know
➜ **Area Code** ☑+421 2
➜ **Location** 55km east of Vienna
➜ **Tourist Office** (☑161 86; www.visitbratislava.eu; Klobučnícka 2; ⊗9am-7pm Apr-Oct, to 6pm Nov-Mar)

SIGHTS

MUNICIPAL MUSEUM   MUSEUM
(☑5910 0812; www.muzeum.bratislava.sk; Hlavné nám; adult/child €6/3; ⊗10am-5pm Tue-Fri, 11am-6pm Sat & Sun) Occupying a group of buildings in the heart of the city centre, including the 14th-century town hall and the 18th-century rococo Apponyi Palace, this excellent museum deals with myriad

Bratislava

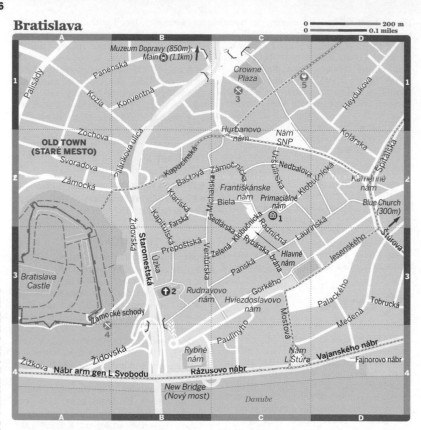

0 ━━━ 200 m
0 ━━━ 0.1 miles

Bratislava

◉ Sights
1 Municipal Museum C2
2 St Martin's Cathedral B3

⊗ Eating
3 Bratislavský Meštiansky Pivovar C1
4 Modrá Hviezda A4

🍸 Drinking & Nightlife
5 Slovak Pub C1

local themes including Carpathian viti-culture, traditional industries, Bratislava's numerous rulers, Hungarian coronations and the city's status as Slovak capital. The magnificent town hall interiors have been crisply renovated and a climb to the top of the tower provides views of the (closed) castle.

MUZEUM DOPRAVY   MUSEUM
(Transport Museum; ☎5244 4163; www.muzeum-dopravy.com; ul Šancová 1/A; admission €3.30; ☺10am-5pm Tue-Sun) Velorex, Tatra, Jawa, ES-KA, Böhmerland, Praga, Škoda...if these names mean anything to you, then visit Bratislava's outstanding, nostalgia-inducing transport museum, Slovak museum of the year 2010. As well as parades of polished classics and veterans, there's also a mock-up of a communist-era driving school, a couple of lumbering steam trains and tons of rail-way hardware, some of it in service until just a few years ago.

ST MARTIN'S CATHEDRAL   CHURCH
(Dóm sv Martina; cnr Kapitulská & Staromestská; ☺9-11.30am & 1-4pm Mon-Sat, 1.30-4pm Sun) A relatively modest interior belies the glo-rious occasions witnessed by St Martin's Cathedral: 11 Austro-Hungarian monarchs (10 kings and one queen, Maria Theresia) were crowned in this 14th-century church.

BLUE CHURCH
CHURCH

(Kostol Svätej Alžbety; Bezručova 2) The 1911 Church of St Elizabeth, known as the Blue Church, is a bouncy-castle-like Secessionist confection by Ödön Lechner, decorated with mosaics and cool shades of azure and ultramarine. Opposite the church, the school by the same architect is almost as impressive.

The Blue Church is located around 500m east of the old town – any street heading west off ul štúrova will get you close.

✖ EATING & DRINKING

★MODRÁ HVIEZDA
SLOVAK €

(www.modrahviezda.sk; ul Beblavého 14; mains €8-20; ☺11am-11pm; 🛜) Claiming to have been filling bellies for 250 years, the 'Blue Star' serves upmarket Slovak fare such as venison steak, roast rabbit and venison pâté with cranberries and gingerbread. The folksy dining room or rock-cut cellar space are the perfect backdrops for a few after-dinner shots of slivovitz accompanied by some fast-tempo Carpathian violin music.

BRATISLAVSKÝ MEŠTIANSKY PIVOVAR
SLOVAK €

(🖉0944512265; www.mestianskypivovar.sk; Drevená 8; mains €5.50-19; ☺11am-midnight Mon-Thu & Sat, to 1am Fri, to 11pm Sun) The local meat-dumpling-beer combination is best executed by this large, modern microbrewery serving Bratislava's freshest suds and monster platters of Slovak fare.

SLOVAK PUB
SLOVAK

(Obchodná 62; mains €3-10; ☺10am-midnight Mon-Thu, 10am-2am Fri & Sat, noon-midnight Sun; 🛜) With 600 seats and a warren of differently styled rooms and halls, this slightly touristy pub is the biggest in the Slovak capital, but also one of the best. The menu features almost every national dish going and some of what goes into the pot hails from the owner's organic farm.

DAY TRIPS FROM VIENNA BRATISLAVA (SLOVAKIA)

Sleeping

From youth hostels to design hotels or luxury establishments where chandeliers, antique furniture and original 19th-century oil paintings abound, Vienna's lodgings cover it all. In between are homely Pensionen and less ostentatious hotels, plus a small but smart range of apartments.

Reservations & Cancellations

It's wise to book ahead at all times. In the winter and autumn low and shoulder seasons (except for Christmas and New Year's) a day or two is usually sufficient for most places, but for the best value, especially in the centre, a few weeks ahead is advisable. From around Easter to September you will need to book at least several weeks in advance for these places, and some in the centre are booked out a month or more ahead. When you book direct with the hotel, some places require email confirmation following a telephone reservation, but many places are also bookable online. Confirmed reservations in writing are binding, and cancellations within several days of expected arrival often involve a fee or full payment.

Hotels & Pensionen

Two stars Expect functional rooms costing around €50/90 single/double close to the centre. It's often better to stay in a hostel.

Three stars Most hotels and *Pensionen* (guesthouses) are in this category. Expect to pay about €70/130 single/double, less in winter or when booking online. Rooms should be clean, with a decent buffet breakfast, wi-fi, minibar and flat-screen TV and have pleasant showers. Some have bath-tubs.

Four & five stars Rooms in four-star hotels are generally larger than three-star rooms and should have sound insulation and contemporary or quality furnishing; some have wellness facilities. Five-star hotels have premium wellness facilities.

Hostels & Student Residences

Vienna has a smattering of *Jugendherbergen*, private hostels or hostels affiliated with Hostelling International (HI). In the former, no membership is required.

Academia Hotels (Map p260; ☑40 176 55; www.academiahotels.at; 08, Pfeilgasse 3a; s/d/tr €62/86/111; ☑rooms Jul-Sep; ☑46 Strozzigasse) handles bookings for its residences in Vienna (as well as Graz and Salzburg). Book on the website or call well in advance.

Apartments & Longer-Term Rentals

The advantage of an apartment is that you have a kitchen and can save on food costs. Most central apartments cost from €120.

The following websites are useful:

Craig's List (http://vienna.de.craigslist.at) Search under 'Ferienwohnungen' in 'Wien'.

Apartment.at (www.apartment.at) A broad selection from a group of owners.

oh-vienna.com (www.oh-vienna.com) Many inexpensive options.

waytostay (www.waytostay.com) Online and telephone booking.

Lonely Planet's Top Choices

25hours Hotel (p204) Offbeat circus theme and prime location.

Hotel Kärntnerhof (p202) Viennese charm and style.

Das Triest (p203) Luxury with design touches.

my MOjO vie (p204) Hostel with upbeat style.

DO & CO (p202) Sexiest hotel in the centre.

Hollmann Beletage (p202) Finely styled and filled with extras.

Best by Budget

€

my MOjO vie (p204) Hostel with bright flair.

Schweizer Pension (p201) Central and friendly.

Pension Kraml (p202) Large rooms in a historic *Pension*.

€€

Hollmann Beletage (p202) Stylish with perks.

Hotel Kärntnerhof (p202) Viennese charm.

Boutiquehotel Stadthalle (p205) Cosy and eco-aware.

€€€

Radisson Blu Palais Hotel (p202) Palatial luxury.

Das Triest (p203) Sir Terence Conran interior design.

Hotel Imperial (p203) Favourite for European royalty.

Best Design Hotels

Radisson Blu Style Hotel (p201) Elegant nuances of art nouveau and art deco.

Das Triest (p203) The hotel that planted the design hotel seed in Vienna.

Hotel Rathaus Wein & Design (p204) An oenologist's delight: minimalist-chic rooms themed by wine and vine.

25hours Hotel (p204) All the fun of the circus bundled into a slick, design-minded hotel.

Altstadt (p204) Razor-sharp design and original art bring this historic hotel bang up to date.

Best Luxury Hotels

Radisson Blu Palais (p202) A combination of two former fin de siècle palaces.

Das Triest (p203) Sir Terence Conran left his designer imprint on this historic-meets-contemporary retreat.

DO & CO (p202) Swanky, sexy, central and some rooms with jacuzzi.

Hotel Sacher (p201) A baroque gem with modern conveniences.

Hotel Imperial (p203) Where royalty stays when visiting Vienna.

Best Classic Viennese Pensionen

Schweizer Pension (p201) Homely and won't break the budget.

Hotel Drei Kronen (p203) Old-fashioned flair in an art-nouveau *Pension*.

Angel's Place (p206) Heaven in the shape of a wine cellar–turned-guesthouse.

Best Hostels

my MOjO vie (p204) Closest thing to a designer hostel, with everything from netbooks to musical instruments.

Wombat's (p206) Aussie charm and a lounge vibe.

Believe It Or Not (p204) Lounge-style Neubau hostel.

NEED TO KNOW

Price Ranges
Each sleeping option has been given a price symbol, indicating the room price at double occupancy.

€	less than €80
€€	€80 to €200
€€€	under €200

Check-in & Check out
Check-in is mostly at 2pm or 3pm. Earlier check-in is usually possible with advance notice. Check out is at 11am or noon.

Tipping
Only bell hops and room service in luxury hotels (€1 or €2).

Breakfast
Included in all prices, often not in upmarket hotels. We say when it's not.

Parking
Indicated when on premises. Usually costs between €6 and €30 for 24 hours. Some places have deals with nearby parking garages.

Wi-Fi
Almost always free.

Websites
➡ **Booking.com** (www.booking.com)

➡ **Hotel.de** (www.hotel.de)

➡ **Hostelworld.com** (www.hostelworld.com)

➡ **Hostelling International** (www.hihostels.com)

➡ **Lonely Planet** (www.lonelyplanet.com/hotels) Reviews, author recommendations and online booking.

SLEEPING

Where to Stay

Neighbourhood	For	Against
The Hofburg & Around	Central, close to the Hofburg, some accommodation close to MuseumsQuartier	More expensive, packed with tourists
Stephansdom & the Historic Centre	Close to key sights and restaurants	More expensive, high tourist density and green spaces only on fringes
Karlsplatz & Around Naschmarkt	Close to Naschmarkt, good bars and restaurants, less expensive	More travel time is needed to get to sights from outlying areas
The Museum District & Neubau	Great neighbourhood, especially closer to Ringstrasse, near museums, the Hofburg, bars and restaurants	Relatively low hotel density, dependence on trams in some parts
Alsergrund & the University District	Uni feel in parts, handful of good, inexpensive hotels	Transport to other districts often indirect unless near Ringstrassse
Schloss Belvedere to the Canal	Quiet and close to the palace	Few sights except Belvedere, limited restaurants and bars
Prater & East of the Danube	Quiet character, good transport to centre and to the Prater, couple of good markets	Limited sights except the Prater, very few outstanding restaurants and bars
Schloss Schönbrunn & Around	Some parts are close to Schönbrunn, others to the lively Brunnenmarkt eating and drinking area	Light on sights except for Schönbrunn, some sections along the Gürtel are sleazy and unattractive

🛏 The Hofburg & Around

PENSION A UND A   BOUTIQUE HOTEL $$
Map p254 (☑8905 128; www.aunda.at; 01, Habsburgergasse 3; r €139-159, ste €259-269; ⬤; Ⓜ Herrengasse, Stephansplatz) This small and elegant hotel offers excellent value close to Hofburg in rooms with parquet floors and large suites sleeping up to four people.

PENSION NOSSEK   PENSION $$
Map p254 (☑533 70 41-0; www.pension-nossek. at; 01, Graben 17; s €80-100, d €125; ✳ @ ⬤; Ⓜ Herrengasse, Stephansplatz) This *Pension* offers a prime location close to the Innere Stadt sights, coupled with typical Viennese service (professional and polite, if a little stiff); rooms are spotless, generally spacious and enhanced with baroque-style furnishings. The hotel does not accept credit cards. WLAN costs €5 per stay.

PENSION PERTSCHY   PENSION $$
Map p254 (☑534 49-0; www.pertschy.com; 01, Habsburgergasse 5; s €83-119, d €91-228; ⬤; Ⓜ Herrengasse, Stephansplatz) It's hard to find fault with Pension Pertschy. Its quiet yet central location, just off the Graben, is hard to beat, staff are exceedingly able, willing and friendly, and children are welcomed with gusto (toys for toddlers and high chairs for tots are available). Rooms are not only spacious but filled with a potpourri of period pieces and a rainbow of colours.

AVIANO   PENSION $$
Map p254 (☑512 83 30; www.secrethomes.at; 01, Marco-d'Aviano-Gasse 1; s €87-112, d €127-187; ⬤; Ⓜ Stephansplatz) Aviano offers a supremely central position, high standards and all-round value for money. Rooms are small (there are no bath-tubs) without being claustrophobic and feature high ceilings, decorative moulding and whitewashed antique furnishings; corner rooms have a charming alcove and bay window. The breakfast room is sunny and bright, and in summer utilises a small balcony on the courtyard.

★ STEIGENBERGER
HOTEL HERRENHOF   HOTEL $$$
Map p254 (☑534 040; www.steigenberger.com/ en/wien; 01, Herrengasse 10; r €189-209, ste €600-700, without breakfast; ✳ @ ⬤; Ⓜ Herrengasse) Decorated throughout in subtle and subdued aubergine colours, Steigenberger Hotel Herrenhof offers style and great value in 24- to 28-sq-metre superior rooms and 35-sq-metre deluxe rooms, complemented by free use of the spacious wellness area extending over two floors with sauna, steam bath and fully equipped gym. Corner deluxe rooms have extra large windows.

★ RADISSON BLU
STYLE HOTEL   DESIGN HOTEL $$$
Map p254 (☑22 780 0; www.radissonblu.com/ stylehotel-vienna; 01, Herrengasse 12; r €185-255, ste €310; ✳ ⬤; Ⓜ Herrengasse) This elegant hotel is a contender for the title of 'most fashionable hotel address' in Vienna; it has overtones of art nouveau and art deco and is decorated throughout in demure grey shades. The least expensive rooms don't include breakfast (€23 per person). Rates can be lower, depending on demand.

HOTEL SACHER   LUXURY HOTEL $$$
Map p254 (☑514 560; www.sacher.com; 01, Philharmonikerstrasse 4; r €480-1350, ste €1600-2900; ✳ @ ⬤; Ⓜ Karlsplatz, ⬚ D, 1, 2, 71 Kärntner Ring/Oper) Walking into the Sacher is like turning back the clocks 100 years. The reception, with its dark-wood panelling, deep red shades and heavy gold chandelier, is reminiscent of an expensive fin de siècle bordello. The smallest rooms are surprisingly large and suites are truly palatial. Junior suites/doubles cost from €480 to €1350.

As well as extras such as original oil paintings throughout and a tiny cube of the hotel's famous *Sacher Torte* on arrival, there's a hi-tech spa complex, with herbal sauna, ice fountain and fitness room.

🛏 Stephansdom & the Historic Centre

SCHWEIZER PENSION   PENSION $
Map p252 (☑533 81 56; www.schweizerpension. com; 01, Heinrichsgasse 2; s €56-75, d €75-98; Ⓜ Schottentor, ⬚1 Salztorbrücke) 🗷 Rooms at this pleasant little *Pension* are super clean, and while they're not flush with the most up-to-date amenities, everything you find inside – from big, comfy beds to ornamental ceramic stoves – has a cosy, homely feel to it. The feeling of well-being extends to low-allergy rooms and bio-breakfasts. The 11 rooms fill up quickly, so book ahead.

★**HOLLMANN BELETAGE** PENSION $$

Map p252 (✆961 19 60; www.hollmann-beletage.
at; 01, Köllnerhofgasse 6; d €159-230, tr €179-279,
q €199-300, ste from €390; @📶; MSchweden-
platz, 🚊1, 2 Schwedenplatz) This minimalist
establishment offers style and clean lines
throughout. Rooms are slick units, with
natural wood floors, bare walls, simple,
classic furniture and designer lamps and
door handles. A terrace and lounge where
you can enjoy free snacks at 2.30pm and
6pm are bonuses, as are the small hotel cin-
ema and free use of an iPad.

★**OPERA SUITES** PENSION $$

Map p252 (✆512 93 10; www.operasuites.at; 01,
Kärntner Strasse 47; r without breakfast €149-165,
apt €168; @📶; MKarlsplatz, 🚊D, 1, 2 Kärntner
Ring/Oper) Located directly across from the
famous Hotel Sacher and close to the major
sights, Opera Suites offers well-priced and
comfortable standard and superior rooms,
some of which have cooking facilities and
are more like apartments or holiday flats.
Book well ahead, and expect to pay from
€4.80 to €9.80 for breakfast if you want it.

PENSION RIEDL PENSION $$

Map p252 (✆512 7919; www.pensionriedl.at; 01,
Georg-Coch-Platz 3; s/d without breakfast from
€69/85; 📶; MStubentor, 🚊1, 2 Julius-Raab-Platz)
Rooms are generally large and bedecked
with mismatched furniture (bathrooms are
on the small side) in this traditional *Pen-
sion*. Rooms 6 and 7 have tiny balconies
overlooking Georg-Coch-Platz, while the
balcony in room 8 enjoys views of the inner
courtyard. Reception hours are 7.30am to
11.15am and 4pm to 8pm.

HOTEL KÄRNTNERHOF HOTEL $$

Map p252 (✆512 19 23; www.karntnerhof.com; 01,
Grashofgasse 4; s €99-129, d €135-195, tr €199-235,
ste €279-299; @📶; MStephansplatz) This tall
treasure fuses old Vienna charm with cosy
ambience, from the period paintings lining
the walls to the wood- and frosted-glass-
panelled lift to the surprising roof terrace.

HOTEL AUSTRIA HOTEL $$

Map p252 (✆515 23; www.hotelaustria-wien.at; 01,
Fleischmarkt 20; s €79-144, d €110-190, tr €225;
@📶; MStephansplatz, Schwedenplatz, 🚊1, 2
Schwedenplatz) This popular hotel with a
tasteful interior offers some of the best value
in the Innere Stadt during the low and shoul-
der seasons. Well-sized, cosy rooms have
kettles for tea and coffee. Book well ahead.

RADISSON BLU
PALAIS HOTEL LUXURY HOTEL $$$

Map p252 (✆515 17-0; www.radissonblu.com; 01,
Parkring 16; s from €109, r from €139, without
breakfast; 📶; MStubentor, Stadtpark, 🚊2 Weihburggasse) Spread across two historic palace
buildings, this is one of the top addresses in
town and a preferred option among visiting state dignitaries. Single and doubles as
well as suites and maisonettes are tastefully furnished with hints of the fin de siècle
epoch, with maisonettes that are vast and
span two levels (from about €239). Prices
vary considerably according to demand, so
check the internet.

★**DO & CO** LUXURY HOTEL $$$

Map p252 (✆241 88; www.doco.com; 01,
Stephansplatz 12; r without breakfast €350-370;
@📶; MStephansplatz) This swanky and
sexy hotel in the heart of the historic cen-
tre offers superb views of Stephansdom in
a selection of exquisite rooms with quality
sound and entertainment systems. Several
rooms have their own jacuzzi, but guests
should be aware that bathrooms (but not
the toilets) have transparent glass walls.

TOPAZZ VIENNA DESIGN HOTEL $$$

Map p252 (✆1532 22 50; www.hoteltopazz.com;
01, Lichtensteg 3; r €228-258; ❋📶; MStephansplatz) Added to Vienna's hotel scene in late
2012, this design hotel has decorations
and furnishings inspired by the Wiener
Werkstätte period around the turn of the
20th century. Gentle browns permeate the
rooms and foyer, and almost all rooms have
large, padded porthole windows that you
can repose in. Prices vary according to size
of the rooms (superior, deluxe and prestige).

Directly across the road is the sister hotel,
Lamée Vienna (Map p252; www.hotellamee.at;
Rotenturmstrasse 15, 01; r €238-308, ste €408; 📶;
MStephansplatz), which is €10 more expensive
in all categories and decorated in the 1930s
art deco style. This place also has suites, and
in both hotels the minibar is restocked daily
for free in the higher categories.

🛏 Karlsplatz & Around Naschmarkt

PENSION KRAML PENSION $

Map p256 (✆587 85 88; www.pensionkraml.at;
06, Brauergasse 5; s €35, d €56-76, tr €78-87, q
€120; @📶; MZieglergasse) Tucked peacefully

CHEZ CLICHÉ

Ever fancied having a friend who lives right in the heart of Vienna? Well, **Chez Cliché** (☑943 69 48; www.chezcliche.com; d €169-239; ☜) is the next best thing. In tune with the 'live like a local' zeitgeist, you can now stay in the home of a fictional Viennese friend in one of eight uberstylish apartments, decorated with a mishmash of design pieces and flea-market finds. They are scattered across the city, from the Innere Stadt's backstreets to student-flavoured Alsergrund.

Each apartment has been designed with a razor-sharp eye for detail to reflect a specific persona. Sophie, the botanist's pad, for instance, has medicinal plants and kitchen herbs in the kitchen, floral dresses hanging on rails, wellies and plenty of pot plants. Beat, the music freak, has hip white-walled digs complete with a disco ball and record player. Or you could opt to stay in the contemporary, art-slung home of Koloman, the theatre buff, the gracefully art nouveau abode of Therese, the classical music enthusiast, or the travel-themed apartment of Bella, the flight attendant.

down a backstreet five minutes' walk south of Mariahilfer Strasse, this family-run *Pension* looks back on 150 years of history and prides itself on old-school hospitality and comfort. Rooms are surprisingly large, accommodating twin beds, bedside tables and a solid wardrobe, while leaving plenty of room for a close waltz. Internet is only available in the common areas.

DAS TYROL   HOTEL $$
Map p256 (☑587 54 15; www.das-tyrol.at; 06, Mariahilfer Strasse 15; s €109-229, d €149-259; ✱☜; ⓂMuseumsquartier) Design is the word at Das Tyrol. Done out in zesty yellow and green hues, the spacious rooms feature original artworks, such as Dieter Koch's playful Donald and Daisy Duck paintings, and Nespresso machines. Corner rooms have small balconies overlooking Mariahilfer Strasse. Breakfast, with eggs cooked to order and prosecco, will keep you going all morning.

The gold-tiled spa has a sauna and a 'light therapy' shower where you can watch fish blub in the aquarium.

HOTEL DREI KRONEN   PENSION $$
Map p256 (☑587 32 89; www.hotel3kronen.at; 04, Schleifmühlegasse 25; s/d €79/109; @☜; ⓂKettenbrückengasse) Within stumbling distance of the Naschmarkt (some rooms overlook it), this family-owned abode is one of Vienna's best-kept secrets. Tiny palatial touches (shiny marble, polished brass, white-and-gold wallpaper) are distinctly Viennese, but nonetheless a casual feel prevails. Rooms are fitted with *Jugendstil* (art nouveau) furniture and art (including many prints by Klimt).

The breakfast buffet is huge, with pastries, cereals, bacon and free-range eggs, as well as *Sekt* (sparkling wine), an unheard-of luxury in a three-star *Pension*.

★HOTEL IMPERIAL   HOTEL $$$
Map p256 (☑501 100; www.luxurycollection. com/imperial; 01, Kärntner Ring 16; r from €350; @☜; ⓂKarlsplatz, ⒹD, 2 Karlsplatz) The merest whisper of the Imperial makes most Viennese nod in awe. This former palace, with all the marble and majesty of the Habsburg era, has service as polished as its crystal. The Fürsten Stiege, with rich red carpet, is a flamboyant opening, leading from the reception to the Royal suite.

Suites are filled with 19th-century paintings and genuine antique furniture (and come with butler service), while 4th- and 5th-floor rooms in Biedermeier style are far cosier and may come with a balcony.

DAS TRIEST   HOTEL $$$
Map p256 (☑589 18; www.dastriest.at; 04, Wiedner Hauptstrasse 12; s/d €229/296; @☜; ⓂKarlsplatz, Kettenbrückengasse) This Sir Terence Conran creation is a symbiosis of history and modern design. The 300-year-old former stables is now a cutting-edge hotel, with an overall nautical theme; portholes replace spy holes and windows, and stairwell railings would be at home on the *Queen Mary 2*. Rooms reveal a clean aesthetic and muted tones, with little touches like fresh flowers polishing the scene off.

On the ground floor is Restaurant Collio (p104), serving Italian food and centered on a pretty inner courtyard.

SLEEPING KARLSPLATZ & AROUND NASCHMARKT

🛏 The Museum District & Neubau

MY MOJO VIE
HOSTEL $

Map p260 (✆0676-551 11 55; http://my-mojovie.at; 07, Kaiserstrasse 77; dm/d/tr/q €26/58/84/108; @📶; MBurggasse Stadthalle) An old-fashioned cage lift rattles up to these incredible backpacker digs. Everything you could wish for is here: design-focused dorms complete with dressing tables and snug-as-a-bug rugs, a kitchen with free supplies, netbooks for surfing, guidebooks for browsing and even musical instruments for your own jam session.

BELIEVE IT OR NOT
HOSTEL $

Map p260 (✆0676-550 00 55; www.believe-it-or-not-vienna.at; 07, Myrthengasse 10; dm €25-30; @📶; MVolkstheater) It may seem nondescript on the face of things, but you really won't believe what a cosy, homely hostel this is. We love the dorms with mezzanine-style beds, laid-back lounge, kitchen with free basics and laptops for guest use. Lily, your South African host, puts on a great spread at breakfast.

KAISER 23
HOSTEL, GUESTHOUSE $

Map p260 (✆523 41 81; www.kaiser23.at; Kaiserstrasse 23, 07; s €37, d €47-52, tr €60; @📶; MWestbahnhof) Though it's just a two-minute walk from Mariahilfer Strasse, the vibe is delightfully mellow at this hostel-guesthouse, part of a 19th-century convent. You might well bump into a friendly nun on your way to one of the bright, parquet-floored rooms, with pared-down furniture and splashes of lime adding a contemporary touch. Breakfast costs an extra €8.

PENSION WILD
PENSION $

Map p260 (✆406 51 74; www.pension-wild.com; 08, Lange Gasse 10; s €41-69, d €53-90, tr €114; MRathaus, Volkstheater) Wild is one of the few openly gay-friendly *Pensionen* in Vienna, but the warm welcome extends to all walks of life. The top-floor 'luxury' rooms are simple yet appealing, with light-wood furniture and private bathrooms, and are a big advantage over Wild's other two categories. All, however, are spotlessly clean and kitchens are there for guests to use.

ALTSTADT
PENSION $$

Map p260 (✆522 66 66; www.altstadt.at; 07, Kirchengasse 41; s €125-175, d €145-215, ste €195-350;

@📶; MVolkstheater) Otto Ernst Wiesenthal has poured his passion and impeccable taste into creating one of Vienna's most outstanding guesthouses in Spittelberg. Design elements by Vitra and Philippe Starck merge seamlessly with original art from the likes of Andy Warhol and Prachensky. The individually decorated rooms are charming and quirky (without being overcooked), with high ceilings, plenty of space and natural light.

The devil is in the detail here: from the free afternoon tea with homemade cakes to the lavish breakfast with salmon, antipasti and *Sekt*, and an open fire where you can nurse a glass of red. Staff bend over backwards to please – whatever you need, just say the word.

25HOURS HOTEL
DESIGN HOTEL $$

Map p260 (✆521 51; www.25hours-hotels.com; 07, Lerchenfelder Strasse 1-3; r €100-130, ste €150-190; 📶; MVolkstheater) Roll up, roll up... OK, you're not going to find any performing elephants or trapeze artists at this circus-themed high-rise hotel, but staff do jump through hoops to please. The groovy Dreimeta-designed rooms are decked out in bold colours, with big-top-style murals, pod-shaped rugs and welcome touches such as iPod docking systems.

Top whack suites come with terraces commanding grandstand views of the Hofburg. The Dachboden rooftop bar, Mermaid's Cave sauna area and free use of electro-bikes for whizzing about town make this all in all a class act.

HOTEL RATHAUS
WEIN & DESIGN
BOUTIQUE HOTEL $$

Map p260 (✆400 11 22; www.hotel-rathaus-wien.at; 08, Lange Gasse 13; s/d/tr €150/210/240; ✺ @📶; MRathaus, Volkstheater) Each stylish room in this boutique hotel is dedicated to an Austrian winemaker and the minibar is stocked with premium wines from the growers themselves. The open-plan, minimalist-chic rooms reveal a razor-sharp eye for design and clever backlighting, especially the opalescent ones with hybrid beds and bath-tubs. Some rooms peer out onto the inner courtyard space.

The hotel offers wine tastings in its chandelier-lit bar, and excursions to Austria's nearby winegrowing regions. Wine is also a theme at breakfast (€17), with wine-based cheese, preserves and cakes alongside a tempting array of mueslis, fruit, fish and cold cuts.

BOUTIQUEHOTEL STADTHALLE   HOTEL **$$**
Map p260 (☎982 42 72; www.hotelstadthalle.
at; 15, Hackengasse 20; s €78-138, d €118-198;
🖘; ⓂSchweglerstrasse) 🌿 Welcome to Vi-
enna's most eco-aware hotel, which makes
the most of solar power, rainwater collec-
tion and LED lighting, and has a roof fra-
grantly planted with lavender. Bursts of
purple, pink and peach enliven rooms that
are a blend of the modern with polished an-
tiques. An organic breakfast is served in the
ivy-draped courtyard garden.

HOTEL FÜRSTENHOF   HOTEL **$$**
(☎523 32 67; www.hotel-fuerstenhof.com; 07,
Neubaugürtel 4; s €79-89, d €89-170, tr €148-185,
q €159-200; 🖘; ⓂWestbahnhof) This family-
run affair overflowing with personality has
been the choice of touring alternative bands
for years – see the reception for proof. Don't
be surprised if you encounter a burgeoning
rock star in the reception lounge, which
doubles as a library. Rooms are basic, with
blood-red carpets, full-length curtains and
deep colours creating a warm feel.

The house dates from 1906, so ceilings
are higher than normal and the lift is a museum piece (thankfully, the motor isn't).

🛏 Alsergrund & the University District

BENEDIKTUSHAUS   GUESTHOUSE **$$**
Map p262 (☎534 98 90 0; www.benediktushaus.
at; 01, Freyung 6a; s €70, d €99-115, tr €119-135, q
€139-155; 🖘; ⓂSchottentor) Rest your weary
head in a Benedictine monastery – you'd
never guess you're in the heart of the action
when you peer out your window into the
tranquil, tree-filled courtyard. It's run by
the Scottish Abbey next door and the tidy

rooms are solid and frill-free, though a few
period antiques line the halls. There are no
TVs in the rooms.

🛏 Schloss Belvedere to the Canal

SPIESS & SPIESS   PENSION **$$**
Map p268 (☎714 85 05; www.spiess-vienna.at;
03, Hainburger Strasse 19; s €105-145, d €140-
180, ste €205-255; ✹ @🖘; ⓂRochusgasse) The
Spiess family goes out of its way to make
you welcome at this elegant, well-positioned
Pension. The spacious, crisp white rooms
have been designed with care and utmost
taste; the pricier ones come with fireplaces
and balconies. Breakfast is a tempting
smorgasbord of fresh fruit salad, bacon and
eggs, cereals and pastries.

HOTEL PRINZ EUGEN   HOTEL **$$**
Map p268 (☎505 17 41; www.austria-hotels.at; 04,
Wiedner Gürtel 14; s €69-100, d €69-120; ✹ @🖘;
ⓂSüdtiroler Platz) Though not as flash as the
chandelier-lit marble lobby might suggest,
this is nevertheless a sound pick, bang op-
posite the Hauptbahnhof and five minutes'
walk from Belvedere. Rooms are dressed in
plush fabrics, wood furnishings and muted
tones, and those on higher floors look out
across Vienna's rooftops. The huge buffet
breakfast will keep you going most of the
day.

🛏 Prater & East of the Danube

GAL APARTMENTS   APARTMENT **$**
Map p266 (☎0650-561 19 42; www.apartmentsvi-
enna.net; 02, Grosse Mohrengasse 29; d/tr/q apt

ESCAPE TO THE COUNTRY

For a touch of Tyrol a mere jaunt uphill from the city, look no further than the thick,
whitewashed walls, rows of flowering pot plants and creeping vines of **Landhaus
Fuhrgassl-Huber** (☎440 30 33; www.fuhrgassl-huber.at; 19, Rathstrasse 24; s/d/q
€85/138/195; 🅿 @🖘; 🚍35A). Set amid the neatly tended vines and *Heurigen* (wine tav-
erns) of Neustift, this country *Pension* features wood-panelled ceilings, folk art, orna-
mental carpets and warm tiled floors, and all staff don traditional garb. The huge buffet
breakfast, taken in the secluded garden on warm mornings, makes you feel far, far
away from anything urban...but you're only a 30-minute bus ride from the city centre.

To reach Landhaus Fuhrgassl-Huber, take tram line 38 from Schottentor to Gatter-
burggasse, then bus 35A to the Neustift am Walde stop, which is a three-minute walk
from the guesthouse. The U6 station Nussdorfer Strasse also connects to bus 35A.

€89/99/119; @📶; MNestroyplatz, Taborstrasse) For a superb home away from home, check into these roomy apartments smack in the action of up-and-coming Leopoldstadt. Occupying a renovated Biedermeier house, the apartments are dressed in modern furniture and *Jugendstil*-inspired paintings. It's a short walk to the Karmelitermarkt, the Prater and the Augarten, and the subway whips you to the centre of town in less than 10 minutes.

HOTEL CAPRI   HOTEL $$

Map p266 (📞214 84 04; www.hotelcapri.at; 02, Praterstrasse 44-46; s €75-105, d €109-149, tr €119-168, q €139-199; P📶; MNestroyplatz) This midranger looks nondescript on the face of things, but its merits are many: it's five minutes' walk from Prater, two U-Bahn stops from Stephansplatz, and staff bend over backwards to please. Done up in pastel colours, rooms are streamlined and immaculate, all with flat-screen TVs and kettles. Breakfast is a wholesome spread of fruit, cereals, cold cuts and eggs.

🛌 Schloss Schönbrunn & Around

ANGEL'S PLACE   GUESTHOUSE $

Map p270 (📞0650-512 1 646; www.angelsplace-vienna.eu; 15, Weiglgasse 1; d €56-78, ste €100; 📶; MSchönbrunn) A wine cellar has been converted into this cute guesthouse, a 10-minute stroll from Schloss Schönbrunn's gates. The warm-hued basement rooms are incredibly homely, with wood floors and eye-catching original touches like brick vaulting. There's a shared kitchen if you want to rustle up a snack, and continental breakfast costs an extra €6.

WOMBAT'S   HOSTEL $

Map p270 (📞897 23 36; www.wombats-hostels.com; 15, Mariahilfer Strasse 137; dm €22-25, d €72-76; P@📶; MWestbahnhof) For a dash of Aussie charm in Vienna, Wombat's is where savvy backpackers gravitate. The interior is a rainbow of colours, common areas include a bar, pool tables, music and comfy leather sofas, and the modern dorms have en suites. The relaxed staff hand you a drink and a useful city map on arrival, and bike hire can be arranged.

ALTWIENERHOF   HOTEL $$

Map p270 (📞892 60 00; www.altwienerhof.at; 15, Herklotzgasse 6; s €50-65, d €89-99, q €125; @; MGumpendorfer Strasse) This pseudo-plush family-run hotel, just outside the Gürtel ring, offers ridiculously romantic abodes that hark back to a bygone era. Miniature chandeliers, antique pieces, floral bed covers and couches, and lace tablecloths do a fine job of adding a touch of old-fashioned romance. Breakfast is taken either in the conservatory or in the large inner courtyard on summer days.

Understand Vienna

Vienna Today

While Vienna enjoys one of the highest standards of living in the world, the financial crisis in the euro zone has triggered moderate discussion about the wisdom of the euro. At the same time, it remains one of the world's most stable capitals, with a government committed to improving an already excellent infrastructure... oh, and the humble *Käsekrainer* sausage has been saved from extinction.

Best in Film

The Third Man (director Carol Reed, screenplay Graham Greene; 1949) One of the oldest and still most atmospheric films about Vienna.

Before Sunrise (director Richard Linklater, screenplay Richard Linklater and Kim Krizan; 1995) Well-crafted kitsch verging on the pathetic, but the city scenes couldn't have been done better by Vienna's tourist board.

Letter from an Unknown Woman (director Max Ophüls, based on novella by Stefan Zweig; 1948) Unrequited love set in Vienna, underscoring the fragility of the human psyche.

Best in Books

The Piano Teacher (Elfriede Jelinek; 1983) By the Nobel Prize–winning author, about a repressed pianist and a sadomasochistic relationship, which is to say, Vienna through and through.

The Road into the Open (Arthur Schnitzler; 1908) The story of an affair, set in Vienna, with insights into Viennese society and culture in the early 20th century.

The World of Yesterday (Stefan Zweig; 1943) An autobiography of Zweig's life up to WWII, describing lots of well-known Viennese.

Crisis, What Crisis?

Despite the woes of the euro currency, Vienna and Austria as a whole have remained in relatively good economic shape, with continuing high disposable income and a quality of life that is the envy of many other Europeans. Vienna also hasn't experienced a real-estate bubble similar to those in the US, UK and Spain, even if locals grumble about the rising cost of rental. While the country has substantial debt and banks are vulnerable to economies in eastern Europe, the Viennese mostly remain unconcerned, seeing the problems as being elsewhere.

A Stable Government

Vienna is a city-state, which means the mayor doubles as the head of a state government. Astoundingly, the capital has been governed by the Sozialdemokratischen Partei Österreichs (Social Democratic Party of Austria; SPÖ) and headed by an SPÖ mayor uninterrupted since 1945. The SPÖ has also won an outright majority of votes in the state elections all but twice since 1945 – once in 1996, and again in the 2010 election, when the right-wing populist Freiheitliche Partei Österreichs (Fredom Party of Austria; FPÖ) managed to scoop up 25% of the vote. While the FPÖ fought this election on its hobby horse of local 'foreigner' issues (misuse of asylum laws, assimilation of foreigners), the SPÖ successfully wooed voters on its good record and longer-term infrastructure and quality-of-life issues, and today the SPÖ governs Vienna in coalition with the Greens party. At national level, the rise of the populist euro-sceptic Frank Stronach (Team Stronach) might well pan out into fewer votes for the FPÖ at the next national election, due to be held in late 2013.

Building a Contemporary City

Vienna has been the scene of some enormous infrastructure projects in recent years. The one with the most impact on visitors is its new Hauptbahnhof (main train station), which is part of a massive project to transform the formerly down-at-heel – if not outright sleazy – Südbahnhof area into a bright new quarter called the Sonnwendviertel (Solstice Quarter), complete with the station, about 5000 new apartments, shops and its own kindergarten and schools. By about 2015 almost everyone arriving by train in Vienna will step out here. Meanwhile, numerous other key projects and initiatives such as a Gender Mainstreaming initiative – shaping the city so it's just as safe and usable for women as well as men – are ensuring that Vienna remains highly liveable and retains its cultural edge.

Changing Face of the City

Vienna's face is changing east of the Danube Canal where a new campus of the Vienna University of Economics and Business is opening up in 2013, just a stone's throw from the Prater's emblematic Ferris wheel. This is unleashing a wave of Austrian and international business students on the Leopoldstadt area and will pep up the district considerably.

Europe Going East & 'Save the Käsekrainer'

Vienna is one of the better Europeans in terms of accepting the edicts of the EU, but it also has a strong grassroots democracy, with regular referendums on anything from lowly parking to lofty issues of government. An important one saw a rejection of any steps leading to a privatisation of essential services, taking aim at a directive by the EU that looks set to open the way for privatisation of water supplies across Europe.

At the same time, Vienna is active in promoting integration with eastern neighbours, such as through Centrope Europaregion, a cross-border cultural and economic initiative with parts of Austria, the Czech Republic, Hungary and Slovakia to create an integrated region.

At European level *'es ging um die Wurst'* (it came to a crunch) in 2012 when Slovenia sought EU protection for its Kranjskaja Klobasa as a regional food. This is the humble forebear of the Viennese *Käsekrainer* (Krainer Wurst) sausage and – spare the thought! – almost compelled a name change at sausage stands around town. The dispute turned out to be a flash in the frying pan, however; a compromise was reached, according to which Slovenians would continue to eat their regional *Kranjskaja Klobasa*, while the Viennese would bite into their own *Krainer*.

if Vienna were 100 people

78 would be Austrian
18 would be other European
4 would be other

belief systems
(% of population)

Roman Catholic   Atheist   Muslim

Protestant   Jewish   other or unknown
5   0.5   12.5

population per sq km

VIENNA   AUSTRIA

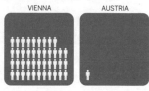

♦ ≈ 100 people

History

From its humbled beginnings as a Roman outpost, Vienna developed into the hub of the Holy Roman Empire, was for several centuries the last bastion of the Occident against Ottoman Turks, and experienced a creative explosion of high culture from the 18th century. War, the abolition of the monarchy, uprising, Austro-fascism and another world war followed before Vienna finally emerged in the mid-20th century to become what it is today – the capital of a modern Austrian state.

Early Vienna

When Richard the Lionheart was captured and held to ransom in 1192 while passing through Austria on his return from one of the Crusades, part of the ransom paid for his release was used to build a new city wall on today's Ringstrasse.

The early history of Vienna dates back to the Palaeolithic age around 35,000 years ago, evidence of which is the 25,000-year-old statuette, the Venus of Willendorf, which is today exhibited in the Naturhistorisches Museum.

Vienna, situated at a natural crossing of the Danube (Donau), was probably an important trading post for the Celts when the Romans arrived around 15 BC. The Romans established Carnuntum as a provincial capital of Pannonia in AD 8, and around the same time created Vindobona, a second military camp that was located in what today is Vienna's Innere Stadt. A civil town flourished in the 3rd and 4th centuries, and around this time a visiting Roman Emperor, Probus, introduced vineyards to the hills of the Wienerwald (Vienna Woods). During this early period, Vindobona developed into a town of around 15,000 inhabitants and was important for trade and communication within the Roman Empire. Today, you can find remnants of this Roman town on Hoher Markt and Michaelerplatz.

The Babenberg Dynasty

In the year 976 a so-called Bavarian Ostmark (Bavarian Eastern March) was established along the Danube River, and this gradually expanded to the north and east, lending greater importance to Vienna. The Eastern March was ruled by the Babenbergs, a wealthy Bavarian dynasty that held onto power until 1248. During their reign, the Babenbergs expanded their sphere of influence to include modern-day Lower Austria and Vienna, Styria and much of Upper Austria. In 1156, under the

TIMELINE	AD 8	5th Century	1137
	Vindobona, the forerunner of Vienna's Innere Stadt, becomes part of the Roman province of Pannonia.	The Roman Empire collapses and the Romans are beaten back from Vindobona by invading Goth and Vandal tribes.	Vienna is first documented as a city in the Treaty of Mautern between the Babenburgs and the Bishops of Passau.

Babenberg monarch Heinrich II 'Jasmirogott,' the Eastern March was elevated to a duchy (ie with its own duke and special rights) and Vienna became the capital. In 1221, two decades before the Babenberg dynasty died out, Vienna was granted its charter, achieving the status of a city.

Habsburg Vienna: Late Middle Ages & Renaissance

The Babenbergs moved their residence to Vienna in the mid-12th century, setting the stage for Vienna to grow considerably. By the late 12th century it had become a significant trading capital with links to Central and Western European capitals, Kiev (Ukraine) in the east, and Venice in the south.

In 1273 Rudolf von Habsburg was elected king of the Romans (Rudolf I), ruling over the Holy Roman Empire and beginning the era of the Habsburgs. The dynasty would retain power until the 20th century.

In the 14th century, Vienna struggled under a string of natural disasters that made everyday life more difficult for many residents; first a plague of locusts in 1338, then the Black Death in 1349, which wiped out one third of the city's population, followed by a devastating fire. Despite these setbacks, the centuries following the rise of the Habsburg Dynasty to power gave Vienna a new scope of power. This was due in no small part to clever politicking on the part of monarchs and even cleverer marriages that catapulted this family of rulers to new heights.

In 1453 Friedrich III was elected Holy Roman Emperor and in 1469 persuaded the pope to raise Vienna to a bishopric. Friedrich's ambition knew few bounds – his motto *'Austria est imperator orbi universo'* (AEIOU) expressed the view that the whole world was Austria's empire.

On the whole, the Habsburgs proved to be more adept at marriage than waging war. Maximilian I, the son of Friedrich III, acquired Burgundy through a clever marriage, while his son Philip the Handsome acquired Spain (and its overseas territories). The marriages of Maximilian's grandchildren brought the crowns of Bohemia and Hungary. This prompted the proverb, adapted from Ovid: 'Let others make war; you, fortunate Austria, marry!'

Maximilian, a ruler on the cusp of the Middle Ages and the Renaissance, encouraged the teaching of humanism in Vienna's university and also founded the Vienna Boys' Choir.

Everyday Life

Everyday life in Vienna in the late Middle Ages and early Renaissance was, of course, far removed from the pomp and circumstance of its Habsburg rulers. Hoher Markt was not only the city's most important

Vienna of the 9th century was a handful of Slavic and Avar tribal settlements, with the former Roman military road running through and Roman ruins which served the Carolingian rulers as a basis for constructing a small fortress.

The Holy Roman Empire grew out of the Frankish Reich, which was seen as the successor to the Roman Empire. It began life in 962 and finally collapsed in 1806 when Kaiser Franz II abdicated. Except for the period 1291–98, the Habsburgs ruled the Empire from 1273.

1155–56	1273–76	1529	1670
Vienna becomes a residence of the Babenbergs; a new fortress is built on Am Hof and Babenberg's Margavate is elevated to Duchy.	Otakar II hands the throne to a little-known count from Habichtsburg (read: Habsburg); Rudolf I of Habsburg resides in Vienna and the Habsburg dynasty commences.	The first Turkish siege of Vienna takes place but the Turks mysteriously retreat, leaving the city. Vienna survives and fortification of the city walls begins.	The second expulsion of Jews is ordered by Leopold I; the financial strength of Vienna is severely weakened and Jews are soon invited back to the city.

marketplace, it doubled as a site for Vienna's many public executions for political as well as criminal activities. Being beheaded or quartered was the usual method there. At other sites around the city, convicted criminals were executed by drowning in the Danube or were burned alive.

In terms of improved health among the Viennese, the first public bath appeared around 1300. First mention of a public bath in Vienna is in 1300, and the first stone houses were erected around 1250. Fire and flooding were usual, and three earthquakes struck the city between 1267 and 1356. Furthermore, the rapid growth of Vienna led to the establishment of mendicant orders to feed the poor. These orders began arriving in Vienna in the mid-13th century, establishing monasteries and churches inside the city walls, such as the Minoritenkloster (Minoritenkirche), the Dominikanerkloster (later replaced by today's church) and an Augustine monastery that was later replaced by another in the Hofburg. These monasteries also cared for travellers and pilgrims.

In comparison with other European cities, Vienna was one of the most stable, largely thanks to privileges (*Ratswahlprivileg;* the city council election privilege) introduced in 1396 that saw the city council divided up equally among patricians, merchants and tradesmen, creating a wise balance of interests.

Turks & Religious Troubles

The 16th and 17th centuries – a time in Vienna's history that included the high Renaissance and early Baroque – were marked by attempts by the Ottoman Turks to take the capital, by the Reformation and Thirty Years' War, plague and, ultimately, an end to the Turkish threat, paving the way for high baroque.

The era began badly when Karl V became Holy Roman Emperor and left the governing of the Austrian territories in the hands of his younger brother, Ferdinand I. Ferdinand, a Spaniard by birth who did not even speak German, was an unpopular ruler who soon had to deal with attacks from the Ottoman Turks. The Turks, having overrun the Balkans and Hungary, were on the doorstep of Vienna by 1529. The city managed to defend itself under the leadership of Count Salm, but the 18-day siege highlighted glaring holes in Vienna's defences. Against this background, Ferdinand moved his court to Vienna in 1533 (he'd spent most of his time outside it until then) and fortified the city's walls, which now boasted bastions, *ravelins* (star-shaped reinforcements attached to the outer wall) and ramparts, as well as a ditch running around a perimeter, all of which followed the course of today's Ringstrasse. He rebuilt the Hofburg in the 1550s, adding the Schweizer Tor (Swiss Gate) you see today, with his own royal titles engraved on it.

CITY WALL

Vienna received its first city wall around 1200, with main gates that today live on as names along the city's Ringstrasse (Ring Road): Stubentor, Kärntner Tor, Schottentor and Rotenturmtor.

1683	1740–90	1805 & 1809
The Turks are repulsed at the gates of Vienna for the second time; Europe is free of the Ottoman threat and Vienna begins to re-establish itself as the Habsburg's permanent residence.	Under the guidance of Empress Maria Theresia and her son Joseph II, the age of reform, influenced by the ideas of the Enlightenment, kicks into gear.	Napoleon occupies Vienna twice and removes the Holy Roman Emperor crown from the head of Franz II, who reinvents himself as Kaiser Franz I.

IMAGNO / GETTY IMAGES ©

Maria Theresia with her children

THE TURKS & VIENNA

The Ottoman Empire viewed Vienna as 'the city of the golden apple', though it wasn't the *Apfelstrudel* (apple strudel) they were after in their two great sieges. The first, in 1529, was undertaken by Suleiman the Magnificent, but the 18-day endeavour was not sufficient to break the resolve of the city. The Turkish sultan subsequently died at the Battle of Szigetvár in 1566, but his death was kept secret for several days in an attempt to preserve the morale of the army. This subterfuge worked – for a while. Messengers were led into the presence of the embalmed body, which was placed in a seated position on the throne, and unknowingly relayed their news to the corpse. The lack of the slightest acknowledgement of his minions by the sultan was interpreted as regal impassiveness.

At the head of the Turkish siege of 1683 was the general Kara Mustapha. Amid the 25,000 tents of the Ottoman army that surrounded Vienna he installed his 1500 concubines. These were guarded by 700 black eunuchs. Their luxurious quarters may have been set up in haste, but were still overtly opulent, with gushing fountains and regal baths.

Again, it was all to no avail. Mustapha failed to put garrisons on the Kahlenberg and was surprised by a quick attack from a German/Polish army rounded up by Leopold I, who had fled the city on news of the approaching Ottomans. Mustapha was pursued from the battlefield and defeated once again, at Gran. At Belgrade he was met by the emissary of the sultan. The price of failure was death, and Mustapha meekly accepted his fate. When the Austrian imperial army conquered Belgrade in 1718 the grand vizier's head was dug up and brought back to Vienna in triumph, where it gathers dust in the vaults of the Wien Museum.

From 1517, the year Martin Luther called for Church reforms, the Reformation quickly spread to Austria. The nobility embraced the Reformation, and about four of every five burghers became practising Protestants. Soon after the Turkish siege of 1529, however, Ferdinand went about purging Vienna of Protestantism. He invited the Jesuits to the city, one step in the Europe-wide Counter-Reformation that ultimately led to the Thirty Years' War (1618–48).

Towards the end of the 17th century Vienna suffered terribly. The expulsion of the Jews left the imperial and city finances in a sorry state, and a severe epidemic of bubonic plague killed between 75,000 and 150,000 in 1679. One visible reminder of this today is the baroque Pestsäule, built shortly afterwards as a reminder of the bubonic plague. In 1683, four years after plague stuck, the city was once again under siege from the Turks. Vienna rebuffed this attack, however, and the removal of the Turkish threat helped bring the city to the edge of a new golden age.

1815–48	1857	1866–67	1910–14
The Metternich system, aimed at shoring up the monarchies of Austria, Russia and Prussia, ultimately begins the 19th-century middle-class revolution.	City walls are demolished to make way for the creation of the monumental architecture today found along the Ringstrasse.	Austria suffers defeat at the hands of Prussia (paving the way for a unified Germany without Austria) and is forced to create the dual Austro-Hungarian monarchy.	Vienna's population breaks the two million barrier, the largest it has ever been. The rise is mainly due to high immigration numbers, the majority of whom are Czechs.

The Golden Age of an Imperial City

When the Turks were beaten back from the gates of Vienna for the last time in 1683, the path was clear for Vienna to experience a golden age of baroque culture and architecture throughout the 18th century. During the reign of Karl VI from 1711 to 1740, baroque architectural endeavours such as Schloss Belvedere, the Karlskirche and the Peterskirche transformed Vienna into a venerable imperial capital.

When in 1740 the Habsburg dynasty failed to deliver a male heir, Maria Theresia ascended the throne (the first and only female Habsburg ever to rule). Maria Theresia took up residence in Schloss Schönbrunn, which she enlarged from its original dimensions dating from 1700, gave a rococo style, and had painted in her favourite colour (the distinctive 'Schönbrunn yellow'). Although her rule was marred by wars – she was challenged by Prussia, whose star was on the rise, and by others who questioned the Pragmatic Sanction that gave her the right to the throne – Maria Theresia is widely regarded as the greatest of the Habsburg rulers. During her 40-year reign, Austria began to take the form of a modern state.

The talented joined the wealthy and the great who frequented the opulent Schönbrunn palace during the reigns of Maria Theresia and the reform-minded Joseph II. A six-year-old Wolfgang Amadeus Mozart and his 10-year-old sister performed in the palace's Spiegelsaal in 1762, Josef Haydn and other composers worked in the palace theatre, and Vienna in the latter half of the 18th century (and beginning of the 19th) witnessed a blossoming musical scene never before or since found in Europe. During this time, Christoph Willibald Gluck, Haydn, Mozart, Ludwig van Beethoven and Franz Schubert all lived and worked in Vienna, producing some of their most memorable music.

Vienna in the Biedermeier Period

When in the early 19th century Napoleon swept across Europe, he triggered the end of the anachronistic Holy Roman Empire and the *Kaiser* who ruled it. The Habsburg Kaiser, Franz II, reinvented himself in 1804 as Franz I, Austria's first emperor, and formally dissolved the Holy Roman Empire two years later, following Napoleon's victory over Russian and Austrian troops in the Battle of Austerlitz (1805).

Vienna was occupied twice by Napoleon (1805 and 1809), and the cost of war caused the economy to spiral into bankruptcy. Following the defeat of Napoleon at the Battle of Waterloo in 1815, the European powers pieced together a post-Napoleonic Europe in the Congress of Vienna. The Congress was dominated by the skilful Austrian foreign minister, Klemens von Metternich. The period between the Congress of Vienna and 1848, the year a middle-class revolution took hold of Europe, is known as

When Napoleon occupied Vienna he established his headquarters in Schloss Schönbrunn, sleeping in what is today known as the Napoleonzimmer (Napoleon Room). In 1810 he even married the daughter of Franz I, Marie Louise. He also demolished part of Vienna's city walls, creating space for Burggarten and Volksgarten a few years later.

1914–18	1918	1919	1938
WWI rumbles through Europe and Vienna experiences a shortage of food and clothes. War-induced inflation destroys the savings of many middle-class Viennese.	The Austrian Republic is declared on the steps of Vienna's parliament; white and red are chosen as the colours of the nation's flag.	The Treaty of St Germain is signed; the Social Democrats take control of the Vienna City Council, marking the beginning of a period known as Rotes Wien (Red Vienna).	Hitler invades Austria in the *Anschluss* (annexation) to Germany; he is greeted by 200,000 Viennese at Heldenplatz. Austria is officially wiped off the map of Europe.

THE JEWS OF VIENNA

Historically, Vienna has had an ambivalent relationship with its Jewry, who first settled in the city in 1194 and by 1400 numbered about 800, mostly living in the Jewish quarter centred on a synagogue on Judenplatz.

In 1420 the Habsburg ruler Albrecht V issued a pogrom against the Jews, who later drifted back into the city and prospered until the arrival of bigoted Leopold I and his even more bigoted wife, Margarita Teresa, who blamed her miscarriages on Jews: in 1670 Jews were expelled from the city and their synagogue destroyed, but this weakened the financial strength of Vienna, and the Jewish community was invited back.

The following centuries saw Jews thrive under relatively benign conditions and in the 19th century they were given equal civil rights and prospered in the fields of art and music. The darkest chapter in Vienna's Jewish history began on 12 March 1938 when the Nazis occupied Austria; with them came persecution and curtailment of Jewish civil rights. Businesses were confiscated (including some of Vienna's better-known coffee houses) and Jews were banned from public places, obliged to wear a Star of David and go by the names of 'Sara' and 'Israel'. Violence exploded on the night of 9 November 1938 with the November Pogrom, when synagogues and prayer houses were burned and 6500 Jews were arrested. Of the 180,000 Jews living in Vienna before the *Anschluss* (annexation), more than 100,000 managed to emigrate before the borders were closed in May 1939. Another 65,000 died in ghettos or concentration camps and only 6000 survived to see liberation by Allied troops.

the Biedermeier period. During this period Franz I and von Metternich oversaw a period of repression that saw the middle classes retreat into private life to cultivate domestic music and a distinctive style of interior architecture, clothing and literature known as Biedermeier for its staidness and stuffiness (the word *bieder* means 'staid' or 'stuffy').

The lower classes suffered immensely, however: the Industrial Revolution created substandard working conditions, disease sometimes reached epidemic levels, and Vienna's water supply was completely inadequate.

Vienna in the Late 19th & Early 20th Century

The repressive mood of the Biedermeier period in first half of the 19th century in Vienna culminated in reaction and revolution among the middle classes, with calls for reform and especially freedom of expression. In March 1848 the war minister was hanged from a lamppost. Klemens von Metternich, the Austrian who was decisive in shaping the repressive Biedermeier period, fled to Britain and Emperor Ferdinand I abdicated to be replaced by the 18-year-old Franz Josef I.

1938–39	1945	1955	1972–88
In the Pogromnacht (Program Night) of November 1938, Jewish businesses and homes are plundered and destroyed; 120,000 Jews leave Vienna over the next six months.	WWII (1939–45) ends and a provisional government is established in Austria; Vienna is divided into four occupied quarters: American, British, Soviet Union and French.	Austria regains its sovereignty – the Austrian State Treaty is signed at the Schloss Belvedere; over half a million Austrians take to the streets of the capital in celebration.	The Donauinsel (Danube Island) is created to protect the city against flooding. Today it serves as one of the city's recreation areas, with parks, river beaches, trails and forest.

This liberal interlude was brief, however, with the army reimposing an absolute monarchy. In 1857 Franz Josef instigated the massive Ringstrasse developments around the Innere Stadt. In 1854 he married Elisabeth of Bavaria, affectionately nicknamed Sisi by her subjects. The couple lived together in the Kaiserappartements of the Hofburg, where today you'll find the Sisi Museum.

The Austrians: A Thousand Year Odyssey (Gordon Brook-Shepherd) is a highly readable take on Austrian history.

In the latter half of the 19th century and going into the 20th century, Vienna enjoyed a phase of rapid development, including massive improvements to infrastructure. Universal male suffrage was introduced in Austro-Hungarian lands in 1906. Culturally, the period was one of Vienna's richest; the years produced Sigmund Freud, Gustav Klimt, Oskar Kokoschka, Gustav Mahler, Johannes Brahms, Egon Schiele and Johann Strauss, as well as Otto Wagner, the most influential architect in fin de siècle Vienna and whose legacy is found throughout the city today.

Vienna: Capital of a Modern Republic

Vienna enjoyed enormous growth in the early 20th century. The century, however, is marked by two cataclysmic wars – WWI (1914–18) and WWII (1939–45) – as well as a 'Red Vienna' period in the 1920s, when left- and right-wing political forces clashed on Vienna's streets, the *Anschluss* (annexation) by Hitler that saw Vienna and the Austrian Republic as a whole become part of the Third Reich, liberation by the Soviet Union and occupation by the Allied powers, and finally the proclamation of Austria as a neutral, independent country in 1955. Most of these events are associated with one or more iconic features of the capital.

Vienna's neo-Gothic Rathaus is closely tied to the Social Democrats, who, following the collapse and abdication of the Habsburg monarchy in 1918, gained an absolute majority in all free elections from 1919 to 1996. The Palace of Justice, which was set on fire in 1927 by left-wing demonstrators following the controversial acquittal of members of the Frontkämpfervereinigung (a right-wing paramilitary group) on charges of assassination, perhaps best symbolises the political struggle of the era. This struggle culminated in several days of civil war in 1934. Hitler, who had departed Vienna many years before as a failed and disgruntled artist, returned to the city in triumph and held a huge rally at Heldenplatz (in the Hofburg) on 15 March 1938 in front of 200,000 ecstatic Viennese. A Holocaust memorial is dedicated to the Jews who suffered under Fascism.

Vienna and the Jews, 1867–1938 (Steven Beller) describes the role of Vienna's Jews in Viennese cultural and intellectual life.

In March 1945 the Soviet Union liberated Vienna, today celebrated by the Russian Heroes' Monument on Schwarzenbergplatz, while Vienna's UNO-City best symbolises the city's post-WWII neutrality and evolution into a modern nation (even if in the 21st century its neutrality is somewhat lost beneath membership of the EU).

1980	1986	1995	2012–3
A third UN headquarters is opened up in Vienna. It is the headquarters for the International Atomic Energy Agency, Drugs & Crime office, and other functions.	Vienna ceases to be the capital of the surrounding *Bundesländ* of Niederösterreich (Lower Austria), replaced by Sankt Pölten.	After resounding support from its populace and a referendum in which 60% voted 'Yes' to joining, Austria enters the EU.	Vienna heads the UN *State of the World Cities* 2012–13 report, judged on factors such as quality of life, infrastructure, social equity and environmental sustainability.

City of Music

Vienna is the world capital of opera and classical music. Who else can claim Mozart, Beethoven, Strauss and Schubert among their historical repertoire? The rich musical legacy that flows through the city is evident everywhere, whether it be buskers hammering out tunes on the streets or a formal performance in one of the capital's renowned venues.

Habsburg Musical Tradition

The Habsburgs began patronising court musicians as far back as the 13th century, and by the 18th and 19th centuries they had created a centre for music that was unrivalled in the world. Many of the Habsburgs themselves were accomplished musicians. Leopold I (1640–1705) stroked a violin, his daughter Maria Theresia (1717–80) played a respectable double bass, while her son Joseph II (1741–90) was deft hand at the harpsichord.

Hofmusik

Hofmusik (music of the royal court) had its beginnings in the Middle Ages when it developed as a form of music to accompany church Masses. From around 1300 a tradition of choirs with multiple voice parts established itself in Austria. The Habsburgs adopted this tradition and, with the collapse of the Habsburg monarchy, the Austrian state took over the Hofkapelle, which today includes members of Vienna's Philharmonic Orchestra, the Vienna State Opera and, above all, the young boys who traditionally provided the 'female' voice parts, the Wiener Sängerknaben – the Vienna Boys' Choir (p47). This tradition lives on with Sunday performances of the Vienna Boys' Choir in the Burgkapelle (p61) inside the Hofburg, and other venues.

Baroque Music

The first dedicated theatre for opera north of the Alps was built in Innsbruck in 1650, but opera was also playing a role in Vienna's cultural scene as early as the 1620s, capturing the hearts of the Habsburg rulers through its paraphernalia of excess – elaborate costumes and stage props, and performers who sang, danced and acted great dramas on stage. Today the baroque era of music is most audible in performances of the two German masters of baroque church music, Johann Sebastian Bach (1685–1750) and Georg Friedrich Händel (1695–1759), performed in many churches around town.

Vienna's Philharmonic

An unmissable Viennese musical experience is a visit to the Vienna Philharmonic (www.wienerphilharmoniker.at), which mostly performs in the Grosser Saal of the Musikverein (p108). The Philharmonic has the privilege of choosing its conductors, whose ranks have included the likes of Mahler, Richard Strauss and Felix Weingartner. The instruments used by the Philharmonic generally follow pre-19th-century design and more accurately reflect the music Mozart and Beethoven wrote.

The Klangforum Wien (www.klangforum.at), an ensemble of 24 artists from nine countries, is a unique collaboration between conductors and composers, who perform at various venues. See the website for current performances.

Downloads

Fifth Symphony in C Minor – Beethoven

Cradle Song, Op 49, No 4 – Brahms

The Creation – Haydn

The Magic Flute – Mozart

COMPOSERS AT A GLANCE

Vienna and music go hand in hand. The following is a selection of composers who came from Vienna or who lived and worked in the capital.

Christoph Willibald Gluck (1714–87) Major works include *Orfeo* (1762) and *Alceste* (1767).

Wolfgang Amadeus Mozart (1756–91) Wrote some 626 pieces; among the greatest are *The Marriage of Figaro* (1786), *Don Giovanni* (1787), *Così fan tutte* (1790) and *The Magic Flute* (1791). The *Requiem Mass*, apocryphally written for his own death, remains one of the most powerful works of classical music. Have a listen to Piano Concerto Nos 20 and 21, which comprise some of the best elements of Mozart: drama, comedy, intimacy and a whole heap of ingenuity in one easy-to-appreciate package.

Josef Haydn (1732–1809) Wrote 108 symphonies, 68 string quartets, 47 piano sonatas and about 20 operas. His greatest works include Symphony No 102 in B-flat Major, the oratorios *The Creation* (1798) and *The Seasons* (1801), and six Masses written for Miklós II.

Ludwig van Beethoven (1770–1827) Studied briefly with Mozart in Vienna in 1787; he returned in late 1792. Beethoven produced a lot of chamber music up to the age of 32, when he became almost totally deaf and, ironically, began writing some of his best works, including the Symphony No 9 in D Minor, Symphony No 5 and his late string quartets.

Franz Schubert (1797–1828) Born and bred in Vienna, Schubert was a prolific composer whose best-known works are his last symphony (the Great C Major Symphony), his Mass in E-flat and the Unfinished Symphony.

The Strausses and the Waltz The early masters of the genre were Johann Strauss the Elder (1804–49) and Josef Lanner (1801–43). Johann Strauss the Younger (1825–99) composed over 400 waltzes, including Vienna's unofficial anthem, 'The Blue Danube' (1867) and 'Tales from the Vienna Woods' (1868).

Johannes Brahms (1833–97) At the age of 29, Brahms moved to Vienna, where many of his works were performed by the Vienna Philharmonic. Best works include *Ein Deutsches Requiem*, his Violin Concerto and Symphony Nos 1 to 4.

Gustav Mahler (1860–1911) Known mainly for his nine symphonies; best works include *Das Lied von der Erde* (The Song of the Earth) and Symphony Nos 1, 5 and 9.

Vienna Classic

Wiener Klassik (Vienna Classic) dates back to the mid- and late 18th century and saw Vienna at the centre of a revolution that today defines the way we perceive classical music. Music moved away from the churches and royal courts into the salons and theatres of upper-middle-class society. The period is associated with composers such as Wolfgang Amadeus Mozart (1756–91), Joseph Haydn (1732–1809), Ludwig van Beethoven (1770–1827) and Franz Schubert (1797–1828), later giving way to a new wave of classical composers in the 19th century, such as Franz Liszt (1811–86), Johannes Brahms (1833–97) and Anton Bruckner (1824–96).

Contemporary Sounds

Vienna's impact on international jazz, rock or pop music is minimal, but it has an interesting scene. Artists on G-Stone Records (www.g-stoned.com) such as Kruder & Dorfmeister, Patrick Pulsinger and Erdem Tunakan have proved a powerful source for new electronic music. In the last few years the city's scene has experienced a revival, with old and new artists once again creating waves in the electronic genre. Tosca, a side project of Richard Dorfmeister, is well regarded; DJ Glow is known for his electro beats; the Vienna Scientists produce tidy house compilations; the Sofa Surfers' dub-hop tracks are often dark but well received; and the likes of Megablast, Makossa and Stereotype are going from strength to strength.

Visual Arts & Architecture

Vienna is one of the world's most interesting capitals when it comes to the visual arts and architecture. The Habsburg monarchs fostered and patronised the arts in grand style, leaving us a legacy of fine historic paintings, sculptures and buildings, complemented by modern and contemporary works, all of which are visible at every turn when you walk through the streets today.

Baroque & Rococo

Unwittingly, the Ottomans helped form much of Vienna's architectural make-up seen today. The second Turkish siege was the major catalyst for architectural change; with the defeat of the old enemy (achieved with extensive help from German and Polish armies), the Habsburgs were freed from the threat of war from the east. Money and energy previously spent on defence was poured into urban redevelopment, resulting in a frenzy of building in the baroque period in the 17th and early 18th centuries.

Learning from the Italian model, Johann Bernhard Fischer von Erlach (1656–1723) developed a national style called Austrian baroque. This mirrored the exuberant ornamentation of Italian baroque with a few local quirks, such as coupling dynamic combinations of colour with undulating silhouettes. Johann Lukas von Hildebrandt (1668–1745), the other famous architect of the baroque era, was responsible for a number of buildings in the city centre.

Rococo, an elegant style incorporating pale colours and an exuberance of gold and silver, was all the rage in the 18th century. It was a great favourite with Maria Theresia, and Austrian rococo is sometimes referred to as late-baroque Theresien style.

Fresco painting in Austria dates back to the 11th century, and the oldest secular murals in the capital, from 1398, are the Neidhart-Fresken. The dizzying heights of fresco painting, however, were reached during the baroque period, when Johann Michael Rottmayr (1654–1730), Daniel Gran (1694–1757) and Paul Troger (1698–1762) were active in Vienna and across the country.

Rottmayr is Austria's foremost baroque painter, spending his early years as a court painter to the Habsburgs in Salzburg before moving to Vienna in 1696, where he became the favoured painter of the architect Fischer von Erlach. He worked on many of von Erlach's projects and is often compared to the Flemish painter Peter Paul Rubens, bringing together Italian and Flemish influences.

Like Rottmayr, the fresco painter Daniel Gran studied in Italy, but his style reined in most of the extravagant elements you find in Rottmayr and offered a foretaste of neoclassicism – best illustrated in a magnificent ceiling fresco in the Nationalbibliothek.

Medieval & Earlier

....

Michaelerplatz
(Roman ruins)

....

Hoher Markt
(Roman ruins)

....

Ruprechtskirche
(Romanesque)

....

Stephansdom
(Gothic)

....

Maria am Gestade
(Gothic)

....

Michaelerkirche
(Gothic)

....

Museum Judenplatz
(Jewry)

....

Dom- & Diöz-esanmuseum
(religious art)

What to See

It's hard to turn a corner in the Innere Stadt without running into a baroque wall. Much of the Hofburg is a baroque showpiece; In der Burg square is surrounded on all sides by baroque wings, but its triumph is the Nationalbibliothek by Fischer von Erlach, whose Prunksaal (grand hall) was painted by Daniel Gran and is arguably one of the finest baroque interiors in Austria.

Herrengasse, running north from the Hofburg's Michaelertor, is lined with baroque splendour, including Palais Kinsky at No 4. The Peterskirche is the handiwork of Hildebrandt, with frescoes by Rottmayr, but its dark interior and oval nave is topped by Karlskirche, another of Erlach's designs with Rottmayr frescoes – this time with Byzantine touches. The highly esteemed Schloss Belvedere is also a Hildebrandt creation, which includes a large collection of masters from the baroque period, featuring works by Rottmayr, Troger, Franz Anton Maulbertsch (1724–96) and others.

Nicolas Pacassi is responsible for the masterful rococo styling at Schloss Schönbrunn, but the former royal residence is upstaged by its graceful baroque gardens.

The Habsburgs were generous patrons of the arts, and their unrivalled collection of baroque paintings from across Europe is displayed at the Kunsthistorisches Museum.

Sculpture's greatest period in Vienna was during the baroque years – the Providentia Fountain by George Raphael Donner and Balthasar Permoser's statue *Apotheosis of Prince Eugene* in the Unteres Belvedere are striking examples. The magnificent Pestsäule (1692) was designed by Fischer von Erlach.

Neoclassical, Biedermeier & the Ringstrasse

From the 18th century (but culminating in the 19th), Viennese architects – like those all over Europe – turned to a host of neoclassical architectural styles.

The end of the Napoleonic wars and the ensuing celebration at the Congress of Vienna in 1815 ushered in the Biedermeier period (named after a satirical middle-class figure in a Munich paper). Viennese artists produced some extraordinary furniture during this period, often with clean lines and minimal fuss. Ferdinand Georg Waldmüller (1793–1865), whose evocative, idealised peasant scenes are captivating, is the period's best known artist.

In the mid-19th century, Franz Josef I called for the fortifications to be demolished and replaced with a ring road lined with magnificent imperial buildings. Demolition of the old city walls began in 1857.

Magnificent buildings were created by architects such as Heinrich von Ferstel, Theophil von Hansen, Gottfried Semper, Karl von Hasenauer, Friedrich von Schmidt and Eduard van der Nüll. Some of the earlier buildings are Rundbogenstil (round-arched style, similar to neo-Roman) in style, but the typical design for the Ringstrasse is High Renaissance. This features rusticated lower stories and columns and pilasters on the upper floors. Some of the more interesting ones stray from this standard, however; Greek Revival, neo-Gothic, neo-baroque and neo-rococo all play a part in the boulevard's architectural make-up.

What to See

The Hofmobiliendepot has an extensive collection of Biedermeier furniture, and more can be seen in the Museum für angewandte Kunst

---

Johann Michael Rottmayr's frescoes adorn the Karlskirche, where a lift ascends 70m into the cuppola for a close-up view, the Peterskirche and – outside town – Stift Melk in the Danube Valley. A ceiling fresco he painted in Schloss Schönbrunn was lost during work on the palace in the 1740s.

Top Museums & Galleries

Kunsthistorisches Museum

Albertina

Österreichische Galerie at Schloss Belvedere

Leopold Museum

MUMOK

Secession

(MAK). Ferdinand Georg Waldmüller's Biedermeier paintings hang in the Wien Museum and Oberes Belvedere and one of the few uniformly Biedermeier houses is the Geymüllerschlössel.

Taking a tram ride around the Ringstrasse provides a quick lesson in neoclassicism. High Renaissance can be seen in Theophil von Hansen's Palais Epstein, Gottfried Semper's Naturhistorisches Museum and Karl von Hasenauer's Kunsthistorisches Museum.

Von Hansen also designed the Ring's Parlament, one of the last major Greek Revival works built in Europe. Von Ferstel's Votivkirche is a classic example of neo-Gothic, but the showiest building on the Ring, with its dripping spires and spun-sugar facades, is Friedrich von Schmidt's unmissable Rathaus in Flemish-Gothic. The most notable neo-baroque example is Eduard van der Nüll's Staatsoper, though it's also worth having a look at Gottfried Semper's Burgtheater.

While Franz Josef was Emperor he had a new wing, the Neue Burg, added to the Hofburg. Gottfried Semper (1803–1879) was instrumental in the planning of the Neue Burg and its museums, and the architect, Karl von Hasenauer, stuck very closely to a traditional baroque look, though there are some 19th-century touches – a certain heavy bulkiness to the wing – that reveal it is actually neo-baroque.

Must-See Buildings

....

Stephansdom

....

Schloss Belvedere

....

Hofburg

....

Schloss Schönbrunn

....

Rathaus & Ringstrasse

Jugendstil & the Secession

Vienna's branch of the Europe-wide art nouveau movement, known as *Jugendstil* ('Youthful Style'), had its genesis from within the Akademie der bildenden Künste (Academy of Fine Arts). The academy was a strong supporter of neoclassicism and wasn't interested in supporting any artists who wanted to branch out, so in 1897 a group of rebels, including Gustav Klimt (1862–1918), seceded. Architects, such as Otto Wagner, Joseph Maria Olbrich (1867–1908) and Josef Hoffman (1870–1956), followed.

By the second decade of the 20th century, Wagner and others were moving towards a uniquely Viennese style, called Secession, which stripped away some of the more decorative aspects of *Jugendstil*. Olbrich designed the Secession Hall, the showpiece of the Secession, which was used to display other graphic and design works produced by the movement. The building is a physical representation of the movement's ideals, functionality and modernism, though it retains some striking decorative touches, such as the giant 'golden cabbage' on the roof.

Hoffman, who was inspired by the British Arts and Crafts movement, led by William Morris, and also by the stunning art nouveau work of Glaswegian designer Charles Rennie Mackintosh, ultimately abandoned the flowing forms and bright colours of *Jugendstil* in 1901, becoming one of the earliest exponents of the Secession style. His greatest artistic influence in Vienna was in setting up the Wiener Werkstätte design studio, which included Klimt and Kolo Moser (1868–1918), and which set out to break down the high-art-low-art distinction, bringing *Jugendstil* into middle-class homes. In 1932 the WW closed, unable to compete with the cheap, mass-produced items being churned out by other companies.

No-one embraced the sensualism of *Jugendstil* and Secessionism more than Klimt. Perhaps Vienna's most famous artist, Klimt was traditionally trained at the Akademie der bildenden Künste but soon left to pursue his own colourful and distinctive, non-naturalistic style.

A contemporary of Klimt's, Egon Schiele (1890–1918) is considered to be one of the most notable early existentialists and expressionists. His gritty, confrontational paintings and works on paper created a huge

Egon Schiele was controversial in his own time. In 1912 he was held in custody for three weeks and later found guilty of corrupting minors with his erotic drawings and paintings. At one stage he fled to Bohemia with his 17-year-old model and lover 'Wally' Neuzil to escape a furore.

The Fin-de-Siècle Years
....
Klimt –
Beethoven Frieze;
The Kiss
....
Loos – *Loos Haus*
....
Schiele –
Anything in the
Leopold Museum
....
Wagner – *Kirche*
am Steinhof;
Postsparkasse

stir in the early 20th century. Alongside his sketches, he also produced many self-portraits and a few large, breathtaking painted canvases. The other major exponent of Viennese expressionism was playwright, poet and painter Oskar Kokoschka (1886–1980), whose sometimes turbulent works show his interest in psychoanalytic imagery and baroque-era religious symbolism.

The last notable Secessionist – and the one most violently opposed to ornamentation – was Czech-born, Vienna-based designer Adolf Loos. Up until 1909, Loos mainly designed interiors, but in the ensuing years he developed a passion for reinforced concrete and began designing houses with no external ornamentation. The result was a collection of incredibly flat, planar buildings with square windows that offended the royal elite no end. They are, however, key works in the history of modern architecture.

What to See

As well as 35 of Vienna's metro stations, Otto Wagner's works include the Stadtbahn Pavillons at Karlsplatz, and the Kirche am Steinhof, in the grounds of a psychiatric hospital.

A prolific painter, Klimt's works hang in many galleries around Vienna. His earlier, classical mural work can be viewed in the Kunsthistorisches Museum, while his later murals, in his own distinctive style, grace the walls of the Secession, where you'll find his famous *Beethoven Frieze*, and MAK. An impressive number of his earlier sketches are housed in the Leopold Museum, and his fully-fledged paintings are in the Leopold Museum, Wien Museum and Oberes Belvedere.

The largest collection of Schiele works in the world belongs to the Leopold Museum. More of his exceptional talent is on display at the Wien Museum, Albertina and Oberes Belvedere; Kokoschka can also be seen at the Oberes Belvedere and Leopold.

One of the most accessible designs of Loos' is the dim but glowing Loos American Bar, a place of heavy ceilings and boxy booths. Also worth a look are his public toilets on Graben. The Loos Haus is his most celebrated work. The Wien Museum provides a look into the personal world of Loos, with a reconstruction of a room from the architect's own

OTTO WAGNER

Otto Wagner (1841–1918) was one of the most influential Viennese architects at the end of the 19th century (also known as the fin de siècle). He was trained in the classical tradition, and became a professor at the Akademie der bildenden Künste. His early work was in keeping with his education, and he was responsible for some neo-Renaissance buildings along the Ringstrasse. But as the 20th century dawned he developed an art nouveau style, with flowing lines and decorative motifs. Wagner left the Academy to join the looser, more creative Secession movement in 1899 and attracted public criticism in the process – one of the reasons why his creative designs for Vienna's Historical Museum were never adopted. In the 20th century, Wagner began to strip away the more decorative aspects of his designs, concentrating instead on presenting the functional features of buildings in a creative way.

The most accessible of Wagner's works are his metro stations, scattered along the network. The metro project, which lasted from 1894 to 1901, included 35 stations as well as bridges and viaducts. All of them feature green-painted iron, some neoclassical touches (such as columns) and curvy, all-capitals fin-de-siècle fonts. The earlier stations, such as Hüttledorf-Hacking, show the cleaner lines of neoclassicism, while Karlsplatz, built in 1898, is a curvy, exuberant work of Secessionist gilding and luminous glass.

house. Pieces by the Wiener Werkstätte are on display at the MAK and can be bought from Woka and Altmann & Kühne.

Modern Architecture

WWII brought an end not only to the Habsburg empire, but also to the heady fin-de-siècle years. Vienna's Social Democrat leaders set about a program of radical social reforms, earning the city the moniker 'Red Vienna'; one of their central themes was housing for the working class, best illustrated by Karl-Marx-Hof. Not everyone was pleased with the results; some of Vienna's leading architects, Adolf Loos included, criticised the government for failing to produce a unified aesthetic vision.

Since the late 1980s a handful of multicoloured, haphazard-looking structures have appeared in Vienna; these buildings have been given a unique design treatment by maverick artist Friedensreich Hundertwasser. Hundertwasser felt that 'the straight line is Godless' and faithfully adhered to this principle in all his building projects, proclaiming that his uneven floors 'become a symphony, a melody for the feet, and bring back natural vibrations to man'. Although he complained that his more radical building projects were quashed by the authorities, he still transformed a number of council buildings with his unique style.

What to See

The municipality buildings of Red Vienna are scattered throughout the city. The most famous is Karl-Marx-Hof. Hundertwasserhaus attracts tourists by the busload, as does the nearby KunstHausWien, but Hundertwasser's coup d'état is the Fernwärme incinerator; opened in 1992, it's the most nonindustrial-looking heating plant you'll ever see.

Of the 21st-century architectural pieces, the MuseumsQuartier impresses the most, with its integration of the historic and the postmodern into the city's most popular space. Gradually taking shape on a 109-hectare site near Südtyroler Platz, Vienna's Hauptbahnhof is as large as the Josefstadt district and goes beyond its functional role as a station to form a city district in itself for 30,000 people, with about 5000 flats, a large park, offices, schools and a kindergarten. A 70m-high Bahnorama platform affords views over the site.

Contemporary Arts

Vienna has a thriving contemporary arts scene with a strong emphasis on confrontation, pushing boundaries and exploring new media – incorporating the artist into the art has a rich history in this city. Standing in stark contrast to the more self-consciously daring movements such as Actionism, Vienna's extensive Neue Wilde group emphasises traditional techniques and media.

The artist Eva Schlegel works in a number of media, exploring how associations are triggered by images. Some of her most powerful work has been photos of natural phenomena or candid street shots printed onto a chalky canvas then overlaid with layers and layers of oil paint and lacquer; they manage to be enjoyable on both a sensual and intellectual level.

One of Vienna's best-known contemporary artists, Arnulf Rainer, worked during the 1950s with automatic painting (letting his hand draw without trying to control it). He later delved into Actionism, footpainting, painting with chimpanzees and the creation of death masks.

Vienna's Akademie der Bildenden Künste (Academy of Fine Arts) is famous for rejecting a painter by the name of Adolf Hitler. One hundred and twenty-eight artists applied for admission in 1907 and Hitler was one of the 100 who failed. His entrance exam themes included 'expulsion from Paradise', 'building workers' and 'death'.

Hans Hollein has been one of Vienna's influential architects since the 1960s. Works include Retti Candleshop (Kohlmarkt 8-10); two jewellery stores designed for Schullin (Graben 26), which have been described as 'architectural Fabergés'; and Haas Haus, whose facade seems to be peeling back to reveal the curtain wall of glass below.

Vienna in Print & on Film

Viennese writing and cinema is often bowed down by the weight of personal and national histories. Living under an autocratic empire, dealing with the end of an autocratic empire, the guilt of *Anschluss*, the horror of Nazism, the emotional legacy of WWII, neo-Nazism, misanthropy, religious upbringing and a real or imagined bleakness of life are all very, very popular themes.

Top Books

The Play of the Eyes, Elias Canetti (1985)

The Radetzky March, Joseph Roth (1932)

The Third Man, Graham Greene (1950)

Across, Peter Handke (1986)

Measuring the World, Daniel Kehlmann (2005)

Literature

19th to Mid-20th Century

Austria's literary tradition really took off around the end of the 19th century. Karl Kraus (1874–1936) was one of the period's major figures; his apocalyptic drama *Die letzten Tage der Menschheit* (The Last Days of Mankind) employed a combination of reports, interviews and press extracts to tell its tale. Peter Altenberg (1859–1919) was a drug addict, an alcoholic, a fan of young girls and a poet who depicted the Bohemian lifestyle of Vienna. Whenever asked where he lived, he reputedly always gave the address of Café Central, where you find his paper mâché figure adorning the room today. Two of his collected works are *Evocations of Love* (1960) and *Telegrams of the Soul: Selected Prose of Peter Altenberg* (2005).

Robert Musil (1880–1942) was one of the most important 20th-century writers, but he only achieved international recognition after his death, when his major literary achievement about Belle Époque Vienna, *Der Mann ohne Eigenschaften* (The Man without Qualities), was – at seven volumes – still unfinished. Stefan Zweig (1881–1942), another of the greatest writers in German, was born in Vienna and in his autobiography *Die Welt von Gestern* (The World of Yesterday, 1942–3) he vividly describes Vienna of the early 20th century. A poet, playwright, translator, paranoiac and pacifist, Zweig believed Nazism had been conceived specifically with him in mind and when he became convinced in 1942 that Hitler would take over the world, he killed himself in exile in Brazil.

Arthur Schnitzler (1862–1931), a friend of Freud, was a prominent Jewish writer in Vienna's fin de siècle years. His play *Reigen* (Hands Around), set in 1900 against a Viennese backdrop, was described by Hitler as 'Jewish filth'; it gained considerable fame in the English-speaking world as Max Ophul's film *La Ronde*. Joseph Roth (1894–1939), primarily a journalist, wrote about the concerns of Jews in exile and of Austrians uncertain of their identity at the end of the empire. His book *What I Saw: Reports from Berlin* is part of an upsurge of interest in this fascinating writer; his most famous works, *Radetzky March* and *The Emperor's Tomb,* are both gripping tales set in the declining Austro-Hungarian Empire.

Modern & Contemporary

Perhaps it's something in the water, but the majority of modern and contemporary Viennese authors (at least those translated into English) are grim, guilt-ridden, angry and sometimes incomprehensibly avant-garde. Thomas

Bernhard (1931–89) was born in Holland but grew up and lived in Austria. He was obsessed with disintegration and death, and in later works like *Holzfällen: Eine Erregung* (Cutting Timber: An Irritation) turned to controversial attacks against social conventions and institutions. His novels are seamless (no chapters or paragraphs, few full stops) and seemingly repetitive, but surprisingly readable once you get into them.

Peter Handke's (born 1942) postmodern, abstract output encompasses innovative and introspective prose works and stylistic plays. His book *The Goalie's Anxiety at the Penalty Kick* (1970) brought him acclaim, helped along by a film based on the book and directed by Wim Wenders. His essay on the Balkan wars of the 1990s, *A Journey to the Rivers: Justice for Serbia* (1997), took an unpopular stance on Serbia and further cemented his reputation for being controversial.

The provocative novelist Elfriede Jelinek (born 1946), winner of the Nobel Prize for Literature in 2004, dispenses with direct speech, indulges in strange flights of fancy and takes a very dim view of humanity. Her works are highly controversial, often disturbingly pornographic, and either loved or hated by critics. Jelinek's *Women as Lovers* (1994) and *The Piano Teacher* (1983) are two of her most acclaimed works. Her controversial *Greed* (2000) focuses on gender and the relationships between men and women.

The most successful of the contemporary writers is arguably Daniel Kehlmann (born 1975), who achieved national and international acclaim with his *Measuring the World*, based on the lives of Alexander von Humboldt and Carl Friedrich Gauss. Kehlmann was born in Munich and grew up in Vienna. A film based on the book was released in 2012, directed by the idiosyncratic German director and actor Detlev Buck.

Many Viennese authors are also playwrights – perhaps the Viennese fondness for the avant-garde encourages the crossing of artistic boundaries. Schnitzler, Bernhard, Jelinek and Handke have all had their plays performed at the premier playhouse in Austria, Vienna's own Burgtheater.

Cinema

Modern Viennese cinema is a bleak landscape of corrupt and venal characters beating their children and dogs while struggling with a legacy of hatred and guilt. That might be a slight exaggeration, but contemporary film does seem to favour naturalism over escapism, violent sex over flowery romance, ambivalence and dislocation over happy endings.

The film industry is lively and productive, turning out Cannes Film Festival–sweepers like Michael Haneke, whose *The Piano Teacher* (2001, based on the novel by Elfriede Jelinek), *Funny Games* (2008), *The White Ribbon* (2009) and *Amour* (2012) have all picked up prizes at Cannes. *Amour* also won the Academy Award for Best Foreign Film.

A healthy serving of government arts funding keeps the film industry thriving, as does the Viennese passion for a trip to the *Kino* (cinema). Local, independent films are as well attended as blockbusters by Graz-boy-made-good, Arnie Schwarzenegger. A yearly festival, Viennale (p47), draws experimental and fringe films from all over Europe, keeping the creative juices flowing, while art-house cinemas like the gorgeous *Jugendstil* **Breitenseer Lichtspiele** (☑982 21 73; Breitenseer Strasse 21, 14) keep the Viennese proud of their rich cinematic history.

That history has turned out several big names ('big' in that they've moved to America and been accepted by Hollywood). Fritz Lang made the legendary *Metropolis* (1926), the story of a society enslaved by technology, and *The Last Will of Dr Mabuse* (1932), during which an incarcerated madman spouts Nazi doctrine. Billy Wilder, writer and director of hits like *Some Like it Hot*, *The Apartment* and *Sunset Boulevard*, was Viennese, though he moved to the US early in his career. Hedy Lamarr – Hollywood glamour girl and inventor of submarine guidance systems – was also born in Vienna. Klaus Maria Brandauer, star of *Out of Africa* and *Mephisto*, is another native. And Vienna itself has been the star of movies such as *The Third Man*, *The Night Porter* and *Before Sunrise*.

Vienna's oldest theatres that still exist include the Burgtheater, founded in 1741, the two *Vorstädte* theatres, Theater in der Josefstadt (1788) and Theater an der Wien (1801), and the Volkstheater (1889).

Documentary-maker Ulrich Seidl has made *Jesus, You Know*, following six Viennese Catholics as they visit their church for prayer, and *Animal Love*, an investigation of Viennese suburbanites who have abandoned human company for that of pets. Lately he has branched into features with *Dog Days*. Jessica Hausner has earned a strong reputation by directing films such as *Lovely Rita*, the story of a suburban girl who kills her parents in cold blood, and *Lourdes*, which is about an atheistic woman with multiple sclerosis who makes a pilgrimage to Lourdes.

The Third Man

'I had paid my last farewell to Harry a week ago, when his coffin was lowered into the frozen February ground, so that it was with incredulity that I saw him pass by, without a sign of recognition, among the host of strangers in the Strand.' Thus wrote Graham Greene on the back of an envelope. There it stayed, for many years, an idea without a context. Then Sir Alexander Korda asked him to write a film about the four-power occupation of postwar Vienna.

Greene had an opening scene and a framework, but no plot. He flew to Vienna in 1948 and searched with increasing desperation for inspiration. Nothing came to mind until, with his departure imminent, Greene had lunch with a British intelligence officer who told him about the underground police who patrolled the huge network of sewers beneath the city, and the black-market trade in penicillin. Greene put the two ideas together and created his story.

Shot in Vienna in the same year, the film perfectly captures the atmosphere of postwar Vienna using an excellent play of shadow and light. The plot is simple but gripping; Holly Martin, an out-of-work writer played by Joseph Cotton, travels to Vienna at the request of his old school mate Harry Lime (played superbly by Orson Welles), only to find him dead under mysterious circumstances. Doubts over the death drag Martin into the black-market penicillin racket and the path of the multinational force controlling Vienna. Accompanying the first-rate script, camera work and acting is a mesmerising soundtrack. After filming one night, director Carol Reed was dining at a *Heuriger* (wine tavern) and fell under the spell of Anton Karas' zither playing. Although Karas could neither read nor write music, Reed flew him to London to record the soundtrack. His bouncing, staggering 'Harry Lime Theme' dominated the film, became a chart hit and earned Karas a fortune.

The Third Man was an instant success, and has aged with grace and style. It won first prize at Cannes in 1949, the Oscar for Best Camera for a Black and White Movie in 1950, and was selected by the British Film Institute as 'favourite British film of the 20th century' in 1999. For years, the Burg Kino has screened the film on a weekly basis.

The film's popularity has spawned the Third Man Private Collection (p100). True aficionados may want to take the Third Man Tour (p28) in English. It covers all the main locations used in the film, including a glimpse of the underground sewers, home to 2.5 million rats.

Important figures in the modern era of theatre were the playwright Franz Grillparzer (1791–1872), Johann Nestroy (1801–62) and Ferdinand Raimund, whose works include *Der Alpenkönig* (King of the Alps) and *Der Menchenfiend* (The Misanthrope).

Theatre

The roots of theatre in Vienna date back to religious liturgies and passion plays of the mid- and late Middle Ages. Baroque operas staged from the late 16th century were very much influenced by Italian styles, and under Habsburg monarchs such as Ferdinand III and Karl VI, baroque theatre of the royal court rose to its zenith. In 1741 Maria Theresia paved the way for abroad theatre audience when she had a hall used for playing the tennis-like game *jeu de paume* converted into the original Burgtheater on Michaelerplatz. This later moved to the Ringstrasse into the premises of today's Burgtheater.

Survival Guide

Transport

ARRIVING IN VIENNA

Vienna International Airport (VIE; www.viennaairport.com) has good connections worldwide, but some travellers might find it more convenient to use international flights to Frankfurt am Main or Munich (Germany), Budapest (Hungary) or Zürich (Switzerland) and travel on by train. There are excellent high-speed rail connections and advance booking deals between Vienna and all of these cities except Bratislava (Slovakia):

➡ Budapest (three hours, €77)

➡ Bratislava (regional express only; one hour, €16)

➡ Frankfurt am Main (seven hours, €136)

➡ Munich (via Salzburg; four hours, €89)

➡ Zürich (eight hours, €106)

For more about flights to/from Vienna, go to the Vienna International Airport website. For railway timetables and prices, see the **ÖBB** (Austrian National Railways; www.oebb.at) website or the **Deutsche Bahn** (German National Railways; www.bahn.de) website.

Vienna has no central bus station. Südtiroler Platz (alongside *Hauptbahnhof*) is the closest thing to one. **Eurolines** (☑798 29 00; www.eurolines.com; Erdbergstrasse 200; ☺6.30am-9pm) uses its own terminal at the U3 U-Bahn station Erdberg, along with Südtiroler Platz and a few other stops. It has bus connections with the rest of Europe.

Flights, cars and tours can be booked online at lonely planet.com.

Vienna International Airport

Train

City Airport Train (CAT; www.cityairporttrain.com; return adult/child €19/free; ☺departs airport 5.36am-11.06pm) services connect Wien-Mitte railway station and the airport every 30 minutes from early morning to late at night (€12, 16 minutes). See the website or www.viennaairport.com for exact times. The S7 (€3.80, 30 minutes) does the same journey to the airport. See www.oebb.at for times.

Bus

Vienna Airport Lines (Map p252; www.postbus.at) has three services connecting different parts of Vienna with the airport. The most central is to/from the Vienna Airport Lines bus stop at Morzinplatz/Schwedenplatz (bus 1185; one way €8, 20 minutes), running via Wien-Mitte. A service also runs to/from Wien Dörfelstrasse (Wien-Meidling Bahnhof) while the *Hauptbahnhof* is being completed. See the website for the latest on routes to/from *Hauptbahnhof* once that is completed.

Taxi

A standard taxi to/from the airport costs about €36 if you call ahead or go directly to the yellow **40 100 Taxi Service** (☑40 100; www.taxi40100.at) in the arrival hall near the bookshop. **C&K Airport Service** (☑444 44; www.cundk.at) has a similar deal, though its desk service at the airport costs a few euros more. Otherwise expect to pay about €50.

Airport Bratislava (Letisko)

Airport Bratislava (Letisko; ☑+421 (2) 3303 3353; www.airportbratislava.sk) is located 60km east of Vienna.

Bus

Buses leave outside the airport arrival hall between 8.25am and 9.25pm daily, travelling via Vienna International Airport to Vienna's Südtiroler Platz.

From Vienna to Airport Bratislava almost hourly buses depart Südtiroler Platz between approximately 6am and 11pm daily, going via Vienna International Airport (one way/return €8/14.50, two hours; return tickets valid 180 days).

The bus also stops at the Eurolines terminal in Erdberg on the way. Book online at www.slovaklines.sk or at www.eurolines.com. For information and reservations by telephone call:

➡ Wien Südtiroler Platz
☑+43 (1) 504 6430

➜ Bratislava
☑ +421 (2) 55 422 734

You can also take the bus to the centre of Bratislava and pick up a frequent train from Bratislava train station to Vienna.

Wien Hauptbahnhof

The Wien Hauptbahnhof is expected to be fully completed in January 2015.

➜ **S-Bahn** S1, S2 and S3 connect *Hauptbahnhof* with Wien Meidling, Wien-Mitte and Praterstern.

➜ **U-Bahn** U1 to/from Karlsplatz and Stephansplatz.

➜ **Tram** O to Praterstern, 18 to Westbahnhof and Burggasse/ Stadthalle. Tram D connects Hauptbahnhof-Ost with the Ringstrasse.

➜ **Bus** 13A runs through Vienna's *Vorstädte* (inner suburbs) Margareten, Mariahilf, Neubau and Josefstadt, all between the Ringstrasse and the Gürtel.

Wien Meidling

You are only likely to arrive here if coming from Graz or other parts of southern

VIENNA BY BOAT

The Danube is a traffic-free access route for arrivals and departures from Vienna. Eastern Europe is the main destination; **Twin City Liner** (☑ Vienna 01-588 80; www.twincityliner.com; Schwedenplatz, 01, Vienna; one-way adult €20-35; ☾ late Mar-early Nov) connects Vienna with Bratislava in 1½ hours, while **DDSG Blue Danube Schiffahrt** (☑ 588 80; www.ddsg-blue-danube. at; 02, Handelskai 265, Reichsbrücke; one way €99-109, return €125) links Budapest with Vienna from May to October, departing Vienna Tuesday and Thursday, departing Budapest Monday and Wednesday. DDSG tickets may also be obtained or picked up at Twin City Liner.

The Slovakian ferry company **LOD** (☑ 421 2 529 32 226; www.lod.sk; departs Quai 6, Reichsbrücke; one way/ return €23/38) has hydrofoils between Bratislava and Vienna, 1½ hours, five to seven days per week from late April to early October. It's best value on weekends and for return trips. Booking is online unless you call Bratislava to reserve and then pay cash on the ship.

For boat trips through the Wachau region northwest of Vienna, see p183.

Austria. Eventually long-distance services will shift to *Hauptbahnhof*.

➜ **S-Bahn** S1, S2 and S3 connect *Hauptbahnhof* with Wien Meidling, Wien-Mitte and Praterstern.

➜ **U-Bahn** U6 (Wien Meidling/ Philadelphiabrücke). Connections with Westbahnhof and the Gürtel stations.

Wien Westbahnhof

➜ **U-Bahn** U6 runs along the Gürtel, U3 to Stephansplatz (for Stephansdom) via Herrengasse (for the Hofburg).

GETTING AROUND VIENNA

U-Bahn

The U-Bahn is a quick, efficient and inexpensive way of getting around the city. There are five lines: U1 to U4 and U6 (there is no U5). Stations have lifts as well as escalators. Platforms have timetable information and signs showing the exits and nearby facilities.

The U-Bahn runs all night on Friday and Saturday; it runs from approximately 5am to 12.30am other days of the week.

VIENNA'S NEW HAUPTBAHNHOF

Vienna's new *Hauptbahnhof* (main train station) went partially into service in 2012 and should go into full service by early 2015. Services to/from Bratislava, Znojmo, Wiener Neustadt and a few other regions of Lower Austria and Burgenland have been using a new section of the station since late 2012. Until *Hauptbahnhof* goes into full service, trains mostly servicing western Austria and international trains to/from European neighbours west of Austria's borders will continue to use Westbahnhof. (This will eventually get only minor regional trains.) Wien-Meidling (Meidling-Philadelphiabrücke U-Bahn, NOT Meidling Hauptstrasse) is for an interim period being used for trains mostly serving southern cities such as Graz. For the current situation, always consult the timetables on www.oebb.at – and look at your ticket closely!

TRANSPORT GETTING AROUND VIENNA

TRANSPORT TICKETS & PASSES

Tickets and passes for **Wiener Linien** (☎7909-100; www.wienerlinien.at) services (U-Bahn, trams and buses) can be purchased at U-Bahn stations and on trams and buses, in a *Tabakladen* (*Trafik; tobacco kiosk*), as well as from a few staffed ticket offices. They must be validated as you enter the station or board a tram or bus.

➧ **Single Ticket** (*Einzelfahrschein*) €2; good for one journey, with line changes; costs €2.20 if purchased on trams and buses (correct change required).

➧ **Short Trips & Children** (*Kurzstrecken*) For one, two or four trips either for children between six and 15 years (ID or passport required) or on short trips (eg two U-Bahn stations). Tickets cost €1 (or €1.10 on tram or bus), €2 and €4 respectively.

➧ **24-/48-/72-hour Tickets** (*24-/48-/72-Stundenkarten*) €6.70, €11.70 and €14.50 respectively. Require validation.

➧ **Eight-Day Ticket** (*8-Tage-Klimakarte*) €33.80; valid for eight days, but not necessarily eight consecutive days; punch the card as and when you need it.

➧ **Weekly Ticket** (*Wochenkarte*) €15; valid Monday to Sunday only.

➧ **Monthly Ticket** (*Monatskarte*) €45; valid from the first day of the month to the last day of the month.

➧ **Vienna Card** (*Die Wien-Karte*) €19.90; 72 hours of unlimited travel from time of validation plus discounts.

➧ **Vienna Shopping Card** (*Wiener Einkaufskarte*) €5.40; for use between 8am and 8pm Monday to Saturday; only good for one day after validation.

➧ **Senior Citizens** Those over 60 years of age can buy a €2.50 ticket that is valid for two trips; enquire at transport information offices.

Tram

There's something romantic and just plain good about travelling by tram, even though they're slower than the U-Bahn. Vienna's tram network is extensive and it's the perfect way to view the city on the cheap. Trams are either numbered or lettered (eg 1, 2, D) and services cover the city centre and some suburbs.

Bus

Bus connections can be useful for outlying parts of town or for travellers with limited physical mobility. Some services are very limited or nonexistent at night and on weekends. U-Bahn and tram services get you close to most sights, especially in the centre and fringing *Vorstadt* areas (ie between the Ringstrasse and Gürtel).

Regular buses 13A runs north–south through the *Vorstädte* between *Hauptbahnhof* and Alser Strasse. 2A connects Schwarzenbergplatz, Stephansplatz, Schwedenplatz and Michaelerplatz. 3A connects Börsenplatz and Schottentor with Stephansplatz and Stubentor.

Night buses *Nightline* routes cover much of the city and run every half-hour from 12.30am to 5am. Note that on early Saturday and Sunday mornings (eg after midnight Friday and Saturday) the U-Bahn runs all night. Schwedenplatz, Schottentor and Kärntner Ring/Oper are stopping points for many night bus services; look for buses and bus stops marked with an 'N'. All transport tickets are valid for *Nightline* services. N25 runs around the Ringstrasse then via Schwedenplatz, Leopoldstadt to Kagraner Platz and beyond weekdays.

Bicycle

Vienna is a fabulous place to get around by bike. Bicycles can be carried free of charge on carriages marked with a bike symbol on the S-Bahn and U-Bahn from 9am to 3pm and after 6.30pm Monday to Friday, after 9am Saturday and all day Sunday. It's not possible to take bikes on trams and buses. The city also runs a City Bike program, with bike stands scattered throughout the city.

S-Bahn

S-Bahn trains, designated by a number preceded by an 'S', operate from train stations and service the suburbs or satellite towns. If you're travelling outside of Vienna, and outside of the ticket zone, you'll probably have to purchase an extension on your standard Vienna transport ticket or buy a ticket from a machine at the station; check on maps posted in train stations.

Taxi

Taxis are reliable and relatively cheap by Western European standards. City journeys are metered; the minimum charge is roughly €3.80 from 6am to 11pm Monday to Saturday and €4.30 any other time, plus a small per kilometre fee. A telephone reservation costs an additional €2.80. A small tip of 10% is expected.

Taxis are easily found at train stations and taxi stands all over the city, or just flag them down in the street. To order one, call ☑140 100 or ☑60 160. These accept common credit and debit cards (check before hopping in, though).

Car & Motorcycle

Driving

You may consider hiring a car to see some of the sights but in Vienna itself it's best to stick with the excellent public transport system.

HIRE

Car-hire rates start at around €80 per day and all the big names in car hire are present in Vienna (and have desks at the airport). A couple of major companies in the city include:

Europcar (☑866 16 1633; www.europcar.at; Schubertring 9; ☺7.30am-6pm Mon-Fri, 8am-1pm Sat, 8am-noon Sun)

Hertz (☑512 8677; www. hertz.at; 01, Kärntner Ring 17; ☺7.30am-6pm Mon-Fri, 9am-3pm Sat & Sun)

Megadrive (☑05 01 05 4124; www.megadrive.at; 03, Erdbergstrasse 202; ☺7am-7pm Mon-Fri, 8am-2pm Sat, 8am-1pm Sun; Ⓜ Erdberg)

Directory A–Z

Discount Cards & Concessions

Vienna Card (*Die Wien-Karte;* €20) Three days' unlimited travel on the public transport system (including night buses) and discounts at selected museums, cafes, *Heurigen* (wine taverns), restaurants and shops across the city, and on guided tours and the City Airport Train (CAT). The discount usually amounts to 5% to 10% off the normal price. Purchased at Tourist Info Wien, the city's main tourist office, the Airport Information Office and many concierge desks at the top hotels.

Concession prices Many museums and sights have concessions for families and children (generally for children under 16 years), which are listed in this book along with practical details. Many museums in Vienna are free for anyone under 19 years. Some places also have reduced student and senior citizen admission prices, which are generally slightly higher than the child's price. Children under 12 years usually receive a substantial discount on rooms they share with parents; ask when booking. Children also travel at reduced rates on public transport.

Electricity

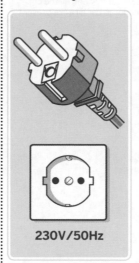

230V/50Hz

Emergency

In case of emergency, the general number for ambulance, fire and police is 112.

Ambulance (Rettung; ☏144)
Fire (Feuerwehr; ☏122)
Police (Polizei; ☏133)

Internet Access

Many of the main streets leading away from the city centre outside the Gürtel are lined with cheap, albeit slightly grungy, call centres doubling as internet cafes. Expect to pay anything from €4 to €8 per hour. Additionally, a large number of coffee houses, cafes and also some bars have free wi-fi, called WLAN (*vee-lan*) in German.

Free wi-fi hotspots can be found at Tourist Info Wien (p235) as well as the Prater, Rathausplatz, Naschmarkt, Donauinsel, Westbahnhof (main hall), Museums-Quartier, and most likely *Hauptbahnhof* when it opens fully. To connect, you often need to go to a website and confirm (*Bestätigen*) conditions or click the connect (*Verbinden*) button.

Most hotels in the mid-range and upwards have wi-fi, usually for free. Sometimes you will need to ask for a password.

For online lists of places with wi-fi check www.free wlan.at and www.freewave.at/en/hotspots.

It can be useful to have a Skype or other calling app installed on your smart phone to use in places with wi-fi.

While there are sufficient free hotspots to rely on around town if you have a mobile device with wi-fi capabilities, if you don't want to use hotspots you can buy prepaid SIM cards without formalities. This will allow you to surf with your tablet computer, surf stick or mobile phone (if there is no SIM lock). Drop into any shop selling SIM cards and ask what's currently the best deal.

Money

Austria's currency is the euro, which is divided into 100 cents. There are coins for one, two, five, 10, 20 and 50 cents, and €1 and €2. Notes come in denominations of €5, €10, €20, €50, €100, €200 and €500.

For the latest exchange rates, check out www.oanda.com. Note that travellers cheques are no longer commonly exchanged in Austria.

ATMs

*Bankomat*s (ATMs), which accept credit cards and debit cards such as Maestro, are never very far away in Vienna – just look for a neon sign with two green and blue stripes sticking out from a bank facade. *Bankomat*s can also be found in the main train stations and at the airport. Many ATMs close at midnight, but many of those located inside a foyer operate 24 hours, including Bank of Austria branches on Stephansplatz.

Check with your home bank before travelling to see how much the charge is for using a *Bankomat* in Vienna; normally there's no commission to pay at the Austrian end.

Changing Money

Banks are the best places to exchange cash, but it pays to shop around as exchange rates and commission charges can vary a little between them. Typically, there's a charge of about 3% on currency exchange, with a minimum charge, so it's best to exchange larger amounts at one time.

There are plenty of exchange offices in the Innere Stadt, particularly around Stephansplatz and on Kärntner Strasse. Commission charges are around the same here as at banks, but quite often the exchange rates are uncompetitive.

Credit Cards

Visa, EuroCard and Master-Card are accepted a little more widely than American Express and Diners Club, although a surprising number of shops and restaurants refuse to accept any credit cards at all. Boutiques, high-end shops and restaurants will usually accept cards, though, and the same applies for hotels. Train tickets can be bought by credit card in main stations.

Opening Hours

The hours provided in this book are for the summer months, which is the peak period. Many places have reduced hours from November to March, when it can sometimes be useful to check ahead.

Banks 8am or 9am to 3pm Monday to Friday, with extended hours until 5.30pm on Thursday. Many smaller branches close from 12.30pm to 1.30pm for lunch.

Cafes 7am or 8am to 11pm or midnight, some traditional coffee houses and cafes close at 7pm or 8pm.

Post Offices 8am to noon and 2pm to 6pm Monday to Friday; some also open 8am to noon Saturday, and many are open all day Monday to Friday. The main post office (Fleischmarkt 19) and branch at Franz-Josefs-Bahnhof have extended hours.

Pubs & Clubs Opening times vary; closing is normally between midnight and 4am throughout the week.

Restaurants Generally 11am to 2.30pm or 3pm and 6pm to 11pm or midnight. Some kitchens are open all day.

Shops Usually open 9am to 6.30pm Monday to Friday and until 5pm Saturday. Some have extended hours until 9pm on Thursday or Friday.

Supermarkets Among the most widespread, Billa is open from 7.15am to 7.30pm Monday to Friday and until 6pm Saturday. Hofer is open from 8am to 7pm Monday to Friday and until 6pm Saturday. All close Sunday.

Public Holidays

The only establishments remaining open on holidays are bars, cafes and restaurants. Museums are usually open except for New Year's Day, Christmas Day and sometimes May Day. The big school break is July and August; most families go away during this time, so you'll find the city is a little quieter, but the downside is that a high percentage of restaurants and entertainment venues close.

New Year's Day (Neujahr) 1 January

Epiphany (Heilige Drei Könige) 6 January

Easter Monday (Ostermontag) March or April

Labour Day (Tag der Arbeit) 1 May

Ascension Day (Christi Himmelfahrt) Sixth Thursday after Easter

Whit Monday (Pfingstmontag) Sixth Monday after Easter

Corpus Christi (Fronleichnam) Second Thursday after Pentecost

Assumption (Maria Himmelfahrt) 15 August

National Day (Nationalfeiertag) 26 October

All Saints' Day (Allerheiligen) 1 November

Immaculate Conception (Mariä Empfängnis) 8 December

Christmas Eve (Heiligabend) 24 December; everything closed afternoon

Christmas Day (Christfest) 25 December

St Stephen's Day (Stephanitag) 26 December

Telephone

Country code Austria's country code is ☑0043.

Area code Vienna's area code is ☑01. When calling from overseas drop the zero in the Vienna code; eg the number for Vienna's main tourist office is ☑0043 1 245 55. When calling from inside Austria but outside Vienna, use the ☑01 area code.

Directory assistance For domestic assistance dial ☑11 88 77, for international assistance ☑0900 11 88 77.

Mobile phones Begin with ☑0650 or higher up to ☑0699.

Roaming Network works on GSM 1800 and is compatible with GSM 900 phones. US mobile phones (cell phones) will only work here if they are at least tri-band. Japanese phones need to be quad-band (world phone).

Prepaid SIM cards Phone shops sell prepaid SIM cards for making phone calls or SIM cards capable of being used on smart phones for data (ie surfing) as well as making calls. Typically, you pay about €15 for a SIM card and receive about €10 free credit. To use one, your mobile phone should be without a SIM lock.

Surfing & wi-fi on mobile phones Make sure the data transfer capability is deactivated while you are roaming. Austria has lots of wi-fi hotspots which can be used for surfing on smart phones with wi-fi capability.

Free phones Numbers starting with ☑0800 are free, numbers starting with ☑0810 cost €0.10 per minute, whereas ☑0820 numbers cost €0.20 per minute; other ☑08XX numbers are relatively inexpensive, while numbers starting with ☑09XX are exorbitant and best avoided.

Phone booths These take either coins or phone cards and a minimum of €0.30 is required to make a local call. Many post offices have phone booths where both international and national calls can be made. Another option is a call centre; they're generally found outside the centre and offer very competitive phone-call rates.

To reverse the charges (ie call collect), you have to call a free phone number to place the call. Ask directory assistance for more numbers.

Australia ☑0800 200 202
Ireland ☑0800 200 213
New Zealand ☑0800 200 222
South Africa ☑0800 200 230
UK ☑0800 200 209
USA (AT&T) ☑0800 200 288

Time

Austrian time is on Central European time, one hour ahead of GMT/UTC. If it's noon in Vienna it is 6am in New York and Toronto, 3am in San Francisco, 9pm in Sydney and 11pm in Auckland. Clocks go forward one hour on the last Saturday night in March and back again on the last Saturday night in October.

Note that in German *halb* is used to indicate the halfhour before the hour, hence *halb acht* (half-eight) means 7.30, not 8.30.

Tourist Information

Airport Information Office (◷6am-11pm) Full services, with maps, Vienna Card and walk-in hotel booking. Located in the Vienna International Airport arrival hall.

Jugendinfo (Vienna Youth Information; Map p256;☑4000 84 100; www.jugendinfowien. at; ☺2-7pm Mon-Wed, 1-6pm Thu-Sat; ⓂMuseumsquartier, 🚋Burgring) Jugendinfo is tailored to those aged between 14 and 26, and has tickets for a variety of events at reduced rates for this age group. Staff can tell you about events around town, and places to log onto the internet. It's on the corner of Babenbergerstrasse and Burgring.

Rathaus Information Office (Map p260;☑525 50; www.wien.gv.at; 01, Rathaus; ☺8am-6pm Mon-Fri; ⓂRathaus, 🚋D, 1, 2 Rathaus) City Hall provides information on social, cultural and practical matters, and is geared as much to residents as to tourists. There's a useful info-screen.

Tourist Info Wien (Map p254;☑245 55; www.wien.info; 01, Albertinaplatz; ☺9am-7pm; 🕾; ⓂStephansplatz, 🚋D, 1, 2, 71 Kärntner Ring/Oper) Vienna's main tourist office, with a ticket agency, hotel booking service, free maps and every brochure under the sun.

WienXtra-Kinderinfo (Map p260;☑4000 84 400; www. kinderinfowien.at; 07, Museumsplatz 1; ☺2-6pm Tue-Fri, 10am-5pm Sat & Sun; ⓂMuseumsquartier) Marketed firstly at children (check out the knee-high display cases), *then* their parents, this tourist office has loads of information on activities for kids and a small indoor playground. It's located inside the courtyard, near the Mariahilfer Strasse entrance.

Travellers with Disabilities

Vienna is fairly well geared for people with disabilities (*Behinderte*), but not exceptionally so. Ramps are common but by no means ubiquitous; most U-Bahn stations have wheelchair lifts. All U-Bahn stations have guiding strips for the blind. All buses these days have ramps (the driver will assist) and tilt technology, and half of the trams in service have low-floor access allowing entry in a wheelchair. A symbol on the arrival board at tram stops indicates trams with low-floor access. Traffic lights 'bleep' to indicate when pedestrians can safely cross the road.

Tourist Info Wien can give advice and information. Its detailed booklet *Accessible Vienna*, in German or English, provides information on hotels and restaurants with disabled access, plus addresses of hospitals, medical equipment shops, parking places, toilets and much more. Send an email (info@ wien.info) for more details. It's available for download at www.wien.info/en/travelinfo/accessible-vienna.

Organisations

Bizeps (Map p260;☑01-523 89 21; www.bizeps.at; Schönngasse 15-17, Vienna; ⓂMuseumsquartier, 🚋49 Siebensterngasse/Stiftgasse) A centre providing support and self-help for people with disabilities. Located three blocks behind the MuseumsQuartier.

Faktor i (Map p256;☑01-274 92 74; www.faktori.wuk. at; 05, Rechte Wienzeile 81; ⓂPilgramgasse) Faktor i offers information to young people with disabilities. Located just north of the Pilgramgasse U-Bahn station.

Visas

Visas for stays of up to 90 days are *not* required for citizens of the EU, the EEA (European Economic Area) and Switzerland, much of Eastern Europe, Israel, USA, Canada, the majority of Central and South American nations, Japan, Malaysia, Singapore, Australia or New Zealand. All other nationalities, including nationals of China and Russia, require a visa.

The Ministry of Foreign Affairs (www.bmaa.gv.at) website has a list of Austrian embassies where you can apply, and the Austrian embassy in Washington (www. austria.org/visa-residence-/ do-you-need-a-visa) lists all visa-free nationalities. For some nationals a biometric passport is required.

Austria is part of the Schengen Agreement, which includes all EU states (minus Britain and Ireland) and Switzerland. In practical terms this means a visa issued by one Schengen country is good for all the other member countries. You can stay for a maximum of 90 days within a time frame of 180 days.

Czech Republic & Slovakia

Both the Czech Republic (for Znojmo) and Slovakia (for Bratislava) are part of the Schengen Agreement. A Schengen visa allows travel to both countries.

Language

German is the national language of Austria. It belongs to the West Germanic language family and has around 100 million speakers worldwide.

German is easy for English speakers to pronounce because almost all of its sounds are also found in English. If you read our coloured pronunciation guides as if they were English, you should be understood just fine. Note that kh sounds like the 'ch' in 'Bach' or in the Scottish *loch* (pronounced at the back of the throat), r is also pronounced at the back of the throat, zh is pronounced as the 's' in 'measure', and ü as the 'ee' in 'see' but with rounded lips. The stressed syllables are indicated with italics in our pronunciation guides. The markers 'pol' and 'inf' indicate polite and informal forms.

BASICS

Hello.	Guten Tag./ Servus.	goo·ten tahk/ zer·vus
Goodbye.	Auf Wiedersehen.	owf vee·der·zay·en
Bye.	Tschüss./ Tschau.	chüs/ chow
Yes.	Ja.	yah
No.	Nein.	nain
Please.	Bitte.	bi·te
Thank you.	Danke.	dang·ke
You're welcome.	Bitte.	bi·te
Excuse me.	Entschuldigung.	ent·shul·di·gung
Sorry.	Entschuldigung.	ent·shul·di·gung

WANT MORE?

For in-depth language information and handy phrases, check out Lonely Planet's *German phrasebook*. You'll find it at **shop.lonelyplanet.com**, or you can buy Lonely Planet's iPhone phrasebooks at the Apple App Store.

How are you?
| Wie geht es Ihnen/dir? (pol/inf) | vee gayt es ee·nen/deer |

Fine. And you?
| Danke, gut. Und Ihnen/dir? (pol/inf) | dang·ke goot unt ee·nen/deer |

What's your name?
| Wie ist Ihr Name? (pol) | vee ist eer nah·me |
| Wie heißt du? (inf) | vee haist doo |

My name is ...
| Mein Name ist ... (pol) | main nah·me ist ... |
| Ich heiße ... (inf) | ikh hai·se ... |

Do you speak English?
| Sprechen Sie Englisch? (pol) | shpre·khen zee eng·lish |
| Sprichst du Englisch? (inf) | shprikhst doo eng·lish |

I don't understand.
| Ich verstehe nicht. | ikh fer·shtay·e nikht |

ACCOMMODATION

guesthouse	Pension	pahng·zyawn
hotel	Hotel	ho·tel
inn	Gasthof	gast·hawf
youth hostel	Jugend- herberge	yoo·gent· her·ber·ge

Do you have a ... room?	Haben Sie ein ...?	hah·ben zee ain ...
double	Doppelzimmer	do·pel·tsi·mer
single	Einzelzimmer	ain·tsel·tsi·mer

How much is it per ...?	Wie viel kostet es pro ...?	vee feel kos·tet es praw ...
night	Nacht	nakht
person	Person	per·zawn

Is breakfast included?
| Ist das Frühstück inklusive? | ist das frü·shtük in·kloo·zee·ve |

DIRECTIONS

Where's ...?
Wo ist ...?   vaw ist ...

What's the address?
Wie ist die Adresse?   vee ist dee a·*dre*·se

How far is it?
Wie weit ist es?   vee vait ist es

Can you show me (on the map)?
Können Sie es mir   *ker*·nen zee es meer
(auf der Karte) zeigen?   (owf dair *kar*·te) *tsai*·gen

How can I get there?
Wie kann ich da   vee kan ikh dah
hinkommen?   *hin*·ko·men

EATING & DRINKING

I'd like to   *Ich möchte*   ikh *merkh*·te
reserve a   *einen Tisch für*   ai·nen tish für
table for ...   *... reservieren.*   ... re·zer·*vee*·ren

   (eight)   *(acht) Uhr*   (akht) oor
   o'clock

   (two) people   *(zwei)*   (tsvai)
      Personen   per·*zaw*·nen

I'd like the menu, please.
Ich hätte gern die   ikh *he*·te gern dee
Speisekarte, bitte.   *shpai*·ze·kar·te *bi*·te

What would you recommend?
Was empfehlen Sie?   vas emp·*fay*·len zee

I'm a vegetarian.
Ich bin Vegetarier/   ikh bin ve·ge·*tah*·ri·er/
Vegetarierin. (m/f)   ve·ge·*tah*·ri·e·rin

That was delicious.
Das hat hervorragend   das hat her·*fawr*·rah·gent
geschmeckt.   ge·*shmekt*

Cheers!
Prost!   prawst

Please bring the bill.
Bitte bringen Sie   *bi*·te *bring*·en zee
die Rechnung.   dee *rekh*·nung

Key Words

bar (pub)	*Kneipe*	*knai*·pe
bottle	*Flasche*	*fla*·she
breakfast	*Frühstück*	*frü*·shtük
cold	*kalt*	kalt
cup	*Tasse*	*ta*·se
desserts	*Nachspeisen*	*nahkh*·shpai·zen
dinner	*Abendessen*	*ah*·bent·e·sen
drink list	*Getränke-karte*	ge·*treng*·ke·kar·te
fork	*Gabel*	*gah*·bel
glass	*Glas*	glahs
hot (warm)	*warm*	warm

NUMBERS

1	*eins*	ains
2	*zwei*	tsvai
3	*drei*	drai
4	*vier*	feer
5	*fünf*	fünf
6	*sechs*	zeks
7	*sieben*	*zee*·ben
8	*acht*	akht
9	*neun*	noyn
10	*zehn*	tsayn
20	*zwanzig*	*tsvan*·tsikh
30	*dreißig*	*drai*·tsikh
40	*vierzig*	*feer*·tsikh
50	*fünfzig*	*fünf*·tsikh
60	*sechzig*	*zekh*·tsikh
70	*siebzig*	*zeep*·tsikh
80	*achtzig*	*akht*·tsikh
90	*neunzig*	*noyn*·tsikh
100	*hundert*	*hun*·dert
1000	*tausend*	*tow*·sent

knife	*Messer*	*me*·ser
lunch	*Mittagessen*	*mi*·tahk·e·sen
market	*Markt*	markt
plate	*Teller*	*te*·ler
restaurant	*Restaurant*	res·to·*rahng*
spoon	*Löffel*	*ler*·fel
with/without	*mit/ohne*	mit/*aw*·ne

Meat & Fish

beef	*Rindfleisch*	*rint*·flaish
carp	*Karpfen*	*karp*·fen
fish	*Fisch*	fish
herring	*Hering*	*hay*·ring
lamb	*Lammfleisch*	*lam*·flaish
meat	*Fleisch*	flaish
pork	*Schweinefleisch*	*shvai*·ne·flaish
poultry	*Geflügelfleisch*	ge·*flü*·gel·flaish
salmon	*Lachs*	laks
sausage	*Wurst*	vurst
seafood	*Meeresfrüchte*	*mair*·res·frükh·te
shellfish	*Schaltiere*	*shahl*·tee·re
trout	*Forelle*	fo·*re*·le
veal	*Kalbfleisch*	*kalp*·flaish

Fruit & Vegetables

apple	Apfel	ap·fel
banana	Banane	ba·nah·ne
bean	Bohne	baw·ne
cabbage	Kraut	krowt
capsicum	Paprika	pap·ri·kah
carrot	Mohrrübe	mawr·rü·be
cucumber	Gurke	gur·ke
grapes	Weintrauben	vain·trow·ben
lemon	Zitrone	tsi·traw·ne
lentil	Linse	lin·ze
lettuce	Kopfsalat	kopf·za·laht
mushroom	Pilz	pilts
nuts	Nüsse	nü·se
onion	Zwiebel	tsvee·bel
orange	Orange	o·rahng·zhe
pea	Erbse	erp·se
plum	Pflaume	pflow·me
potato	Kartoffel	kar·to·fel
spinach	Spinat	shpi·naht
strawberry	Erdbeere	ert·bair·re
tomato	Tomate	to·mah·te
watermelon	Wasser-melone	va·ser·me·law·ne

Other

bread	Brot	brawt
cheese	Käse	kay·ze
egg/eggs	Ei/Eier	ai/ai·er
honey	Honig	haw·nikh
jam	Marmelade	mar·me·lah·de
pasta	Nudeln	noo·deln
pepper	Pfeffer	pfe·fer
rice	Reis	rais
salt	Salz	zalts
soup	Suppe	zu·pe
sugar	Zucker	tsu·ker

Drinks

beer	Bier	beer
coffee	Kaffee	ka·fay
juice	Saft	zaft
milk	Milch	milkh
orange juice	Orangensaft	o·rang·zhen·zaft
red wine	Rotwein	rawt·vain
tea	Tee	tay
water	Wasser	va·ser
white wine	Weißwein	vais·vain

EMERGENCIES

Help!	Hilfe!	hil·fe
Go away!	Gehen Sie weg!	gay·en zee vek

Call the police!
Rufen Sie die Polizei! — roo·fen zee dee po·li·tsai

Call a doctor!
Rufen Sie einen Arzt! — roo·fen zee ai·nen artst

Where are the toilets?
Wo ist die Toilette? — vo ist dee to·a·le·te

I'm lost.
Ich habe mich verirrt. — ikh hah·be mikh fer·irt

I'm sick.
Ich bin krank. — ikh bin krangk

I'm allergic to ...
Ich bin allergisch gegen ... — ikh bin a·lair·gish gay·gen ...

SHOPPING & SERVICES

I'd like to buy ...
Ich möchte ... kaufen. — ikh merkh·te ... kow·fen

Can I look at it?
Können Sie es mir zeigen? — ker·nen zee es meer tsai·gen

How much is this?
Wie viel kostet das? — vee feel kos·tet das

That's too expensive.
Das ist zu teuer. — das ist tsoo toy·er

There's a mistake in the bill.
Da ist ein Fehler in der Rechnung. — dah ist ain fay·ler in dair rekh·nung

ATM	Geldautomat	gelt·ow·to·maht
post office	Postamt	post·amt
tourist office	Fremden-verkehrsbüro	frem·den·fer·kairs·bü·raw

Signs

Ausgang	Exit
Damen	Women
Eingang	Entrance
Geschlossen	Closed
Herren	Men
Offen	Open
Toiletten (WC)	Toilets
Verboten	Prohibited

TIME & DATES

What time is it?
Wie spät ist es? vee shpayt ist es

It's (10) o'clock.
Es ist (zehn) Uhr. es ist (tsayn) oor

At what time?
Um wie viel Uhr? um vee feel oor

At ...
Um ... um ...

morning	*Morgen*	mor·gen
afternoon	*Nachmittag*	nahkh·mi·tahk
evening	*Abend*	ah·bent
yesterday	*gestern*	ges·tern
today	*heute*	hoy·te
tomorrow	*morgen*	mor·gen
Monday	*Montag*	mawn·tahk
Tuesday	*Dienstag*	deens·tahk
Wednesday	*Mittwoch*	mit·vokh
Thursday	*Donnerstag*	do·ners·tahk
Friday	*Freitag*	frai·tahk
Saturday	*Samstag*	zams·tahk
Sunday	*Sonntag*	zon·tahk

TRANSPORT

boat	*Boot*	bawt
bus	*Bus*	bus
metro	*U-Bahn*	oo·bahn
plane	*Flugzeug*	flook·tsoyk
train	*Zug*	tsook

At what time's *Wann fährt* van fairt
the ... bus? *der ... Bus?* dair ... bus

first	*erste*	ers·te
last	*letzte*	lets·te
next	*nächste*	naykhs·te

A ... to *Eine ... nach* ai·ne ... nahkh
(Linz). *(Linz).* (lins)

1st-/2nd- *Fahrkarte* fahr·kar·te
class *erster/* ers·ter/
ticket *zweiter Klasse* tsvai·ter kla·se

one-way *einfache* ain·fa·khe
ticket *Fahrkarte* fahr·kar·te

return ticket *Rückfahrkarte* rük·fahr·kar·te

Does it stop at ...?
Hält es in ...? helt es in ...

What station is this?
Welcher Bahnhof vel·kher bahn·hawf
ist das? ist das

What?	*Was?*	vas
When?	*Wann?*	van
Where?	*Wo?*	vaw
Who?	*Wer?*	vair
Why?	*Warum?*	va·rum

What's the next stop?
Welches ist der vel·khes ist dair
nächste Halt? naykh·ste halt

I want to get off here.
Ich möchte hier ikh merkh·te heer
aussteigen. ows·shtai·gen

Please tell me when we get to ....
Könnten Sie mir bitte kern·ten zee meer bi·te
sagen, wann wir in zah·gen van veer in
... ankommen? ... an·ko·men

Please take me to (this address).
Bitte bringen Sie mich bi·te bring·en zee mikh
zu (dieser Adresse). tsoo (dee·zer a·dre·se)

platform	*Bahnsteig*	bahn·shtaik
ticket office	*Fahrkarten-*	fahr·kar·ten·
	verkauf	fer·kowf
timetable	*Fahrplan*	fahr·plan

I'd like to *Ich möchte* ikh merkh·te
hire a ... *ein ... mieten.* ain ... mee·ten

bicycle	*Fahrrad*	fahr·raht
car	*Auto*	ow·to

How much *Wie viel kostet* vee feel kos·tet
is it per ...? *es pro ...?* es praw ...

day	*Tag*	tahk
week	*Woche*	vo·khe

bicycle pump	*Fahrradpumpe*	fahr·raht·pum·pe
child seat	*Kindersitz*	kin·der·zits
helmet	*Helm*	helm
petrol	*Benzin*	ben·tseen

Does this road go to ...?
Führt diese Straße fürt dee·ze shtrah·se
nach ...? nahkh ...

Can I park here?
Kann ich hier parken? kan ikh heer par·ken

Where's a petrol station?
Wo ist eine Tankstelle? vaw ist ai·ne tangk·shte·le

I need a mechanic.
Ich brauche einen ikh brow·khe ai·nen
Mechaniker. me·khah·ni·ker

Are there cycling paths?
Gibt es Fahrradwege? geept es fahr·raht·vay·ge

Behind the Scenes

SEND US YOUR FEEDBACK

We love to hear from travellers – your comments keep us on our toes and help make our books better. Our well-travelled team reads every word on what you loved or loathed about this book. Although we cannot reply individually to postal submissions, we always guarantee that your feedback goes straight to the appropriate authors, in time for the next edition. Each person who sends us information is thanked in the next edition – the most useful submissions are rewarded with a selection of digital PDF chapters.

Visit **lonelyplanet.com/contact** to submit your updates and suggestions or to ask for help. Our award-winning website also features inspirational travel stories, news and discussions.

Note: We may edit, reproduce and incorporate your comments in Lonely Planet products such as guidebooks, websites and digital products, so let us know if you don't want your comments reproduced or your name acknowledged. For a copy of our privacy policy visit lonelyplanet.com/privacy.

OUR READERS

Many thanks to the travellers who used the last edition and wrote to us with helpful hints, useful advice and interesting anecdotes:

John Carroll, Albert Castell, Lene Cools, Graham Courtenay, Cristina Domínguez, Daniel Hammerl, Alessandra Ongaro, Cristian Polescu, Amanda Raffaelli, Martin Rauch, Glenn van der Knijff, Daniel Ward

AUTHOR THANKS

Anthony Haywood

Many thanks to the many Viennese who helped with expert knowledge and advice while this book was being researched and written – including staff at the Vienna Tourist Board, Tom Venning and Ishimitsu Takako for interviews, Reini Weissensteiner for offering tips, and the folks at the galleries around town who gave insights into the art scene. Huge thanks to coauthor Kerry Christiani for her fantastic work on the book, and commissioning editor Dora Whitaker, Annelies Mertens and the rest of the Lonely Planet team.

Kerry Christiani

A big *Dankeschön* in Vienna to Astrid Pockfuss and her team at the Vienna Tourist Board.

Huge thanks also to the fantastic folk I met and interviewed: shopping maven Lucie Lamster-Thury, coffee-house connoisseur Eugene Quinn, Kay Fröhlich at Café Central, Rainer Staub at Café Sperl and Vienna Guides Service tour guide Gertrude Frantal. I'd also like to say *Danke* to my Vienna friends Chiara and Karin for invaluable tips, Monika Christiani for being a fun travel companion, and coordinating author Anthony Haywood for being a star to work with. Finally, thanks go to Dora Whitaker for giving me the gig and the entire Lonely Planet production team.

Marc Di Duca

Firstly, I am forever indebted to the dedicated staff at tourist offices in Krems, Znojmo, Bratislava and Melk who helped me along the way. A huge thank you to my Ukrainian parents-in-law for their free child-care services, and to my wife and two sons, for all the days we spend apart.

ACKNOWLEDGMENTS

Vienna U- & S-Bahn map © 2013 Wiener Linien

Cover photograph: Schloss Belvedere, Colin Dutton/4Corners ©.

THIS BOOK

This 7th edition of Lonely Planet's *Vienna* guidebook was researched and written by Anthony Haywood, Kerry Christiani and Marc Di Duca. The 6th edition was written by Anthony and Caroline Sieg. The 5th edition was written by Neal Bedford with assistance from Janine Eberle. This guidebook was commissioned in Lonely Planet's London office, and produced by the following:

Commissioning Editor Dora Whitaker

Coordinating Editors Carolyn Boicos, Gabrielle Innes

Senior Cartographers Mark Griffiths, Anthony Phelan

Coordinating Layout Designer Wibowo Rusli

Managing Editors Sasha Baskett, Annelies Mertens

Senior Editor Catherine Naghten

Managing Layout Designer Jane Hart

Assisting Editors Janice Bird, Tali Budlender

Assisting Cartographer Alison Lyall

Cover Research Naomi Parker

Internal Image Research Gerard Walker

Language Content Branislava Vladisavljevic

Thanks to Laura Crawford, Ryan Evans, Larissa Frost, Chris Girdler, Genesys India, Jouve India, Trent Paton, Kerrianne Southway, Ross Taylor

BEHIND THE SCENES

See also separate subindexes for:

✗ **EATING P245**

🍷 **DRINKING & NIGHTLIFE P246**

☆ **ENTERTAINMENT P247**

🔒 **SHOPPING P247**

🏃 **SPORTS & ACTIVITIES P248**

🛏 **SLEEPING P248**

Index

Vienna Maps

Sights
- Beach
- Bird Sanctuary
- Buddhist
- Castle/Palace
- Christian
- Confucian
- Hindu
- Islamic
- Jain
- Jewish
- Monument
- Museum/Gallery/Historic Building
- Ruin
- Sento Hot Baths/Onsen
- Shinto
- Sikh
- Taoist
- Winery/Vineyard
- Zoo/Wildlife Sanctuary
- Other Sight

Activities, Courses & Tours
- Bodysurfing
- Diving
- Canoeing/Kayaking
- Course/Tour
- Skiing
- Snorkelling
- Surfing
- Swimming/Pool
- Walking
- Windsurfing
- Other Activity

Sleeping
- Sleeping
- Camping

Eating
- Eating

Drinking & Nightlife
- Drinking & Nightlife
- Cafe

Entertainment
- Entertainment

Shopping
- Shopping

Information
- Bank
- Embassy/Consulate
- Hospital/Medical
- Internet
- Police
- Post Office
- Telephone
- Toilet
- Tourist Information
- Other Information

Geographic
- Beach
- Hut/Shelter
- Lighthouse
- Lookout
- Mountain/Volcano
- Oasis
- Park
- Pass
- Picnic Area
- Waterfall

Population
- Capital (National)
- Capital (State/Province)
- City/Large Town
- Town/Village

Transport
- Airport
- Border crossing
- Bus
- Cable car/Funicular
- Cycling
- Ferry
- Metro station
- Monorail
- Parking
- Petrol station
- Taxi
- Train station/Railway
- Tram
- U-Bahn/Underground station
- Other Transport

Note: Not all symbols displayed above appear on the maps in this book

Routes
- Tollway
- Freeway
- Primary
- Secondary
- Tertiary
- Lane
- Unsealed road
- Road under construction
- Plaza/Mall
- Steps
- Tunnel
- Pedestrian overpass
- Walking Tour
- Walking Tour detour
- Path/Walking Trail

Boundaries
- International
- State/Province
- Disputed
- Regional/Suburb
- Marine Park
- Cliff
- Wall

Hydrography
- River, Creek
- Intermittent River
- Canal
- Water
- Dry/Salt/Intermittent Lake
- Reef

Areas
- Airport/Runway
- Beach/Desert
- Cemetery (Christian)
- Cemetery (Other)
- Glacier
- Mudflat
- Park/Forest
- Sight (Building)
- Sportsground
- Swamp/Mangrove

DONAUSTADT 22

Wasserpark

Obere Alte Donau

Donaupark

Donauinsel

Neue Donau

Danube

Danube Canal

Unterer Prater
Fasangarten

2 km
1 miles

0
0

N

SIMMERING 11

LANDSTRASSE 3

Schweizer
Garten

BRIGITTENAU 20

LEOPOLDSTADT 2

Wien

Augarten

Stadtpark

Schloss
Belvedere

FAVORITEN 10

INNERE
STADT 1

Karlsplatz

WIEDEN 4

UNTERDÖBLING

OBERDÖBLING

ALSERGRUND 9

Rathausplatz

Volksgarten

MARIAHILF 6

MARGARETEN 5

GERSTHOF

JOSEFSTADT 8

NEUBAU 7

DÖBLING 19

UNTERSIEVERING

GERSTHOF

RUDOLFSHEIM-
FÜNFHAUS 15

Auer-
Welsbach-
Park

Wien

MEIDLING 12

NEUSTIFT
AM WALD

PÖTZLEINSDORF

WÄHRING 18

Pötzleinsdorfer
Schlosspark

DORNBACH

HERNALS 17

OTTAKRING 16

PENZING 14

Fasangarten

Tiroler
Garten

HIETZING 13

MAP INDEX

STEPHANSDOM & THE HISTORIC CENTRE Map on p252

STEPHANSDOM & THE HISTORIC CENTRE

N
0   200 m
0   0.1 miles

LEOPOLDSTADT 2

Nestroyplatz ⓤ

Zirkusgasse
Praterstr
Ferdinandstr
Aspernbrückengasse
Grosse Mohrengasse
Prinzengasse

Aspernbrücke

Uraniastr

Julius-Raab-
Platz

86

(Ringstrasse)

Oskar
Kokoschka
Platz

Georg-Coch-
Platz

7 🏛 96
37
25

Rosenburserstr
Biberstr

Postgasse

Dominikanerbastei

See map
p266

Taborstr

Untere Donaustr
Schweden-
brücke
Franz-Josefs-Kai (Ringstrasse)

Gredlerstr
Lilienbrunngasse
Hollandstrasse

Obere Donaustr

Danube Canal

Marien-
brücke

Salztor-
brücke

Franz-Josefs-Kai (Ringstrasse)

Franz-Josefsgasse
Heinrichsgasse
89

98

Gonzagagasse

Wiedtelorgasse

Börsegasse
Börseplatz
Börseplatz

Salzgries

Salvatorgasse
Gölsdorfgasse

Rudolfsplatz

Passauer
Platz

Vienna Airport
Lines Bus Stop

Morzinplatz
19

Rabensteig
44

27 ✚ 60
28
Seitenstetten-
gasse

Schwedenplatz ⓤ
Schwedenplatz
Night Bus Stop
87
88

Rotenturmstr

Franz-Josefs-Kai

Hafnersteig

Fleischmarkt
Grashofgasse
91
93
41 ✖ 14
Wollzeile

Drachgasse

Drachenfelsgasse
Bäckerstr
Köllnerhof
70
31
43
55

Drachgasse
92
74
33
59
80
47
69
16
6 🏛 11

10 ✚

Barbaragasse

Sonnenfelsgasse

Heiligenkreuzerhof

Lugeck
Rotenturmstr
94
Rauhensteingasse
Kärntnerstr
Strobelgasse

Essiggasse
38
67
30
51
39
9

81

Lichtensteg
Landskrongasse

26 🏛
Brandstätte

77

Jasomirgottstr

84

INNERE
STADT 1

36

Marc-Aurel-Str
Vorlaufstr
Sterngasse
Judengasse
Ruprechtsstiege
65
73
32
79

Hoher Markt
4
40
22 ✚
71

Wipplingerstr
Salvatorgasse
5
78

Judenplatz
8

Bauernmarkt

Schultergasse
Kurrentgasse

29

17 ✚
34
35
42
68

Farbergasse

Schulhof

Drahtgasse
3
Am Hof

Tuchlauben
Bognergasse

Naglergasse

Heidenschuss

Strauchgasse

Freyung

Tiefer Graben
Wipplingerstr
Hohenstaufengasse
Rennweg
Herrengasse

ⓤ Herrengasse

See map
p262

Schottenring (Ringstrasse)

Wallnerstr

Graben
12 🏛
45
24 ✚
50

15 🏛
21
18 ✚

Seilergasse

Schottenring
(Ringstrasse)

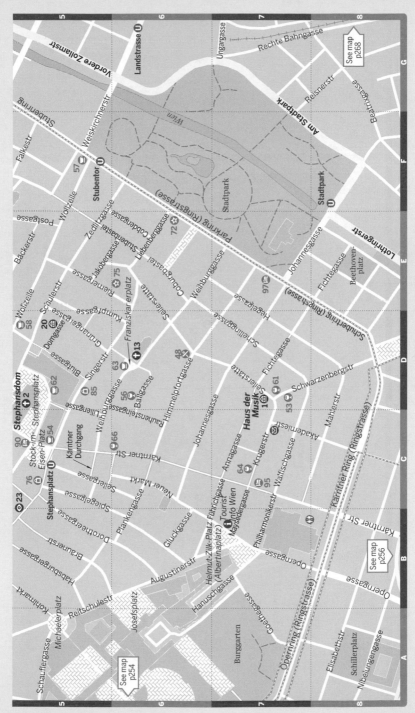

Vordere Zollamtst

Landstrasse Ⓤ

Rechte Bahngasse

Ungargasse

See map
p268

Reisnerstr

Beatrixgasse

Stubenring

Falkestr

Am Stadtpark

Wien

57

Stubentor Ⓤ

Weiskirchnerstr

Parkring (Ringstrasse)

Stadtpark

Stadtpark Ⓤ

Lothringerstr

Beethoven-
platz

Postgasse

Bäckerstr

Wolzeile

Zedlitzgasse

Stubenbastei

Liebenberggasse

Cobdengasse

72

Coburgbastei

Weihburggasse

Johannesgasse

Fichtegasse

Schubertring (Ringstrasse)

Wolzeile

Schulerstr

Riemergasse

Jakobergasse

Grünangergasse

75

Franziskarerplatz

Seilerstätte

Weihburggasse

Schellinggasse

97

Hegelgasse

Fichtegasse

58

20

Domgasse

Singerstr

13

63

Kumpfgasse

48

Blutgasse

61

Schwarzenbergstr

Stephansdom

2

Stephansplatz

62

85

56

Ballgasse

Rauhensteingasse

Himmelpfortgasse

Johannesgasse

Seilerstätte

Haus der
Musik

1

53

Mahlerstr

90

Stock-im-
Eisen-Platz

54

Lilliengasse

Weihburggasse

Kärntner
Durchgang

66

Kärntner Str

Annagasse

Krugerstr

64

Akademiestr

Stephansplatz Ⓤ

76

Seilergasse

Neuer Markt

Führichgasse

Kärntner Ring (Ringstrasse)

23

Spiegelgasse

Plankengasse

Gluckgasse

Helmut-Zilk-Platz
(Albertinaplatz)

Maysedergasse

Tourist
Info Wien

95

Philharmonikerstr

Walfischgasse

Kärntner Str

See map
p256

Dorotheergasse

Bräunerstr

Augustinerstr

Hanuschgasse

Operngasse

Opernring (Ringstrasse)

Operngasse

Habsburgergasse

Josefsplatz

Goethegasse

Burggarten

Elisabethstr

Schillerplatz

Nibelungengasse

Kohlmarkt

Schauflergasse

Michaelerplatz

Reitschulestr

See map
p254

THE HOFBURG & AROUND

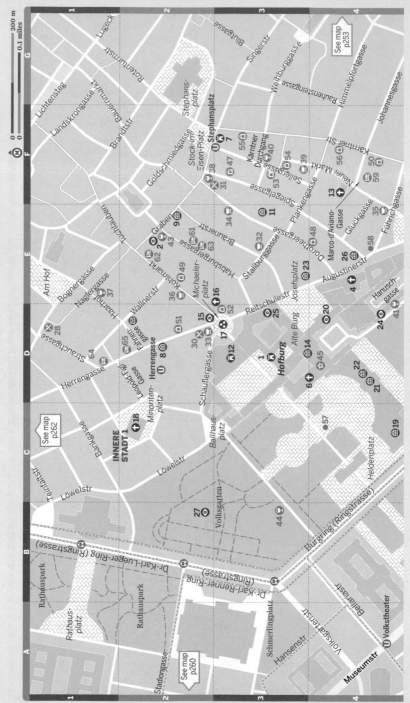

THE HOFBURG & AROUND

255

◎ Top Sights (60)
1 Hofburg D3

◎ Sights (p66)
2 Adolf' Public Toilets E2
3 Albertina E5
4 Augustinerkirche E4
5 Burggarten D5
6 Burgkapelle D4
7 Equitable Palais F3
8 Esperantomuseum .... (see 8)
9 Globenmuseum D2
9 Grabenhof E2
10 Helmut-Zilk-Platz E5
11 Jüdisches Museum E3
12 Kaiserappartements D4
13 Kaisergruft D3
14 Kaiserliche Schatzkammer D3
Kapuzinerkirche .... (see 13)
15 Loos Haus D2
16 Michaelerkirche E3
17 Michaelerplatz (Roman Ruins) D3
18 Minoritenkirche C2
Monument Against War & Fascism .... (see 10)
19 Museum für Volkerkunde C4
20 Nationalbibliothek Prunksaal D4
21 Neue Burg Museums .... (see 8)
22 Papyrusmuseum D2
23 Phantastenmuseum E2
Schmetterlinghaus .... (see 12)
24 Schmetterlinghaus D4
Sisi Museum .... (see 12)
25 Spanish Riding School D3
26 TheaterMuseum E4
27 Volksgarten B2

◎ Eating (p68)
28 Akakiko D1
29 Bitzinger Würstelstand am Albertinaplatz E5
30 freshii D2
Restaurant Herrlich .... (see 65)
31 Trzesniewski F3

◎ Drinking & Nightlife (p69)
32 Café Bräunerhof E3
33 Café Griensteidl D2
34 Café Leopold Hawelka E3
Café Sacher .... (see 60)
35 Café Tirolerhof E4
36 Demel E2
37 Esterházykeller E1
38 Fledermaus F2
39 Le Bol F3
40 Loos American Bar E4
Palffy Club .... (see 23)
41 Palmenhaus E4

◎ Entertainment (p71)
42 Passage C5
43 Villon E2
Volksgarten
ClubDiskothek .... (see 44)
44 Volksgarten Pavilion B3

◎ Entertainment (p71)
45 Hofburg Concert Halls D4
46 Österreichisches Filmmuseum E5
Vienna Boys' Choir Tickets .... (see 6)

◎ Shopping (p71)
47 Augarten Wien F3
48 Dorotheum E4
49 Freytag & Berndt E2
50 J&L Lobmeyr Vienna F4
51 Kabul Shop D2
52 Loden-Plankl D3
53 Mühlbauer F3
54 Oberlaa F3
55 Österreichische Werkstätten F3
United Nude .... (see 51)
56 Wolford F4

◎ Sports & Activities (p28)
57 Oldtimer Bus Tours C4
58 Redbus City Tours E4

◎ Sleeping (p201)
59 Aviano F4
60 Hotel Sacher E5
61 Pension a und a E2
62 Pension Nossek E2
63 Pension Pertschy E2
64 Radisson Blu Style Hotel C1
65 Steigenberger Hotel Herrenhof D2

Key on p258

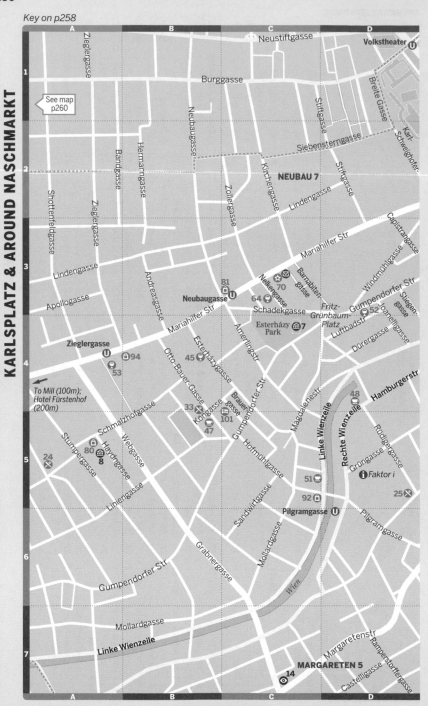

Neustiftgasse

Volkstheater

Burggasse

See map
p260

Zieglergasse

Bandgasse

Hermanngasse

Shottenfeldgasse

Zieglergasse

Lindengasse

Apollogasse

Andreasgasse

Neubaugasse

Zollergasse

Kirchengasse

Siebensterngasse

Stiftgasse

Breite Gasse

Karl-Schweighofer-

NEUBAU 7

Lindengasse

Stiftgasse

Mariahilfer Str

Capistrangasse

Windmühlgasse

Gumpendorfer Str

81

Neubaugasse

Nelkengasse

70

Barnabiten-gasse

Stiegen-gasse

64

Schadekgasse

Fritz-
Grünbaum-
Platz

52

Loquaiplatz

Luftbadstr

Durergasse

Esterházy
Park

7

Zieglergasse

94

53

Mariahilfer Str

Otto-Bauer-Gasse

Esterházygasse

45

Amerlingstr

Brauer-gasse

Gumpendorfer Str

Magdalenenstr

Linke Wienzeile

Rechte Wienzeile

48

Hamburgerstr

To Mill (100m);
Hotel Fürstenhof
(200m)

Schmalzhofgasse

Webgasse

Stumpergasse

80

8

Haydngasse

Liniengasse

33

Königseg

101

47

Hofmühlgasse

Rüdigergasse

Grüngasse

24

Sandwirtgasse

51

Faktor i

92

Pilgramgasse

25

Gumpendorfer Str

Grabnergasse

Mollardgasse

Wien

Pilgramgasse

MARGARETEN 5

Mollardgasse

Margaretenstr

Ramperstorffergasse

Linke Wienzeile

14

Castelligasse

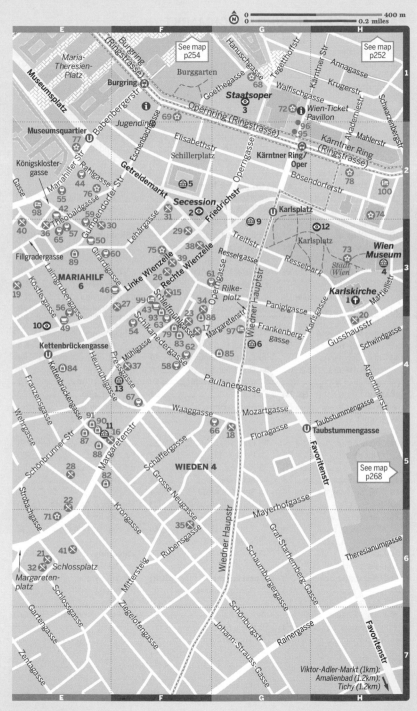

KARLSPLATZ & AROUND NASCHMARKT *Map on p256*

MUSEUM DISTRICT & NEUBAU *Map on p260*

MUSEUM DISTRICT & NEUBAU

Key on p259

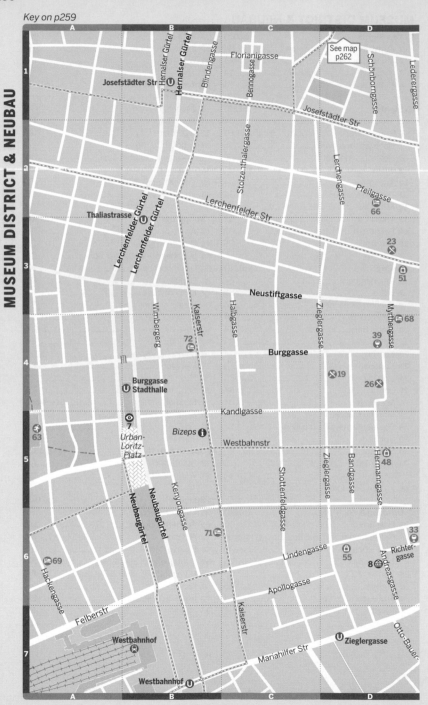

See map
p262

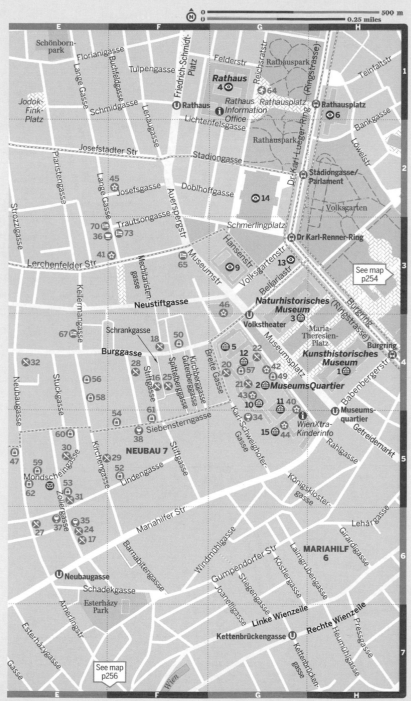

See map p254

See map p256

Key on p264

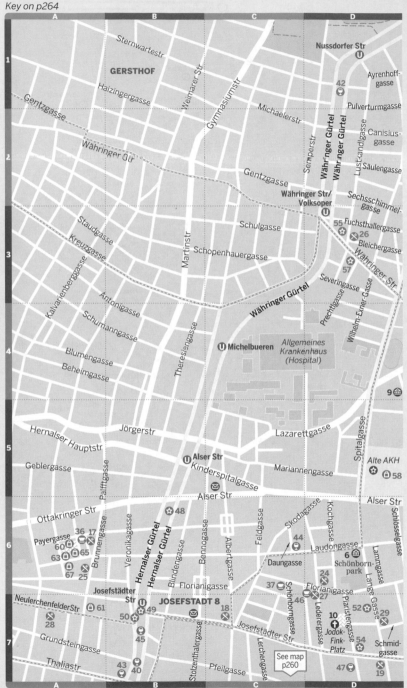

See map p260

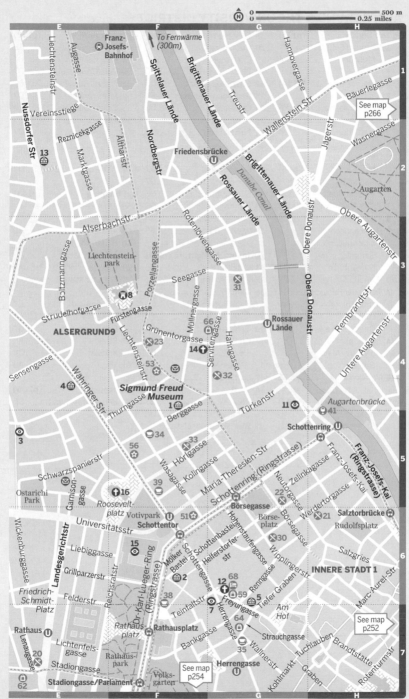

ALSERGRUND & THE UNIVERSITY DISTRICT Map on p262

PRATER & EAST OF THE DANUBE *Map on p266*

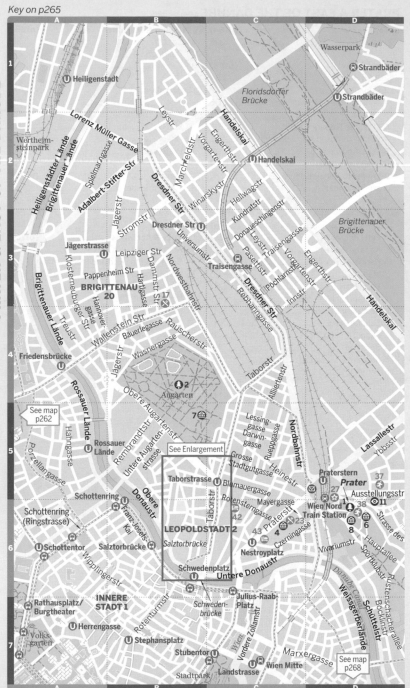

PRATER & EAST OF THE DANUBE

Wasserpark

Heiligenstadt

Strandbäder

Strandbäder

Floridsdorfer
Brücke

Wertheim-
steinpark

Lorenz Müller Gasse

Heiligenstädter Lände
Brigittenauer Lände

Spielmanngasse

Leystr

Marchfeldstr

Vorgartenstr

Engerthstr

Handelskai

Handelskai

Adalbert-Stifter-Str

Dresdner Str

Winarskystr

Hellwagstr

Kundratstr

Brigittenauer
Brücke

Jägerstr

Stromstr

Dresdner Str

Universumstr

Donaueschingenstr

Leystr

Traisengasse

Vorgartenstr

Engerthstr

Handelskai

Jägerstrasse

Leipziger Str

Traisengasse

Pasettistr

Pöchlarnstr

Innstr

Pappenheim Str

Hartgasse

Dammstr

Nordwestbahnstr

BRIGITTENAU
20

Hannover
gasse

Klosterneuburger Str

Wallenstein Str

Bäuerlegasse

Rauscherstr

Dresdner Str

Rebhanngasse

17

Brigittenauer Lände

Treustr

Jägerstr

Wasnergasse

Taborstr

Alliertenstr

Friedensbrücke

Rossauer Lände

Hahngasse

Obere Augartenstr

Untere Augarten
strasse

2
Augarten

Lessing-
gasse

Darwin-
gasse

Rueppgasse

Heinestr

Nordbahnstr

Lassallestr

Ybbsstr

See map
p262

Porzellangasse

Rembrandtstr

7

Grosse
Stadtgutgasse

Praterstern

Prater

37

Rossauer
Lände

Taborstrasse

Blumauergasse

Rotensterngasse

Mayergasse

Praterstr

Wien Nord
Train Station

27

Ausstellungsstr

1
38

11

Strasse des

Schottenring

Franz-Josefs-
Kai

See Enlargement

Taborstr

42

43

4

23

Czerningasse

8

6

Schottenring
(Ringstrasse)

Schottentor

Salztorbrücke

LEOPOLDSTADT 2

Salztorbrücke

Nestroyplatz

Vivariumstr

Hauptallee

Sportklub

Wipplingerstr

Obere
Donaustr

Schwedenplatz

Untere Donaustr

Danube Canal

Rüstenschacherallee

Böcklinstr

INNERE
STADT 1

Rathausplatz/
Burgtheater

Herrengasse

Rotenturmstr

Schweden-
brücke

Julius-Raab-
Platz

Weissgerberlände

Schüttelstr

Volks-
garten

Stephansplatz

Stubentor

Wien

Vordere Zollamtsstr

Wien Mitte

Marxergasse

See map
p268

Landstrasse

Stadtpark

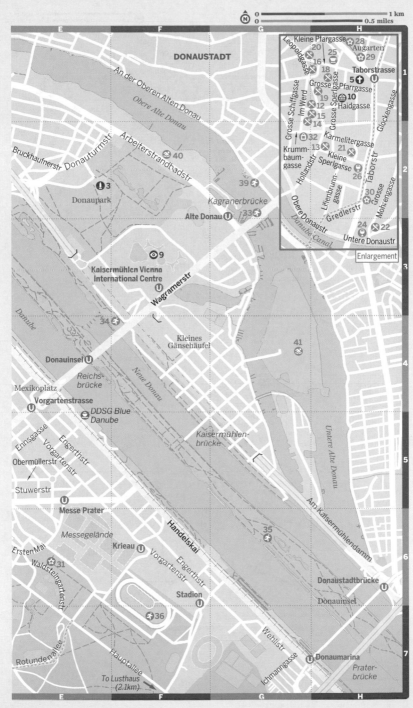

0 _____ 1 km
0 _____ 0.5 miles

DONAUSTADT

An der Oberen Alten Donau

Obere Alte Donau

Arbeiterstrandbadstr

Bruckhaufnerstr Donauturmstr

40

39

Kagranerbrücke

Donaupark

3

Alte Donau U 33

9

Kaisermühlen Vienna International Centre

Wagramerstr

34

Kleines Gänsehäufel

41

Donauinsel U

Reichs-brücke

Mexikoplatz

Vorgartenstrasse U

DDSG Blue Danube

Ennsgasse

Vorgartenstr

Engerthstr

Obermüllerstr

Neue Donau

Stuwerstr

Kaisermühlen-brücke

Messe Prater U

Messegelände

Krieau U

Handelskai

ErstenMai

Waldsteingartenstr

31

Stadion U

36

Rotundenallee

Hauptallee

To Lusthaus (2.1km)

Wehlistr

Vorgartenstr

Engerthstr

Am Kaisermühlendamm

Untere Alte Donau

35

Donaustadtbrücke U

Donauinsel

Ichmanngasse

Donaumarina U

Prater-brücke

Enlargement

Kleine Pfarrgasse

Leopoldsgasse

20

25

28

Augarten 29

16

18

Taborstrasse

Grosse Sperlgasse

5

U

Pfarrgasse

Grosse Schiffgasse

19

Im Werd

12

10

Haidgasse

15

14

Grosse Sperlgasse

Glockengasse

Karmelitergasse

32

13

21

Krumm-baum-gasse

Kleine Sperlgasse

Hollandstr

Lilienbrunngasse

26

30

Taborstr

Grosse Mohrengasse

Gredlerstr

24

22

Obere Donaustr

Untere Donaustr

Danube Canal

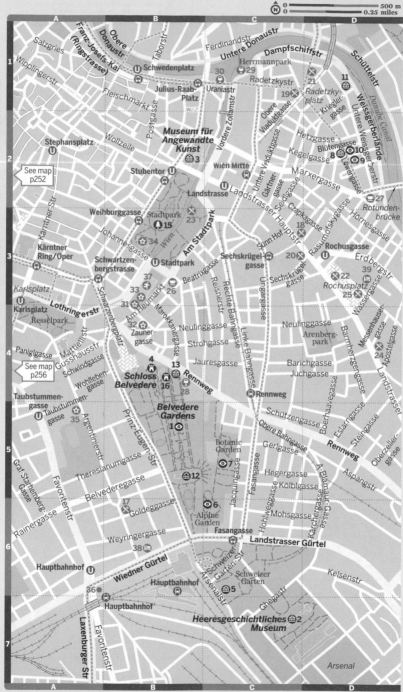

0 500 m
0 0.25 miles

A B C D

Wipplingerstr
Salzgries
Franz-Josefs-Kai (Ringstrasse)
Obere Donaustr
Taborstr
Schwedenplatz
Ferdinandstr
Untere Donaustr
Dampfschiffstr
Herrmannpark
Radetzkystr
Schüttelstr
Fleischmarkt
Julius-Raab-Platz
Uraniastr
30
29
21
11
19
Radetzky-platz
Kriedler-gasse
Weissgerberstr
Weissgerberlände
Danube Canal
Untere Weissgerberstr
Postgasse
Wollzeile
Museum für Angewandte Kunst
Vordere Zollamtstr
Obere Zollamtstr
Obere Viaduktgasse
Hetzgasse
Kegelgasse
Blütengasse
10
8
9
Stephansplatz
See map p252
3
Stubentor
Wien Mitte
Untere Viaduktgasse
Gärtner-gasse
Geusaugasse
Marxergasse
Landstrasse
Landstrasser Hauptstr
27
Rotunden-brücke
Weihburggasse
Stadtpark
23
Am Stadtpark
Sünn Hof
Crapkagasse
18
Rasumofskygasse
Hörnesgasse
Kärntner Ring/Oper
Johannesgasse
34
15
Wien
Sechskrügel-gasse
Rochusgasse
Erdbergstr
Karlsplatz
Schwartzen-bergstrasse
Stadtpark
Beatrixgasse
Reisnerstr
Sechskrügel-gasse
20
Rochusplatz
22
39
25
Karlsplatz
Lothringerstr
Resselpark
37
33
26
31
Am Heumarkt
Ungargasse
Rechte Bahngasse
Marokkanergasse
Neulinggasse
Linke Bahngasse
Neulinggasse
Arenberg-park
Taubstummen-gasse
Schwarzenbergplatz
32
Zauner-gasse
Strohgasse
Jauresgasse
Barichgasse
Juchgasse
Barmherzengasse
See map p256
Mattiellistr
Gusshausstr
Schwindgasse
Wohllebeng.
4
Schloss Belvedere
16
13
Rennweg
28
Rennweg
Schützengasse
Obere Bahngasse
Boerhaavegasse
Eslanggasse
Steingasse
Rennweg
24
Apostelgasse
Taubstummen-gasse
35
Argentinierstr
Prinz-Eugen-Str
Belvedere Gardens
1
Botanic Garden
Gerlgasse
Fasangasse
Hegergasse
Kölblgasse
A.Blamauer-Gasse
Oberzeller-gasse
Theresianumgasse
Belvederegasse
17
Goldeggasse
12
7
6
Alpine Garden
Jacquingasse
Hohlweggasse
Mohsgasse
Karcheargasse
Grat-Starhemberg-Gasse
Rainergasse
Weyringergasse
38
Fasangasse
Landstrasser Gürtel
Kelsenstr
Hauptbahnhof
Wiedner Gürtel
36
Hauptbahnhof
Hauptbahnhof
Schweizer Garten-Str
Arsenalstr
Schweizer Garten
5
Ghegastr
Laxenburger Str
Favoritenstr
Heeresgeschichtliches Museum
2
Arsenal

A B C D

See map p266

SCHLOSS BELVEDERE TO THE CANAL

SCHLOSS SCHÖNBRUNN & AROUND

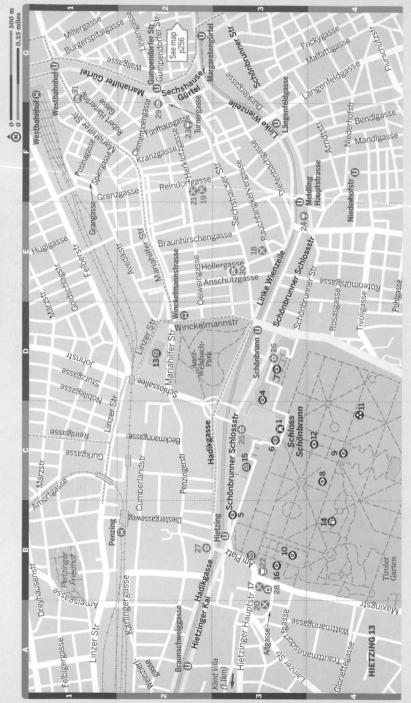

SCHLOSS SCHÖNBRUNN & AROUND

Our Story

A beat-up old car, a few dollars in the pocket and a sense of adventure. In 1972 that's all Tony and Maureen Wheeler needed for the trip of a lifetime – across Europe and Asia overland to Australia. It took several months, and at the end – broke but inspired – they sat at their kitchen table writing and stapling together their first travel guide, *Across Asia on the Cheap*. Within a week they'd sold 1500 copies. Lonely Planet was born.

Today, Lonely Planet has offices in Melbourne, London, Oakland and Delhi, with more than 600 staff and writers. We share Tony's belief that 'a great guidebook should do three things: inform, educate and amuse'.

OUR WRITERS

Anthony Haywood

Coordinating Author, The Hofburg & Around and Stephansdom & the Historic Centre Anthony is a freelance journalist and has been based in Germany for over two decades. While travelling to Moscow in the very early 1990s he detoured to Vienna, the first of very frequent travels to the Austrian capital. This was the start of a fascination with Vienna, which he loves for its unusual contrasts of high and low culture, and of course for the Viennese themselves and their humour, the famous *Wiener Schmäh*. While writing this new edition of the city guidebook he explored the capital under snow in double-digit subzero temperatures – Vienna from one of its most beautiful sides. He has coordinated and coauthored numerous guidebooks and written a cultural history of Siberia (useful for surviving cold snaps). Anthony wrote most of the Plan Your Trip section, along with the Neighbourhoods at a Glance and Sleeping chapters and the Understand Vienna and Survival Guide sections. For more, visit www.anthonyjhaywood.com.

Read more about Anthony at:
lonelyplanet.com/members/anthonyhaywood

Kerry Christiani

Karlsplatz & Around Naschmarkt, The Museum District & Neubau, Alsergrund & the University District, Schloss Belvedere to the Canal, Prater & East of the Danube, Schloss Schönbrunn & Around Ever since her first postgrad trip to Austria, Kerry has seized every available chance to return to Vienna. For this edition she spent several snowy, subzero weeks in the Austrian capital, wallowing in the richness of the city's palaces and Klimt-crammed museums, waltzing through hidden backstreets to sniff out the best restaurants and newest boutiques, and having her cake and eating it (again, and again) while road-testing scores of Vienna's best coffee houses. Kerry has authored or coauthored some 20 guidebooks, including Lonely Planet's *Austria*, *Germany*, *France* and *Switzerland* guidebooks. She tweets @kerrychristiani and lists her latest work at www.kerrychristiani.com. Kerry also wrote the Coffee Houses & Cake Shops, Drinking & Nightlife, Shopping, Sports & Activities and Sleeping chapters, and the Salzburg section of Day Trips from Vienna.

Read more about Kerry at:
lonelyplanet.com/members/kerrychristiani

Marc Di Duca

Day Trips from Vienna Marc's troublingly nostalgic obsession with the Austro-Hungarian Empire goes back over 25 years, during which time he has visited many of its most far-flung corners. Hence, a week-long border-hopping expedition between three countries for the Day Trips from Vienna chapter was just the ticket, and saw Marc hiking trails deep into the snowbound Podyjí National Park, clambering through the vineyards of the Wachau and crossing the Danube more times than a Viennese taxi driver. This is Marc's 25th contribution for Lonely Planet.

Read more about Marc at:
lonelyplanet.com/members/madidu

Published by Lonely Planet Publications Pty Ltd
ABN 36 005 607 983
7th edition – November 2013
ISBN 978 1 74179 938 5
© Lonely Planet 2013   Photographs © as indicated 2013
10 9 8 7 6 5 4 3 2
Printed in China